Nietzsche and Architecture

Nietzsche and Architecture

The Grand Style for Modern Living

LUCY HUSKINSON

BLOOMSBURY VISUAL ARTS
LONDON • NEW YORK • OXFORD • NEW DELHI • SYDNEY

BLOOMSBURY VISUAL ARTS
Bloomsbury Publishing Plc
50 Bedford Square, London, WC1B 3DP, UK
1385 Broadway, New York, NY 10018, USA
29 Earlsfort Terrace, Dublin 2, Ireland

BLOOMSBURY, BLOOMSBURY VISUAL ARTS and the Diana logo are trademarks of Bloomsbury Publishing Plc

First published in Great Britain 2024

Copyright © Lucy Huskinson, 2024

Lucy Huskinson has asserted her right under the Copyright, Designs and Patents Act, 1988, to be identified as Author of this work.

For legal purposes the Acknowledgements on p. xv constitute an extension of this copyright page.

Cover design: Eleanor Rose
Cover image: Forty-four by Jeff Battersby. Oil on canvas. © Jeff Battersby

All rights reserved. No part of this publication may be reproduced or transmitted in any form or by any means, electronic or mechanical, including photocopying, recording, or any information storage or retrieval system, without prior permission in writing from the publishers.

Bloomsbury Publishing Plc does not have any control over, or responsibility for, any third-party websites referred to or in this book. All internet addresses given in this book were correct at the time of going to press. The author and publisher regret any inconvenience caused if addresses have changed or sites have ceased to exist, but can accept no responsibility for any such changes.

A catalogue record for this book is available from the British Library.

A catalog record for this book is available from the Library of Congress.

ISBN:	HB:	978-1-3504-1290-3
	PB:	978-1-3504-1291-0
	ePDF:	978-1-3504-1293-4
	eBook:	978-1-3504-1292-7

Typeset by Integra Software Services Pvt. Ltd.
Printed and bound in India

To find out more about our authors and books visit www.bloomsbury.com and sign up for our newsletters.

For Jeff and Rusty Reg

CONTENTS

List of illustrations viii
Acknowledgements xv
List of abbreviations xvi

Introduction 1

PART ONE Nietzsche's philosophy of architecture 21

1. The problematic lack of style 23
2. Architecture in the grand style 37
3. Nietzsche's architectural influences. Gottfried Semper and festive theatre 61

PART TWO Nietzsche's ambiguous architectural legacy 87

4. Buildings to 'honour' Nietzsche 89
5. Nietzsche and the new style 154
6. The grand style in modern architecture 171
7. Modern architecture inspired by Nietzsche 192

Notes 221
Bibliography 235
Index 248

ILLUSTRATIONS

Introduction

I.1 Naumburg town hall and fountain of Wenceslas (Wenzelsbrunnen). Author's photograph 4

I.2 The 'miserable' building, Naumburg. (The former episcopal residence in front of Stadtkirche St. Wenzel/ St. Wenceslaus Church.) Postcard from *c.*1900 4

I.3 Galleria Subalpina, Turin. Interior (b.1873–4, Pietro Carrera). Illustration from the magazine *L'Illustrazione Universale*, year 2, no. 17, 31 January 1875. De Agostini Picture Library. © Getty Images 6

I.4 Galleria Subalpina, Turin. Interior. Looking up to Nietzsche's apartment. Author's photograph 7

I.5 Palazzo Madama, Turin (b.1721, Filippo Juvarra). View from south-west, showing also Casaforte degli Acaja. © Giancarlospillo 7

Chapter 2

2.1 Genoa Palazzi. Strada Nuova/Via Giuseppe Garibaldi (b.1558–83). Perspective view, above street level of various palazzi. © Superchilum 46

2.2 Palazzo Pitti, Florence (b.1458, Luca Fancelli). Front elevation. Photograph. Michael Maslan/Corbis/VCG. © Getty Images 48

2.3 Mole Antonelliana, Turin (b.1863–89, Alessandro Antonelli). Front elevation. Author's photograph 55

2.4 Mole Antonelliana. Detail of its pinnacle. Author's photograph 59

Chapter 3

3.1 Semperoper, Dresden (b.1870–78, Gottfried Semper). Front elevation. Photograph, 1888. Hulton Archive. © Getty Images 71

3.2 Semperoper. Detail of the quadriga with Bacchus/Dionysus and Ariadne (1871, Johannes Schilling). © Paulae 73

3.3 *Dionysos, von den Musen Apollos erzogen.* Watercolour (*c.*1832–36, Bonaventura Genelli) © Nationalarchiv der Richard-Wagner-Stiftung, Bayreuth 77

3.4 Richard Wagner Festspielhaus, Bayreuth (b.1872–6). Illustration, Nineteenth Century. Clu. © Getty Images 82

Chapter 4

4.1 Silberblick Villa, Nietzsche-Archiv building (renovations 1902–3, van de Velde). Front elevation. Author's photograph 93

4.2 Front cover of original guidebook, *Nietzsche Archiv: Das Nietzsche-Archiv in Weimar* (Paul Kühn, 1904). Author's photograph 99

4.3 Nietzsche-Denkmal. Temple des Lesben/'Temple of Life'. Charcoal sketch (Fritz Schumacher, 1898) 105

4.4 Ernst Abbe-Denkmal, Jena (b.1908–11, Henry van de Velde). Exterior view from the South. Author's photograph   106

4.5 Nietzsche-Archiv main room, with Nietzsche herm (1905, Max Klinger) and detail of vertical wooden strips and cavetto moulding by van de Velde. Author's photograph   110

4.6 Nietzsche Temple design (1911–12, Henry van de Velde). Phase 1. Sketch of front elevation resembling Doric temple, with *Feststraßen* and statue, 1911. Collection ENSAVE – La Cambre, Bruxelles, inv.1503. © Henry van de Velde Foundation (Pays-Bas)   123

4.7 Nietzsche Temple design. Phase 1. Sketch of front and side elevations with statue, 1911. Collection ENSAVE – La Cambre, Bruxelles, inv.4519. © Henry van de Velde Foundation (Pays-Bas)   124

4.8 Nietzsche Temple design. Phase 2. Sketch of front elevation with *Feststraßen*, 1912. Collection ENSAVE – La Cambre, Bruxelles, inv. 4521. © Henry van de Velde Foundation (Pays-Bas)   128

4.9 Nietzsche Temple design. Phase 3. Perspective sketch with stadium behind, 1912. Collection ENSAVE – La Cambre, Bruxelles, inv.1505. © Henry van de Velde Foundation (Pays-Bas)   130

4.10 Nietzsche Temple design. Phase 3. Sketch, plan of lower floor with gallery, 1912. Collection ENSAVE – La Cambre, Bruxelles, inv.2213. © Henry van de Velde Foundation (Pays-Bas)   130

4.11 Nietzsche Temple design. Phase 4. Perspective sketch, 1912. Collection ENSAVE – La Cambre, Bruxelles, inv.1508. © Henry van de Velde Foundation (Pays-Bas)   132

4.12 Nietzsche Temple design. Phase 4. Sketch of front elevation with *Feststraßen*, 1912. Collection ENSAVE – La Cambre, Bruxelles, inv.1507. © Henry van de Velde Foundation (Pays-Bas) 133

4.13 Nietzsche Temple design. Phase 4. Sketch of site plan, 1912. Collection ENSAVE – La Cambre, Bruxelles, inv. 2210. © Henry van de Velde Foundation (Pays-Bas) 133

4.14 Nietzsche Memorial, Kröller-Müller's 'Museum Park', Holland (1925, Henry van de Velde). Sketch. Collection ENSAVE – La Cambre, Bruxelles, inv.4583. © Henry van de Velde Foundation (Pays-Bas) 136

4.15 Nietzsche Memorial Hall, Weimar. Main entrance. View from Luisenstrasße (now Humboldstraße). Author's photograph 138

4.16 Nietzsche Memorial Hall and the Nietzsche Archiv, Villa Silberblick. View from Luisenstrasße (now Humboldstraße). Author's photograph 139

4.17 Nietzsche Memorial Hall and Villa Silberblick with connecting building, Weimar. Sketch by Paul Schultze-Naumburg, March 1935. © Goethe und Schiller Archiv. Foto: Klassik Stiftung Weimar. GSA 72/2599 144

4.18 Nietzsche Memorial Hall and Villa Silberblick, with connecting building, from the East (top left). Cross section of Philosopher's walkway from East (top right). Memorial Hall, showing the Philosopher's walkway, from the North (bottom). Plans by Paul Schultze-Naumburg, March 1935. © Goethe und Schiller Archiv. Foto: Klassik Stiftung Weimar. GSA 72/2602 145

4.19 Nietzsche Memorial Hall, Weimar. View from the Philosopher's walkway, looking towards the apse in the Main Hall. Photograph, 1943. © Goethe und Schiller Archiv. Foto: Klassik Stiftung Weimar, 1943. GSA 72/2610 145

4.20 Nietzsche Memorial Hall, Weimar. Festive room with apse. Photograph, 1943. © Goethe und Schiller Archiv. Foto: Klassik Stiftung Weimar. GSA 72/2620 146

4.21 Nietzsche Memorial Hall, Weimar. Model, with figures of Apollo and Dionysus flanking the main entrance. Photograph, January 1937. © Goethe und Schiller Archiv. Foto: Klassik Stiftung Weimar. GSA 72/2610 147

4.22 Nietzsche Memorial Hall, Weimar. Model, showing apse. Photograph, January 1937. © Goethe und Schiller Archiv. Foto: Klassik Stiftung Weimar. GSA 72/2610 148

4.23 Nietzsche Memorial Hall, Weimar. Ground floor plan of final design. July 1937. © Goethe und Schiller Archiv. Foto: Klassik Stiftung Weimar. GSA 72/2602 149

4.24 Nietzsche Memorial Hall. Topping out ceremony, 3 August 1938. Photograph. © Goethe und Schiller Archiv. Foto: Klassik Stiftung Weimar. GSA 72/2610 151

Chapter 5

5.1 Opening ceremony, Darmstädt Colony, *Das Zeichen*, 1901, with Ernst Ludwig House (1900–01, Joseph Olbrich). Photograph. © Institut Mathildenhöhe, Darmstädt Municipal Art Collection 160

Chapter 6

6.1 Guaranty building (later Prudential building), Buffalo, NY (b.1894–5, Louis H. Sullivan). East elevation. Author's photograph 181

6.2 Marshall Field and Co. Wholesale Store, Chicago, IL, 1887. Henry Hobson Richardson, Shepley, Rutan and Coolidge. J.W. Taylor, photographer. J.W. Taylor Photograph Collection, Ryerson and Burnham Art and Architecture Archives © Art Institute of Chicago. Digital file #199303_120806_032 185

6.3 Wainwright building, St.Louis (b.1891, Louis H. Sullivan), East elevation. © Reading Tom (flickr), 2011 186

Chapter 7

7.1 Theatre, Werkbund Exhibition, Cologne (b.1914, Henry van de Velde). Front perspective. Photograph, 1914. © Bildarchiv Foto Marburg 194

7.2 Theatre, Werkbund Exhibition, Cologne. Plan, 1913. Henry van de Velde. © Rheinisches Bildarchiv Cologne, RBA 194 095 196

7.3 Frontispiece for an edition of Nietzsche's *Dionysos Dithyramben*. Henry van de Velde, 1914. Author's photograph 196

7.4 Peter Behrens' House, Darmstädt. Northeast elevation. © Bildarchiv Foto Marburg/Norbert Latocha 199

7.5 *Hamburger Vorhalle*, Exposition of the Decorative Arts, Turin (b.1902, Peter Behrens) © Bildarchiv Foto Marburg 202

7.6 AEG Turbine Building, Berlin (b.1909, Peter Behrens). Photograph, 1910. © Bildarchiv Foto Marburg 203

7.7 *Monument des Neuen Gesetzes* (1919, Bruno Taut). Illustrated letter with a drawing of a project for the Monument to the Dead. © Canadian Center for Architecture 214

7.8 *Glashaus*, Werkbund Exhibition, Cologne (b.1914, Bruno Taut), front elevation. © Bildarchiv Foto Marburg 218

7.9 *Glashaus*, Werkbund Exhibition, Cologne (b.1914, Bruno Taut), interior. © Bildarchiv Foto Marburg 218

ACKNOWLEDGEMENTS

The cover of this book depicts *Forty-four*, a painting in oils on canvas by Jeff Battersby. Jeff's abstract compositions express a dynamic interplay of forms not unlike architecture in the 'grand style'. In *Forty-four* I am reminded of Nietzsche's enjoyment of walking mountainous pathways, and Bruno Taut's alpine architecture where mountains and caves morph into glittering caverns and crystal peaks. See http://jeffbattersby.blogspot.com for more of his paintings.

Antony Gormley kindly allowed me to use an image of a sculpture by him for the cover of my first book about Nietzsche. *Nietzsche and Architecture* is dedicated in part to another sculpture by him – one who is very much a character in his own right. Following Reg's gaze across the Sound to the ocean beyond has helped sharpen many thoughts in this book. But the book itself is dedicated in full to Jeff, who draws my gaze further still, to horizons infinite and joyful, to laughter and love.

Several others must be thanked. Not least, Régine Carpentier, bibliothécaire at *Ecole nationale supérieure des arts visuels de La Cambre* in Brussels for her efficiency and kindness in assisting me with various images. Josephine Liesegang at *JenaKultur* for taking the time to show me inside the Ernst Abbe memorial building in Jena. Martin Gledhill for indulging me in many long and wide-ranging conversations about architectural obscurities. Seilesh Khumanthem for his copy editing. And a big thank you to notable others who have inspired me in other but no less meaningful ways, including Josh Andrews, Jim Battersby, Paul Bishop, Andrei Constantin, Teresa Crew, Gareth Evans-Jones, Rachel Hughes, Thomas Hughes, Janet Huskinson, Bethan Loftus, Theresa Nally, Steve Nash, Aidy Phillips, Charmaine Rodwell, Peter Shapely, Kevin Symonds and Farhaan Wali. Finally, special thanks to David Sullivan for his patience in accompanying me to faraway places to check out the smallest of architectural details. To Ludo and of course, to Mark, to whom Zarathustra owes his best dance moves.

ABBREVIATIONS

Friedrich Nietzsche

AC   F. Nietzsche, *The Antichrist: Curse upon Christianity*, in The Complete Works of Friedrich Nietzsche, vol. 9, trans. Carol Diethe and Adrian Del Caro, Stanford University Press: Stanford, CA, 1888/2021. Cited with aphorism number.

BGE   F. Nietzsche, *Beyond Good and Evil: Prelude to a Philosophy of the Future*, in The Complete Works of Friedrich Nietzsche, vol. 8, trans. Adrian Del Caro, Stanford University Press: Stanford, CA, 1886/2014. Cited with aphorism number.

BT   F. Nietzsche, *The Birth of Tragedy: Out of the Spirit of Music*, trans. Shaun Whiteside, ed. Michael Tanner, Penguin: Middlesex, 1872/1993. Cited with section number.

CW   F. Nietzsche, *The Case of Wagner: A Musicians' Problem*, in The Complete Works of Friedrich Nietzsche, vol. 9, trans. Carol Diethe and Duncan Large, Stanford University Press: Stanford, CA, 1888/2021. Cited with section number.

D   F. Nietzsche, *Daybreak*. Edition cited is *Dawn: Thoughts on the Presumptions of Morality*, in The Complete Works of Friedrich Nietzsche, vol. 5, trans. Brittain Smith, Stanford University Press: Stanford, CA, 1881/2011. Cited with aphorism number.

EH   F. Nietzsche, *Ecce Homo: How One Becomes What One Is*, in The Complete Works of Friedrich Nietzsche, vol. 9, trans. Carol Diethe, Duncan Large, Adrian Del Caro and Alan D. Schrift, Stanford University Press: Stanford, CA, 1888/2021. Cited with chapter number and corresponding abbreviation of book title, and section number.

FS   F. Nietzsche, *Frühe Schriften: Jugendschriften, 1854–1869*, ed. Hans Joachim, 5 vols, Deutscher Taschenbuch Verlag: Munich, 1994. Cited with volume and page reference.

GM	F. Nietzsche, *On the Genealogy of Morality: A Polemic*, in The Complete Works of Friedrich Nietzsche, vol. 8, trans. Adrian Del Caro, Stanford University Press: Stanford, CA, 1887/2014. Cited with treatise number and section number.
GMD	F. Nietzsche, *The Greek Music Drama,* trans. Paul Bishop, New York: Contra Mundum Press, 1870/2013. Cited with page number.
GS	F. Nietzsche, *The Gay Science, with a Prelude in German Rhymes and an Appendix of Songs*, trans. Josefine Nauckhoff and Adrian Del Caro, ed. Bernard Williams, Cambridge University Press: Cambridge, 1882/2001. Cited with aphorism number.
GSA	*Goethe Schiller Archiv* Weimar.
HHI	F. Nietzsche, *Human All Too Human I: A Book for Free Spirits,* in The Complete Works of Friedrich Nietzsche, vol.3, trans. Gary Handwerk, Stanford University Press: Stanford, CA, 1878/1995. Cited with aphorism number.
KSA	F. Nietzsche, *Sämtliche Werke: Kritische Studienausgabe*, ed. G. Colli and M. Montinari, 15 vols, De Gruyter: Berlin and New York; Deutscher Taschenbuch Verlag: Munich, 1967–77 and 1988. Cited with volume, fragment number and page reference.
KSB	F. Nietzsche, *Sämtliche Briefe: Kritische Studienausgabe*, ed. G. Colli and M. Montinari, 8 vols, De Gruyter: Berlin and New York; Deutscher Taschenbuch Verlag: Munich, 1975–84. Cited with volume, letter number and page reference.
NCW	F. Nietzsche, *Nietzsche Contra Wagner: Documents of a Psychologist,* in The Complete Works of Friedrich Nietzsche, vol. 9, trans. Carol Diethe and Adrian Del Caro, Stanford University Press: Stanford, CA, 1889/2021. Cited with chapter number, section number and page reference.
OM	*Mixed Opinions and Maxims*, 1879, in *Human All Too Human II and Unpublished Fragments from the Period of 'Human, All Too Human II' (Spring 1878–fall 1879),* in The Complete Works of Friedrich Nietzsche, vol. 4, trans. Gary Handwerk, Stanford University Press: Stanford, CA, 1880/2013: 11–144. Cited with aphorism number.
TI	F. Nietzsche, *Twilight of the Idols: or How to Philosophize with a Hammer,* in The Complete Works of Friedrich Nietzsche, vol. 9, trans. Carol Diethe, Duncan Large, Adrian Del Caro and Alan D. Schrift, Stanford University Press: Stanford, CA, 1888/2021. Cited with chapter number, section number and page reference.

UM   F. Nietzsche, *Untimely Meditations*. Edition cited is *Unfashionable Observations*, in The Complete Works of Friedrich Nietzsche, vol. 2, trans. Richard T. Gray, Stanford University Press: Stanford, CA, 1873–76/2001. Cited with essay number, section number and page reference.

WS   F. Nietzsche, *The Wanderer and His Shadow*, in *Human All Too Human II and Unpublished Fragments from the Period of 'Human, All Too Human II' (Spring 1878–Fall 1879)*, The Complete Works of Friedrich Nietzsche, vol. 4, trans. Gary Handwerk, Stanford University Press: Stanford, CA, 1880/2013: 145–296. Cited with aphorism number.

Z   F. Nietzsche, *Thus Spoke Zarathustra*, trans. R.J. Hollingdale, Penguin Books: Harmondsworth, 1883–1885/1969. Cited with part number, chapter number, section number and page reference.

Harry Graf Kessler and Henry van de Velde

KV   *Harry Graf Kessler–Henry Van de Velde: Der Briefwechsel*, Antje Neumann (editorial and commentary), Vandenhoeck & Ruprecht: Göttingen, 2015. Cited with letter number and page reference.

Introduction

When Nietzsche claimed 'only ideas *won by walking* have value' (TI I, 34), he cemented his position among the ranks of many a philosopher who professed the need to walk to think well. While the peripatetic school, founded by Aristotle, derived their name from the covered and colonnaded walkways (*peripatoi*) of the Lyceum where members met, Nietzsche's walking philosophy is most often associated with treacherous mountainous paths and icy peaks. Much has been written, for instance, of his love of the alpine shores of Lake Silvaplana in the Upper-Engadine valley of Grisons in Switzerland, where his contemplation of a pyramid-shaped boulder led him to one of his most important ideas – the eternal recurrence, an idea he referred to as '6000 feet beyond people and time' to honour the location that encouraged it (EH, IX, Z.1).

Nietzsche goes on to attribute the ideas of his most popular work, *Thus Spoke Zarathustra* (1883–5) to his rural jaunts. The first book 'stole upon' him near Genoa, on his morning walks along 'the glorious road' from Rapallo to Zoagli, which took him past pine trees and granted him vast views of the sea, and on his afternoon strolls around the entire bay, from Santa Margherita right up to Porto Fino (EH, IX Z.1). The second book was conceived in the same 'hallowed spot where the first lightning bolt of *Zarathustra* had hit me' – on those two pathways, and a third which he 'discovered beneath the halcyon sky of Nice'. Nietzsche singles out an unforgettable moment, when his 'creative energy was in full flow', enabling him at one and the same time to climb from the station to Eza (a Moorish chateau) and to discover 'On Old and New Law Tables' ['Von alten und neuen Tafeln'], a key section for book three (EH, IX Z.4). This section will feature several times in the investigation that follows, as a passage of *Zarathustra* favoured by notable early-twentieth-century architects who sought to translate Nietzsche's 'new law' into their architectural designs.

'Almost every proposition' in his book *Daybreak* (1881) was 'thought up, *caught up*' [erdacht, erschlüpft] in a tangle of rocks near Genoa, 'where I was alone and still shared secrets with the sea' (EH, VII D.1; cf.GS, 310). And, trees, too, shared their secrets with him by shedding their 'truths' like fruits falling in the wind (EH, XII TI.2). Malwida von Meysenbug (1816–1903), a mutual friend of Nietzsche and Richard Wagner, recounts how Nietzsche would regularly stand underneath a particular tree in the orange groves of Sorrento to receive its ideas (D'Iorio 2012:67). Occasionally, natural features from these rural landscapes would find their way into his writings, such as the volcanic island of Ischia, which became the model for the 'Blissful Islands' – the isles of the future, of hope and youth for which Zarathustra yearned.[1] Some have gone on to argue that the topography of the mountain-form, which so captured Nietzsche's imagination, impressed upon him his deep-seated understanding of culture as having a hierarchical structure, with exemplary artists or creators placed at the heights of the summit and the inferior herd, residing like sheep in the valleys below.

Thus Spoke Zarathustra was instrumental in popularizing the romantic image of the lonely wanderer venturing forth on treacherous icy mountain paths of self-discovery. At the turn of the twentieth century, the book sparked waves of tourists to Nietzsche's favourite mountain paths. As Aschheim notes, thanks to this book '*Einsamkeitserlebnis* – the experience of being alone – was transformed into a mass business!' And alongside this, a wider 'cult of mountains' developed with 'Nietzsche and Nietzschean imagery', specifically 'Zarathustrian imagery', at its heart (Aschheim 1994:35; Krause 1984). Of course, Nietzsche would have been horrified by such mass-consumerism and branding of his ideas. But what of Nietzsche's – and Zarathustra's – walks in the various towns and cities he visited and of the architectural designs, styles and features he inevitably experienced along the way? Relationships between Nietzsche's philosophy and the natural world/rural environments are well documented. Sadly, the same cannot be said for architecture and the built environment, where scholarship is relatively scant in both quality and extent. One hopes this relative silence is not indicative of outmoded romantic assumptions that glorify rural environments as the only place where one can feel revived, inspired and replenished. The chapters that follow will dispel this assumption unreservedly from a Nietzschean perspective. We shall see, for Nietzsche, architecture and urban environments provide the platform for spiritual and cultural renewal. Through the immediacy of their material forms, we find ourselves in place and more in touch with our instinctual needs and aspirations; and through the rhythmic play of *good* architectural design, we find ourselves integrated and uplifted. Furthermore, we shall see that the pyramidal stratification of culture was no less present for Nietzsche in the towering heights and cavernous depths of architecture as it was in the precipice of the mountain. As Wolfgang Pehnt reminds us, 'the topography of the superman' comprises an intimate 'connection between tower and cave' [Turm und Höhle] and 'almost all reading and thinking artists of the era' were aware of this (1994:58). By examining Nietzsche's relationships with architecture – and their interpretation by architects at the turn of the twentieth century – we acquire a veritable resource to draw from to shed new light on some of his most prevalent ideas about the elevation of culture, and to begin to consider their efficacy for evaluating our own built environments.

Nietzsche does not present us with a conclusive philosophy of architecture. There are a few aphorisms and comments in his published works that refer explicitly to architecture and the built environment. But when these are read in the context of other relevant topics – such as his metaphors of building and of transformation through stone, his discussions on historicism and the significance of style – specifically building in the grand style (*grossen Stil*) – and his letters of correspondence to colleagues, friends and family which comment on his experiences of cities, specific buildings and architects – we uncover a rich repository of insights about architectural design which are suggestive of the beginnings of a distinctive theory of the cultural and existential significance of architecture as well as the merits and pitfalls of specific building types, features and designs.

Arguably, Nietzsche was interested in architecture throughout his life as a vehicle for the transformation of character and culture. In one of his earliest bibliographical accounts, at the age of fifteen, Nietzsche reflects on his 'love of architecture' [*Liebe zur Baukunst*]. He explains how it manifested itself initially when very young through his construction of model buildings, which enabled him 'through much practice' to learn 'all the finer points of building'. He recalls constructing a little chapel, and later, 'magnificent temples with several rows of columns, high towers with winding staircases, mines with underground lakes and interior lighting, and finally castles' (FS I:152). Upon his move to Naumburg from the village of Röcken, he became captivated by the town's 'beautiful wide streets with their ancient houses' (notably, Jakobstraße), its marketplace with its fountain and 'large' town hall – 'How big it is! What extension!' he exclaims. 'Let me always look at it with awe' (see Figure I.1). To the left of the townhall is the 'high, venerable city church protruding' (St. Wenzel), but 'in front of it, see the miserable [erbärmliche] building standing there! Oh, if it were torn away, does it not inhibit the whole view of the church?!' (FS I:7, 16–18; see Figure I.2).

Nietzsche's observations of architecture and the built environments of towns and cities continued throughout his life, initially in Germany, then Switzerland and Italy. Following his resignation from his post at the University of Basel in 1879, Nietzsche becomes something of a flâneur, taking up lodgings in various urban and rural locations where he would walk and write, and alternating between places according to seasonal climates in the hope of alleviating the ailments brought on by his increasingly poor health. Prior to his resignation, he confides in Malwida von Meysenbug about his general 'mistrust of large cities' – Rome, Nice and Zürich in particular – as places which 'make me irritable, gloomy [...] uncertain, despondent,

FIGURE I.1 Naumburg town hall and fountain of Wenceslas (Wenzelsbrunnen). Author's photograph.

FIGURE I.2 The 'miserable' building, Naumburg. (The former episcopal residence in front of Stadtkirche St. Wenzel/St. Wenceslaus Church.) Postcard from $c.$1900.

unproductive, and sick' (May 1887; KSB,8[845]:69). His later stays in Italy, especially the cities of Genoa and Turin, would challenge his view and arguably overturn it, on account of their architectural delights.

To his friend, Franz Overbeck, Nietzsche lays claim to Genoa as 'my city' for it is 'bursting with vitality' (October 1881; KSB,6.158:134). To his mother and sister, he alludes to the 'beautifully paved paths' of this 'great, bustling sea town', which 'gives me peace and being for myself' (November 1880; KSB,6.68:51). To his friend, Heinrich Köselitz, he asserts that to leave

Genoa is to leave oneself behind (April 1888; KSB,8.1013:285). Genoa was the home of Christopher Columbus, and from where he set sail in search of the 'new world'. Centuries later it would become a place of self-discovery and revival for Nietzsche and Nietzschean philosophy, from where he composed *Daybreak* [*Morgenröte*] and started to write *The Gay Science* [*Die fröhliche Wissenschaft*]. But it is with the tall Baroque residential palazzi of former wealthy merchants where his aspirations find greatest affinity. To Nietzsche's mind, each palace has impressed into its design the nobility of its merchant-creators – a singular taste that sets itself apart from its neighbour as distinctive and self-sufficient, and when these palaces are viewed together, they express a loathing for the tedium of laws, and a will to overcome them (GS, 291). In a curious slip – perhaps of wishful thinking – Nietzsche mentions to his sister, Elisabeth, that his lodgings in the city (on the relatively non-descript street, *Salita delle Battistine*) are set among a street of palaces (December 1880; KSB,6,69:52). This theme returns as a haunting image with his final residence – Villa Silberblick in Weimar – where the now-deteriorating Nietzsche, living under the care of his sister, took his final walks. Elisabeth would recount how he 'wandered everywhere' within the house, 'saying always "Palazzo, palazzo, palazzo!"' (Kessler 1880–1918/2011:187).

But it was the architectural delights of Turin, which Nietzsche writes most effusively about. 'This really is the city I need! This is palpable and was almost from the first moment', he writes to Köselitz. 'What a dignified and serious city! Not a big city, not at all modern, as I had feared. Rather, a princely residence of the 17th century which has only one commanding taste everywhere, that of court and nobility. An aristocratic calm is preserved in everything: there are no shabby suburbs'. There is 'a unity of taste' that filters down even to its colour, for the 'whole city is yellow or redbrown' (April 1888; KSB,8.1013:285; cf. KSB,8.1018:293). To his mother, Nietzsche writes in the same month that Turin 'is the only city I like living in'. Its 'magnificent, spacious portici, colonnades and hallways' run 'along all the main streets', connecting streets to squares and 'stretching far and wide through the city for a total of 10,020 meters' (KSB,8.1023:301). And these enabled Nietzsche to walk – and subsequently to think – undisturbed for hours at a time and apparently in supercharged fashion: 'half an hour in one breadth'! (KSB,8.1018:293). Turin was simply, 'paradise for the feet' (KSB,8.1016:292).

Arguably, Turin's streets were more productive for Nietzsche than mountain pathways. In August 1888, Nietzsche attributes his inability to write his long-anticipated work, *The Will to Power* (*Der Wille zur Macht*), to the rain-washed summer he had spent in Sils Maria where his philosophical project, he says, 'literally fell into the water' ['wörtlich "in Wasser" gefallen ist'] (KSB,8.1098:406; cf. Gleiter 2009:103). By contrast, in Turin, he could walk unimpeded whatever the weather, and his writing was prolific; from Turin he wrote, *Ecce Homo*, *Twilight of the Idols* [*Götzen-Dämmerung*], and *The Antichrist* [*Der Antichrist*]. In Turin Nietzsche found himself living in lodgings conjoining the palatial, Galleria Subalpina (b.1873–4) – 'the most beautiful and elegant space of its kind that I know of' – high up, near its iron and glass roof 'in a magnificent high-ceilinged room' (December 1888; KSB,8 [1192]:528; see Figures I.3 and I.4). From there he had views into the arcade (towards his favourite café, *Caffe Baratti & Milano*) and across to Piazza Carlo, and from his writing desk he could hear the muffled music from the *Teatro Carignano* located at the other end of the Galleria. A walk through the Galleria would take him to Piazza Castello and to Palazzo Madama – 'my palazzo' as he called this curious hybrid of a 'grand castle' (*Casaforte degli Acaja*) built at the end of the thirteenth century conjoined with a Baroque residential palace designed by members of the Savoy family (December 1888; KSB,8.1227:565; see Figure I.5). But it was the Mole Antonelliana, just a ten-minute walk from his apartment that captivated him most (see Figure 2.3).

Upon its completion in 1889, the Mole, at 167.5 metres high, was the tallest brick construction in Europe, and for Nietzsche 'the most ingenious structure that might ever have been built' (December 1888; KSB,8.1227:565). Nietzsche mentioned this in a letter to his friend, Köselitz, written just before

FIGURE I.3 Galleria Subalpina, Turin. Interior (b.1873–4, Pietro Carrera). Illustration from the magazine *L'Illustrazione Universale*, year 2, no. 17, 31 January 1875. De Agostini Picture Library. © Getty Images.

FIGURE I.4 Galleria Subalpina, Turin. Interior. Looking up to Nietzsche's apartment. Author's photograph.

FIGURE I.5 Palazzo Madama, Turin (b.1721, Filippo Juvarra). View from southwest, showing also Casaforte degli Acaja. © Giancarlospillo.

Nietzsche's fateful collapse in Turin – in a street or palazzo, depending on which account you believe.[2] Nietzsche continues to describe the Mole as built 'out of an absolute desire for the heights' [Höhentrieb], and, as such, it reminded him of nothing other than 'my Zarathustra'. The building at the time had no name – only later would it become known as the Antonelliana, after its architect, Alessandro Antonelli (1798–1888). Nietzsche subsequently takes it upon himself to 'christen it' with the name '"Ecce Homo"', and he 'mentally surround[s] it with an immense open space' (December 1888; KSB,8.1227:565). Ecce Homo, 'behold the man', was the title of Nietzsche's final work, akin to a quasi-autobiography, where Nietzsche interprets his own significance through his published works. To name the Mole after this book indicates the intimate connection Nietzsche felt towards the building. In a postscript to his letter, Nietzsche draws attention to the fact that Antonelli 'lived just as long, until Ecce Homo, the book was finished – The book and the human being'. After his collapse, in the last of Nietzsche's so-called 'delusional letters' (Wahnbriefe), he wrote to his former colleague, Jacob Burckhardt (1818–97) on 6 January 1889 to imply that he had once been Antonelli, the building's architect, before telling Burckhardt that he really ought to come to Turin to see this building for himself (January 1889; KSB,8.1256:579).[3] The timing of Nietzsche's physical and mental collapse shortly after declaring his intimate and direct identification with the building and its architect presents us with a curious symbolism, or ironic twist perhaps, to the link Nietzsche himself proposed between the death of Antonelli and the ending or completion of his 'autobiographical' narrative. Whatever one makes of this, it is indisputable that architecture is a poignant presence for Nietzsche, from his early years when he felt compelled to master the design and construction of model buildings, to his final years, from the point of his collapse. As Fritz Neumeyer puts it, 'architecture stands before Nietzsche's eyes as a parable when entering the world of thought and when leaving it' (2001/2004:10).

Sadly, few scholars have written about Nietzsche and architecture. Discussions of Nietzsche's relationship with architecture tend to be fleeting and within broader analyses of Nietzsche and art or alongside sculpture and the plastic arts generally. When the built environment is described within bibliographical accounts of Nietzsche, it is usually presented as an incidental backdrop to the events and ideas that preoccupied him.[4] The few monographs on the topic are in German without English translation. They include *Der bauende Geist. Friedrich Nietzsche und die Architektur* (*The Building Spirit. Nietzsche and Architecture*) by Markus Breitschmid (2001); *Der Klang Der Stein: Nietzsches Architekturen* (*The Sound of Stones: Nietzsche's Architectures*) by Fritz Neumeyer (2001/2004); *Nietzsches Italien: Städte, Gärten und Paläste* (*Nietzsche's Italy: Cities, Gardens, and Palaces*) by Tilmann Buddensieg (2002a); and *Der philosophische Flaneur: Nietzsche und die Architektur* (*The Philosophical Flâneur: Nietzsche and Architecture*) by Jörg H. Gleiter (2009).

INTRODUCTION

The works of Breitschmid and Neumeyer were the first to give serious scholarly consideration to Nietzsche's relationship with architecture. Breitschmid's study examines the notions of 'building-thought' (Gedankengebäude) and 'thought buildings' (Baugedanken) as central to Nietzsche's philosophy of the creative spirit. The creative spirit is compelled to make its ideas a living reality, and architecture – both material and metaphorical – provided Nietzsche with a viable image or mental container with which to organize and evoke his ideas. Breitschmid discusses Nietzsche's conception of architecture as a manifestation of the will to power and, according to Breitschmid, this is most clearly expressed in Nietzsche's interests in Classical architecture due to Nietzsche's desire to revive the creative spirit of classical antiquity. Neumeyer, by contrast, examines Nietzsche's interests in Renaissance architecture within his early and middle writings, which were encouraged by Nietzsche's readings of Gottfried Semper (1803–79) and Jacob Burckhardt. According to Buddensieg, Nietzsche's ideas anticipated modern, ornament-free architecture, and encouraged the birth of the American skyscraper thanks to Nietzsche's influence on Louis H. Sullivan (1856–1924) and the Chicago School. Gleiter presents a useful critical account of the literature on Nietzsche and architecture up until 2009. In his summation, the three works above fail to account for Nietzsche's consideration of physiological experience, which, for Gleiter, is central to the subject. Gleiter seeks to rectify their oversight by highlighting Nietzsche's ambiguous reception of modernity and its architecture, which is due, Nietzsche argued, to the modern tendency towards physiological degeneration and decadence. I will consider and critique these works at various points in my study, alongside relevant conclusions reached in other, related works, such as Hartmut Böhme's (2001) 'Architektur im post-religiösen Zeitalter' ('Architecture in the Post-Religious Age'). According to Böhme, the appropriation of Nietzsche's idea of the heroic master builder did less to inspire architectural modernism than provide a representative architecture of the totalitarian social regimes of the twentieth century.

There is one work of note in English: *Nietzsche and 'An Architecture of Our Minds'* (1999) edited by Alexandre Kostka and Irving Wohfarth. This anthology of essays is drawn from a conference on the broad theme of 'Nietzsche's reception by the protagonists of modernity', held in 1994 in Weimar, and sponsored by the *Getty Research Institute for the History of Art and the Humanities*. Three essays are worth mentioning here: Buddensieg on Nietzsche's notion of 'empty form' and its impact on architects; Neumeyer's account of Nietzsche's influence on modern architecture, specifically the work of Ludwig Mies van der Rohe (1886–1969), Ludwig Hilberseimer (1885–1967), and Bruno Taut (1880–1938); and Alexandre Kostka's assessments of Henry van de Velde's (1863–1957) renovations for the Nietzsche-Archiv (1902–3), and his collaborative project with Count Harry Graf Kessler for a Nietzsche temple-stadium complex (built in 1910–14). Aside from these essays, the volume takes a tangential approach to the subject, with a meandering array of topics that place Nietzsche in the midground or background to other artists, architectural themes and metaphors.[5] Because of its broad and eclectic focus, the work ignores central topics, such as the theatre – the architectural type that Nietzsche wrote most about – and the influence of Gottfried Semper on Nietzsche's ideas: a man whom Nietzsche celebrates in 1870 as 'the most significant living architect' (GMD:18; KSA,1:522).

There is a raft of works written for audiences interested in the history of architecture and architectural theory, which allude briefly to Nietzsche's ideas, but often with little understanding of them. They tend towards a caricature of the most familiar and misunderstood of Nietzschean ideas, notably the *Übermensch* or superman and will to power. Understandably, these works seek to understand, not Nietzschean philosophy, but the works of architects who have been linked to Nietzsche, either because they have referred directly to his ideas or have been associated with them in a common desire to elevate culture through their own creations and designs. These most often focus on the architectural writings and designs of Louis H. Sullivan, Henry van de Velde, Peter Behrens (1868–1940), Paul Schultze-Naumburg (1869–1949), Bruno Taut, Walter Gropius (1883–1969) and Charles-Édouard Jeanneret or Le Corbusier (1887–1965), among others. There is often a 'pick and mix' approach to Nietzsche's philosophy where his ideas are pitched against each other either to uphold or undermine ideological positions across architectural schools of thought. For instance, Nietzsche's call for 'empty forms', when interpreted as a forms devoid of ornament and historical reference, may be used to uphold values of the Bauhaus school of architecture (1919–33), of radical and modernist designs, and so-called 'international' styles (1932–1970s). By contrast, Nietzsche's desire to revive the German spirit can be interpreted as a need to return to styles rooted in German folk traditions. Nietzsche's name has subsequently been cited in attempts to justify philosophically the eradication of so-called 'degenerate' and 'Bolshevik' architecture, and their replacement with designs primed for the Third Reich – a proposal which comprised a disorganized contradiction of styles, culminating in Albert Speer's (1905–81) grandiose plans for *Germania*, capital city of the world. Although scholarship written for an audience that is interested in architecture rather than Nietzschean philosophy tends to mislead with its crude and often erroneous presentation of Nietzsche and Nietzschean ideas, they are nonetheless vital in capturing Nietzsche's architectural legacy. The place architects and their commentators give to Nietzsche's ideas – for better or worse – is important for making sense of Nietzsche's contributions to architectural theory and design.

Nietzsche's fears that he would be misunderstood or, worse, pronounced holy (EH, XIV) were borne out after his death at the hands of his entrepreneurial sister, Elisabeth Förster-Nietzsche, who helped to cultivate a 'cult following' around a mythologized image of him, as a saintly hero and prophet of a new Germany. It was this vision of Nietzsche which many architects and artists at the turn of the twentieth century sought to emulate. Several appealed directly to Nietzsche's ideas for philosophical justification of their innovative designs or their personal and professional standing, believing themselves to be the heroic individual or genius who could elevate culture to new creative heights through their unique design style.

Nietzsche was widely recognized as having identified the problem and potential solution to the demise of German culture. The modern mindset was, he maintained, too invested in the acquisition of facts and knowledge of the historical past, which meant it could only relate to itself in abstract terms. It lacked the instinctual awareness to apply this knowledge effectively for living in the present. It had become desensitized to the immediacy of its material environments and out of touch with its instinctual needs, and this is evident, he claims, in 'the chaotic mishmash of all styles' [*dem chaotischen Durcheinander aller Stile*]. Every time a German 'glances at their clothes, their room, and their house' or 'walks through the streets of their cities', they are reminded of the 'grotesque juxtaposition and jumbling of all possible styles. The German person amasses around themselves the forms, colours, products, and curiosities of all ages and climes, and thereby produces that carnival motley' of the 'modern' world (UM, I:1). In unpublished fragments from 1873, Nietzsche notes: 'Dwellings, rooms, clothes, manners, theatres, museums' are 'proof of the most absolute absence of style' (KSA,14.161:60); 'it will be evident from your buildings that they have been *amassed* rather than *assembled*' (KSA,7.29.58:653). Zarathustra becomes a mouthpiece for Nietzsche's frustrations. Upon seeing a row of new houses, Zarathustra asks 'What do these houses mean?' for 'truly, no great soul put them up as its image!' He continues, 'Did a silly child perhaps take them out of its toy-box? If only another child would put them back into its box! And these sitting rooms and bedrooms: are *men* able to go in and out of them? They seem to have been made for dolls.' He longs to return home to the heights of his mountain cave where, 'I shall no longer have to stoop *before the small men*!' (Z, III, 5[1]:187). Modern designs are derivative. There is nothing distinctive or instinctive about them, as such they consolidate the underlying problem, as Nietzsche saw it, by failing to capture the imaginations of the people, and presenting instead through their uninspiring façades, allusions to an outmoded past.

Nietzsche was also recognized and revered for the remedy he proposed: to stop replicating historic styles and to enlist the creative spirit that gave rise to these once-powerful buildings as legitimate expressions of the will and aspirations of the people of that time and place. Knowledge of the past can be useful, Nietzsche maintained, only if it is used critically and constructively and not acquired as an end unto itself. Rather than regurgitating information and replicating past styles, we must seek to 'unmask' the creative spirit that gave rise to them in the hope of reawakening this spirit to enable us to build effectively in the present. What is needed are buildings that express the will, desires and aspirations of its people. 'What is missing primarily in our big cities', he writes, are 'quiet and wide, expansive places for reflection – places with long, high-ceilinged arcades [...] buildings that give expression to the sublimity of contemplation' and a stepping aside to take thought for oneself (GS, 280).

Ancient Greek culture was Nietzsche's prototype for the grand style that he envisioned for the future of Germany, not with the intention of replicating its classical art and architecture, but of exposing its capacity to evoke the noble spirit of its people. Nietzsche understood this creative achievement as the dynamic tensions between Apollonian and Dionysian impulses. The modern mindset, he claimed, had become too entrenched in Apollonian approaches to art and architecture, and desperately required compensatory readjustment through the revival of Dionysian instincts. Following Nietzsche's rejection of Wagner and Wagner's music, architecture came to displace music for Nietzsche as the foundation for the unification of all other arts. While Nietzsche did not reject music fully, he came to realize that the idea of Gesamtkunstwerk, a total artwork, must start with architecture.[6] Only an architecture in the grand style could evoke the creative spirit of the people and their collective will to power, and thereby enrich and elevate their aspirations and the quality of their everyday experiences.

Nietzsche's revised approach to music leads him to modify his understanding of the creative tensions between Apollonian and Dionysian impulses in architectural forms. Hitherto, music was considered by Nietzsche as a pure Dionysian art due to its non-figurative form, while architecture, by contrast, as an art that is wholly reliant on the immediacy of its material form, was pure Apollonian art. Architecture in the grand style, however, will maximize the creative tensions of both. No longer a plastic form that is perceived at a distance, architecture in the grand style becomes a rhythmic interplay of forms to entice our bodily identification with its design. Perhaps best described as an architectural *event* rather than *object*, buildings in the grand style encourage a festive experience, inviting us to participate in their design as a celebration of cultural achievement.

To investigate Nietzsche's call for architecture in the grand style inevitably involves consideration of his relationship with Wagner and Wagner's music, given, that is, the strength of Nietzsche's commitment to the musician early in his career, and the profound repercussions his rejection of Wagner would come to have on his philosophy, following his realization that Wagner was not the creative genius he once believed him to be. Similarly, Nietzsche's burgeoning interests in architecture were probably encouraged by his interests in the ideas of Jacob Burckhardt and Gottfried Semper – two prominent architectural theorists, who helped Nietzsche to develop his understanding of architecture in the grand style and as festive celebration, and whom – not insignificantly – both shared a common desire to distance themselves from Wagner.[7]

Burckhardt's praise for the Palazzo Pitti in Florence (built in 1458 by Luca Fancelli) in *Der Cicerone* (1855) and *Geschichte der Renaissance in*

Italien (1867/1868) made a strong impression on Nietzsche. Here was a building, Burckhardt wrote, of 'highest will power', the 'most ambitious' private building ever to have been commissioned (1867/1868:54,14). It is 'colossal' and can only have been created by 'superhuman beings' (*'übermenschliche Wesen'*) (1855:177; 1867/1868:54; see also 1867/1987:42). Crucially, it achieves its powerful status not from its large dimensions or its position on elevated ground, but 'the relationship of its forms', its 'rejection of all decoration' and its distance from 'anything pleasing or delicate'. For Nietzsche, the Palazzo Pitti arguably becomes the antidote he required to alleviate his profound disappointment at the loss of music. To the musicologist, Carl Fuchs (1838–1922), Nietzsche writes, the Palazzo Pitti has 'the *grand style'*, as it expresses 'the most intense form of the art of melody' (April 1886; KSB,7.688:177). Nietzsche's discussions of this building led him to begin to consider the architectural features and qualities of the grand style more formerly. The Palazzo Pitti suggested to him a raw will to power through its unambiguous style and rhythmic formal arrangement that is free from ornament and resistant to the charms of sentimentality (KSA,9.197:520, KSA,3.226:511). It was the kind of architecture that could encourage an immediate and uplifting bodily response. Nietzsche would come to supplement his understanding of architecture in the grand style with other buildings that captivated him, culminating in his impressions of the Mole Antonelliana as 'the greatest work of genius ever built'.

In the Mole, Nietzsche found architectural expressions of height instinct [*Höhentrieb*] and the defeat of gravity – not simply because the building was tall, but because it expressed the unwavering will to power of its architect, Antonelli, who stubbornly refused to compromise on its design even when the money ran out and his benefactors withdrew. He built ever higher because he willed to go beyond the dictates of architectural convention. Prior to Nietzsche's stays in Turin, he wrote of both Zarathustra's disappointment at the stunted houses of the modern city which he had to stoop to enter, for their lack of height conveyed to him the city's lack of aspiration, and Zarathustra's contrasting joy, with his celebration of life expressed as a towering building,

> Life wants to build itself high with columns and stairs; it wants to gaze into the far distance and out upon joyful splendour – *that* is why it needs height! And because it needs height, it needs steps and conflict between steps and those who climb them! Life wants to climb and in climbing overcome itself. [...] Here he who once towered aloft his thoughts in stone, knew as well as the wisest about the secret of life! [...] How divinely vault and arch here contrast one another in the struggle: how they strive against one another with light and shadow, these divinely-striving things.
>
> (Z, II, 29:125)

In the Mole Antonelliana, Nietzsche's metaphor turns to concrete reality. This building, he asserts, has 'been built out of an absolute desire for the heights – suggestive of nothing other than my Zarathustra' (KSB,8.1227:656).

Semper's analysis of the festive roots of architecture helped to shape Nietzsche's understanding of the instinctual potentials of architecture. Nietzsche was already familiar with Semper's writings when his own friendship with Wagner was at its height, and he may have taken more than a passing interest in the breakdown of Wagner's relationship with Semper several years earlier in the wake of their disastrous collaboration for a Theatre in Munich (a project enthusiastically supported – in word but not monetary funds – by the newly crowned King Ludwig II of Bavaria). Contrary to Joseph Rykwert's (1989/2010) claims, it is unlikely that Semper and Nietzsche met, and although we do not know whether Semper was familiar with Nietzsche's ideas, they demonstrate remarkable similarities in their respective depictions of Dionysus. In an unconventional move for their times, both sought to elevate Dionysus above Apollo as the anointed god of music and the arts, and master of the Muses. Thus, it is striking to find Nietzsche's notion of Dionysus depicted so boldly as it appears to do atop of Semper's renovated opera house, the Semperoper in Dresden, as its crowning feature. Semper was working on his design for the Semperoper at the same time Nietzsche was developing his conception of Dionysus in *The Birth of Tragedy* (*Die Geburt der Tragödie*). This building may point to something akin to a 'Nietzschean architecture', but whether it embodies architecture in the grand style is another matter.

The Chapters

This investigation is divided into two parts. The first analyses the extent of Nietzsche's philosophy of architecture, and the second, Nietzsche's ambiguous architectural legacy. I begin in Chapter 1 with the problematic lack of style which Nietzsche identifies at the root of the cultural malaise that has infiltrated modern German culture, expressed clearly in its stagnant and decadent architecture. According to Nietzsche, the 'One thing needful' is 'to give style to one's character', but Germany's lack of a unifying instinct means its cultural achievements are fragmented and in disarray (GS,290). Its architecture is simply a masquerade of historic styles, which, at best, allure us superficially with their sentimental charm and dazzling spectacle, or worse, alienate us from ourselves and each other. I analyse three problematic building types described by Nietzsche to illustrate these modern problems – the labyrinth, mausoleum and an uninhabitable garden house (*Gartenhaus*). Nietzsche presents Wagner as the master of the labyrinth and David Strauss (1808–74) as the metaphysical builder (*metaphysichen Baumeister*) of the garden house.

Chapter 2 begins to outline Nietzsche's architectural remedy for these problems with his notion of architecture in the grand style – an idea that is examined throughout the book. The grand style is brought into being by an 'organising power of will', the will to power of the architect, who is in touch with the cultural needs of their time and is subsequently able to render these needs into 'eloquent' plastic forms, which, in turn, uplift and revive those who experience them (TI IX.11:94). Attempts have been made to explain Nietzsche's account of the transformative power of architecture and the passage of the will to power from architect to onlooker. (For example, in Chapter 4, I evaluate an effusive explanation of Nietzsche's account given by Paul Kühn (1904) in the official guidebook for the Nietzsche-Archiv, which was intended as a philosophical critique of van de Velde's renovations of the building that housed the archives in Weimar.) I continue in Chapter 2 to explore the empathic relationship Nietzsche proposes between architectural forms and physiological experiences, which underpins Nietzsche's presentation of the evocative power of architecture – ideas he presents ahead of comparable studies, such as Heinrich Wölfflin's (1864–1945) influential work, *Prolegomena zu einer Psychologie der Architektur* (*Prolegomena to a Psychology of Architecture*) (1886). I go on to examine various elements of the grand style identified by Nietzsche, each of which contributes to a building's capacity to elicit a person's physiological engagement with its design, and subsequently to encourage a person to reflect on themselves rather than consider at a distance the material features of the building. Elements of the grand style include Nietzsche's notions of empty form, rhythmic form and height instinct. I examine these alongside Nietzsche's accounts of the Palazzo Pitti in Florence, palazzi in Genoa and the Mole Antonelliana in Turin.

I conclude Part I by evaluating Nietzsche's architectural influences. Here I consider the extent to which Wagner and Semper impacted on his notion of the grand style. I examine the significance of the theatre and festive celebration, and the importance of architectural surfaces as places of human interaction. Crucial to making sense of the dynamic and animating qualities of architecture proposed by Semper and Nietzsche is an understanding of the relationship between Apollo and Dionysus as contrasting aesthetic principles and creative forces. Nietzsche's early accounts of their relationship are most prominent in *Birth of Tragedy* (1872), but the genesis of his ideas can be traced to earlier public lectures that he gave in 1870 and their preparatory notes, which involve Nietzsche's annotations of works by Semper on architectural style. I examine the extent of Semper's influence on Nietzsche and consider whether this influence went both ways by assessing, amongst other instances, whether Semper's unconventional decision to give pride of place to Dionysus atop his Semperoper was an explicit nod to Nietzsche's philosophy. I end this chapter by investigating another, no less significant depiction of Dionysus, which inspired Nietzsche, Semper and Wagner alike – a composition known as *Bacchus unter Musen* (*Bacchus among the Muses*) by the German artist, Bonaventura Genelli (1798–1868). A watercolour version of this composition hung in Wagner's drawing room in Tribschen, where it would enthral Nietzsche during his visits. Many have speculated about the impression this painting made on Nietzsche, and whether Wagner had directly contributed to Nietzsche's understanding of Dionysus and Apollo from the many discussions they probably had while gazing at Genelli's painting. But what many if not most of these accounts fail to realize is that Genelli produced several compositions of the same theme. There is a tendency – evident even in esteemed scholarly accounts – to mistake Wagner's version of the painting for the most common composition in the series, and this is a costly error with unfortunate repercussions for Nietzschean scholarship, because the watercolour image that came into Wagner's possession differed not only in title (*Dionysos, von den Musen Apollos erzogen/Dionysus educated by Apollo's Muses*), but more significantly, in its composition. Many discussions have focused on the incorrect image. I draw attention to the repercussions of this error before explaining how Genelli's *Bacchus unter Musen* also inspired Semper, who desired its image as a stage curtain for his first opera house in Dresden. I propose that Genelli's Dionysus was more integral to Nietzsche and to Semper than often realized.

I end this chapter by analysing the Festspielhaus in Bayreuth as an embodiment of the deep-seated problems that Nietzsche sought to overcome with his remedy of architecture in the grand style. As such Wagner's theatre serves as an additional Nietzschean architectural metaphor of modern decadence and the antithesis of architecture in the grand style. The Festspielhaus in Bayreuth was apparently insulting also to Semper's architectural sensibilities, for it is in large part a distorted version of Semper's earlier designs for his failed Munich Theatre project, taken by Wagner without permission.

Part II begins with a comprehensive philosophical survey of architectural designs that have been created with the explicit intention of commemorating Nietzschean philosophy. Many of these seek to represent or to evoke central tenets of Nietzschean philosophy. I address the inherent problems of constructing a distinctly *Nietzschean architecture* before examining the significance of the temple as the most prominent building type conceived for these designs. I scrutinize the following designs in turn to ascertain how they sought to incorporate Nietzsche's ideas and whether they meet requirements for an architecture in the grand style. Renovations of Villa Silberblick for the Nietzsche-Archiv in Weimar that take place between 1902 and 1903; plans made by van de Velde in 1910 for a 'modest Nietzsche Temple' situated just below Villa Silberblick; a sketch of a temple to Nietzsche by Fritz Schumacher in 1898; a Temple Stadium Complex proposed for Weimar by van de Velde with direction from Count Harry Graf Kessler between 1911 and 1913 – conceived first as a small *temenos* in 1911, then, in the same year, as four variations of a larger temple with various sculptural figures, and finally, as a large international Centre for culture and sport, replete with horse shoe stadium; and a Nietzsche memorial for Kröller-Müller's 'Museum Park' in Holland, conceived in 1925 by van de Velde. The final design I consider is a Nietzsche memorial hall in Weimar, conceived and built between 1934 and 1944 by Paul Schultze-Naumburg, intended as a cultural Centre for the Third Reich. Hitler initially contributed financially from his private funds, but the building would soon become an ambiguous priority for Hitler. This building project is a useful case study for assessing Hitler's perception of Nietzsche's philosophy and the extent to which he valued Nietzsche's legacy as a political commodity. Furthermore, it exposes the conflict between an architecture designed to convey Nazi ideology and Nietzsche's intentions for the grand style.

Chapter 5 gives an overview of some of the ideological concerns that were common to Nietzsche and to early modern architects and design movements at the turn of the twentieth century. This prepares us to evaluate more effectively the extent to which Nietzsche influenced the ideas and designs of architects who have been associated with his name, and subsequently to ascertain whether Nietzsche was an explicit influence on them or simply a common voice in the background. Germany was a fertile country for developments and experiments in modern architectural designs due in large part to its identity crises in the lead up to the First World War and the Weimar Republic that followed. Rapid industrialization and technological innovations in the production and use of new materials for building construction informed the search for a 'new style' to elevate German culture and revive its ailing spirit. Inevitably, this search sparked political and ideological rifts and heated debates over aesthetic details of this innovative new style. Should architecture be radically new and abstracted entirely from its historical traditions? Ought it be distinctly German or be open to international influence? I address these questions from a Nietzschean perspective by drawing on his views on German nationalism and the appropriate use of history. I subsequently critique from a Nietzschean perspective an array of designs that have been presented as examples of the 'new style' – from utilitarian cubic or modular styles promoted by socialist and internationalist agendas to 'German' styles rooted in conservative narratives of race. The competitive struggle for styles may have appealed to Nietzsche's perspectivism and his desire for creative tensions, but equally, he would have insisted that no style or approach could credibly lay claim to being a definitive expression of the new style. My analysis considers the aims, ethos, and aesthetic approaches of key organizations and movements that have been associated with the origins of modern architecture and with the philosophical ideas of Nietzsche. They include the Deutscher Werkbund (1907–38), the Darmstädt Colony (1899–1901) and the Bauhaus (1919–33), alongside their respective critics.

Chapter 6 delves deeper into relationships between Nietzsche's ideas and common themes in the early developments of modern architecture. Here I identify how key elements of the grand style are evident in the concerns of several prominent architects and designers who have been associated with Nietzschean philosophy. I evaluate, in turn, the elements of empty form (and lack of ornament), festive rhythm, height instinct, physiological affect and the importance of the architect as a heroic figure of the grand style, alongside ideas and designs of Le Corbusier, Oskar Schlemmer (1888–1943), Henry van de Velde and Louis H. Sullivan, among others.

The book ends with Chapter 7 with a close analysis of specific designs of modern architecture which have been identified by scholars as making explicit reference to Nietzschean ideas. I draw upon the findings from previous chapters to evaluate their claims. The works considered include Henry van de Velde's Theatre for the 1914 Werkbund Exhibition in Cologne; Peter Behrens' 'Zarathustra house' devised and built between 1899 and 1901 at the Darmstädt Artist Colony; Behrens' *Hamburger Vorhalle* for the Exposition of Decorative Arts in Cologne in 1902; Behrens' AEG Turbine building built in 1909 in Berlin; and Bruno Taut's various crystal houses, conceived in his illustrated works, *Alpine Architektur* (1919) and *Die Stadtkrone* (1919/2015), together with his celebrated *Glashaus*, exhibited at the 1914 Werkbund exhibition in Cologne, hundreds of yards away from van de Velde's Theatre – and finally, Taut's *Monument des Neuen Gesetzes*, sketched in 1919. Perhaps most insightful for this investigation is Taut's attempts in *Die Stadtkrone* to establish an architectural template for a city that maximizes and elevates the creative aspirations of its citizens in accordance with Taut's ideas about social hierarchy. Each citizen is instinctively drawn to their respective zones in the city, which radiate outwards and downwards from a large *Kristallhaus*, where the exemplary artists dwell. The *Kristallhaus* is 'quiet and empty' and has no purpose other than to inspire every citizen. It radiates its light onto every building in the city, right down to the simplest hut, and imparts to each one the 'depth and power' of its 'philosophy of life', causing them to 'shimmer' in its brilliance (1919/2015:76). In Taut's plans we may have found a city to meet Zarathustra's approval.

* * *

To read Nietzsche productively is a tricky path to negotiate. Nietzsche's writings are replete with symbols, metaphors and contradictions, which encourage multiple interpretations and perspectives, understandings and misunderstandings. It is a style that reinforces his philosophical aims by encouraging his readers to consider viewpoints that contrast with their own. 'The worst readers', Nietzsche writes, 'are those who behave like plundering soldiers: they take the few things they can use, leave the rest dirty and disordered, and slander the whole' (OM,137). It is tempting to assemble edifices from the 'building blocks' Nietzsche provides, and to create a haphazard mishmash of styles akin to those he criticizes. This study is not so misguided as to imagine itself as a definitive work on Nietzsche and architecture, but neither does it refrain from calling attention to the misinterpretations of others, not least those architects – or their commentators – who portrayed themselves as superhuman figures or creators of a distinctly 'Nietzschean architecture'. Ultimately, it is simply hoped that this study encourages discussion on its intriguing subject.

PART ONE

Nietzsche's philosophy of architecture

CHAPTER ONE

The problematic lack of style

Nietzsche asserts, 'One thing is needful – to "give style" to one's character – a great and rare art!' (GS,290). Similarly, it is 'in art' that 'the human relishes themselves as perfection' (TI, IX,9:93). To have 'grand style' therefore suggests one has exceptional character and artistic prowess. I wish to argue that the figure of the architect in Nietzsche's writings is primed for the grand style, and is in many ways, a precursor to Nietzsche's Übermensch. In an unpublished note from March/April 1888, Nietzsche describes the architect as 'a great act of willing in its most convincing and proudest form'. By the same token, architecture is 'edifices of power', which embodies 'the eloquence of the will in spatial form' (KSA,14[117]:425). Nietzsche's use of architectural imagery to convey features of the grand style is evocative and striking and is often employed by him to pass comment at one and the same time on the characters of people, cultures and buildings, both real and imagined.

Nietzsche invokes the work of the builder or sculptor through his metaphors of 'philosophizing with a hammer'. Zarathustra describes each person as a raw, unhewn stone, within which sleeps the most noble edifice, woken only by 'the hammer' that is used forcibly by Zarathustra's 'creative will' (EH,IX,Z.8). The work of the artist or architect is difficult and ongoing for it is linked to Nietzsche's determination to smash and raze all outmoded values and idols. It is also dangerous work, for Nietzsche warns those who attempt to topple idols and to invert values to be sure they do not fall back on them: 'Take care, lest a falling statue [or building] strike you dead!' (Z, I,22[3]:103). The building and self that is conjointly perfected in the grand style are hammered instinctively into a shape that is absent of frivolous ornament and is not excessive in volume. At the end of *The Birth of Tragedy,* Nietzsche suggests a person's perfected shape is reflected to them in the 'pure and noble lines' and 'gleaming marble' of 'tall Ionic columns' (BT,25), but, as I will argue, architecture in the grand style is not necessarily of the Ionic order, and nor is it restricted to the classical style. Similarly, it is neither explicitly Renaissance, Baroque, nor modern in style. It emulates no preconceived style or building type but is driven by the instinctual desires and will of its creator, and this will is subsequently in tune with the present needs and aspirations of the culture and people for whom the architect creates. Architecture in the grand style is free from the dictates of outmoded conventions and traditions. 'Good architecture', in this context, Neumeyer writes, is 'the stone physiognomy and the built image of bold, hungry active people, who have faith in themselves, and who value it highly and enough to immortalize themselves in buildings' (2001/2004:167). 'Bad architecture', by contrast, will inevitably deflect from the aspirations of people with a parody of power, with designs that are often overly complex, and with elaborate façades that confuse and inhibit self-expression and self-reflection.

Throughout this book I identify and seek to explain various connections Nietzsche makes between architectural designs and the character of individuals and cultures to illuminate Nietzsche's notion of 'grand style' and his understandings of the creative relationships we have with ourselves, others and the places we inhabit. These connections and relationships are principally grounded in our physiological engagement with the material fabric of architectural design – specifically their rhythmic play of form – which facilitates our heightened self-awareness. In *Twilight of the Idols: or How to Philosophise with a Hammer* (1888/2021), Nietzsche defines art and 'any aesthetic doing and seeing' as a physiological experience of 'increased strength and fullness'. A person who feels uplifted in this manner is compelled, he says, to enrich 'everything' ('whatever one sees, whatever one wills') with 'fullness' until these things are similarly transformed, and 'mirror' the person's feelings (TI, IX,8–9:92–3). Architecture in the grand style invites us to engage with its material forms instinctively, but, as Nietzsche argues, our capacity to do so is severely limited because modern culture has sought to repress our instinctive sensibilities, conditioning us to respond to the world intellectually with a view to understand rather than experience. Consequently, the modern mindset is largely estranged from physiological experiences and desensitized to the material world. Architecture in the grand style is a much-needed remedy to heal this division, and to re-orientate people to place.

Nietzsche seeks a new type of person with an attitude that cannot be distracted by unhelpful approaches to life, which hinder the discovery of enriching experiences and values. In parallel, he seeks a new architecture, with buildings that embody the will of the architect and the people, and which encourages creativity and self-reflection in all who use them. But he laments the fact that both scenarios are improbable so long as the modern mindset continues to be entrenched in unhelpful conventions that systematically enslave us, preventing the cultivation of new values and styles. By submitting to the dictates of ideology and institutional thought – such as religious dogma, scientific code or other certitudes – we forfeit our individual freedoms and our social responsibility to discover our own values and truths relevant to our time and place. Nietzsche was firmly opposed to Hegel's understanding of the modern state as the institutional grounds to which human spiritual energies should aim. For Nietzsche this is a decadent approach to life that establishes a 'herd' mentality where the blind leads the blind into deluded ways of being. The state, he maintained is better regarded as a means to a more valuable goal – the cultivation of genius and enrichment of culture.

Much of what Nietzsche has to say about the problematic modern mindset and its remedy underpins his ideas about architecture and the built environment. Architecture in the grand style expresses and encourages the character and qualities of the creative mindset. We would undermine Nietzsche's position if we sought to prescribe how a creative person ought to behave, and in similar vein it is futile to posit what a 'Nietzschean building' looks like. He does not present us with a definitive architectural blueprint for the grand style. The grand style is achieved not emulated. 'Good style *in itself*', he maintains, is 'pure folly, mere "idealism"' (EH III.4). An examination of Nietzsche's account of architecture and its place within his wider philosophy needs first to address the problems that Nietzsche had identified at the root of Germany's cultural decay, for these are the problems Nietzsche sought to remedy with his conception of the grand style. To this I now turn.

Germany's stylistic masquerade and mishmash of architectural styles

Nietzsche's sustained 'attack', as he referred to it, on German culture first appears in the first of his *Untimely Meditations* from 1873, where he equates it with 'mere "public opinion"': 'without meaning, without substance, without aim' (EH, V,UM.1). In the second Meditation from 1874, he criticizes the German predilection for rationalizing human experience and appraising it according to past experiences through the accumulation of historical facts and results of scientific endeavour – an approach he brandishes 'inhuman', 'dangerous', a 'sickness' and 'poison to life' (EH, V,UM.1). According to Nietzsche, nineteenth-century Europe, more generally, had endorsed a brutalized version of eighteenth-century Enlightenment values by prioritizing reason and logical method with little recourse to human instinctual experiences as an equally valid source of meaning and value. Reason and instinct, he argues, must be allowed to inform each other in our quest for meaning and a flourishing life. Reason depends on instincts for its continuous renewal, and the instincts depend on reason as a vehicle for their expression. One without the other leads to a stagnant, neurotic life.

Nietzsche's philosophy is often admired for its psychological insights, and their influence can be traced in the ideas of notable psychologists such as Sigmund Freud (1856–1939). Perhaps most influential in this context was Nietzsche's account of the repression of instincts and its repercussions for individuals, groups and whole cultures. According to Nietzsche, repressed instincts can lead to feelings of frustration and resentment towards those who appear more satisfied and freely able to express their desires. A life of repressed instincts is a stagnant life, one severely limited in creative resources, and impeded in its capacity to 'give style' to character. The repression of instincts, Nietzsche says, is the 'most dangerous blasting and explosive material' (GM, III:15). It can lead to a fragmented character, and as Freud would later convey in his theories of psychoses, to fragmented experiences of reality.

Earlier I mentioned that Nietzsche lauded ancient Greek culture for its ability to harness the tensions between reason and instincts to highly creative ends. Nietzsche initially thought a similar approach could be revived in modern Germany through the music of Wagner, with its powerful mythological narrative, but he soon came to criticize Wagner and his music as symptomatic of the decadent values that had infected modern Europe. In an essay from 1888 written as an attack on Wagner, Nietzsche explains how modern-day Germany is unable to respond effectively to the all-important 'question of *style*' due to its inability to cultivate a *unified* sense of style. The key problem, as Nietzsche saw it, is the lack of a unifying instinct within German culture, which results in poor achievements that are fragmented and riddled with chaotic and confusing styles. The essential unity or 'whole' is replaced by a 'composite' of 'little units' – an 'anarchy of atoms' – that establish a 'calculated, artificial' and 'unnatural product' (CW,7).

Nietzsche regarded architecture as a useful medium with which to observe and assess the values and artistic priorities of the culture that created it. He refers to the vernacular architecture of modern Germany to make his point, by citing its designs as evidence of the fragmented and chaotic sense of style that informed it. To the architects, who are desensitized to people's psychological and somatic needs, Nietzsche writes, 'it will be evident from your buildings that they have been *amassed* rather than *assembled*' (KSA,7.29[58]:653). The disintegration of modern German culture, he continues, is available for all to see through the 'chaotic mishmash of all styles'. Every time a German 'glances at their clothes, their room, and their house' or 'walks through the streets of their cities' they are reminded of the 'grotesque juxtaposition and jumbling of all possible styles. The German amasses around themselves the forms, colours, products, and curiosities of all ages and climes, and thereby produces that modern carnival motley of the modern world [...] They calmly seat themselves in the midst of this tumult of styles' (UM I.1). Our 'dwellings, rooms, clothes, manners, theatres, museums', he says, are 'proof of the most absolute absence of style' (KSA,14.161:60). According to Markus Breitschmid, 'For Nietzsche, the cities and their houses seem to be the most important testimonies of the desolate cultural situation of the nineteenth century' (2001:15).

Historical style revivalism: Façades and disembodied selves

Nietzsche's account can be read as a reaction to the historicism and style-revivalism that were popular in Germany at the time. During the second half of the nineteenth century, Germany was an industrial world-leader, competing internationally in science, technology and commerce. Following a large influx of capital from war reparations of the Franco-Prussian war (1870–1) and its subsequent unification into the German Empire, the nation enjoyed considerable economic boom. This period of prosperity led to a call for more housing, and a national drive to elevate the quality of mass-produced artistic goods to ensure they were more stylish and aesthetically pleasing. To that end, green fields were transformed into housing developments, often comprising large buildings of four to six storeys, with finely decorated façades in an array of revivalist styles.

For Nietzsche, the mimicry of historical styles in vernacular architecture exposes the absence of creative spirit. The German spirit reveals its weakness by emulating ideas of greatness from the past, rather than seeking through risk and experiment innovative design principles and styles more suited to the present. According to Nietzsche, modern German culture is grounded less in greatness but in a superficial pretence – of pretending to be great for appearance's sake. 'Just take a stroll through any German city', he writes, 'everything is colourless, worn out, badly copied, slipshod; everyone does as they like' but without consideration and in haste, and according to 'the universal addiction to comfort' (UM II.4). The modern German mindset was, he thought, so steeped in the weight of facts and knowledge that it could only relate to itself in abstract terms. It was as if it were disembodied and uprooted from its immediate and material environment. Nietzsche subsequently defined German culture as 'essentially inward', and the modern mindset as a 'walking encyclopaedia' – 'on the outside' cover of which, 'the bookbinder has printed': a "Handbook of Inward Cultivation for Outward Barbarians" (UM II.4) The inner life of the modern German could be richer and wiser had it not lacked the instinctual awareness to employ its knowledge critically for effective living in the here and now. Its lack in this regard makes it 'arrogantly clumsy, and meekly slovenly' (UM II.4). Modern German culture in Nietzsche's eyes is a dead culture, a mere repository of facts related to past cultures. Although the accumulation of knowledge for knowledge's sake fails to transform people, modern people take pride in it, seeking to furnish their inwardness in ever-greater forensic details and nuances.

Contemporary German architecture is opposed to the grand style because it encourages people to hide behind façades – both psychological and architectural – where they become entrenched and lost in abstract ideals, disconnected from their instinctual and aesthetic needs. Their built environments proffer few opportunities for self-reflection and self-discovery because their preference for an architecture that makes explicit reference to past styles and designs inevitably distracts people from themselves, encouraging them to contemplate instead the architectural masquerade before them. In one of Nietzsche's most recognizable comments about architecture, he laments, 'we no longer understand architecture', 'we have lost touch with the symbolism of lines and figures'. 'What is the beauty of a building to us now?' – it is 'masklike' (HH I,218). Decorated façades sporting a mishmash of historical styles are indeed masklike. They function for appearance's sake, as a caricature of culture. The symbolism of the lines and figures that inform their design fails to engage or move the onlooker beyond superficial flights of fancy.

Superfluous designs and their neurotic effects

Nietzsche outlines some problematic consequences of an architecture devised by a culture that is weak and fragmented. In Nietzsche's critique the modern German mindset is at some level aware of its discord and its desensitized relationship with the material world, for it finds itself drawn to things and experiences that grant temporary satisfaction and fleeting sensations of connection and completion. Nietzsche's psychological insights into this situation are significant to our discussion. For instance, those who are disengaged from their instinctual needs, he says, will go in search of sublime experiences and theatrical affects, and will, in turn, be easily distracted and captivated by superficial displays of emotion. Furthermore, their penchant for abstract reasoning will attract them to idealistic ways of thinking, and to the misguided belief that life can be understood, mastered and improved upon through intellectual reasoning. In both instances a person will attempt to compensate for their inability to manage the natural expression of their instincts by seeking out grandiose experiences in things outside of them. These external sources are sought to provide energy and vitality, but they are poor substitutes for a person's own instinctual resources – their 'unifying instinct', as Nietzsche refers to it – which they had come to repress. These external sources provide a 'quick fix', with a fleeting sense of elation and a delusory sense of power. As such, the desire for larger-than-life experiences compounds the problem, encouraging a person to depend on external resources for their self-affirmation.

According to Nietzsche, instincts cannot be wholly denied when repressed. They continue to generate a strong – potentially 'explosive' – energetic charge, which propels them eventually to overcome their censorship and to break into consciousness as sudden outbursts of emotion. The modern mindset is therefore susceptible to emotional turbulence. Had instincts been granted their natural expression, they would be more manageable and available for creative use. Instead, the modern person is emotionally vulnerable and easily distracted by situations that provoke emotion. They are defined by an 'over-boisterousness in the smallest details; emotion at any price; sophistication as expression of *impoverished* life; always more nerves in place of flesh' (CW, Second Postscript).

The most distracting figure in the modern era, Nietzsche claims, is the actor or theatrical 'stage-player' with their ability to 'awaken *great* enthusiasm' (CW,11). Nietzsche pitches the actor against the architect. 'When actors become masters', he says, 'great architects' become 'ever more disadvantaged' and 'finally made impossible'. Above all, 'the strength to build becomes paralysed' (GS,356). Architects can no longer build, they merely 'assemble', becoming actors themselves through their imitation of historical styles and pretence of power. Once the mask or façade of their creations is removed, the fragmented foundations are exposed. Nietzsche criticizes modern architecture for sensationalizing power and creativity in various ways. For instance, its proclivity for gigantic buildings that overwhelm the onlooker with their vastness – after all, it is easier, he notes, to move the masses by being gigantic than beautiful (CW,6). And its appetite for architectural ruins, which arouses feelings for the picturesque. The picturesque is a forced and exaggerated image of something, a superficial experience of the desire simply to experience something (KSA,12.110:398–9).

Labyrinths, mausoleums and garden houses

According to Nietzsche, German culture was underpinned by a nationalistic fervour, which presented a significant obstacle for its creative achievements by inspiring fragmentation and contempt among its people. The lack of a unifying instinct leads, he claimed, to a collective grandiosity and to a 'sacred compulsion' to establish an unhealthy compensation in the form of a united German nation at all costs, united 'in nature and soul'. Nietzsche considers this another symptom of the ailing modern German mindset and a displaced desire caused by the failure to engage with the root of the problem. Germany's need for creative spirit is greater, he asserts, than its need for political unity; creative genius, not citizenship, he claims, is the highest expression of cultural achievement. Exemplary figures of the nineteenth century, he says, have risen above their nation, and he cites as cases in point, Beethoven, Goethe, Napoleon, Stendhal, Heinrich Heine, Schopenhauer and Wagner (even though Wagner misunderstood his genius) (BGE, 256). Because the German mindset had restricted the instinctual resources made available to it, its understanding of cultural unity is similarly constrained and weakened. Subsequently, modern Germany barely looks beyond itself towards its potential enrichment as a more expansive 'European' culture, where it could 'digest' and 'absorb' cultural tendencies of other nations, such as France – 'the seat of the most spiritual and sophisticated culture in Europe and the preeminent school of taste' (cf. BGE, 251,254). Nietzsche suggests, '[we] present ourselves fearlessly as *good Europeans* and in our actions work for the melting together of nations' (HH I.475). Modern German nationalism establishes an attitude of 'us versus them' – a 'pathological alienation' of others (BGE, 256) – which dampens creative spirit rather than cultivating its exemplary artists. It imagines itself as a superior nation and invents elaborate justifications for its superiority, with recourse to mythologies and complex symbols, discoverable only to the initiated. 'The German soul contains passages and inter-passages, there are caves, hideouts and dungeons in it [...] and Germans know the secret paths to chaos' (BGE, 244). '*Let us be idealists!*' exclaims the modern German, for if we are to elevate ourselves, 'we ourselves must be sublime. Let us walk above the clouds, let us harangue the infinite, let us place huge symbols all around us!' (CW,6).

Arguably, the architecture that Nietzsche most disliked and sought to eradicate in his discussions of the grand style were designs that incorporated extensive symbolic ornament. Indeed, later I discuss how Nietzsche's ideas were cited by architects of the Bauhaus School and others linked to the 'Internationalist style' as philosophical justification for their own stark designs, free from ornament. In this respect, buildings replete with ornament stand alongside those that parade a mishmash of historical styles as Nietzschean architectural metaphors for the ailing modern mind. To these we might add others described by Nietzsche, including unhabitable houses, mausoleums and labyrinths.

In the first of his *Untimely Meditations*, Nietzsche questions whether the 'metaphysical builder' [*metaphysichen Baumeister*], David Friedrich Strauss (1808–74), understands how to construct a house. Nietzsche's essay is an attack on Strauss' recent work, *The Old and the New Faith: A Confession* (1873) – a work Nietzsche upheld as an exemplar of modern German thought with its promotion of scientific understanding, which Strauss employs in his book to further the idiotic ideology, as Nietzsche sees it, of the progress of Christianity and history. Nietzsche compares Strauss' problematic approach to a clumsy architect, who designs defective buildings.

> Once [...] the edifice itself has been erected in harmonious proportions, there is still much left to be done: how many minor defects must be corrected, how many gaps filled; here and there provisional partitions or scaffolds have had to suffice for the time being; everywhere you turn there is dust and rubble, and wherever you look you see the signs of problems and ongoing labour. The house as a whole is still uninhabitable and unhomey; all the walls are naked, and the wind whips through the open windows.
>
> (UM I.9)

Nietzsche suggests it is unhelpful to ask 'whether Strauss has constructed this building with sound proportions and with an eye for totality' because Strauss follows the scholarly customs of his time, and merely assembles his edifice 'out of bits and pieces'. He thereby 'trust[s] that these bits and pieces have a coherence unto themselves', and inevitably confuses 'logical and artistic coherence'. Indeed, according to Nietzsche, the overall design is less of a 'temple' or 'residence', and more of a summer pavilion or 'garden house' [*Gartenhaus*]. Its architecture lacks vision and is concerned primarily with calculated aesthetic effects to manufacture mysterious feelings. For Nietzsche, this is a fundamentally flawed approach, 'just as we might view some irrational thing – let us say, the ocean – from the vantage point of the most ornamental and rationally constructed terrace' (UM I.9).

Nietzsche treats his reader to a guided tour of the interior of Strauss' house, while at the same time commenting on sections of Strauss' book. The overriding impression Nietzsche gives is of a house of uncoordinated design and aesthetic effect, and precarious engineering. While the inhabitants enjoy the comforts of its furnishings, its structure is defective. It is unfinished with gaps and holes exposed to the elements. The mismatch between its structural integrity and the experience of its inhabitants suggests only those in a deluded state of mind can live there. Nietzsche begins his tour of the garden house in the dark 'gloom' of its 'theological catacombs', which are clothed with 'convoluted and Baroque ornamentation'. From there we step immediately into a hall that is brightly lit with artificial overhead lighting. The walls of the hall are covered with mathematical tables and celestial charts, and the room houses scientific instruments and is furnished with cabinets filled with skeletons, stuffed apes and anatomical specimens. 'From here we amble on, feeling for the first time genuinely happy, into the total comfort of those who dwell in our garden house.' We find other residents 'surrounded by their wives and children, engrossed in their newspapers and mundane political discussions [...] and it strikes us that we could not possibly rattle off the rosary of public opinions more quickly than they do'. Finally, 'a brief visit to the library and the music room' reveals 'only the best books line the shelves, and only the most celebrated compositions are on the music stands'. In conclusion, 'the owner of this garden house praises himself and expresses the opinion that anyone who is not happy here is beyond help and not ripe for his standpoint' (UM I.9).

If the garden house emphasizes the decadence of a comfortable life led in accordance with truth and certainty, Nietzsche's allusions to the mausoleum and the labyrinth emphasize the alienated and oppressive nature of this modern condition. 'A completely modern person who wants to build themselves a house', he says, 'feels as if this would be the same as wanting to entomb their living body in a mausoleum' (HH I.22). Such a person has cut themselves off from the vital instincts that would otherwise nourish their values and replenish their lives. Nietzsche employs a similar architectural metaphor in his parable of the *madman*, who enters the marketplace to proclaim the death of God to the bemusement of his secular audience (GS,125). 'What after all are these churches now if they are not the tombs and sepulchres of God?' the madman asks. The buildings that once housed the metaphysical values of God lie dormant, waiting for new inhabitants to repurpose them with viable, life-sustaining values.

God had to die, Nietzsche claimed, to eradicate the metaphysical grounding of values which seduce us with their promise of unchanging truth and remove from us the responsibility of creating our own values according to our own experiences. But as Nietzsche laments, modern people lack the instinctual intelligence to embrace this situation and create for themselves. They continue to favour abstract ideals and metaphysical propositions, effectively keeping God alive, often substituting God for another idol, such as a faith in scientific progress – a move that perpetuates the problem. The underlying 'will to truth' must be eradicated and replaced by a will to power. The remedy to this modern condition is to appreciate our somatic response to things and to attune ourselves to our material environments. The modern German mindset, by contrast, is conditioned to become captivated by 'hidden secrets', facts and abstract ideas. It is analogous to the labyrinth – to an architecture that entraps its inhabitants within complicated and concealed interiors (D,169). The labyrinth induces anxiety and bewilderment through its meandering paths that suggest a way forward but lead without direction and without orientation. The labyrinth is a daunting prospect. It threatens from its dark passageways the sudden revelation of something monstrous – the threat, perhaps, of 'explosive' instincts about to break through into consciousness. The madman's words could be applied to the bewildering and uncanny experience of the labyrinth: 'Whither are we moving?', 'Are we not plunging continually? Backward, sideward, forward, in all directions? Is there any up or down? Are we not straying as through an infinite nothing? Do we not feel the breath of empty space? Has it not become colder? Is not night continually closing in on us?' (GS,125).

Wagner: Master of the labyrinth

According to Nietzsche, 'Wagner is the *modern artist par excellence*.' His art mixes, 'in the most seductive way', the 'three great stimulants of the exhausted; the *brutal*, the *artificial*, and the *innocent* (idiotic)'. His art leads not to style but to 'neurosis' and to 'hysterics' problems' (CW I.5). Wagner has an 'incapacity for any style whatsoever', and in him his followers have the 'best practiced guide for the labyrinth of modern soul' (CW,7; CW, *Foreword*). This is not to suggest that Wagner can help others find their way out of the labyrinth, but on the contrary, he can draw their attention more closely to its hidden secrets, distracting them further.

As I mentioned in the Introduction, Wagner is at the centre of Nietzsche's account of architecture in several respects, and any serious examination of the subject must consider his role carefully. It is in Nietzsche's rejection of Wagner's music that Nietzsche discovers architecture as a valuable resource and antidote to the demise of modern German culture. It is Wagner's watercolour painting, *Dionysos, von den Musen Apollos erzogen* by Giovanni Buonaventura Genelli, displayed at Wagner's house in Tribschen, which sparked conversations between Wagner and Nietzsche about the Dionysian spirit, and, arguably, encouraged Nietzsche to develop his account of the significance of Dionysus and Apollo for an elevated culture. Nietzsche was also party to the design and construction of Wagner's Festspielhaus in Bayreuth – which took as its template, theatre designs by Gottfried Semper, whom Nietzsche regarded as 'the most significant living architect' (GMD:18; KSA,1:522). Although it is unlikely that Nietzsche met Semper – despite some suggesting without evidence that Wagner personally introduced them to each other – we know that Nietzsche was influenced by Semper's writings, and his interest in Semper was encouraged by Wagner and his wife, Cosima. In Chapter 3, I explore these points in turn.

Wagner was initially revered by Nietzsche. Nietzsche regarded him as a mentor, believing him to be a genius who could restore power to German culture in similar manner to ancient Greek tragedy through his creative fusion of history and myth. Nietzsche's early work, *The Birth of Tragedy: Out of the Spirit of Music* (1872/1993), which he dedicated to Wagner, proposed a reform of German culture founded on the metaphysics of art and the rebirth of tragic myth. He would later regret the work, as he did his relationship with Wagner, regarding both as misguided and naïve. Nevertheless, the book includes important themes that continue to develop throughout his work, nonetheless so than the creative tensions between Dionysian and Apollonian approaches to art and life, and arguably also the importance of myth, without which, he writes, 'every culture loses its healthy and natural creative power: only a horizon defined by myths can unify an entire cultural movement' (BT,23). The grand Wagnerian festival at Bayreuth in August 1876 was hotly anticipated by Nietzsche as an event to mark the beginning of a profound rebirth of Germany as an artistic culture. But it proved to be catastrophic for Nietzsche. It expressed to him all the problems it had set out to overcome. It was decadent, depressing and artificial (KSA, 8.40[11]:580). Nietzsche escaped to Sorrento to recover. From thereon, his friendship with Wagner deteriorated rapidly, and he sought to undermine the value of metaphysics, which for him had been closely intertwined with Wagner's music. And it was arguably at this time that Nietzsche began to lose trust in the value of music more generally, with its powerful capacity to seduce a person into unbounded states of reverie and flights of fancy, and to find solace in the corporeal immediacy of architecture as a more credible remedy to the cultural problem. Architecture could provide a person with a crucial grounding and containment, helping them to engage with the immediacy of things in a meaningful way. Nietzsche describes his objections to Wagner's music as 'physiological objections'. The body complains when it listens to Wagner's music – one 'no longer breathes easily', one's 'foot soon resents it and rebels' because it needs the 'easy, bold, exuberant self-assured rhythms' and 'all those delights which are found in *good* walking, striding, leaping, and dancing' (GS,368). In Wagner's music one swims in an infinite nothingness – a disorientation reminiscent of the nihilistic pronouncements of Nietzsche's madman. As we know, good walking was vital for Nietzsche, and dancing was no less crucial for his Zarathustra. As I will argue, rhythm and movement are key components of architecture in the grand style.

Looking back on his relationship with Wagner, Nietzsche explains, 'I needed Wagner to get free from the Germans' with their overly rational mindset. But 'Wagner is the counter-poison to everything German par excellence – still poison. I do not dispute it' (EH, II.6). Wagner was unable to unify German culture because he, too, lacks an 'organising idea', and 'organising energy', and is ultimately incapable of creating 'organic form'. In that respect, he is just as toxic as the modern German mindset. Wagner was 'admirable', Nietzsche says, only in his capacity to master 'microscopic features of the soul' (CW,7). Wagner invents 'little unities' and 'animates them, inflates them, and renders them visible'. But by doing so, 'his power exhausts itself' and presents a 'complete degeneration' of 'rhythmical feeling', with '*chaos* in place of rhythm' (CW,7; CW, *Postscript*). Wagner's music manages to compress 'into the smallest space an infinitude of meaning and sweetness' (CW,7.). The result is a 'theatrical pose', stage-playing and pantomime to achieve mere '*effect* and nothing more' (NCW IX.1:393).

Wagner is a master of the labyrinth because he entices people into constricted places to play a 'game of hide-and-seek among a hundred symbols' (CW,10). In another architectural analogy, Nietzsche portrays Wagner as a self-conflicted person, divided against himself. One part of him wants to disregard small details and design 'great walls and daring frescos', but the other part enjoys nothing more than sitting quietly in the corners of 'collapsed buildings', where 'hidden' and 'hidden from himself, he paints his real masterpieces, which are all very brief, often only a single bar long' (NCW I:389).

Nietzsche's Wagner, as 'the *modern artist par excellence*', personifies for Nietzsche the failings of modern German culture. The problem with Wagner and his followers, Nietzsche asserts, is their hunger for something sublime to arouse them and make them feel alive. They do not need to seek clarity about themselves when they are bowled over with the mere imitations that Wagner provides (CW,6).

> That which Wagner and the 'others' have in common – I shall spell it out: a deterioration of organising powers; misuse of traditional methods without the ability to provide a *justification* or purpose; counterfeiting in imitation of grand forms for which nobody nowadays is strong, proud,

confident, *healthy* enough; over-boisterousness in the smallest things; emotion at any price; sophistication as the expression of *impoverished* life; always more nerves in place of flesh.

(CW, Second Postscript)

He continues, Wagner 'is a master of imitation'. Furthermore, all 'that makes pretensions to the "grand style" in music today is therefore *either* false toward us *or* false toward itself'.

Architecture as remedy

In Nietzsche's reading, we find nineteenth-century Germany stuck in an uncreative cycle, due in large part to its compulsion to acquire knowledge for knowledge's sake and its ineffective management of instinctual resources otherwise available to it. Modern German culture cannot begin to mine the creative potentials of human living. Its creative output is sterile due to its naïve conception of aesthetic value, and this leads to architectural designs that are merely pleasing to the eye, superficial in dramatic effect or intellectually distracting. Buildings of this nature will help to establish desensitized environments, and these in turn continue to stultify the inhabitants' general well-being, providing further obstacles to their creative development. It is a cycle Nietzsche wants to break.

On the one hand Nietzsche is keen to accelerate the decline of German culture in its current state, and on the other he seeks the means to revitalize it. He is subsequently regarded at one as the same time as a cultural critic and a 'prophet' for a new approach to design (Breitschmid 2001:15; Garnham 2013:71). Nietzsche's desire for cultural reform and for a new beginning without a return to defunct, once-powerful architectural designs, does not mean a total break with historical forms, as I will come to explain. Rather, his vision for a new culture sits alongside the old. Although he rejects historicism – the most popular approach to cultural criticism in Germany at the time, expressed in its vernacular architectural designs – he encourages more critical approaches to history. For instance, he suggests that much can be learnt from contemplating powerful cultures of the past through their historic monuments, but importantly, the knowledge acquired needs to be put to good use (UM II.2). Modern German culture will not discover its greatness by imitating the once-powerful designs of these monuments, but through careful investigation of the instinctual sources that gave rise to them, and a subsequent evaluation of whether these sources can be revived for present times.

Nietzsche's remedy to the problem is an architecture built in the grand style, which will reunite a person with their instinctive selves and their material environments, re-sensitizing them to their corporeal needs and to rich textures and experiences of the world. In other words, an architecture that expands the creative resources available to us, fostering in the process a fuller, richer, self-awareness. While music transports the listener from their material world to dream-like reveries, architecture in the grand style will bring a person back to themselves, to an embodied experience of themselves, reoriented in relation to their material environments.

The architecture Nietzsche seeks has a 'necessary' design. In other words, its design will respond to our needs, and, to recall, the *one thing needful* is to give style to our character. This architecture will help to unify a person, organizing and harnessing otherwise chaotic and fragmentary experiences that beset modern culture. It will have a new-found sense of 'rhythm' and 'ritual' that will not transport a person away from themselves but draw them meaningfully to themselves. Its design will subsequently be devoid of unnecessary distractions: of unhelpful aesthetic effects and ornamental 'chatter'. Instead, 'quiet and wide, expansive places with long, high-ceilinged arcades' will be cultivated, with buildings that express 'the sublimity of contemplation and stepping aside' to take thought for oneself (GS,280). Next I analyse architecture in the grand style as the remedy Nietzsche proposes to revitalize the creative spirit, before examining key architectural influences for his ideas.

CHAPTER TWO

Architecture in the grand style

Nietzsche proposes architecture in the grand style as a remedy to the fragmented disarray of modern German culture. In Nietzsche's summation, the modern German mindset relies predominantly on knowledge as its source of meaning to the detriment of more instinctual modes of experience. This results in a distant and desensitized relationship to the material world and a tendency towards emotional turbulence. Modern Germany had become sterile, entrenched, and lost among a bewildering array of styles and aesthetic inclinations derived from times passed. It needed to discover its own style to affirm its presence in the world and allow it to begin to create more boldly and effectively for itself. The grand style remedies the situation by emphasizing the immediacy of corporeal forms to dislodge the ailing mindset from its 'barbaric' preoccupation with 'inwardness' and invite it to engage freely and spontaneously with the material, concrete world. By doing so, Nietzsche attempts to heal unhealthy splits between body and mind and perceived 'inner' and 'outer' worlds. The intended result is an enriched culture that encourages people to experience themselves more fully, by having greater resources to self-reflect and to create more authentically.

The grand style is brought into being by a unifying instinct, the will to power or 'organizing power of will'. Through the exercise of will to power a person can harness tensions between competing and fragmentary ideas, perceptions and feelings. Nietzsche speaks of it as the 'central organizing power' (BGE,242), which gives all instincts their 'way and measure' (KSA, 12,9[169]:435). It is the 'one yoke' under which all seemingly contradictory experiences are gathered (KSA,12,9[166]:433; cf.GS,113). While the cultural approach of modern Germany sought merely to 'assemble' fragments into a pretence of a whole, the grand style exercises a will to power that organizes fragments into a cohesive and unified whole. The will to power enables a person to master their chaotic experiences and to give style to their character. A person who exercises their will to power will create in the register of the 'grand style', and by the same token, architecture in the grand style will express the power of those who shape, sculpt or construct themselves in accordance with their will. Architecture in the grand style will elicit a rhythmic force – an artistic '*grand* rhythm' – with a 'rise and fall' of 'superhuman passion' (EH, II.4).

Early in the development of his thought, Nietzsche regarded architecture alongside sculpture and epic poetry as an example of Apollonian aesthetics in its purest form due to its rationalized structure, which is explicit and immediately conveyed (BT,1). He contrasted these artistic examples with music as a Dionysian art form of the purest kind due to its frenzied, non-figurative and more intuitive qualities. Later, in *Twilight of the Idols* (1888/2021), Nietzsche identifies architecture as a special aesthetic type, linked specifically to the will to power. Sculpture and epic poetry continue to exemplify Apollonian visionary art, while music – following his quarrel with Wagner – resembles 'just the leftovers of a much fuller realm of emotional expression, a mere *residuum* of Dionysian histrionics'. It fails to embody 'the normal Dionysian state', due to its 'immobilization' of 'a number of senses' and 'above all, the muscular sense' (TI, X.10:94). According to Nietzsche, while these various art forms have gradually evolved into distinctive types while continuing to subscribe generally to either an Apollonian or Dionysian approach and affect, the work of the '*architect* represents neither a Dionysian nor an Apollonian state'. Architecture is no longer conceived by Nietzsche as a pure Apollonian art form, but rather, a 'great act of will, the will that moves mountains, the intoxication of the great will that craves for art'. He goes on:

> The mightiest humans have always inspired the architect; the architect was always prone to the suggestion of power. An edifice is intended to display pride, victory over gravity, the will to power; architecture is a kind of power eloquence in forms that are now persuasive, even flattering, now simply imperative. The highest feeling of power and security is expressed in whatever has *grand style*. Power that no longer needs any excuse; that scorns giving pleasure; that answers gravely; that does not need to be corroborated; that exists without being conscious that it is being contradicted; that reposes within *itself*, fatalistically, a law among laws: *that* speaks of itself as grand style.
>
> (TI, X.11:94–5)

In unpublished drafts for this passage Nietzsche describes the architect as 'a great act of willing in its most convincing and proudest form', and architecture as 'the edifice of power' and 'the eloquence of the will in spatial forms', where 'the will to power' is 'made visible' and the 'soul's loquacity' is 'writ large' (KSA,14[117]:425). Because architecture in the grand style expresses the will to power, it does not seek justification or permission for its design, it does not seek to please, and it does not emulate or imitate other designs. It answers only to itself; it is self-secure. Fritz Neumeyer notes that Nietzsche in this passage commits to architecture as the most powerful art form. Architecture for Nietzsche, he says, is an unconditional obligation to this world, an 'architecture of being' and the security of being within oneself is the 'hallmark of grand style' (2001/2004:183).

Architecture in the grand style denotes the art of giving style to one's character. Crucially, Nietzsche does not intend this architecture to be enjoyed by the architect in isolation from others. Its design will express the unified will of the architect, but the architect who designs in the grand style is in touch with the existential needs of their society and designs to meet those needs. Buildings in the grand style express the will to power of their architect and subsequently empower those who come to use them. Unsurprisingly, Nietzsche does not explain the causal relations that underpin this architectural experience. But we know from his definition of art that it involves physiological experiences of increased strength and fullness of the kind he ascribes to the powerful will. He suggests that an architect or artist in this position will 'lend to', 'force' and 'enrich' their designs until their designs are similarly 'swelled' and 'overloaded with strength', and come eventually to express distinctive features, reflecting the architect's or artist's will in spatial form (TI, IX,8–9:93).

We can also deduce from Nietzsche's comments that people who exercise their will to power are better placed to recognize architecture in the grand style, and more attuned or receptive to its transformative effects. To exercise will to power is to give style to one's character, and this involves continual self-scrutiny to ascertain 'what is necessary in things' and to 'take delight' in the necessities one imposes on oneself (GS, 276,335; TI IX,9:93). 'Grand style' requires, he says, 'the will to economy' (AC, Foreword). But to maintain such concentration is not easy and wholly improbable for those who are weak of will, and who otherwise depend on the decadent comforts of modern living. Such self-scrutiny requires honesty, a robust intellectual conscience and daily practice (GS,290; HH I, 163).[1]

Scholars have attempted to explain Nietzsche's account of the transformative power of architecture and the passage of will to power from architect to inhabitant or onlooker. Perhaps most notable is Paul Kühn's account (1904), in his analysis of Henry van de Velde's architectural renovations of Villa Silberblick in Weimar for the official guidebook of the *Nietzsche-Archiv*. Kühn draws upon van de Velde's theory of 'line-force' (1902a)[2] to explain how the Belgian architect fashions his materials into a rhythmic composition which both empowers and unifies the instincts of the onlooker. Van de Velde's use of patterned lines was not intended by him as mere decorative ornament, but as a rhythmic power, which would accentuate the distinctive characteristics of his design materials, and in turn, uplift the spirits of those who perceived them. In Chapter 4, I consider

Kühn's account more closely as well as van de Velde's line theory and his architectural renovations of Villa Silberblick in relation to the grand style.

According to Nietzsche, the human body is a vital philosophical organ through which we discover and master our values and take delight in ourselves and our creations. The body is the 'great reason' [*grosse Vernunft*], a 'mighty commander' and 'sage', who creates beyond itself, a bridge to the Superman (Z, I,4:62). 'Our most sacred convictions' and 'the unchanging elements of our supreme values are', he writes, 'judgements of our muscles' (KSA,13.11[376]:169). Through our bodily sensations we can comprehend and evaluate ourselves without the kinds of unnecessary distractions that arise from our rational deliberations. By using physiology as a guiding principle, a person can become more attuned to their immediate needs without succumbing to external pressures or conforming to the dictates of others – and architecture in the grand style will help to facilitate this.

Nietzsche's suggestion that the formal qualities of architecture impact on the onlooker physiologically and psychologically can be read as a forerunner to similar ideas that rose to prominence after his death, which are widely cited in the history of architecture. Of note is Heinrich Wölfflin's doctoral thesis (1886/2021), *Prolegomena zu einer Psychologie der Architektur* (*Prolegomena to a Psychology of Architecture*), which argued for an empathic relationship between architectural form and bodily experience. What 'we want', Nietzsche says, is 'to have ourselves translated into stone', 'to have ourselves to stroll in' as we would a building (GS,280), for we have 'value and meaning only insofar as [we are] a *stone in a great edifice*' (GS,356). Wölfflin similarly asserts, 'to resolve the whole edifice into functioning members' is 'to wish as it were to feel every muscle in one's body' (cited in Buddensieg 1999:267). Both thinkers continue the tradition – traceable to the writings of Roman architect, Vitruvius – of finding correspondences between architectural forms and the human body. Nietzsche also ascribes to buildings the ability to speak and converse with people, as we find in his descriptions of ecclesiastical buildings, which 'speak much that is too emotional and too partisan' (GS, 280), and the occasion when he imagines 'a soul' speaking from within the colossal stones of a Greek temple at Paestum (HH I,145).[3] Buildings may distract and mislead with their bewildering assemblage of ideas and false utterances, but a person who exercises their will to power will be able to discern from the cacophony insights that are useful for their own creative reflections.

The rest of this chapter will address aspects which Nietzsche identifies as necessary to an architecture in the grand style. As we shall see, each fosters a physiological engagement with the built environment. I examine them in turn, starting with Nietzsche's notion of 'empty form', which, as I argue, emphasizes the organic character of a building, its raw materials, plain surfaces and unambiguous designs free from distracting ornament. Following this, I revisit the significance Nietzsche ascribes to powerful, rhythmic forms especially in vast buildings that otherwise appear inert. By way of examples, I examine Nietzsche's accounts of the palazzi in Genoa and the Palazzo Pitti in Florence. My analysis continues with Nietzsche's notion of height instinct with its defeat of gravity, which he identifies with the Mole Antonelliana in Turin – the building which disclosed to Nietzsche an image of himself perfected in stone.

Empty form: 'More stone than stone before'

Architecture in the grand style utilizes the will to power to gather and unify fragments of experience into a distinctive and distinguished whole. The architectural forms of this style are by necessity 'empty' to allow people to use them for their own musings and self-reflections. An architecture with empty form, as Nietzsche sees it, is a new type of architecture that will help restore a more visceral engagement with the material world and revitalize people's creative outlooks in the process. Gone are the distracting signifiers that speak of times passed, other worlds and misleading ideologies. What remains are the raw components of the building to encourage greater physiological identifications with it.

According to Buddensieg, Nietzsche changes his mind about the value of empty form significantly from *Human, All Too Human* in 1878, where it represents a painful loss, to the occasions of Nietzsche's visits to Genoa and Turin a few years later, where he comes to celebrate its liberating nature (1999:263). Thus, in the aphorism titled, *'Stone is more stony than before'* (HH I,218), Nietzsche criticizes modern culture for habitually failing to appreciate the 'inexhaustible significance' of buildings and their enchanting beauty. Consequently, once-evocative buildings – such as 'Greek or Christian buildings' – are transformed by the modern mindset into stones devoid of significance. Modern culture is no longer roused by the power of architecture; its buildings are empty forms. But from 1880, following his stays in Genoa and later Turin, whereupon Nietzsche discovers the delights of secular Italian urban architecture with its piazzas, plazas and arcaded streets, he revises his position on the inherent power of empty forms. The loss of symbolic ornamentation becomes a cultural gain, now denoting potential liberation for people as an enabler of self-discovery. Nietzsche had lamented the loss of deciphering Christian buildings and others replete with ornament, but now he berates their 'intercourse with another world', regarding these buildings as speaking too emotive and constrained a language 'for us godless people to think *our thoughts*' in them (GS,280). These buildings had outworn their masks, and their masks subsequently had to be removed. There was no longer a place for hidden features and magical secrets. Buildings must be made visible, open, simple, vivid, honest and grounded in the present to allow a person to stroll within themselves without being distracted by the thoughts of others. Nietzsche's call for an architecture of empty form contrasts starkly with the architectural examples discussed in the previous chapter, which exemplified for him the failings of modern culture with its tendency to mislead and suppress: the decadent garden house, assembled from bits and pieces which expose gaps and defects in its construction; labyrinthine buildings with convoluted pathways; the collapsed house of Wagner; and the mausoleum that is closed off from life.

Rather than have those buildings that speak of unhelpful ideals and distant worlds razed to the ground, Nietzsche sets about cleansing them so they can be reused and reinterpreted and subsequently become more responsive to contemporary needs.[4] Nietzsche could be regarded as an iconoclast. Indeed, Buddensieg suggests Nietzsche may have been influenced by the systematic 'purification' of Naumburg Cathedral (1874–8), which saw some of its Baroque features removed and replaced with decoration in the Romanesque/Gothic revivalist style to imitate its original mediaeval appearance (1999:265). Nietzsche was certainly very familiar with the cathedral having attended the Domgymnasium, the cathedral's grammar school, housed in a building attached to the cathedral, and he would return to Naumburg with its 'disturbing' and 'gloomy streets', and its 'disturbingly long cobbled streets' as he describes them, throughout his life, principally to visit his mother who lived there (FS I:7). Above all, Nietzsche sought through the cleansing of architecture the silencing of features that drew unnecessary attention to themselves, with their arbitrary 'chatter'. We must 'avoid today', he writes, the 'noise' of 'democratic chatter' and the 'junk of the marketplace', and to seek instead 'quiet places' where 'we can speak without speaking *out loud*' and do so unobserved (GM, III.8) – and where we can rest 'still and silent', like stone (D,541). Churches, temples, palaces, city streets, marketplaces, indeed *all* built environments when silenced and still, can become for Nietzsche, places for self-reflection, and an *'architecture for the knower'* [*Architektur der Erkennenden*] (GS,280).

Once stripped and emptied, architecture does not lose its capacity to communicate, it simply changes the way it expresses itself. It no longer 'talks' at a person with idle chat but utilizes the will to power to 'command' a person to engage with it and compel them to reflect not on it but on themselves (cf.TI, IX.8:92; GS,291). The commanding presence of a building is emphasized by the solidity of its mass, which becomes most prominent when stripped of unnecessary features and ornamentation (KSA,12.7[7]:290). In this context, the aphorism title, '*Stone is more stony than before*' (HH I, 218) – which has befuddled many Nietzsche scholars – begins to make more sense. As I noted, in this passage Nietzsche questions the contemporary value of historical buildings which speak an outmoded, rhetorical language. A building's 'stony' quality suggests to me the raw materials of its construction. Subsequently, an historic building that is *more stony than before* implies a building that has become increasingly identified with its raw materials to the point where the gaze of a modern person sees only a material object. Gone are the symbolic nuances of its design features that readily impressed upon the onlookers of its day. Read this way, the 'stony' quality of a building signifies the ineffective relationship between historical designs and the people who experience them in the present, which is to say, the building's inability to command a powerful response in people, and the onlooker's inability to be aroused by its design. Later, Nietzsche reversed his position, to revere the 'stony' quality of a building. It would no longer convey a building's passive impact, but the very means to reinvigorate relations between buildings and people. To empty a building of its distracting features and thereby reduce it to its elementary material components is to expose its raw materials and enable the stone to become 'more stoney'. Markus Breitschmid aptly notes:

> [W]ith the shift of the architectural essence or meaning [from the 'interior mind' of intellectual contemplation] to the outside, it is the building's proportions, the outline, the straight and right-angled lines and edges, the surface, the unity of the body, which are decisive.
>
> (2001:93)

Thus, empty form becomes for Nietzsche a vital component of architecture for the modern era. The material components of a building together with its essential (or 'necessary') features – its surfaces, shapes, angles, edges, outlines and proportions – speak for themselves. They reveal a self-evident, unified structure and elicit in the onlooker an immediate visceral response.

Interpretations of Nietzsche's notion of empty form and his appeal to more honest or 'necessary' designs are commonly cited by those who wish to link his ideas to modernist architecture and to architects whose designs are characterized by abstract forms and their material components. By the same token, Nietzsche's vision of the creative artists who can lead ailing Germany to discover its own cultural style became an attractive invitation for several aspiring architects in the early to mid-twentieth century. In Part II, I evaluate Nietzsche's influence in this regard alongside his wider architectural legacy. There I explain that although Nietzsche's ideas have been cited as philosophical justification for specific architectural styles or building types, there is no singular architectural style, or explicit combination of styles or design types that exemplifies his notion of the grand style. Nietzsche does, however, have his favourite buildings, which he describes with great enthusiasm and in conjunction with the grand style. As Buddensieg notes, Nietzsche revised his evaluation of empty architectural forms in response to various buildings he visited in northern Italy, and specifically, I suggest, in the cities of Genoa, Florence and Turin. I will now turn to the buildings that made greatest impression on Nietzsche and to the contribution each made to the development of his idea of grand style. I begin with the palazzi of wealthy Genoese merchants and the Palazzo Pitti in Florence and the contributions they made to Nietzsche's perceived need for designs that express nobility through their material mass and rhythmic play of forms. Following this I analyse Nietzsche's notion of height instinct and its architectural expression in the Mole Antonelliana in Turin.

Noble mass and rhythmic form: Palazzi in Genoa and the Palazzo Pitti in Florence

Nietzsche may seem partial to buildings that seem large or tall, but it is important to note that size and height are not in themselves indicative of the grand style. He does not appreciate buildings for their measurements, but for their boldness and the achievements of their free-standing nature – in other words, the exercise of will to power. Indeed, Nietzsche dislikes buildings that seek to overwhelm the onlooker with displays of 'massiveness' [*Massenhaftigkeit*], 'great quantity' [*grossen Quantität*] (D,169; BGE,241) and 'inflated style' [*aufgeblasene Stil*] (D,332). Buildings that are too vast and lofty, or 'bloated, gigantic, and nervous' [*gedunsen, riesenhaft und nervös*] undermine Nietzsche's search for designs that are self-contained and complete, for their expansive surfaces that extend and disappear into the horizon surpass our own bodily proportions, making them difficult to perceive and appreciate as unified structures (D,161). These vast and lofty buildings nourish unhelpful flights of fancy, while architecture in the 'grand style' involves a 'victory of beauty over the colossal' (WS,96).

Nietzsche favours buildings which have what he considers, dynamic and rhythmic form, which encourage corresponding feelings of vitality within the onlooker, and this capacity is increased, he maintains, when ornamental features are kept to a minimum. To that end, Nietzsche prefers buildings with simple and unified surfaces. Although he does not extol any given architectural style over any other, buildings of Classical, Renaissance or Baroque style are more likely to meet this demand than Gothic designs with their complex and cavernous spaces and ornate tracery.

Genoese Palazzi

Nietzsche visited Genoa several times from November 1880 to April 1881; October 1881 to March 1882; February to May 1883; and September to October 1886. During his earlier stays he lived in *Salita delle Battistine* 8, a building situated near the bottom of a very steep cobbled street, and just a two-minute walk from the palazzi that line *Strada Nuova* [now *Via Garibaldi*]. His room, interno 6, was an unheated 'attic room with an excellent bed' (November 1880; KSB,6.68:51), but he appears to have moved rooms upon his second stay to 'a very bright room with a high ceiling – which is good for my mood' (December 1881; KSB,6.181:151).

In a postcard to Franz Overbeck, Nietzsche describes Genoa as 'my city' – 'the most unmodern [city] I know and yet bustling with life – it's completely unromantic and yet the opposite of vulgar' (October 1881;

KSB,6.158:134). To his mother and sister, he describes it as 'a great, bustling sea city' which 'gives me peace and being-for-myself', and with 'paths with wonderful paving' to satisfy his appetite for walking (November 1880; KSB,6.68:51). To Köselitz, he writes, 'I am here in Genoa, so rich and proud' (November 1881; KSB,6.165:138). Indeed, when walking 'on the heights above Genoa', as he reports to Erwin Rohde, he feels 'moments of courage' like those he imagined Columbus feeling, when he launched his ship from the city's port 'to the sea and the future' (March 1881; KSB,6.96:74). Much later, he reminisces to Köselitz about his intimate connection with the place, and to 'the fate that condemned me', he writes, 'to this hard and sombre city in the years of decadence; to leave it behind is to leave oneself behind' (April 1888; KSB 8.1013:285). He needs his 'Genose Boldness' (*Genueser Kühnheit*) to get through 'terrible times' (To Köselitz, October 1881; KSB,6.162:136–7). Genoa was home to Christopher Columbus, and it was from Genoa's port that Columbus began his voyage of discovery of the 'new world', and it was home too for Nietzsche as a place that came to represent for him his hopes for the dawning of a new culture. It was largely in Genoa that Nietzsche composed *Daybreak* (1881/2011), and the beginnings of *The Gay Science* (1882/2001) – a book which alludes to the architectural delights of Genoa's palazzi (Figure 2.1). It is perhaps no accident that the aphorism, titled, *Genoa*, which describes these palazzi, immediately follows the aphorism, titled '*One thing is needful – To "give style"* to one's character' (GS,290), for Nietzsche's reverential description of the architects of the Genoese palazzi is highly suggestive of those who give style to their character; in other words, of those 'great and rare' artists of 'strong and noble natures' (some of whom 'build palaces'), who are driven by the 'passion of their tremendous will' to create in accordance with their 'single taste' (GS,290). Thus,

> *Genoa* – For a long while now I have been looking at this city, at its villas and pleasure-gardens, and the wide circumference of its inhabited heights and slopes, and in the end, I must say: I see *faces* that belong to past generations; this landscape is strewn with the images of bold and autocratic human beings. They have *lived* and wish to live on – that is what they are telling me with their houses, built and adorned to last for centuries and not for the fleeting hour [...] I keep seeing the builder, how he rests his gaze on everything they have built, near and far, as well as on city, sea, and mountain contours; and how with his gaze he exerts [...] conquering power; he wants to fit all this into *his* plan and finally make it his *possession* by incorporating it into his plan. This whole landscape is overgrown with this magnificent, insatiable selfishness for possession and spoils; and [...] in their thirst for something new, set up a new world alongside the old, so too, at home each rebelled against the other and found a way to express his superiority and place his personal infinity between himself and his neighbour. Each conquered his homeland

FIGURE 2.1 Genoa Palazzi. Strada Nuova/Via Giuseppe Garibaldi (b.1558–83). Perspective view, above street level of various palazzi. © Superchilum.

again for himself by overwhelming it with his architectural ideas and refashioning it, so to speak, into a house that was a feast for his eyes.

(GS,291)

Nietzsche continues to note that 'here you find, upon turning every corner' individuals who loathe the tedium of laws and their neighbours, and who, with 'cunning imagination', would like to put their hands and minds to overcoming all that is old and alien.

Genoa embodied for Nietzsche an antidote to the problematic modern city that failed to accommodate him, and this was viscerally experienced by Nietzsche in their contrasting building designs. Genoese palazzi conveyed to him a strong instinctual desire for a new cultural style, one that learns effectively from the past by channelling its creative spirit, not seeking merely to imitate historic designs with a false pretence of proprietorship.

The palazzi that captured Nietzsche's attention were large and imposing residences built by Genoese aristocracy at the height of their financial, seafaring power in the late sixteenth and early seventeenth centuries. He celebrates the individualistic style of each palazzo, with their 'singular taste' and free-standing nature, set apart from others as distinctive and self-assured.

Each conveys the single-minded plan and mastery of the creator. Importantly, when viewed together, the palazzi conveyed to Nietzsche an overarching unity of style expressed as an organized and creative 'competition' between buildings, rather than the kind of 'chaotic' mishmash of styles that he came to identify with modern German architecture.

Nietzsche was very taken with these palazzi, and it appears he fancied himself as their potential inhabitant, and perhaps, subsequently, fancied also the power he ascribes to them. When describing to his sister the location of his rented Genoese apartment, he writes:

> I have to climb 164 steps in the house to get to my attic room, and the house itself is very high in a steep street of palaces [Pallast-Straße], which is very quiet because of its steepness and because it ends in a great flight of steps.
>
> (December 1880; KSB,6.69:52)

It seems Nietzsche so desired to live in a palace that he pretended to his sister he did. Nietzsche's house, like others on *Salita delle Battistine*, was a non-descript terraced house of between four to five storeys, quite unlike the imposing palazzi of *Strada Nuova*.[5]

Palazzo Pitti, Florence

According to Buddensieg, Nietzsche was desperate to discover a convincing example of his grand style in architectural form and the Genoese palazzi, although expressive of the will to power, did not fully satisfy him in his search (2002a:138). These palaces were impressive in their expression of human achievement and nobility but there was another Italian palace that would come to overshadow all others in Nietzsche's view. This was the Palazzo Pitti in Florence (b.1458), a building that exudes, for Nietzsche, a power of 'superhuman' proportion (Figure 2.2).

The design and construction of this vast Renaissance palace was originally attributed to Filippo Brunelleschi, but is commonly accredited to his understudy, Luca Fancelli. Nietzsche made a trip to Florence in November 1885 primarily to see this building, and this desire was probably fuelled by remarks made about it by Jacob Burckhardt, historian of Italian Renaissance art and architecture, and mentor to Nietzsche at the University of Basel from 1869 to 1879. The two scholars would have much to discuss given their mutual concerns for the decline of modern culture and its possible revival. Burckhardt's principal interest in the Italian Renaissance led him to consider ideas of creativity in relation to the despotic rulers of the era, and perhaps most significant to Nietzsche's philosophy, ideas of autonomous personality, ruthless self-mastery and the socio-political responsibility of power.

FIGURE 2.2 Palazzo Pitti, Florence (b.1458, Luca Fancelli). Front elevation. Photograph. Michael Maslan/Corbis/VCG. © Getty Images.

Nietzsche's admiration of Burckhardt was not reciprocated with equal enthusiasm. Burckhardt maintained a polite and respectful distance from his passionate younger colleague. Nevertheless, they continued to correspond with each other, albeit infrequently after Nietzsche left Basel for his nomadic lifestyle.[6] It was to Burckhardt that Nietzsche composed his final letter before his collapse – a letter urging Burckhardt to visit Turin to see what became for Nietzsche his most exciting architectural discovery of all, the Mole Antonelliana.

Nietzsche made expansive comments in his copies of Burckhardt's works, and some of Burckhardt's ideas about Italian Renaissance architecture are traceable in Nietzsche's remarks about the grand style.[7] For instance, in *Cicerone: Guide to the Enjoyment of the Artworks of Italy* (1855), Burckhardt suggests a building's power comes from its material fabric and not its symbolic meaning because the latter can lead one astray with distracting emotions. He cites the example of early Christian churches, which evoke 'unconscious' fantasies of buildings imbued with 'a mysterious aura' (1855:93). Burckhardt also remarks that the playful ornamentation of fifteenth-century art distracts with so many details which detract from and fragment the beauty of the whole. It was later discovered, he notes, that the absence of detail and ornament increased the impression of power (1855:298). Nietzsche underlines these remarks in his copy of *Cicerone*, singling out the words, 'detail' [Detail], 'absence' [*Wegbleiben*], 'impression of power' [*Eindruck der Macht*]. Neumeyer asserts that these three words make up Nietzsche's formula for a grand style (2001/2004:185).

In *Cicerone* (1855) and *History of the Renaissance in Italy*[8] (1868), Burckhardt turns his attention to the Palazzo Pitti, praising it as 'an image of the highest will power', and the 'most ambitious' private building to have been commissioned (1867/1868:54,14). It achieves the 'highest impression of the sublime that has ever been achieved' [*hat dieser Palast den höchsten bis jetzt erreichten Eindruck des Erhabenen voraus*] (1855:175) – and it owes this less to its 'very large dimensions or its position on sloping ground', and more to its repetitive and simple 'relationship of forms'. The palazzo's façade repeats a series of seven arched apertures (reminiscent of a Roman aqueduct, and expressive of *all'antica* – the manner or style of ancient antiquity which was popular in Florence at the time). This repetition is broken by the elevation of the uppermost floor positioned to the middle of the building, and it is this 'special' feature, Burckhardt says, that evokes the building's 'highest majestic effect'. Anticipating words of Nietzsche, Burckhardt describes the palazzo as the 'highest will power', due to its 'rejection of all decoration' and its distance from 'anything pleasing or delicate'. The building feels 'colossal' to Burckhardt, and – again anticipating Nietzschean ideas – he describes the creators of the palazzo as 'superhuman beings' [*'übermenschliche Wesen'*] (1855:175; 1867/1868:54; cf.70; see also 1867/1987:42).[9]

Burckhardt's comments about the Palazzo Pitti made a strong impression on Nietzsche. In an unpublished note from August 1881, Nietzsche repeats Burckhardt's words as a directive: '"Refuse everything pretty and pleasing as a world-despising violent man" [*weltverachtender Gewaltmensch*] says J. Burckhardt of the Palazzo Pitti' (KSA,9.11[197]:520). In a later note from August/September 1885, Nietzsche praises the architect of Palazzo Pitti with qualities befitting his own vision of Burckhardt's superhuman beings, replacing the emphasis on the colossal with the power of 'leadership' and the capacity to resist the charms of sentimentality with a raw will to power, expressed as the unambiguous simplicity of style (KSA,3.226:511). The rhythmic play of pure formal components of the Palazzo Pitti is for Nietzsche, as it was for his colleague Burckhardt, its most powerful aspect. Indeed, the architecture of Palazzo Pitti comes to signify for Nietzsche a significant antidote to the profound disappointment he felt with the loss of his former love for music. For the Palazzo Pitti, he asserts, achieves 'the *grand style*', as its 'form' conveys 'most intensely' the 'art of melody', which is to say, more than any musician has achieved (letter to Carl Fuchs, April 1886; KSB,7.688:177).

The historian Hippolyte Taine (1828–93) – another scholar whom Nietzsche held in high esteem – characterized the Palazzo Pitti in terms remarkably like Burckhardt's and favourable to Nietzsche's notion of grand style. Nietzsche approved of Taine's criticism of historicism, describing him in an unpublished note from 1885 as 'the first living historian in Europe. A resolute man who is brave even in his despair' (KSA,11,38[5]:598; cf. KSB,7.753:253). He went on to imagine himself, Taine and Burckhardt as 'thoroughly reliant on one another, as three fundamental nihilists' – 'although', he notes, 'I myself still have not abandoned hope of finding the way out' (letter to Erwin Rhode, May 1887; KSB,8.852:80–1). Arguably, the Palazzo Pitti presented to all three thinkers a potential way forward or 'way out' from nihilistic malaise.

Francis Haskell notes that it was not unusual for Taine to include the insights of others in his observations (1993:350) and given the admiration Taine and Burckhardt had for each other, it unsurprising that Taine's travel writings made use of Burckhardt's reflections in *Cicerone* (1855). In *Italy: Florence and Venice* (1866/2020) Taine writes:

> I doubt if there is a palace in Europe more monumental than the Pitti Palace. I have not seen one that leaves such a simple, grandiose impression. Placed on an eminence its entire outline appears in profile against the clear blue sky. [...] But what is unique and carries to an extreme the grandiose serenity of the edifice is the vastness of the material of which it is built. It is not stone, but fragments of rock and almost sections of mountains.
> (1866/2020:151)

Taine's comparison of the building's raw materials to mountains may have further sparked Nietzsche's imagination given Nietzsche's penchant for mountains as places in which to think and self-reflect. These mountainous blocks, Taine continues, are 'as long as five men', and their colossal size – as Burckhardt similarly maintained – are suggestive of a superpower at work, which designs and builds only for itself.

> Scarcely hewn out, rugged and dark, they preserve their original asperity, as would a mountain if torn from its foundations, broken into fragments, and erected on a new site by cyclopean hands. There is no ornamentation to the façade [...] Colossal round arcades support the windows, and each of their vertebrae forms a projection with its primitive irregularities, as if the skeleton of an old giant. [...] Stone reigns supreme here; the eye seeks for nothing beyond variety of reliefs and substantial position; it seems as if it subsisted in and for itself [...] If anything can give an idea of the grandeur, severity and audacity of intellect which the middle ages bequeathed to the free citizens of the renaissance it is the aspect of such a dwelling built by a single individual for his own use [...]
> (1866/2020:151–2)

Vertical achievements: The height instinct

Of all towns and cities Nietzsche visited, Turin made the greatest impression on him. While Nietzsche was initially guided by Burckhardt in his association of the grand style with the rhythmic mass of the Palazzo Pitti, his walks in Turin appear to have encouraged in him a greater awareness and sensitivity to the physiological impact of architecture, which became reflected in his developing concept of grand style. During his time in Turin, the grand style becomes associated with what he calls, 'height instinct' (*Höhentrieb*). By emphasizing height rather than mass, Nietzsche could highlight more clearly the contradistinctions he makes between grand style and decadent values, for he had linked the latter to notions of heaviness and density, to the 'spirit of gravity' and 'great weight'. What better way to convey 'victory' over gravity and weight than the energetic movement of mass upwards? Thus, in *Thus Spoke Zarathustra*, in the chapter 'On the Spirit of Gravity', Zarathustra's remedy to those who are unable to love themselves is to remove the burdens of 'heavy words and values' so that they no longer 'roam about', but 'become light' enough 'to fly'. To learn to fly, he says, one must be proficient at climbing and dancing. He goes on to describe how he himself learnt to climb with guidance from tall architectural structures, suggestive of lighthouses (and ships), from which he learnt to climb upwards 'to many a window', up 'rope ladders' and 'high masts' (Z,III,11[2]:213).

Nietzsche conceptualizes cultural malaise and the exercise of will to power as its remedy in spatial terms, with the latter also portrayed as a dynamic movement upwards, seeking an elevated position. Cultural malaise is without this dynamic propulsion. It is inert, stagnant, and too heavy. It subsequently lacks power to quash and overturn the democratic values which otherwise flatten individual enterprise. By exercising the will to power, individuals rise above and overcome the status quo. This elevated position separates them from unhelpful influences of others and provides them with a panoramic vision of the horizon beyond. This enhanced view encourages their creative vision to extend well beyond those who are compelled at ground level to 'stick their heads heavily into the heavy earth' (Z,III,11[2]:213). Interestingly, Mark Bolland (1996) argues that the mountainous paths that Nietzsche liked to walk were instrumental to the shaping of his ideas. He suggests that rather than employing 'mountain images' as dramatic metaphorical 'dress up' for abstract ideas he had already formulated – such as the will to power or height instinct – Nietzsche derived '*concepts themselves*' from the landscapes in which he walked (1996:18). In this context, urban landscapes, I claim, are no less significant for Nietzsche than rural, mountainous ones.

Earlier I described Nietzsche's walks in urban and mountainous landscapes as integral to the alleviation of his psychosomatic symptoms and to the clarity of his thoughts. His walks empowered and revitalized him. Consequently, one could argue that his ideas about power, the affirmation of life, self-mastery and so on were shaped not simply by the features of the landscapes he walked in but the uplifting feelings they induced in him. His descriptions of height often blend allusions to the empowered self and mountains or tall architectural edifices. 'Life', he asserts, 'wants to build itself high with columns and stairs; it wants to gaze into the far distance and out upon joyful splendour – *that* is why it needs height! And because it needs height, it needs steps [...]. Life wants to climb' (Z, II, 29:125). In response to his question, 'What is noble?', he notes, ' – The collection of precious things, the needs of a high and fastidious soul; to desire to possess nothing in common. One's own books, one's own landscape [*Landschaften*]' (KSA,11,35[76]:544–5). Height instinct is a hallmark of the affirmation of life which Nietzsche seeks, and he discovers it within mountain scenery and architecture in the grand style, and it is his hope that it will be discoverable on any given walk and any pathway or street. We wish to see *ourselves*, he says, 'translated into stone and plants; we want to take walks *in ourselves* when we stroll through [...] buildings and gardens' (GS,280).

The creative power of the heights contrasts with the mass or herd who reside at ground level. In the mountains where Nietzsche walked and where Zarathustra lived, Nietzsche discovered a veritable metaphor for the ordering of culture and the assignment of will to power, with the placement of the exemplary individual at the summit and the decadent mob residing below akin to a herd of sheep grazing in the valleys. Zarathustra comes down from the mountain heights to teach the rabble in the lowlands, but his teachings fall on deaf ears; so enslaved are they to their idols and ideologies that they would rather raze to the ground the creative achievements of individuals and to ensure all achievements are levelled out by the constraints of social customs and norms. Nietzsche identifies among the herd, 'the anarchist and the Christian', who both possess 'the instinct of *lethal hatred* toward everything that stands, that stands tall' (AC, 58; cf.TI,IX.38:112[10]). Exemplary individuals by contrast in Nietzsche's early writings are associated with philosophers, with Heraclitus at the summit, only to be supplanted in his later writings by Zarathustra, or Nietzsche himself, as the solitary thinker alone with his thoughts.

The significance of mountain peaks is, I suggest, equivalent to the architectural forms that captivated Nietzsche on his walks. Nietzsche perceives modern German architecture as a material expression of the decadent culture that shapes it; its architecture is in desperate need of an 'uplift'. 'Suppose I were to step out of my house', he writes, 'and find, instead of peaceful, aristocratic Turin, a small German town: my instinct would have to put up barricades to repel anything assaulting it from this flat and cowardly world' (EH, II.8:242). German towns are stunted and flattened by the weight of the oppressive values that their inhabitants, and all who built these towns, subscribe to. Buddensieg suggests that Nietzsche alludes here to the 'intricately timber-framed cities of modern, medieval domestic architecture – Halle, Naumburg, Cologne, Basel, and Strasbourg – those [Nietzsche] himself had seen as "cowering" beneath the sway of vast cathedrals' (1999:263). One might imagine in contrast to this, a city in the grand style – with a cathedral now stripped of its oppressive power, standing alongside a variety of buildings and other architectural structures, each of them elevated, distinctive, self-assured and in creative competition with one another.

Throughout his writings Nietzsche differentiates between an architecture of mediocrity, which often comprises homogeneous forms on a horizontal plane, and a noble architecture of towering spaces. Nietzsche complains of 'peasant houses' [Bauernhäusern] which he finds impossible to live in due to their 'low and depressed' rooms, which 'always cause restlessness' (letter to Carl von Gersdorff; KSB,6.427:387), and Zarathustra sighs at having to stoop to enter the houses built by modern people. Upon seeing a row of new houses, Zarathustra asks 'What do these houses mean?' For 'truly, no great soul put them up as its image!' He continues, 'Did a silly child perhaps take them out of its toy-box? If only another child would put them back into its box! And these sitting rooms and bedrooms: are *men* able to go in and out of them? They seem to have been made for dolls.' He longs to return home to the heights of his mountain cave where, he says, 'I shall no longer have to stoop *before the small men*!' (Z,III,5[1]:187). Later, Zarathustra laments that even 'higher men' are not 'high' enough, and so he waits in his mountain cave for those who can discover his lofty terrain – 'those who are higher, stronger, more victorious, and more joyful, such as are built right-angled [*rechtwinklig gebaut*] in body and soul' (Z, IV,11:294). Perhaps also for those who are like stone pillars, for earlier he asserts: 'You should aspire to the virtue of the pillar: the higher it rises, the fairer and more graceful it grows, but inwardly harder and able to bear more weight' (Z, II,13:141). Various buildings suggest height instinct to Nietzsche, including the free-standing, self-sufficient Genoese palazzi that exude nobility and self-assurance of those who built them, also Nietzsche's second lodgings in Genoa on Salle delle Battistine with its high ceilings which put him in a 'good mood', and the Sabalpina Gallerie that adjoin his lodgings at Via Carlo Alberto in Turin with its 'splendid heigh ceiling' (letter to Köselitz, December 1888; KSB,8.1192:528). But we shall see, it was the monolithic Mole Antonelliana, which towered above Turin, which expressed the height instinct most viscerally for Nietzsche.

It is important to note that height instinct is not satisfied as soon as a specific altitude is reached; the mountain summit or top of a tall building is not a final stage or end goal for Nietzsche. As Bolland notes, while Nietzsche's writings are saturated with allusions to mountains, he rarely alludes to the mountain summit or to a singular mountain, but mostly to mountain ranges. This suggests there are several places of elevation and no specific terminus or end to the assent; there is always another mountain to climb. Height instinct is identified with the struggle towards the heights, or across the heights as depicted in the prologue to *Thus Spoke Zarathustra* with the dangerous rope bridge positioned high above the ground and tied between two towers, representing ape and *Übermensch* respectively, and the human desire to make the transition across.

To imagine one can reach the end or arrive at the top is to fail to grasp the value Nietzsche ascribes to the heights and height instinct. Height in this context is not a matter of size. If a contemporary skyscraper or high-rise building were to convey Nietzsche's notion of height instinct, it achieves this accolade not because it is a particularly tall building, but because its architect has a voracious will to express and achieve ever-greater feats of engineering. I shall revisit this idea in Chapter 6, where I assess the influence of Nietzsche's ideas on the so-called 'father of skyscrapers', Louis H. Sullivan, who owned a well-read copy of *Thus Spoke Zarathustra*, and on Bruno Taut, who sought, alongside other enthusiasts of 'alpine architecture', to design buildings embedded within mountain ranges, often extending the height of mountain peaks with crowning architectural structures. I end this chapter with the Mole Antonelliana in Turin: Nietzsche's favourite building, which arguably expresses his notion of height instinct most distinctly.

Mole Antonelliana, Turin

According to Buddensieg, the Palazzo Pitti had been for Nietzsche the only figurative and artistic example of the 'grand style' from 1884, until 1888 when he was able to find it more powerfully embodied in another architectural edifice, the Mole Antonelliana (2002a:140). Nietzsche lived in Turin in 1888, from April to June, and then from September until his mental collapse in December. His home was an apartment on the fourth floor of 6 Via Carlo, looking over Piazza Carlo, towards the statue of Carlo Alberto, King of Piedmont, in military uniform, seated upon his horse with his sword raised. Nietzsche's apartment conjoined the Galleria Subalpina, an elegant arcade combining elements in Renaissance and Baroque style with marble pillars and a striking roof of iron and glass (b.1873–4; Pietro Carrera; Figures I.3 and I.4). Two sets of stairs at either end of the arcade led to a balcony that runs along the entire perimeter, from which Nietzsche's apartment was accessible. Nietzsche describes the Galleria as 'the most beautiful and elegant space of its kind that I know of' (December 1888; KSB, 8 [1192]:528). His room was positioned close to its roof, from which he gazed down into the arcade with its various shops, including Nietzsche's favourite coffee house, *Baratti & Milano*, and across to the *Teatro Carignano*, 'where', he writes to Köselitz, 'they play the *Barber of Seville* every evening' (December 1888; KSB, 8 [1192]:528). Just a ten-minute walk from Nietzsche's apartment is the Mole Antonelliana (b.1863–89) (Figure 2.3). Named after its architect, Alessandro Antonelli (1798–1888), the Mole was initially designed as an impressive synagogue for Turin as the capital city of the recently unified Italian state. But the building would never be used for this function, due in large part to the departure of significant numbers of the Jewish community to Florence when Florence replaced Turin as Italy's capital city in 1864. There were also problems with the building's construction – notably escalating costs and delayed timescales enforced by Antonelli – which frustrated its Jewish clients, causing their withdrawal from the project. These problems were exacerbated by Antonelli's insistence on increasing the height of the building ever upwards: 46m higher than originally planned. This delayed its completion on several occasions. City funds were invested in the project from 1877 to resume construction in accordance with Antonelli's developing plans, but Antonelli died before his building was completed.

Upon its completion, the Mole at 167.5 metres high was the tallest brick construction in Europe (and continues to lay claim to the tallest masonry building in the world without a reinforced steel frame or steel floor support). The building is rarely mentioned in scholarly works in the history of architecture. Indeed, as Buddensieg notes, it is often 'ridiculed as a "monster"' for its eclectic design which blends traditional and modern forms and materials into unconventional forms' (1999:266).[11] However, for Nietzsche, it was an impressive building, which, more than any other, exudes the grand style. Its deviation from conventional architectural stylings, its lack of a distinctive name and lack of purpose are indicative of its empty form, and its invitation to Nietzsche to use it for his self-reflections and self-discovery. Significant too is the Mole's dynamic thrust upward and

FIGURE 2.3 Mole Antonelliana, Turin (b.1863–89, Alessandro Antonelli). Front elevation. Author's photograph.

skyward. Contemporaries of Nietzsche and Antonelli regarded the building as a 'formidable stairway to the sky' (Guillén 2006:69).

Nietzsche describes the Mole as 'the greatest work of genius ever built out of an absolute instinct for height – suggestive of nothing so much as my Zarathustra. I have christened it "Ecce Homo" and mentally surrounded it with an immense open space' (Letter to Köselitz, December 1888; KSB,8.1227:565). *Ecce Homo*, 'behold the man', was the title of Nietzsche's final work, a work akin to a quasi-autobiography where Nietzsche recounts the significance of himself, his self-development and his writings. To name the Mole after this book suggests the strong personal bond that Nietzsche felt towards the building. Indeed, in a postscript to his letter to Köselitz, Nietzsche draws attention to the correlation between his book and the architect, who 'lived just as long, until *Ecce Homo*, the book was finished – The book and the human being' (December 1888; KSB,8.1227:565). (Antonelli died on 18 October 1888, and Nietzsche completed his book by 4 November 1888, but he continued to make alterations to it up until 6 January 1889.) Incidentally, this was not the first occasion that Nietzsche had linked the completion of a book to the death of a significant person, for in *Ecce Homo*, Nietzsche mentions that 'the closing section' of *Thus Spoke Zarathustra* 'was completed precisely at that sacred hour when Richard Wagner died in Venice' (EH,IX Z.1). As Gleiter remarks, 'Twice, one of his books became the legacy of an artist: *Zarathustra* and the composer, *Ecce Homo* and the architect' (Gleiter 2009:48, cf.20). Nietzsche had revered both artists, and it seems that Antonelli's legacy through the Mole may have provided Nietzsche with the remedy he sought to overcome the decadent legacy of Wagner's music. While the Palazzo Pitti expressed to Nietzsche an intense melody and bold and merry tempo (KSB,7.688:177), the Mole Antonelliana would later convey to him through its powerful rhythms, the kind of experience he had sought in architecture. In other words, he discovered in this building a place to walk as if in himself, a place to rediscover himself.

Whether he discovered a more fulfilling, healthier version of himself is questionable, for Nietzsche collapsed shortly after he had come to identify himself with the building and its architect – an ironic twist, perhaps, to the symbolic link he proposed between the death of its architect and the end of his 'autobiographical' work. After his collapse, Nietzsche wrote a series of letters known as 'the delusional letters' (*Wahnbriefe*), and in the last of these, written on 6 January 1889 to Jacob Burckhardt, he suggests he had once lived as Alessandro Antonelli, before telling Burckhardt that he really ought to come to Turin to see the building.

To what extent, then, was Mole Antonelliana a building in the grand style? Which aspects or features of the building impressed most upon Nietzsche? Nietzsche spoke of the need for a building to be in creative relationship with its surroundings – something he came to celebrate in the individual styles of the Genoese palazzi, which express noble competition between each other in their variation. The urban environment in which the Mole is situated is subsequently important to consider, and Nietzsche provides us with allusions aplenty to potential sightings of the grand style within Turin. This 'princely city', he writes, 'has only one commanding taste everywhere', and 'a unity of taste' in everything, even 'to the matter of colour (everything is either yellow or red-brown' (KSB,8.1013:285). The covered arcaded streets that extend to over a kilometre around the Mole enable him 'to stroll within [him]self' no matter the weather. 'Evenings on the Po bridge' are 'heavenly! Beyond good and evil!' (KSB,8.1013:285). Even its coffee houses serve 'excellent gelato' of 'the highest culture' (KSB,8.1019:295, 1022:299). And on he goes. The Mole can be construed as the crowning feature of a city that Nietzsche felt very much at home in (a *Stadtkrone* to cite Bruno Taut's term). Nevertheless, Nietzsche describes how he sought to imagine the Mole in isolation from its surroundings by mentally surrounding it with immense open space, which is to say an empty space, perhaps to encourage him to fix his attention solely on it and thus on himself, without distraction.

I wish to suggest that the Mole Antonelliana embodies the grand style for Nietzsche due to its empty form and 'absolute instinct for height' as Nietzsche puts it. According to Neumeyer:

> What Turin's Baroque architecture cultivated to highest theatrical and imitative effect, Antonelli realized in real life. He managed to drive a building to the dizzying heights [*schwindelnde Höhe*] that the Baroque could only stage as an illusion with perspective tricks. No traditional masonry building could be made to go higher.
>
> (2001/2004:248)

The grand style is expressed in the Mole's achievement to rise above imitation and trickery, and to transcend the desire to impress with the kind of superficial spectacle that hampered modern German culture as Nietzsche had claimed. Its height extends further than conventional masonry building of its time, and its design avoids stylistic traditions. Indeed, Gleiter suggests that the 'decisive quality' of the Mole is less its height, and more its stylistic eclecticism, expressed by 'the linearity and arrangement of different architectural elements' (2009:58). Its betrayal of conventional style gives emphasis to its empty form, as does its estrangement from its original religious purpose as a synagogue.

The official *Visitor's Guide* to the Mole Antonelliana emphasizes the heights reached by the building, describing them in terms that complement Neumeyer's assessment of their 'dizzying' effects. A section of the guidebook titled 'Vertigo' describes the Mole as having 'luminously appealing voids', alongside the 'vertigo one feels climbing "up to the blue sky", up the helical stairs inside the ever-narrowing pinnacle, as if the construction technique, taken to its most extreme limits, could emancipate itself from gravity' (Cimorelli 2016:5). The guidebook describes the final cusp of the pinnacle – which measures 19 metres, with eight vertical sides measuring 24 centimetres by 21 centimetres – as imparting to those who dare to venture up its narrow stairs to its four tiny balconies with metal grate flooring, 'chilling feelings of walking in the void' (Cimorelli 2016:10). Terry Kirk describes the interior space of the Mole as 'so lofty and of such overwhelming volume that the rushing absence of scale makes the mind spasm' (2005:164). The bewildering effects of the heights of the Mole may suggest it reaches too high for architecture in the grand style in so far as it disorientates and disembodies us, as participants in its design, as a place without grounding and focus. By the same token, the Mole highlights the dangers and risks involved in creativity and self-discovery – signalling Nietzsche's warning of the fine-line between creativity and madness or 'monstrosity', and the dangers of looking 'into an abyss' for the abyss may look 'into you, too' (BGE,146). Nietzsche's identification with the Mole could be construed as a dangerous risk that Nietzsche was unable to manage creatively. Soon after he identified with the building his body collapsed leading to its paralysis and to death.

The grand style is not conveyed in the material measurements of the Mole's heights, but its height-instinct, which is to say, its desire to 'rise above' convention. The Mole is the achievement of an architect who sought to defy dictates of others despite the palpable risks involved. With little respect for the approved plans and administrative consent to build to a height of 47 metres, Antonelli modified the agreed design to raise it considerably to 167.5 metres. Such radical changes to its design threatened to scupper the entire project. According to Cimorelli, Antonelli was spurred on by 'a never-ending "need" to surpass every limit' established 'either by authorities or by nature'. Antonelli's insatiable drive and sheer determination to accomplish his self-imposed goals, coupled with an inflexible regard for his clients made him 'an obstinate experimenter, a severe, strict innovator, prepared to risk isolation, incomprehension, and criticism' (Cimorelli 2016:5,6). Antonelli's attitude bears the hallmarks of will to power. As Neumeyer notes, Nietzsche identified so intimately with the Mole as a building which bestows on humankind what one *can* build (2001/2004:248).

Antonelli's unappeasable ambition and his desire to repeatedly modify the design is also evident in its eclectic design, and perhaps mostly in the pinnacle of the Mole (Figure 2.4). There we find a variety of heterogeneous forms, stacked one on the other. At the base of the pinnacle is a two-level square lantern with pediments. Upon this sits a truncated cone, where the square section becomes circular. This is followed by a cylindrical tract which divides first into a double ring of fulcrums, then a second ring of fulcrums, and finally into an octagonal pyramid. On top of the pinnacle is a star, which was replaced for several years by a statue of a winged figure (the *Genio Alato*), from 10 April 1889 until 11 August 1904 when the entire pinnacle was destroyed by a tornado. At the time Nietzsche identified himself with the Mole, its exterior was close to completion with the winged figure in place on top of the pyramid. At this time the building was undergoing consolidation works to the spire and the tambour following

ARCHITECTURE IN THE GRAND STYLE

FIGURE 2.4 Mole Antonelliana. Detail of its pinnacle. Author's photograph.

damage caused by a violent earthquake on 23 February 1887. The test of the Mole's integral structure and design at the hands of inclement weather could be construed symbolically as an existential test to its vitality and capacity to remain 'noble', 'upright' and true to itself despite ongoing risks and threats. Indeed, the official guidebook to the Mole suggests that following the damage caused by the tornado to its pinnacle – as its most fragile and less anchored part – the building presented itself 'even more evidently' as having 'a vitality of its own, able to adapt to environmental changes'. The building managed to prove the 'pessimists' predictions wrong' (Cimorelli 2016:12). Nietzsche would have been aware of the building's resilience to the tornado. By resisting the threat of unforeseeable forces and by proving the doubters – or 'nay-sayers' – wrong, the Mole Antonelli is a veritable embodiment of the will to power, to the vital 'yea-saying instinct' and *Amor fati* (Z,III,IV:184–7; GS,276).

According to Nietzsche, the Mole Antonelli is 'the greatest work of genius ever built out of an absolute instinct for height – suggestive of nothing so much as my Zarathustra'. It is architecture of the grand style. Several years before Nietzsche first saw the Mole, he intuits the intimate relationship between Zarathustra and a similar tower-like structure. In a letter to

Overbeck from February 1884, he describes the symphonic composition of *Thus Spoke Zarathustra* as proceeding, 'artistically and step-by-step, like building a tower' [*wie man etwa einen Thurm baut*] (KSB,6:486:475). The similarities between the Mole and Zarathustra continue with Zarathustra's description of the power of life with its incessant desire to build upwards – its *height instinct*. Zarathustra describes a tower with features reminiscent of the Mole Antonelliana. His vision of life prefigures the tower that presents itself to Nietzsche several years later rising out of the streets of Turin:

> Life wants to build itself high with columns and stairs; it wants to gaze into the far distance and out upon joyful splendour – *that* is why it needs height! And because it needs height, it needs steps and conflict between steps and those who climb them! Life wants to climb and in climbing overcome itself. [...] Here he who once towered aloft his thoughts in stone, knew as well as the wisest about the secret of life! [...] How divinely vault and arch here contrast one another in the struggle: how they strive against one another with light and shadow, these divinely-striving things.
> (Z,II, 29:125)

CHAPTER THREE

Nietzsche's architectural influences. Gottfried Semper and festive theatre

While Nietzsche revered individual buildings such as the Palazzo Pitti and Mole Antonelliana, it was the theatre as an architectural type that he discusses most. Gottfried Semper, whom Nietzsche admired as the most significant living architect, was renowned for his theatres and opera houses. In this chapter I consider the extent to which Semper's theory of the origins of architecture in festival performance influenced Nietzsche's notion of the grand style. I go on to question whether Semper was also influenced by Nietzsche through an investigation of the Dionysian iconography showcased in his designs for the Semperoper in Dresden, for its timing and unusual imagery coincides with Nietzsche's studies on Dionysus.

Nietzsche was drawn to Semper's work at a time when Nietzsche was captivated by Wagner, believing him to be a creative genius, and his music, the antidote that German culture desperately needed with its promise of spiritual revival in the image of its people. Semper and Wagner had a tumultuous relationship, of which Nietzsche was undoubtedly aware and perhaps intrigued by given his own struggles with Wagner. Arguably, Semper's alliance with Wagner encouraged Nietzsche to study Semper's ideas in some detail, and perhaps their common frustrations with Wagner led Nietzsche to identify more strongly with Semper's ideas. Certainly, Nietzsche came to promote Semper's discipline of architecture above Wagner's music as the vehicle for cultural revival.

Some have suggested that Wagner introduced Nietzsche to Semper's work,[1] with Joseph Rykwert going so far as to suggest that Wagner arranged a meeting between Semper and Nietzsche at the architect's workshop.[2]

Unfortunately, Rykwert provides no evidence for the meeting, and we know the relationship between Semper and Wagner had started to sour before Nietzsche and Wagner first met in November 1868. It is commonly thought that Semper and Nietzsche were not personally acquainted. Because Semper was a renowned figure in his own right, it is probable that Nietzsche was already familiar with aspects of his ideas before he took a keen interest in Wagner.[3] Other scholars take a different tack, suggesting that Semper was drawn to Nietzsche's work and that Nietzsche's ideas can be traced in Semper's writings.[4] And some suggest Semper was merely aware of Nietzsche's works and may not have read them.[5]

What is certain is that Nietzsche and Semper, together with their mutual acquaintance Wagner, were driven by a common desire to counteract the demise of German culture by mastering the approach of the ancient Greeks, an approach which embodied for them the golden age of creativity where the human spirit was most powerfully expressed. It is inevitable, therefore, that some early ideas of Nietzsche are entwined with those of Semper and Wagner.

Unity of arts and the festive celebration of architecture

Nietzsche, Semper and Wagner believed the decline in the arts was facilitated by their gradual fragmentation into disparate areas of expertise, which diluted their integrity and influence. According to Semper, modern German architecture and art was in decline and impoverished in its character. 'No other century', he lamented, 'is so rich in artists and so poor in art'.[6] This disparity, which prevented architects from creating quality buildings comparable to those of the past, was caused, he claimed, by the 'fatal separation of the arts', causing architecture to become 'a branch set apart'.[7] The key to the revival of all arts was subsequently envisaged in terms of their reunion and synthesis, in what Wagner referred to as Gesamtkunstwerk – a total work of art. Nietzsche, Semper and Wagner regarded this union to be most powerfully expressed in the tragic plays of ancient Greece, with the combination of music, drama and dance. The ancient Greeks ensured, Semper claimed, that 'all the fine arts worked closely together', 'knitted' into a 'harmonious, well-proportioned whole'.[8]

Wagner sought to revive the powerful union of music, drama and dance with his own operatic performances by incorporating mythological narratives of the German people to stir the German soul. And in December 1864 he invited Semper to design an architectural setting worthy of his performances to heighten their rousing effects. With support from the newly crowned King Ludwig II of Bavaria, Semper invested great efforts in his plans for Wagner's building, which he initially envisioned as a Festspielhaus situated on the

Gasteig Hill in Munich to rival Munich's existing Court Theatre, which put on performances of 'ordinary' operas. The project became a saga of fractious communications and bitter resentments between its stakeholders before it finally petered out in January 1869.[9] Semper was poorly treated throughout the project and received no financial compensation for his immense efforts, and little support from his friend, Wagner, after Wagner appeared to lose interest in the project early on. Their friendship appears to have ended on 20 January 1869 when Wagner wrote to Semper to express with bitterness Semper's apparent lack of confidence in him. Semper annotated the letter, 'This letter, of which I could make neither head nor tail, I left unanswered' (Newman 1980:436). Later in this chapter I will consider Semper's proposed design for the Munich Festspielhaus in the context of his Semperoper in Dresden and Wagner's Festspielhaus in Bayreuth.

According to Semper, the separation and weakening of the arts was compounded at the end of the nineteenth century with the rise of industrial production, and with the development of more efficient methods and materials at a rate that outpaced their artistic mastery. This invariably led to products of inferior quality.[10] Semper also identified as a parallel concern, the vast repository of information and data generated by academic research into architectural styles of times past. This research, he surmises, has caused unnecessary confusion for contemporary architects, who now question *which* style they ought to emulate in their own designs. Semper writes:

> Just as the abundance of technical means is an embarrassment to us, even more so are we perplexed by the immense mass of historical knowledge, which increases daily. Every trend of taste is familiar to us, from the times of the Assyrian and Egyptian styles to the age of Louis XVI and beyond. We can do everything; we know everything except ourselves!
> (Semper in Herrmann 1981: MS 88, fol.34)

Semper's complaint reflects Nietzsche's criticism of historicism. Historicism, they both assert, leads to an incoherent mishmash of architectural styles along city streets and prevents styles from emerging organically out of the creative needs and expressions of people living in the here and now. Historicism subsequently establishes significant obstacles to self-reflection and self-knowing. Semper refers to architectural replicas of past styles as 'historical treatises in stone' and 'eerie phantasmagorias'.[11] Echoing Nietzsche's complaint, Semper says they reveal 'the dire poverty of our own ideas and dependence on those of others'.[12] Semper bemoans the fact that in Germany 'architecture as an art has been confined to a beautiful façade, planted there without any attempt at integration'.[13]

To illustrate his point, Semper draws on the problematic methods of the French architect, Jean-Nicholas Louis Durand (1760–1834) whose teachings stressed the need for symmetry and uniformity in contemporary German architecture, as seen in his modelling of town plans at the time (such as Mannheim and Karlsruhe). Durand's method was to draw square grids, on to which plans of buildings were plotted and arranged routinely. This simple system – now termed the 'modular' design – was taught to engineering students from 1795 at the newly founded Ecole Polytechnique in Paris, with the expressed claim that any student in their first year of study could qualify as a fully trained architect after just six months of training in this method, or, as Semper sarcastically writes, ready to perform architectural 'miracles' upon whole cities. The graduate of Durand's School of architecture, Semper maintains, 'loses himself' in the 'lifeless schematism' of his methodology, which both 'combines' and 'lines up things superficially' to establish a 'sort of unity of parts in a mechanical way, instead of showing their organic working together around the primary, animating idea' (Semper 1852/2010:169). Semper sought to counteract this kind of rigid approach to architecture which led to characterless designs by consulting ancient Greek architecture for inspiration. He did so with a view to emulating its more harmonious approach to design that considered the needs of its users and inhabitants. He imagined how this played out in the civic areas of the Greek polis, where buildings were carefully placed to reflect a centre expressive of the cultural needs and political freedom of its people. Buildings were assigned a place more organically, conveying, he says, a 'lyricism of spatial proportions', where no one building dominates, and each has an important role to play in the wider, cultural environment.[14] His consideration of ancient Greek architecture led him to propose the 'great secret of architecture': to design a building 'that has individual character but, at the same time, is in full harmony with itself and the environment'.[15] Perhaps Nietzsche discovered this 'secret', when he came across the Genoese palazzi, which, to his mind, express greatness in their individual character and their affinity with each other.

Crucially, the union of arts that Wagner, Semper and Nietzsche admired in ancient Greek culture evoked an appetite and excitement, which was markedly absent in German culture. Their interpretation of Greek civilization and its arts departed radically from academic conventions of their time, which – since the influential work of art historian, Johann Joachim Winckelmann (1717–68) – generally portrayed the ancient Greeks as people of reason, who were concerned principally with a virtuous life replete with Apollonian ideals of harmony and certainty, and whose architecture mirrored these values with emphasis given to symmetry, proportionate forms and simple lines. In *Das Kunstwerk der Zukunft* [*The Art Work of the Future*] (1849), Wagner draws attention to the religious significance of Greek tragedy and its capacity to arouse irrational fervour in theatre goers, compelling them to participate in the drama, and to conjoin as one people. His operatic performances were conceived with the dynamics of attic tragedy in mind, combining music and myth to stimulate a spiritual response.

Semper's interest in the more dramatic and irrational aspects of ancient Greek culture is first apparent in his contributions to intense debates that questioned whether ancient Greek monuments were coloured or white. Semper realized the extent and importance of ancient polychromy, and to that end he supported the French archaeologist, Antoine-Chrysostome Quatremère de Quincy (1755–1849), in his attack (1815) on Winckelmann's (1756) established ideology of the 'pure' white surface. Winckelmann revered classical architecture of ancient Rome and Greece as the most perfect architectural type, and as such, it ought, he claimed, to be replicated for all time across cultures (1756/1987:33). It achieves its perfection, he maintained, from its rationalized proportions, which means – in contrast to Baroque architecture with its emphasis on passion, tragedy and movement – it expresses the human soul with noble simplicity. The greatness of soul was most appropriately conveyed, Winckelmann argued, in rest, not in passionate movement, and its most vivid expression is in the placid white surfaces of Greek architecture and sculpture. Quatremère rejected this position, citing as evidence, fifth-century texts which allude to brightly coloured chryselephantine sculptures as the highest expression of Greek art. Colour, he argued, was fundamental to ancient Greek art and to the expression of its cultural values, and consequently, the significance of Classical art and architecture rests with colour, and not the weather-washed white sculptures celebrated by his contemporaries. Although Semper admired the ancient Greeks for the harmonious arrangements of their civic buildings, he considered their use of texture and colour as no less vital in establishing the cultural importance of their architecture.

Semper's empirical studies into the colours that originally festooned ancient buildings led him to consider the social significance of coloured surfaces and coverings more generally, and to the conclusion that the historical origins of architecture coincided with the origins of textiles. The first enclosures, he argued, would have been fashioned from woven materials, and these would develop over time to become more sophisticated with the incorporation of coloured patterns. According to Semper, the surface covering or cladding of a building [Bekleidung] expresses its cultural value more vividly than its overall structure. The surface covering is the 'true and legitimate representative of the spatial idea', which 'always and everywhere conveys by itself the nature of the thing' (1860–2/2004:248–50). Semper's view departs from more conventional approaches, which ascertain the origins of architecture according to structural composition, leading many to regard the primitive hut as the original architectural form. Instead, for Semper, the origins and overall significance of architecture is 'festive celebration', and the earliest architectural form, a festive stage,

> [H]ung with tapestries, dressed with festoons and garlands, and decorated with fluttering banners and trophies – is the *motive* for the *permanent* monument, which is intended to proclaim to future generations the festive act or event celebrated.
>
> (1860–2/2004:249)

It is perhaps unsurprising that Semper devoted considerable time designing theatres and opera houses. They include the Dresden Hoftheater (b.1838–41, destroyed by fire in 1869) and its redesign, the new Hoftheater, named Semperoper, after him (b.1871–8); a theatre in the style of a Roman amphitheatre for the central transept of the Crystal Palace, Sydenham, London (1854, never realized); a theatre in Brussels (submitted with Charles Séchan in 1855 for a competition to rebuild the Théâtre Royal de la Monnaie); a theatre in Rio de Janeiro (submitted in 1858 for a public competition); the Vienna K.K. Hoftburgtheatre (b.1874–88, with Karl von Hasenauer); and the Festspielhaus in Munich for Wagner's operatic performances (1864–9). Semper's plans for the Munich theatre were later adapted in part without Semper's permission by Wagner with assistance from architect, Otto Brückwald for the Festspielhaus in Bayreuth (b.1872–5).

For Semper, *all* buildings irrespective of their function find their origins in the colours and textures of the festive, theatrical stage. Both Semper and Nietzsche attach great significance to the architectural surfaces of buildings as social markers of the aspirations and values of their designers, which encourage the onlooker to reflect on their own. One might initially question whether Semper's prioritization of surface cladding and its colourful dressings conflicts with Nietzsche's desire to strip the architectural surface from unnecessary distractions, but I do not think their positions are incompatible. Surfaces are a vital consideration for Nietzsche because they elicit an immediate physiological response in us, and the emptying or stripping of unnecessary decoration from surfaces enhances this response by removing unhelpful distractions. Subsequently, one might imagine Nietzsche tearing down the various festoons, banners and other trophies, which Semper extols as integral to monumental architecture. However, Semper is less concerned with the dressings themselves than he is *the spirit of festivity* conveyed by them. The presence or absence of ornamentation is not the decisive factor here. What matters is the dynamic nature of the surface and its capacity to express a 'festive' atmosphere, and it is this which resonates strongly with Semper and Nietzsche alike. Architecture for Semper, as with Nietzsche, becomes an activity to participate in rather than an object to behold. For Nietzsche, architecture stripped of distracting décor will enable the onlooker to participate in its festivities more effectively. 'Oh, those Greeks!', Nietzsche remarks excitedly, 'They knew how to *live*: what is needed for that is to stop bravely at the surface, the fold, the skin; to adore appearance, to believe in shapes, tones, words – in the whole Olympus of appearance! Those Greeks were superficial – *out of profundity!*' (GS, preface, 4). The empty surfaces Nietzsche seeks are not bland or barren, and if they appear so, it is *out of profundity*, which is to say, they grant us the courage to give style to our character. For both Semper and Nietzsche, the animating principle of the architectural surface is construed as a dynamic interaction of Apollonian and Dionysian artistic impulses.

Apollo and Dionysus

Nietzsche's understanding of the Apollonian and Dionysian as opposing creative forces has gone on to inspire many notable theorists, such as Sigmund Freud (1856–1939) and C.G. Jung (1875–1961), who drew on these ideas in their respective investigations into the unconscious forces that shape human development and behaviour. Nietzsche's influence in this regard is well documented, as is the suggestion that Nietzsche found inspiration for these antithetical forces in the writings of others, such as Jules Michelet (1798–1874), Johann Jakob Bachofen (1815–87), Karl Otfried Müller (1797–1840), Arthur Schopenhauer (1788–1860), Friedrich Hölderlin (1770–1843), Friedrich Schiller (1759–1805), and of course, Richard Wagner. Relatively unacknowledged, however, is the influence of Semper's ideas on Nietzsche's characterization of Apollo and Dionysus, and the influence, therefore, of an architect on Nietzsche's ideas. Nietzsche and Semper were keenly interested at one and the same time in the creative relationship of the Apollonian and Dionysian, and they both expressed the need to accentuate the Dionysian impulse in modern culture where Apollo had come to dominate. Nietzsche argued that human creativity is driven by an interplay of these opposite forces, so that when the tension between them is at its fullest, the most creative and noble human achievements will arise. As with Semper and Wagner, Nietzsche regarded the ancient Greeks as masters of creativity, and he considered their tragic plays as the greatest of artistic expressions because they utilize Apollonian and Dionysian forces at their maximum tension.

In ancient Greek religion every divinity was associated with a set of social functions and personal characteristics, such that Apollo is in many instances a god of higher civilization (e.g. of the arts, medicine, and law), while Dionysus is related to more primordial and chthonic realms (of nature, wine and orgiastic worship).[16] According to Nietzsche, Apollonian forces are associated with reason, order, restraint, clarity, distinction, spatiality, distance and individuality, and with the visual arts due to their immediate, often-unambiguous forms. The Dionysian, by contrast, represents for Nietzsche, non-rational forces and non-figurative art, intoxication, disorder, the dissolution of forms, and a total merger with and obliteration of otherness. The nature of art and human experiences generally will vary according to the extent to which the two forces are active. The Dionysian experience on its own is dangerous and barbaric; it shatters subjectivity and results in something akin to a psychosis, where there is no differentiation between self and other. The Dionysian therefore requires the Apollonian to contain its energy and to harness it for creative ends. Likewise, the Apollonian achievement cannot be appreciated fully until its source of nourishment is recognized; without the Dionysian, the Apollonian is overly determined, rigid and insipid.

At the heart of Germany's cultural decline was its failure to harness the creative tensions between these antithetical forces, and its celebration of Apollonian values at the expense and suppression of Dionysian instincts. This problem was articulated by Semper in his criticism of historicist approaches to architectural design (which sought to emulate styles of the past rather than identify the creative spirit that gave rise to them), and to the rigid techniques employed by Durand's school of architecture. A purely Apollonian approach to architecture will create buildings that are functional and economical, occasionally beautiful, never shocking, and will consider them at a distance, as commodities or objects to critique. A more effective architecture, Nietzsche and Semper would maintain, is dynamic and arresting, it will elevate us and invite us to experience ourselves as if immersed within its material forms and the festivities at its surface. They call for architecture designed with creative tensions of Apollonian and Dionysian forces.

Semper's influence on Nietzsche

Nietzsche's account of Dionysus and Apollo in creative relationship is most prominent in *The Birth of Tragedy* (1872/1993), but the genesis of his idea can be traced to his earlier notes and writings, including two public lectures he gave in Basel in early 1870, 'The Greek Music Drama' [*Das griechische Musikdrama*] and 'Socrates and Tragedy' [*Sokrates und die Tragödie*]; and an essay (also from 1870), 'The Dionysian Worldview' [*Die dionysische Weltanschauung*], which he presented to Cosima Wagner as a Christmas gift. When preparing for these, Nietzsche made notes on Semper's works, including *Style in the Technical and Tectonic Arts; or, Practical Aesthetics* (1860–62/2004) [*Der Stil in den technischen und tektonischen Künsten oder praktische Ästhetik*], and *Preliminary Remarks of Polychrome Architecture and Sculptures in Antiquity* (1834/2010) [*Vorläufige Bemerkungen über farbige Architektur und Plastik bei den Alten*], and his published lecture, 'On Architectural Styles' (1869/2010) [*Ueber Baustyle*].

In the days surrounding Nietzsche's first lecture, 'The Greek Music Drama' (given on 18 January 1870), Semper also happened to be on Nietzsche's mind in a more awkward, personal way. Five days after his lecture, he received a letter from Semper, who apologized for his delayed response to a letter Nietzsche had sent him. Sadly, the content of their correspondence has little to do with their ideas or common cultural interests. Rather, Nietzsche appears to have been manipulated into the correspondence by Cosima Wagner, who used Nietzsche as a go-between to request from Semper a sketch of a lamp he had designed for a synagogue in Dresden. Cosima had taken a fancy to the lamp and wanted a copy made for her husband. Her reticence to ask Semper directly may have been related to the soured relationship between Wagner and Semper. Nietzsche dutifully wrote to

Semper and forwarded Semper's response to Cosima on 25 January. She replied to Nietzsche on 27 January, suggesting amongst other things, that he keep the letter with Semper's valuable signature on it as a form of payment for the favour. One could imagine Nietzsche feeling disheartened by his trivial exchange with Semper, for how insightful and rewarding it might otherwise have been! The nature of their exchange strongly suggests they were not personally acquainted. Undoubtedly, Nietzsche's attentiveness to Semper was heightened at this time.

In 'The Greek Music Drama', Nietzsche refers to Semper as 'the most significant living architect', and he goes on to cite from Semper's *De Stil* (GMD:18; KSA,1:522). Moreover, as Neumeyer has demonstrated, the lecture itself appears to have incorporated the logical structure of Semper's written account of polychromy (1834/2010), with Nietzsche simply substituting Semper's allusions to architecture and sculpture with drama, so that when read together, Nietzsche's lecture and Semper's 'Preliminary Remarks of Polychromy' run in parallel (Neumeyer 2001/2004:37).[17]

Central to Nietzsche's lecture is the assertion that the surviving tragic plays of ancient Greece (notably those of Aeschylus and Sophocles) are poor copies of more complex choral works that preceded them. In Nietzsche's day, music was generally thought to have played a subsidiary role in ancient tragedies, with greater significance and emphasis given to a play's dialogue and plot. But this common view, Nietzsche argued, was founded on an erroneous assumption that distorts the true nature and value of ancient tragedy. To make his point, he compares this error to those who rejected the polychrome of ancient sculpture. Evoking Semper's writings, Nietzsche writes:

> Until recently it was thought to be an unconditional axiom of art that all idealistic sculpture had to be without colour, and that sculpture in antiquity did not permit the use of colour. Quite slowly, and encountering the resistance of these ultra-Hellenists, it has gradually become possible to accept the polychrome view of ancient sculpture, according to which we should no longer imagine that statues were naked but clothed in a colourful coating.
>
> (GMD:8)

Just as Semper had argued that vivacious painted dressings or claddings of ancient architecture expressed the vitality of ancient Greek values, so Nietzsche argued that the musical power of ancient tragedies expresses a vital value that has since been overlooked and neglected not only by historians and scholars of antiquity but by those with a keen interest in contemporary culture and its modern concerns.

Nietzsche goes on to explore what it is that makes ancient choral song so powerful, and he concludes it is its evocation of Dionysian frenzy, which encourages the spectator to become one with the performance. The music uplifts and exalts the human spirit, allowing more primitive human urges to take over. This occurs through the theatrical masking of the spectator's more measured responses. In a preparatory note for his essay, Nietzsche illustrates his point with a phrase taken from a footnote of Semper's *Der Stil*: '"The haze of carnival candles is the true atmosphere of art, Semper, p. 231"' (KSA,7.1[21]:16). Semper employed these words to furnish his own argument about the nature and significance of art. There Semper claims that art is meaningful when it suspends and denies reality, and to this end, it must utilize various techniques of masking and decoration; these are both necessary and enjoyable. Thus, with help from Semper, Nietzsche claims that the vital Dionysian instincts are aroused within the festive atmosphere of the tragic performance – within the haze of carnival candles, the provocative masking of actors and its evocative music.

Nietzsche believed ancient tragic drama achieved its aim through the unified impact of its lyrics, music, orchestral dance, the masks and costumes of its actors, and the design of the stage. In *The Birth of Tragedy*, it is Apollo who provides the masking and decoration to allow the Dionysian instincts to be experienced and harnessed: through Apollo 'the daylight world is veiled and a new world, more distinct, comprehensible and affecting than the other and yet more shadowy, is constantly reborn before our eyes' (BT,8:45). The problem with contemporary German culture, in the eyes of Nietzsche and Semper, was that it had invested too heavily in the Apollonian mask, failing to master it effectively, so that it now hides and represses, not evokes, the Dionysian instincts. In Semper's 'On Architectural Styles' – a public lecture Nietzsche had read and sent to Richard and Cosima Wagner on 19 July 1869 – Semper speaks of the need for the unification of 'two seemingly contradictory cultural forces: namely, striving towards individuality and merging into the collective' (1869/2010:281). These two forces resonate strongly with Nietzsche's Apollo and Dionysus.

In writings of Semper and Nietzsche, we find the art of modern German culture is divested of essential, festive energies, and it subsequently extols an Apollonian distance between subject and artwork. While Nietzsche and Semper sought an architecture of festive play, they regarded modern buildings as rigid façades or stone memorials of times passed.

Dionysus in Dresden

There is no evidence that Semper read Nietzsche's writings, nor, as I noted, to suggest the two ever met. However, there is a curious matter of a Nietzschean-like presentation of the relationship between Dionysus and Apollo, and between Dionysus and the arts, expressed visually in the Semperoper in Dresden – the designs for which Semper prepared while Nietzsche was writing *The Birth of Tragedy*. In this respect, the Semperoper could be regarded as an architectural representation of Nietzschean thought (Figure 3.1).

FIGURE 3.1 Semperoper, Dresden (b.1870–78, Gottfried Semper). Front elevation. Photograph, 1888. Hulton Archive. © Getty Images.

The elevated status that Nietzsche and Semper gave to Dionysus in relation to the arts and to musical performance is regarded by many as somewhat odd. For Apollo is traditionally conceived as master of the arts and leader of the Muses, and consequently, it is Apollo who is more commonly emphasized in the iconography of theatres and opera houses. While images of Dionysus or Bacchus may be apparent in these buildings, they tend to figure less prominently or not at all. It is unusual to find the positions of Apollo and Dionysus reversed, but this is exactly what Semper does with his Semperoper, and confidently so, by establishing Dionysus as the leitmotif of his building, inside and out. A triumphant Dionysus appears in pride of place alongside his bride, Ariadne, in a panther-drawn quadriga, above the building's central exedra and main entrance. Nietzsche, similarly, in *The Birth of Tragedy*, elevates the position of Dionysus within the arts, associating Dionysus with the ecstatic power of music and making him central to tragic performance. Nietzsche's portrayal of Dionysus' link to music was widely ridiculed and criticized by the academic community at the time for its disregard for textual evidence gleaned from ancient Greek texts and scholarly testimony.[18] The most cited and scathing of commentaries, by the Berlin philologist Ulrich von Wilamowitz-Möellendorf (1848–1931), asserted that the error of Nietzsche's unconventional presentation of Dionysus, both in the company of the Muses and in relationship with Apollo, was of such magnitude that it warranted Nietzsche's immediate dismissal from his academic post at Basel University (Wilamowitz 1872:19, fn.18).[19]

Semper was commissioned in 1870 to design the Semperoper in Dresden after its predecessor, the Royal Court Theatre also designed by him (b.1834–41), was destroyed by fire on 21 September 1869. Nietzsche visited the latter on 21 January 1869, eight months before its fateful demise, to attend Dresden's premier of Wagner's *Die Meistersinger*. We do not know what Nietzsche thought of the building, but it undoubtedly contributed to his overwhelming experience of the evening, which he recounts as an experience of being at home both in his surroundings and within himself ['*zu Hause und heimisch zu sein*'] (Letter to Erwin Rohde; KSB,2.625:379). Given the powerful experience he had inside the building, it is disappointing that we have no record of his thoughts on the building's catastrophic demise – an event which made headline news across Europe – nor, indeed, of its 'rebirth' into the Dionysian edifice of the Semperoper, which would undoubtedly have piqued his interest. Nietzsche did not visit Dresden after his trip in 1869.

The Semperoper honours Dionysus throughout. The large bronze crowning sculpture of Dionysus and his bride in their chariot gives the building a sense of animation and movement (Figure 3.2). The panthers are in full stride with raised paws, Ariadne's veil is waving in the rush of wind and the ribbons of Dionysus' Thyrus (staff) are flapping. Stephan notes, 'the Quadriga is like an "allegro con fuoco", a symbol of enthusiasm. Joy and intoxicating power of music, incarnated in the immortal love of the beautiful, eternally cheerful and young god Bacchus [Dionysus] with Ariadne'; the composition is altogether 'rousing' and 'sky-storming' (1996:101, cf.190). Its dynamism establishes a tension with the building's otherwise calming, more 'Apollonian' architecture in high Renaissance style. It is, Neumeyer notes, an Apollonian building with a Dionysian frame (2001/2004:120). The tensions between the Apollonian and Dionysian are suggestive of the 'festive' experience that Nietzsche and Semper desired for the creative revival of German architecture – an architecture that revitalizes the onlooker, inviting them to participate in its spectacle. Semper's Dionysus looks towards his bride and outwards to meet the gaze of those who approach, as if encouraging them to join them in the ensuing festivities. Johannes Schilling describes his sculpture as 'a festive entry among the people', bringing them 'enthusiasm and joy' (cited in Stephan 1996:98). Stephan similarly describes how the eyes of Dionysus look 'out into the country', with a gaze that expresses an awareness of 'freedom' (1996:190). The connection of Dionysus to the people is precisely what Nietzsche desired. Indeed, as Neumeyer aptly remarks, 'The fact that someone had dared to lay an entire city at the feet of Dionysus and his panthers at the same time', as Nietzsche was developing his ideas for *The Birth of Tragedy*, 'would probably have given Nietzsche a solemn feeling of confirmation' (2001/2004:124).

A closer look at the pedestal of the quadriga reveals the masks of satyrs, created by Semper's son, Emanuel (1848–1911),[20] and underneath the quadriga are four of the nine Muses: Melpomene (tragic poetry and

FIGURE 3.2 Semperoper. Detail of the quadriga with Bacchus/Dionysus and Ariadne (1871, Johannes Schilling). © Paulae.

funeral song), Thalia (comic poetry), Terpsichore (dance), and Polyhymnia (hymn and poetry). Usually associated with Apollo, these Muses have become mediators of Dionysus. Further below, underneath the vault of the exedra, we find a depiction of Apollo, relegated to a single side-panel of a painted mosaic, alongside three Graces. Apollo's lyre also features on the rear gable of the stage building. The leitmotif of Dionysus continues inside the building with painted ceilings of the upper, circular foyer depicting the life of Dionysus (his upbringing by the nymphs of Nysa, the discovery of Ariadne, Dionysus punishing the Tyrrhenian pirates and Dionysus torn apart by the Titans). The largest, central painting depicts the rebirth of Dionysus. Semper describes the ceiling as having 'a festive effect' (cited in Magirius 1987:92). An inevitable focal point inside is the stage curtain. Semper was known to have disliked the curtain with its central motif of a female figure riding on a white horse through a forest (a scene from Ludwig Tieck's romantic comedy, *Emperor Octavianus*, painted by Julius Huebner).[21] Semper wanted instead an image of Dionysus and the Muses by Bonaventura Genelli – the artist of the watercolour owned by Wagner, which so enthralled Nietzsche (see Magirius 1987:146; Neumeyer 2001/2004:123). I will consider Genelli's image of Dionysus as a point of connection between Semper and Nietzsche shortly, but beforehand I wish to consider the possibility that Semper's choice of Dionysus as the leitmotif for his Semperoper was directly influenced by Nietzsche's writings on Dionysus.

Nietzsche's Dionysus at the Semperoper?

In his study on the Semperoper, Heinrich Magirius asserts that Semper's choice of 'mythical imagery' for the building was intended 'to illustrate the content and development of human drama', which 'found its ideas' in 'the birth of tragedy in the life of the "natural god" Dionysus' (1987:160). According to Magirius, Semper's intentions dove tail with Nietzsche's: 'Semper's iconography shared the priority of the Dionysian over the Apollonian with Friedrich Nietzsche's *Birth of Tragedy from the Spirit of Music*' (1987:67). A small number of other historians have made similar connections between the building and book. Bärbel Stephan, in her study of Johannes Schilling (1828–1910; the sculptor whom Semper commissioned to create the quadriga sculpture), notes, 'The choice of Bacchus and Ariadne on a panther-drawn chariot comes from Gottfried Semper. Friedrich Nietzsche's book on the Dionysian and Apollonian in art, published in 1872, could have been decisive for this' (1996:97–8). Stephan undermines her claim somewhat when she notes elsewhere in her study that that Schilling received the commission for the Dionysian quadriga a year earlier, on 16 May 1871, which is to say, several months before the publication of *The Birth of Tragedy*. The discrepancy in dates suggests that had Semper been familiar with Nietzsche's accounts of the 'Dionysian and Apollonian in art', it would have been from Nietzsche's earlier works, such as the published public lecture, 'The Greek Music Drama' from 1870. Fritz Neumeyer highlights the fact that the foundation stone of the Semperoper was laid on 26 April 1871, eight months before *The Birth of Tragedy* was first available (2001/2004:121). Harry Mallgrave, in his introduction to his translation into English of Semper's *Der Stil*, concedes that Semper may well have read 'The Greek Music Drama' and *The Birth of Tragedy* when Semper was considering his iconographic themes for the Semperoper. Mallgrave, however, mistakenly gives a later date for Semper's considerations to 'around 1873' (1996:351). Mallgrave regards the similar portrayals of Apollo and Dionysus by Semper and Nietzsche as 'one of those interesting coincidences (though not accidents) of history' (2006:51). Their similar exaltation of Dionysus over Apollo can be explained, he claims, by their common acquaintance, Wagner. Thus, Semper had shared his 'interest in theatricality' with Wagner in the 1840s, and this, Mallgrave suggests, was 'handed down from Wagner to Nietzsche in 1869'. He concludes that Nietzsche 'inherited' an 'intoxicating view of art' that was, 'at least in part, Semperian' (1996:351).

When considering Semper's decision to give Dionysus pride of place in his Semperoper, we ought not treat the Semperoper in isolation from Semper's earlier designs for opera houses and theatres. If we regard the Semperoper as a phase in the evolution of Semper's designs, we find Dionysus is an ever-present prominent feature. For instance, the theatre in Rio de Janeiro, designed in 1858, and the ill-fated Festspielhaus in Munich designed between 1864 and 1869 already indicate Semper's intention to place a large sculpture of Dionysus in a carriage prominently above the main entrance (Habel 1970:310; Habel 1985:128; Neumeyer 2001/2004:213[22]; Sturm 2003:169,154). Furthermore, the painted ceiling of the Semperoper with its depictions of the life of Dionysus 'corresponded exactly', Semper remarks, 'to the ceiling of the old theatre destroyed by fire' (cited in Magirius 1987:92). When considering the evolution of Semper's theatre designs, it is useful to note that Semper intended to crown the new Hofburgtheater in Vienna on the Ringstrasse (b.1888) with a similar quadriga to the Semperoper, with Dionysus and Ariadne in pride of place (see Maigrius 1987:19, plates 11–14). Semper was commissioned to design the layout and interior design of this theatre, with Karl von Hasenauer (1833–94) overseeing its overall design. Had Semper taken charge of the project (or had he not withdrawn fully from it), he may have got his way. After Semper's departure from the project, Hasenauer had Apollo reinstated above the entrance as the ruler of the arts (Mallgrave 1996:336–7; Neumeyer 2001/2004:123) – a move Magirius describes as a rejection of 'human ideals' in favour of a more appropriately 'historical' iconography (1987:164).[23]

Semper's interest in Dionysus was long standing and predated Nietzsche's. It is difficult to ascertain whether Nietzsche was familiar with the Dionysian iconography of the Semperoper. Neumeyer maintains that Nietzsche would have seen Semper's designs for the Munich Festspielhaus when he visited Wagner in Tribschen before he began his essays in preparation for *The Birth of Tragedy* (2001/2004:117). We have no record of this, and this account jars somewhat with Manfred Semper's (1838–1913) assertion that Wagner had not bothered to familiarize himself with the later phases of its design (1906:56–7). And if Nietzsche had seen these designs, it would have been long after the publication of *The Birth of Tragedy*, and in the context of Wagner's design for the Festspielhaus in Bayreuth – a building that would come to incorporate structural elements of Semper's Munich theatre (see below).

It is most probable that Nietzsche and Semper developed similar accounts of Dionysus because they were inspired by a common source – not simply Wagner, as Mallgrave suggests, but a larger, ancient tradition, which linked Dionysus directly to music and to the Muses. Although Nietzsche and Semper were criticized for their controversial break with historical tradition by upholding Dionysus, not Apollo, as the figurehead for theatre and musical drama, they were expressing ancient ideas that had been largely obscured or forgotten since the sixteenth century. To Ernst Julius Hähnels (1811–91), Dresden sculptor and teacher of Johannes Schilling, Semper writes, 'According to a very ancient mythological account, the Muses belong to the immediate entourage, and as it were, the court of Dionysus' (cited in Magrius 1987:144). Similarly, in response to Wilamowitz-Möellendorf's scathing criticisms of *The Birth of Tragedy*, Nietzsche prompts his friend Erwin Rohde to write a critical counter-response, which he does with allusions to this ancient tradition (Rohde 1872). Arguably, only since the Italian high Renaissance, with Raphael's influential depiction of Apollo with the nine Muses in his fresco painting, *The Parnassus* (*c*.1509–11), does Apollo come to predominate as the god of music and master of the arts. Prior to this, Dionysus was traditionally linked to the Muses alongside Apollo, as we find in Ovid's *Metamorphoses* (3:421; 4:18) and his *Epistulae Heroides* [Letters of Heroines] (15:31). Occasionally we find the two gods representing each other or the two merged into one figure, such as Andrea Alciati's *Emblemata* (*c*.1531) where Dionysus and Apollo appear together on a pedestal (emblem XCIX 'In iuventam'/'On youth'), and Martin Poussin's painting *Bacchus-Apollo* (1620–5) depicting a figure as a composite of both gods, or his, *The Triumph of Bacchus* (1635–6), where the two gods are depicted in chariots, running parallel to each other, with Bacchus travelling on the ground and Apollo in the sky. The Semperoper and *The Birth of Tragedy* continue this tradition. Indeed, Schilling's figure of Dionysus is thought by some to resemble the Roman sculpture of Apollo Belvedere (AD 120–40; see Stephan 1996:120).

I end this investigation into the potential links between Nietzsche and Semper with another significant depiction of Dionysus: a painting of Bacchus among the Muses by German artist, Bonaventura Genelli (1798–1868).[24] A version of the painting hung on the wall of Wagner's drawing room in Tribschen, where it enthralled Nietzsche when he came to visit. Many have speculated on the impact it had on Nietzsche and his portrayal of Dionysus in relation to Apollo and the arts, and the extent to which Wagner – in his conversations with Nietzsche about the painting – was a key influence on Nietzsche's presentation of Dionysus in *The Birth of Tragedy*. What is not documented in the context of Nietzsche and Wagner, however, is Semper's interest in Genelli's painting for use as a theatre curtain for his first Dresden opera house (and another painting by Genelli for the stage curtain of the Semperoper). The absence of this discussion is unfortunate because Genelli's image of Dionysus provides us with another curious link between the Semperoper and *The Birth of Tragedy*, and between Semper's architecture and Nietzsche's philosophy more generally.

Genelli's Dionysus: Linking Nietzsche, Semper, and Wagner

Genelli was known for his artistic representations of mythological themes, not least, his depictions of Dionysian or Bacchic adventures gleaned from ancient sources. He repeatedly reworked images of Dionysus in drawings, watercolours and oils, including six different versions over several decades on the theme of Dionysus or Bacchus with the Muses.[25] Discussions of these works tend to neglect the fact that they differ in composition and title, and subsequently, these various works are often referred to as replicas or copies of one and the same composition, titled, *Bacchus unter Musen* [*Bacchus among the Muses*]. This has had unfortunate repercussions for Nietzschean scholarship and for studies that assess relationships between Genelli's work and the ideas of Nietzsche and Wagner. Indeed, several scholars of Nietzsche and of Wagner have fallen into the trap of assuming the painting that was displayed in Wagner's drawing room – which so captivated Nietzsche, and inspired the ideas of both men – was simply a replica of the most common composition in the series (notable among these is Martin Vogel 1966; and M.S. Silk and J.P. Stern 2016[26]). But the watercolour and pen composition, which came into Wagner's possession in 1867, differs to others in the series, not only in title (*Dionysos, von den Musen Apollos erzogen/ Dionysus Educated by Apollo's Muses*) but in quality and composition (Figure 3.3).

In an article from 1869 for the periodical *Unsere Zeit*, Peter Cornelius (1824–74), nephew to Genelli and long-standing friend of Wagner, highlights the exceptional quality of Wagner's painting to another, later version in the series. This later painting, in oil, titled *Bacchus unter den Musen*, was Genelli's final rendition of the theme, commissioned by Adolf

FIGURE 3.3 *Dionysos, von den Musen Apollos erzogen.* Watercolour (*c*.1832–36, Bonaventura Genelli) © Nationalarchiv der Richard-Wagner-Stiftung, Bayreuth. Notice the herm in the top left quarter.

Friedrich Count von Schack (1815–94) in 1866 and completed in 1868. According to Cornelius, one can see the misery Genelli felt from the death of his son immediately prior to its completion. This painting is half-heartedly executed and incomparable, he writes, to the warmth and youthful vibrance reflected in *Dionysos, von den Musen Apollos erzogen*, which graced Wagner's salon at Tribschen.[27] Hans Ebert, in his study of the life and work of Genelli, similarly asserts that the death of Genelli's son paralysed the artist's creativity, causing him great difficulty in completing this painting. The result, he says, lacks spatial depth, and is rather messy (1971:172,174). Siegfried Mandel, a scholar of Nietzsche, describes its figure of Bacchus as 'stodgy', and its overall effect as 'an over-elaborated pastiche' (1990:217). Most significantly, the composition of Wagner's painting differs to Schack's and to several others in the series, with its addition of a prominent and rather menacing herm, who looks out of the painting from behind the drunken figure of Silenus.

In 1838, Semper commissioned Genelli to reproduce his composition, *Bacchus unter den Musen* for the stage curtain of his first opera house in Dresden. It is probable that Semper's interest in Genelli's work was encouraged by Ernst Hähnel, a mutual friend of Semper and Genelli. Hähnel and Genelli exchanged ideas with each other through written correspondence until the end of Genelli's life, and although Hähnel was occasionally critical of certain peculiarities in Genelli's drawings, Genelli's influence can be traced in Hähnel's own work, such as the frieze of the procession of Bacchus he had created for Semper's first opera house in Dresden (destroyed in the fire of 1869), which is thought to reflect Genelli's style, specifically with its rhythmic quality and animated motifs (Ebert 1971:84). Semper had consulted Hähnel on the sculptural and decorative programmes for the two Dresden opera houses, with their overarching Dionysian theme. As well as incorporating statues by Hähnel in both buildings, and utilizing the talents of Hähnel's student, Johannes Schilling, for the crowning quadriga of the Semperoper, Semper expressed his desire to reproduce for the stage curtain of the Semperoper, another image by Genelli, which Hähnel had in his possession (*Die Geburt der Künste aus der Finsternis/The Birth of the Arts out of Darkness*; cited in Magirius 1987:146,88).[28]

Genelli's image of Bacchus and the Muses appears to have been integral to the visions of Dionysus that Nietzsche and Semper sought to express in their respective works. What remains unclear is whether Nietzsche and Semper were inspired by the same composition by Genelli, albeit different copies or variations of a theme. As I noted, Wagner's watercolour version includes a menacing herm, which, as I go on to discuss, is a prominent feature that would inevitably have captivated Nietzsche's attention. But the herm is absent in several other versions by Genelli that go by the same name.

The images of Dionysus that inspired Semper and Nietzsche seem to have originated in a problematic commission Genelli undertook for Hermann Härtel (1803–75), Director and co-owner of Breitkopf & Härtel, the celebrated music publishing house. Härtel sought the services of Genelli in 1832 to create a fresco depicting Bacchus in the company of the Muses to adorn the ballroom ceiling of his newly built Roman-inspired villa in Leipzig (b.1834; destroyed 1945).[29] Härtel originally wanted images from the Odyssey, but Genelli convinced him to have images from the Bacchus myth. From 15 January 1832, Genelli notes his enthusiasm for the project, not least because, to his mind, no ancient artwork had depicted Bacchus in the company of the Muses, but the idea of them together was 'a very sweet thought!'[30] Unfortunately, Genelli's progress was slow and Härtel grew impatient and withdrew the commission in May–April 1834, but not before Genelli had completed various images for it.[31] The project's failure left Genelli in a precarious position financially and professionally. His images for the project were apparently passed over – presumably sold – in 1834 to the book dealers, Friedrich and Heinrich Brockhaus, both of whom were a brother-in-law to Wagner. To redeem his reputation following the termination of his services, Genelli sought a new commission for his Dionysian compositions. To that end, in 1838 he submitted a design for a stage curtain for Semper's first opera house in Dresden, under the title, *Bacchus unter den Musen*. Ernst Hähnel wrote to Genelli from Dresden on 10 January 1839 to inform him that his proposal had been well received and stood every chance of success. But Genelli himself withdrew his proposal a week later, on the grounds that, as he explains to Hähnel, the depiction of Bacchus among the Muses, although suitable for an 'ancient theatre', is inappropriate for a contemporary opera house. He goes on to note that the subject would be misunderstood by the uneducated public, who are unfamiliar with the theme, and who would probably mock Silenus' fat belly. Genelli changed his mind and submitted his design, *Bacchus unter den Musen*, in the summer of 1853 to Franz von Dingelstedt, Director of the Court Theatre in Munich (Nielsen 2005:57, n.198). Genelli thought his design much more appropriate than the image that adorned the stage curtain in this theatre at the time – a copy of Guido Reni's fresco painting, *L'Aurora*, which Genelli thought more suited to an observatory than a theatre (Nielsen 2005:60). Genelli's submission came to nothing. In 1868, the year he died, he completed the composition in oils for Schack. Interestingly, this and Wagner's version of the painting are themselves reminiscent of a theatre curtain with heavily framed borders that resemble a tapestry.[32]

Dionysos, von den Musen Apollos erzogen was sold to Friedrich Brockhaus, husband to Wagner's sister Luise. Wagner recalls how the painting made a 'deep impression on him' in his younger years when he stayed with his sister in Leipzig, and it continued to inspire his ideas later in life. Wagner reminisces about its impact in his autobiography, *Mein Leben*, where he recalls sitting in Café Littéraire in Zürich in the summer of 1849. After a heavy meal, he found himself staring at the café's wallpaper with its motifs of ancient subjects. This triggered for him a dream-like reverie, taking him back to occasions in his youth when he would gaze upon Genelli's painting at his brother-in-law's house (Wagner 1870/1963:439). According to Wagner, this reverie gave birth to his writings that year, including his essays *Das Kunstwerk der Zukunft* ['Artwork of the Future'] and *Die Kunst und die Revolution* [Art and Revolution].

After Friedrich Brockhaus died, Cosima Wagner acquired Genelli's watercolour from Luise in 1867 for Richard as a gift in October of that year. Wagner described it as 'the most beautiful thing we have', and he displayed it in his drawing room in Tribschen, and later in the Purple Salon (Lila Salon) at Wahnfried in Bayreuth (Habel 1985:608; 606, plate 103). On 24 February 1869, Wagner wrote to his benefactor, King Ludwig II, describing his 'splendid masterpiece by the now deceased Genelli (original watercolour), depicting the education of Dionysus by the Muses – it was in the possession of my late brother-in-law, Brockhaus, in whose house as a youth I often regarded it with true enchantment, and from it I received my first vivid impression of the Greek spirit of beauty (cited in Vogel 1966:125).

It was during his twenty-three visits to Tribschen (from May 1869) that Nietzsche became entranced by Genelli's painting, and its depiction of Dionysus subsequently became a discussion point for Wagner and Nietzsche. We know, for instance, between 11 and 13 June 1870, Nietzsche's friend, Erwin Rohde, joined Nietzsche in Tribschen as Wagner's guest, and during this stay, the three of them had lively discussions about the painting. But we do not know what was said. Nietzsche recalls this occasion to Rohde in a letter of 16 July 1872, when urging him to come to his defence against Wilamowitz's criticisms of *The Birth of Tragedy*, especially with regard to the associations Nietzsche had made between Dionysus and the Muses.[33]

The composition of Wagner's painting included an ominous herm, a short stone pillar ending in a grimacing, horned head of a Pan-like figure, who stares out of the image. The figure is reminiscent of the herm in Nicholas Poussin's oil painting, *A Bacchanalian Revel Before a Term* (c.1633). The herm of Pan is traditionally associated with Bacchus, as his companion and guardian, and here its presence appears to contrast with the radiant, Apollo-like figure of Bacchus himself, as if his 'alter ego', as Mandel remarks (1990:223). It accentuates the darker, irrational forces of the Dionysian, and, together with the drunken figure of Silenus and the animated figure of Eros, it forms a company of Dionysian revellers in the left of the image. Our attention is drawn to their side of the composition, aided by Dionysus at the centre whose body is turned towards them directing them in their dance. In stark contrast, to the right of Dionysus are the serene Muses of Apollo, who, according to Mandel, represent an 'Apollonian illusion that dwindles in the face of another art and truth: the intoxication of Dionysus'. Thus, it was the case, he claims, that Nietzsche saw in Genelli's painting, 'the antithetical Dionysiac and Apollonian melt into one another' (Mandel 1990:224). Without the herm, *Bacchus und den Musen*, is a less arresting image. The gaze of the herm meets our own and draws us in, as a much-needed reminder that we, too, are entwined with the Dionysian aspect of life.[34]

Mandel argues that Wagner was resentful – albeit unconsciously – of Nietzsche's understanding of Genelli's painting, compared to his own 'amateurish appreciation' of it (1990:217–19). While Wagner idealized its images of Dionysus and the Apollonian, Nietzsche digested its entire scene with its tensions and contrasts, and 'aesthetically refined it into a view of creative mutuality – a mythic and valid image of human existence' (1990:213). Mandel also questions the accuracy of Wagner's reminiscences about Genelli's painting, and Wagner's claim that it was a long-standing influence on his ideas, finding Wagner's assertions 'tenuous at best', and indicative of Wagner's attempt to lay prior claim to ideas that Nietzsche expounded more explicitly (1990:213, 215). While, as I claim, the Semperoper could be regarded as an architectural representation of Nietzsche's vision of Dionysus in relation to the arts, Genelli's painting – as an inspiration to Semper and Nietzsche alike – could be construed, as Mandel puts it, as 'a detailed and validating emblematic visualization', not only of Nietzsche's work, as Mandel suggests, but of Semper's too.

Bayreuth Festspielhaus

The charge of Wagner's superficial engagement with Genelli's painting anticipates Nietzsche's later criticisms of Wagner's approach to art more generally, and notably, Wagner's preoccupation with theatrical tricks, shocks, and rousing effects that deflect from more meaningful and lasting transformations of the human spirit. Earlier I examined various architectural analogies that Nietzsche employed when discussing the cultural malaise that he sought to remedy. He presents Wagner within a collapsed building, separated from his spirit, and as master of a labyrinth with its 'game of hide-and-seek among a hundred symbols' (CW,10). Wagner exemplifies in Nietzsche's later writings a prime decadent, concerned only with pretence and posturing, with pithy details and superficial effects. In relation to Genelli's painting and within Nietzsche's architectural analogies, Wagner seems out of touch with the bigger picture. Wagner came to construct a theatre of his own, described by him as very close in design to an 'ideal' building to house his artistic vision (Wagner 1873). The Festspielhaus in Bayreuth could subsequently be regarded as emblematic of Wagner's creative instincts, and by the same token, of the deep-seated problems Nietzsche sought to overcome (see Figure 3.4).

While Nietzsche felt an overwhelming sensation of 'being at home' when listening to Wagner's *Die Meistersinger* in Semper's first Dresden opera house, his experience at the opening of Wagner's Festspielhaus was in stark contrast, utterly devastating for Nietzsche, causing him to flee the building and to break his allegiance with Wagner. If the Semperoper resonates with Nietzsche's grand style through its festive spectacle, the Festspielhaus epitomizes Nietzsche's views of decadence. The festivity of

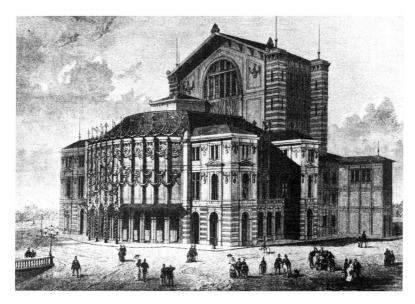

FIGURE 3.4 Richard Wagner Festspielhaus, Bayreuth (b.1872–6). Illustration, Nineteenth Century. Clu. © Getty Images.

the Semperoper is not reduceable to its visual or spatial imagery, but its rhythmic interplay across its surfaces, such as we find in the creative tensions between its excitable Dionysian quadriga and the more measured symmetry of its Apollonian façade. The result is at once calming and frenzied: a unified sense of style. Mallgrave's characterization of Semper's sense of festivity in architecture summarizes it well, as a 'grand unity of effects gleaned from all the fine arts', which exude 'a certain fleshiness or corporality' and 'animate and enliven surfaces' (1996:126). Although Nietzsche does not discuss the design of Wagner's Festspielhaus beyond its orchestra pit, we can identify various features of it that chime with Nietzsche's criticisms of Wagner and modern decadence more generally.

The Festspielhaus was in part a distorted version of Semper's earlier design for the failed Munich project. According to Semper's son, Manfred, Semper was insulted by Wagner's decision to use features of his design without his prior approval (M. Semper 1906:102). Wagner employed the services of another architect, Otto Brückwald (1841–1917), to create the Festspielhaus, which, as Wagner later admitted to Semper, was inferior to Semper's original design, comparably 'clumsy and tasteless' (13 June 1877; Habel 1970:314; M. Semper 1906:105). Neumeyer notes, 'from an architectural point of view, there is hardly anything uplifting to say about it, because nothing really fits together. Even the untrained eye does not miss the blatant lack of relationship between its components' (2004:117). The Festspielhaus thereby reflects the 'modern carnival motley', which so troubled Nietzsche with its architecture in a 'chaotic mishmash of all styles' (UM I.1). The Festspielhaus, Neumeyer remarks, is an 'awkward mix' that is at once 'stubborn' and 'pompous', and more reminiscent of a factory or a purpose-built agricultural or industrial building than a theatre. This he says, is underscored by the fact that it managed to escape being bombed in the Second World War because the allied bomber pilots mistook it for a brewery! (2001/2004:117; see also Sturm 2003:110).

Central to Wagner's overall failure, in Nietzsche's eyes, was Wagner's lack of 'rhythmic feeling' and 'organizing power', which subsequently distorted his artistic achievements, removing the possibility of an organic and unified style in his works, and preventing them from inspiring creative power in others. Wagner's confusing artistry may allure with its fleeting effects, Nietzsche contends, but it ultimately misleads through its 'imitation of greatness'. Wagner consequently compounds the problematic conceptual split of the modern mindset, which Nietzsche identifies and seeks to remedy with his grand style. The Festspielhaus is emblematic of this split with the mismatch of its simplified exterior and the grandiosity of the effects paraded within. Wagner was not interested in its exterior design, choosing to channel his financial resources into the stage machinery and scenery to ensure the building's interior reflected his 'ideal inner work of art – *perfect* in every way'. For the simple timber and brick construction of its exterior, Wagner intended only a 'humble shell', which would be 'solid' enough to 'prevent it from collapsing' (12 April 1872; cited in Baker 1998:60). The disparate approaches to the exterior and interior indicate a lack of creative tension between Apollonian and Dionysian considerations, with an exterior fashioned according to Apollonian precepts of function and restraint, and an interior that grants the Dionysian an unchecked, free rein.

Nietzsche was enthusiastic about the Festspielhaus from its initial design through to the laying of its foundation stone, but his feelings changed significantly when it became fully operational in the summer of 1876. In an unpublished note he writes: 'My mistake was to come to Bayreuth with an ideal. I was forced to experience the bitterest disappointment. The excess of ugliness, distortion, and overexcitement repulsed me vehemently' (KSA, 8.30[1]:522); 'a deep alienation from everything surrounded me there [...] Not one monstrosity is lacking' there (EH, VI.HH.2). In Nietzsche's mind, Wagner had created a grandiose spectacle of delusion. His theatre 'offers us a magnifying glass', Nietzsche writes, 'you look through it and cannot believe your eyes – everything becomes big, *even Wagner*' (CW,3). The sunken orchestra pit, which Brückwald had adapted from Semper's Munich design, contributed to the effect that so riled Nietzsche. It was perhaps this design feature, above others, that encouraged his condemnation of Wagner as a mere 'master of hypnotic tricks' (CW,5).[35] Its intention was to keep the musicians and conductor out of sight, and to give the impression that their music was from another world, from a 'mystical chasm' (Baker 1998:262;

Wagner 1873). Its powerful effects would make spectators feel as if they were being transported to a metaphysical reality, conjoined as one with the performance – a similar approach to the ancient tragic performance, with its use of the Chorus. This communal experience was integral to Wagner's vision of the Gesamtkunstwerk, and his desire to transform individual spectators into a collective audience with a common cultural identity, as *Volk*. This experience was aided by another feature lifted from Semper's earlier design: the linear seating arrangement. This reduced potential distractions from other members of the audience and gave uninterrupted sight of the stage. Coupled with the hidden orchestra, this arrangement gave the impression that the actors on stage were much closer to the audience than they were, imbuing them with an otherworldly character, and 'larger, superhuman stature' (Baker 1998:262; Wagner 1873).

Wagner's ideal architecture is an invisible architecture, and this is problematic for Nietzsche. The various tricks that are supported by an imperceptible architecture are perhaps less of a problem for Nietzsche than the feelings of disembodiment they cultivate. Invisible architecture is bewildering and disorientating; it lacks the solidity we require to ground ourselves and to feel ourselves in place. Invisible architecture allows Dionysus free rein, with the obliteration and dissolution of Apollonian structure and distinctive form. Wagner seeks to eliminate any distractions that might prevent the fabricated illusion of a total merger of audience and performance; he seeks within his building to replace concrete 'reality' with an 'ideal stage world' (Habel 1970:311; Wagner 1873; see also Baker 1998:242).[36] In 1876, prior to the inauguration of the building, Nietzsche describes the effect of Wagner's music positively, as leading the spectator to a 'new mode of understanding and existence, just as if suddenly their senses had become more spiritual and their spirit more sensual' (UM IV.9). But as Nietzsche came to realize, this heightened spiritual experience was, in and of itself, the real distraction: a problematic distraction from oneself. It is akin, he writes, to the 'problems of hysterics' (CW.I.5), and to an existential crisis where one is 'perplexed' by one's 'own being', and '*alienated from*' oneself – 'For it is with precisely this feeling that [one] participates in Wagner's mightiest accomplishments' (UM IV.7). Nietzsche's proposed remedy to overcome such self-alienation was the affirmation of self through bodily experiences – an experience of oneself that is grounded in concrete realities. Nietzsche's grand style calls for an architecture without unnecessary distractions, not to dissolve bodily forms and individual identities, but to cultivate and emphasize them. Architecture grants us through the immediacy of its material forms an awareness of ourselves grounded in the here and now.

'Greek Tragedy' was in many ways a prototype for Nietzsche's grand style. By association, the theatres in which they were performed anticipate architecture in the grand style. Nietzsche initially appreciated Wagner's metaphysical assumptions which emphasized Dionysian mysteries as a counter to the intellectual sterility of modern culture. But the failure of

Wagner's achievements for Nietzsche, with their seductive quackery and quasi-religious idealism, encouraged Nietzsche to ground the grand style in more concrete realities – realities that allow the individual to master their own instinctual and spiritual development. Nietzsche thereby sought to retain the Dionysian in his philosophical outlook, but a Dionysus that is kept in checked by Apollo. And the development of his thought is reflected in his move from music to architecture as his preferred artistic medium of the grand style.

PART TWO
Nietzsche's ambiguous architectural legacy

CHAPTER FOUR

Buildings to 'honour' Nietzsche

Can Nietzsche's philosophical concepts be translated into spatial forms and conveyed effectively in architectural design? Is a *Nietzschean architecture* elusive? The difficulty of rendering abstract ideas into three-dimensional forms is compounded when those ideas, such as Nietzsche's, are themselves riddled with ambiguity and contradiction. In the Introduction I suggested that Nietzsche's writing style encourages confusion in his readers and lends itself intentionally to a variety of competing interpretations. The relatively scant remarks he makes about buildings and architectural design adds another layer of complication. In this respect, Angelika Emmrich's remark seems most apt: 'Various statements by Nietzsche can be interpreted with regard to certain ideas of colour and shape, but a specific "Nietzsche Style" cannot come from this' (2000a:60).

Nietzsche's most explicit comments about the kind of architecture he seeks appear in *The Gay Science* in the aphorism titled 'Architecture of the knower [Architektur der Erkennenden]' (GS,280). Here he celebrates quiet and wide expansive places for reflection, with long, high-ceilinged arcades and buildings that encourage one to wander and wonder. A second passage of note is from the third treatise of *Genealogy of Morals*, where he continues to recommend quiet and concealed places where one can retreat from the distracting 'noise' of 'democratic chatter' and the 'junk' of today (GM,III.8). He alludes to the courtyards and colonnades of the temple of Artemis where Heraclitus retreated from the noise of his day before he laments the absence of such temples today. Nietzsche's complaint is quickly curbed however when he recalls the beauty of Piazza di San Marco in Venice in the springtime, between the hours of ten and noon. This brief reverie leads him to concede that temples of contemplation are perhaps '*not* lacking' after all. He goes on generously to admit, 'at times even a room in a busy, ordinary guest house where one is sure to go unrecognized and can talk with impunity to everyone' will do.

Beyond the specific buildings and architectural features suggested by Nietzsche as worthy places for his own reflections, it is not altogether clear how Nietzsche's call for an architecture of self-reflection translates into a distinctive type. Earlier I argued that it is contrary to Nietzsche's philosophy to promote an ideal type above others and to assume a one-size fits all approach to his ideas. Nietzschean architecture is in the eye of the beholder, as it were – a room in an ordinary guest house and the Piazzo di San Marco are equally worthy in Nietzsche's eyes as *temples* of self-reflection. It is unsurprising that commentators of Nietzsche suggest an array of architectural styles and examples, which, to them at least, exemplify a *Nietzschean* style. There is, as Werner Oechslin puts it, an 'Eldorado' of 'free associations' in the reception of Nietzsche when it comes to architectural images and metaphors (1996:172,263). A Nietzschean architecture has subsequently been associated with a disparate wealth of different architectural styles, including but not limited to Classical, Renaissance and Baroque styles, Brutalism and monolithic monumentalism, Cyclopean style ['Zyklopenstil'] and Internationalist style, and architecture in the styles of medieval monasticism and totalitarian regimes.[1]

Another problematic aspect to the translation of Nietzsche's ideas into spatial forms are his commentators and editors (and translators if his ideas are not read in their original German) who will inevitably interpret his ideas in accordance with their own motivations, agendas and aspirations, no matter how objective or honest they seek to be. In Chapter 5, I outline how Nietzsche's ideas became a political commodity at the turn of the twentieth century for competing groups and organizations who cited them as philosophical justification for their contrasting visions for Germany, refashioned as a powerful nation. Nietzsche's sister Elisabeth was keen to establish herself at the centre of these political dealings, not least those involving public monuments or buildings designed to propagate Nietzsche's legacy in relation to national identity, vitality and power.

In the nineteenth century it was common practice to commemorate people of historic importance with figurative statues depicting their physical likeness, usually seated, standing, or on horseback and coupled with allegorical reliefs and inscriptions to explain the memorial. Around the time of Nietzsche's death, it was becoming increasingly popular to honour a person with a statue or building with more abstract design features that referred to the ideas or events associated with their legacy. A common monument type of this time was the secular temple building on the grounds that it was thought to represent a desire for a different, more fulfilling life in accordance with the ideals of the client or person commemorated by the temple. Although secular, the temple presented itself as a place where ideals are revered, even worshipped.

Several architectural plans were made for the design and construction of buildings in commemoration of Nietzsche between 1898 and 1944 – a period that begins just before his death and is curtailed by the outbreak of the Second World War. Most were temple designs endorsed by Elisabeth Förster-Nietzsche. While Nietzsche himself valued temples as places for self-reflection, he would have rejected temples of worship or indeed any monument that idolized him. In *Ecce Homo*, he asserts: 'I *want* no "believers"; I think I am too malicious to believe in myself; I never speak to masses – I have a terrible fear that one day I will be pronounced *holy*' (EH,XIV). Through his prophetic spokesperson, Zarathustra, he longs not for disciples but listeners. To his unwanted acolytes he says: 'Take care, lest a falling a statue [or building, perhaps] strike you dead!' (Z, I, 22[3]:103).

Nietzsche's sister appears less concerned about her brother's ideas and beliefs as she was his political legacy. Following her marriage to Bernard Förster, she moved with her husband to Paraguay to establish an anti-Semitic, pure-German colony called Nueva Germania. When this failed and her husband killed himself (supposedly on account of accumulating financial debts), she returned to Germany to take care of her ailing brother in Weimar and to channel her energies into establishing the Nietzsche-Archiv. By acquiring the copyright of her brother's works, including his unpublished notebooks and papers, she set about profiting from their sales and establishing her social position in Weimar. Given her differing ideological views and indifferent education, Elisabeth was not the ideal custodian of her brother's works.[2] But she was scrupulous in her attempts to secure financial, intellectual and political support for her brother's legacy, which would help her to fund and promote his archives.

On 2 February 1894, Elisabeth opened the first Nietzsche-Archiv in a room on the ground floor of her mother's house in Naumburg, at *Weingarten* 18. But due to cramped conditions with Nietzsche needing to use the ground floor for his exercise, Elisabeth moved seven months later to larger lodgings in nearby *Grochlitzer Straße* 7. Access to the archives provided intellectual legitimacy to any writer or thinker wanting to make a name for themselves on the cultural scene (Kostka 2000:37). Interestingly for my enquiry, the first person to visit the Nietzsche-Archiv in Naumburg (on 26 October 1895) would come to plan the grandest of temple buildings to honour Nietzsche. This was Count Harry Graff Kessler (1868–1937), a striking figure in the arts, who was well travelled and financially independent.

Kessler was concerned, as so many were, with establishing a new cultural standard for Germany, grounded in his interests for art and aesthetics. To that end he founded the renowned *Cranach Press*, but his arranged visit to the Nietzsche-Archiv was on behalf of the literary journal *PAN* (1895–1900), a lavishly illustrated quarterly devoted to international avant-garde art and literature in Germany.[3] As a member of its editorial board, Kessler set up a meeting with Förster-Nietzsche to negotiate the publication of Nietzsche's musical works within the journal.

Although Kessler was wary of Förster-Nietzsche's motivations for the promotion of her brother's work, his diaries recall him leaving their meeting as an ardent supporter of the Nietzsche-Archiv, keen to contribute to its development. His first act was to finance Förster-Nietzsche's acquisition of the copyright of her brother's works from her mother on 18 December 1895, and thence to help her to relocate the archives – and later her brother – from her mother's house in Naumburg to a house in Weimar.

The decision to move the archive to Weimar was a symbolic and ideological strategy to place Nietzsche's legacy alongside Goethe and Schiller, the heavyweight German thinkers of the Weimar tradition. Weimar was imagined as an ideal place for Nietzsche's ideas to thrive and develop, with its foundation ensconced in the creative spirit of the past, and its sights set on forging a new cultural identity for Germany's future. Förster-Nietzsche was keen to carve out a legacy for Nietzsche that could rival or surpass the Wagner cult in Bayreuth, and to that end she attempted to cultivate an image of her brother as a secular saint, clothing him in white robes. And just as Wagner had his opera house as a place of pilgrimage for his ardent followers, Förster-Nietzsche was keen to establish for her brother's legacy its own Festspielhaus, a veritable temple for the ages.

Förster-Nietzsche employed the Belgium architect, Henry van de Velde to make extensive refurbishments to the archive building in Weimar, and it was at this time that she envisaged a temple building on, or close to, the grounds of the archive building, and she asked van de Velde to design it. She intended the two buildings to be separate but linked by association. Although the temple was never designed or constructed, there are several clues that suggest how it may have looked. We know, for instance, that Förster-Nietzsche was particularly impressed by a drawing of a temple to honour Nietzsche by the architect, Fritz Schumacher (1869–1947), and one designed by van de Velde to commemorate the scientist Ernst Abbe in Jena (b.1909–11). Kessler, so captivated with the idea of constructing a temple to Nietzsche, encouraged van de Velde to design a large building complex that would connect a temple – similar in design to the Abbe memorial – to a vast stadium, to be constructed on hills overlooking the Nietzsche-Archiv building. These ambitious plans would never be put into practice. As if by way of a compensatory response to their sheer scale and ambition, van de Velde would later design a small, humble memorial to Nietzsche for Helene Kröller-Müller (1869–1939), a collector of modern art, but it too would not be built. A memorial hall to honour both Nietzsche and Nazi ideology was constructed several years later next door to the Nietzsche-Archiv building. Designed by Paul Schultze-Naumburg (1869–1949) and funded with Nazi Party money, its shell remains to this day.

I will examine these designs in turn to ascertain the extent to which they sought to incorporate Nietzsche's ideas and appeal to architecture in the 'grand style'. Because their conceptual origins are linked to the refurbished Villa Silberblick, home to the Nietzsche-Archiv, my analysis begins with this building, as the first 'temple' to Nietzsche.

The Nietzsche-Archiv, Villa Silberblick, Weimar

Förster-Nietzsche moved to Weimar in August 1896, setting up the archives in a spacious rented apartment in *Wörthstraße 5* (now, *Thomas-Müntzer-Straße 5*). At this time, Nietzsche was being cared for by their mother in their family home in Naumburg. But following her death on 20 April 1897, Förster-Nietzsche was tasked with finding larger accommodation in Weimar to house herself, the archives and her brother. On 20 May 1897, Meta von Salis-Marschlins (1855–1929), a Swiss aristocrat who befriended Nietzsche in Zürich, purchased for Förster-Nietzsche a three-storey house recently built on the outskirts of the city at *Luisenstraße 30* (now, *Humboldtstraße 36*) (Figure 4.1).[4]

The building was named Villa Silberblick ('Silver View') due to its view of the Silber hill, the city, and mountains beyond. Just a ten-minute walk from the house is the cemetery that houses the tombs of Goethe and Schiller. The building is redbrick, with windows framed by white stucco. The slate mansard roof has a dormer on the entrance side and a flat gable roof on the west side. Prior to its refurbishment the entrance had a wooden roof and a wooden balcony above it. Following his first visit to the house on 7 August 1897, Kessler describes it in his diaries:

FIGURE 4.1 Silberblick Villa, Nietzsche-Archiv building (renovations 1902–3, van de Velde). Front elevation. Author's photograph.

> The house lies on a hill above the city in a newly planted but still rather bare garden. The view over the city and countryside is pretty. Inside it is spacious; parterre, archive, and reception room, in the first floor the private residence of Nietzsche and his sister, in the second my guest room, where there is no longer a featherbed but still a tub. Everything else corresponds to the cultural level, prosperous but decorated without refinement [...] In the reception room on the ground floor there is red velvet furniture and framed family photographs mixed with mementos from Paraguay, lace veils, needlework, Indian majolica. Everything is displayed above all for the interest of its content and not to evoke an aesthetic impression, like the home of a prominent university professor or civil servant.
>
> (Kessler 1880–1918/2011:186–7)

Although Kessler describes a somewhat ordinary domestic dwelling, he recounts how he felt he was stepping on 'holy ground' – and this was precisely the kind of impression Förster-Nietzsche wanted to cultivate for the place. The fact that Nietzsche died in this house, and it accommodated his final bed-ridden years goes some way to imbuing the building with the character of a memorial to the man, or as Cancik puts it, a 'numinous' aura (1987:411). Indeed, *Das Nietzsche-Archiv in Weimar* (1904) – the official guidebook to the Nietzsche-Archiv, which was published a year after its extensive renovations – begins with the idea that Nietzsche's very being permeates throughout the house. 'Anyone who has lingered in these rooms feels the closeness to the life of this great man.' 'We believe we are close to him, and hear his teachings from his mouth, here, where he died, in these rooms' (Kühn 1904:2).[5] The guidebook also portrays the house as analogous to Nietzsche himself, with both house and man 'consecrated for all time' in a 'lonely' prominent position in the 'heights' with wide and unobstructed panoramic views of the horizon (Kühn 1904:3).

According to Förster-Nietzsche, her brother liked the new house: 'from the first moment he entered the lonely house, he showed a happy satisfaction' (Cohn and Förster-Nietzsche 1931:156; Kessler 1880–1918/2011:18). Förster-Nietzsche remarked to Kessler: 'When he arrived, he looked very carefully at the decoration, wandered everywhere without having to be supported, saying always, "Palazzo, palazzo"' (Kessler 1880–1918/2011:187). 'How pleased he was with the beautiful view of Weimar and the mountains beyond, the wide horizon, the cloud formation and the sunsets!' He also enjoyed the relationship between height and light inside the building, with its high ceilings and sunny prospect (Förster-Nietzsche 1914:544). She goes on to note that Nietzsche 'had always said that his nature was set up for air and light', and she suggests the house had a surprising therapeutic effect on his well-being, enabling him to start talking again, to walk unaided, to read and comment on what he had read (Förster-Nietzsche 1914). It is as if the architecture revived his energy or granted new life – ideas that Paul Kühn develops in the official guidebook to the building, which I discuss below.

Soon after moving in, Förster-Nietzsche was keen to renovate the house, and she employed the services of Weimar architect, Rudolf Zapfe (1860–1934), to undertake some basic changes. A veranda was constructed for Nietzsche's bedroom, a bathroom was installed, and a guest room was enlarged by removing the partition wall between two smaller rooms, the kitchen floor was tiled, a new sink ordered and rooms were repainted. She sent the expensive bill directly to von Salis-Marschlins for payment, who responded with outrage at Elisabeth's 'reckless arrogance' (Peters 1977:161). Following an unpleasant exchange of letters, von Salis-Marschlins broke off contact with Förster-Nietzsche and on 1 July 1898 she sold the house to Adalbert Oehler (1860–1943), a family relation of Nietzsche. Förster-Nietzsche bought it from Oehler in April 1902, but not before she put in motion plans for more extensive renovations, with the intention of transforming the house into something 'more monumental', akin perhaps to the grand salon of the Wagners that Förster-Nietzsche had admired in Bayreuth (van de Velde 1995:154). To this end she commissioned the services of Henry van de Velde in the spring of 1902 to extend the building and renovate the entire lower floor.

Van de Velde initially worked as a painter in impressionist and neo-impressionist style but had been devoted to architecture and the decorative arts since 1893. He was a fervent advocate for a 'new style' of art and design, one that could reform and renew life through the aesthetic improvement of everyday objects and domestic settings. By the same token, he rejected the imitation of historical styles and the conservative bourgeois taste that was so widespread. He lectured and published widely on these subjects and his central idea of the significance of figurative lines as the key to successful designs. For him, the line was not intended simply as decorative ornament but as having a distinct power or, 'line-force', which imparts to a design a vital energy or evocative quality, which, in turn, enlivens those who engage it. 'Line-force' is similar in some respects to Nietzsche's idea of will to power, with the line evoking the kind of empowering rhythm that Nietzsche seeks in architecture. I examine this in the next chapter.

Van de Velde was renowned for his interior designs, which include the influential art gallery, Maison de l'Art Nouveau in Paris in 1895 for Samuel Bing in Paris – from where 'Art Nouveau' took its name – and Kessler's apartments in Berlin and Weimar, in 1897 and 1902 respectively. Kessler was instrumental in securing new clients for van de Velde in Berlin, organizing lecture venues for him, and introducing him to various salons, including that of Cornelia Richter where van de Velde first met Förster-Nietzsche in March 1901. In August of that year, he accompanied Förster-Nietzsche and Kessler to her brother's tomb in Röcken on the first anniversary of Nietzsche's death and attended the memorial service at Villa Silberblick. Kessler and Förster-Nietzsche were instrumental in advancing van de Velde's candidacy for the appointment of director of the *Weimarer Kunstschul* (Weimar Art School), which was conferred upon him on 21 December 1901. Before he began his official appointment, Förster-Nietzsche commissioned him to renovate the interior of Villa Silberblick.

It is interesting to note that van de Velde later designed lavish limited editions of Nietzsche's works, including *Thus Spoke Zarathustra* and *Ecce Homo* in 1908, and *Dionysos Dithyramben* in 1914. Each features geometric patterns suggestive of architectural motifs. The 'architectural expression' of his cover for *Thus Spoke Zarathustra*, Sebastian Schultze notes, 'engages the reader and creates a monumental entrance to Zarathustra's formidable prophecies' (2019:23). Later, I address the striking similarities between van de Velde's illustration for the frontispiece of *Dionysos Dithyramben* and his theatre design for the Werkbund Exhibition in Cologne (1914–18).

Van de Velde's refurbishment of Villa Silberblick

Van de Velde was commissioned by Förster-Nietzsche to make Villa Silberblick appear 'more monumental' and 'less banal and bourgeois' (van de Velde 1995:154–5). Kühn's account is more dramatic. According to Kühn, van de Velde subjected the entire ground floor, inside and out, to a radical modernist transformation, culminating in a Gesamtkunstwerk, infused with the spirit of Nietzsche – a 'landmark monument' and 'symbol of a new culture and way of life' (1904:10).

Van de Velde completed his final drawings for the design by July 1902 and the renovation work was completed in July 1903. The most noticeable change to the exterior is the addition of the large two-storey porch that gives greater significance to the street-facing façade. The façade exemplifies van de Velde's idea of 'line-force' with its interplay of curves and right-angles, and above the entrance, 'NIETZSCHE-ARCHIV' is inscribed in a horizontal rectangular strip of red sandstone that cuts across the façade to delineate the two storeys of the porch. This is flanked by two thinner vertical strips of red sandstone that rise upwards to flank two large square windows on the upper storey. These red strips are framed by white plastered surfaces. The right-angled geometric arrangement is interrupted on the lower storey with a curved archway of brown wood that emphasizes the main entrance. The large oak door establishes the top of the arch, and the line of the curve continues by intersecting the frames of two side-windows. The effect of this is a large archway that extends either side of the doorway, which is reminiscent of a sun with the muntin bars in nearby windows appearing like sun beams. The vertical strips with their vertical grooves and warm red colour support this analogy, drawing the eye upwards. The windows on the façade are a mixture of square and arched, which contributes to the overall geometric interplay of curved and right-angled lines. The door itself is heavy oak with curly brass handles. Through the door, the visitor is met with an entrance hall with wooden cladding that continues the geometric play of right-angled forms, and a double-glazed door with a bronze handle. The door features three arches, reminiscent of the arch of the façade. Above the door is a glazed window with a geometric pattern that suggests an image of a lantern. Through the door are a wooden-clad cloakroom and a wide staircase with a stencilled frieze of a patterned line which unites the two areas and continues to the upper floor. The private rooms on the upper floors were untouched by van de Velde.[6]

The ground floor rooms were enlarged by removing the room partitions and replacing them with beams. This enhanced the activities of the Archiv, providing generous space for the library and lecture room (for sixty to seventy-five seated people), an archival room to consult Nietzsche's manuscripts and a dining room. The library room was the focal point. Here the geometric play of lines from the exterior is mirrored by vertical wooden strips that divide the four walls and bend to follow the curvature of the cavetto moulding before stopping at the ceiling area (see Figure 4.5). This makes the room appear taller than it is, and the grooves in the moulding establish a rhythmic play with the contrast of light and shadow (see Emmrich 2000b:74). The integrated bookshelves and cupboards produce right-angled lines that contrast with the sweeping curves of the furniture, and the warm colour schemes – of natural wood, brass fittings, red fabrics, and perfectly white ceiling – reflect the colours of the exterior. The dynamic quality of its lines and colourings were lauded in a review of the renovations by Finnish architect, Sigurd Frosterus (1876–1956). Van de Velde was impressed with the review and cites it in his memoirs: 'There is a force, a suppleness and an excessive elasticity in the severe lines of the furniture, an admirable balance and harmony in the ornaments.' Van de Velde and Frosterus concur that the renovations are 'reminiscent of the reflections of the setting sun' (van de Velde 1995:155).

Van de Velde was known for mirroring exterior design features in the interior, and vice-versa to cultivate an organic unity to his buildings. Some have suggested features of the main room of Villa Silberblick have been incorporated by van de Velde into exteriors of his other buildings, such as Sembach (1989), who identifies its features in the exterior of van de Velde's theatre in Weimar that he designed in 1904, and Kostka (2000) who identifies other aspects of the room with the exterior of the Ernst-Abbe Denkmal, the Abbe memorial building, built in 1909–11.[7] As we shall see, van de Velde's method of incorporating interior features of one building into the exterior of another would come to frustrate Kessler in their collaborative plans for a larger Nietzsche monument.

The main room of Villa Silberblick made explicit reference to Nietzsche through various artefacts and portraits that were displayed, and with the prominent letter 'N' that appears as a brass motif above the fireplace, and which quickly became the corporate logo for the Nietzsche-Archiv, appearing in its publicity materials. A herm of Nietzsche, designed by

German artist Max Klinger (1857–1920), was proudly placed in the west end of the room, raised on a wooden step, and set before a tinted matt glass window.[8] Kessler regarded Klinger as 'one of the greatest living geniuses' (1880–1918/2011:124), and it was Kessler who in 1902 funded and commissioned Klinger's herm made from a single block of Seravezza marble (see Figure 4.5). Van de Velde was not a fan of the herm. Measuring 2.38 metres in height, he felt it dominated the interior. But his dislike could also be construed as a conviction on his part that Nietzsche's ideas are best evoked or represented in abstract forms – such as his line-force – rather than in effigies of Nietzsche's physical likeness.

The inauguration and opening of Villa Silberblick as the newly renovated Nietzsche-Archiv building took place on 15 October 1903 on the anniversary of Nietzsche's birthday. The total cost of the work was just over 50,000 marks, more than the cost of the house itself (40,000 marks). The result is regarded by many as a place of pilgrimage not only for admirers of Nietzsche but also aficionados of van de Velde and modern art more generally. Sigurd Frosterus, whose review so impressed van de Velde, claimed it to be 'without a doubt, the most beautiful thing van de Velde has created, the most unified, the purest, the most substantial work that modern art has so far produced' (van de Velde 1995:155).

The house is described by many as a 'temple to Nietzsche', including Kessler, the sculptor Karl Donndorf (1870–1941), and the artist, Edvard Munch (1863–1944) who refers to Elisabeth Förster-Nietzsche as the 'Priestess of the Temple' (cited in Emmrich 2000a:61). Fritz Schumacher similarly describes the house as a 'realm of a lord of the spirit' (1935/1949:250). Carl Albrecht Bernoulli (1868–1937), a student of Nietzsche's friend Franz Overbeck and a critic of Förster-Nietzsche's use of the Archiv, highlights the curious contradiction of the house as both temple and family home. This point is echoed by later scholars, such as Angelika Emmrich, who makes the point that Förster-Nietzsche's desire to give the main room a more 'homely' atmosphere – by surrounding Klinger's herm and other sculptures with flower pots and bouquets, and filling it with draped tablecloths and cushions – compromised the overall intended aesthetic, ensuring that van de Velde's 'new style' and the idea of the '"new man" – didn't quite work' here (2000a:61).

Nietzschean architecture in the grand style?

Despite the conceptual difficulties of visualizing a 'Nietzschean architecture', several people have suggested that van de Velde's remodelling of Villa Silberblick exemplifies it precisely, and perhaps none more forcibly than Paul Kühn (1904), author of the official guide to its redesign: *Das Nietzsche-Archiv in Weimar* (*The Nietzsche Archive in Weimar*) (Figure 4.2).

FIGURE 4.2 Front cover of original guidebook, *Nietzsche Archiv: Das Nietzsche-Archiv in Weimar* (Paul Kühn, 1904). Author's photograph.

The guidebook's cover depicts a stylized image of the new entrance to the building, and within its pages Kühn sets about explaining correspondences between van de Velde's design and Nietzsche's philosophy. Unsurprisingly, his discussion is wedded to Förster-Nietzsche's own mythological aspirations for her brother. Kühn portrays van de Velde as nothing short of an embodiment of Nietzsche's vision of the creative 'new man' – one who shares in Nietzsche's ideals and has successfully transferred these ideals into the fabric of Villa Silberblick, thereby transforming the building into a veritable Nietzschean architecture. Van de Velde, he says, is a creator of life, a prophet, a spiritual leader and the most modern of all people. As such, he is a 'cultural agitator of the grand style' (1904:34) and is 'ranked' alongside 'the artists who created the Greek temples, the Gothic domes, the Pantheon in Rome' (1904:15) – a position that grants Villa Silberblick an elevated status and places it in formidable architectural company. Kühn's descriptions are dramatic and exaggerated, but some of the basic ideas he draws on are particularly useful to our investigation.

Much of Kühn's discussion tries to explain the powerful effects of van de Velde's abstract design on the visitor, with particular emphasis given to his use of lines, light and shadow, and their capacity to both arouse and organize a person's emotions and instincts into a heightened experience of the kind Nietzsche associates with self-aware and enlightened people. In Kühn's analysis of the merits of Villa Silberblick, we find several key features of the grand style as I have presented it. For instance, he tells us that van de Velde's design does not distract the visitor with superficial ornamentation but expresses only what is 'necessary' to 'give strength and life' to the visitor and to establish for and within them a 'life-awakening function' (1904:23).

Kühn supports van de Velde's rejection of historical styling and subsequently seeks to align van de Velde's ideals of a future artistic age with Nietzsche's (1904:37). To this end, Kühn, on the one hand, is scathing in his assessment of the German Renaissance – which sought to replicate the ornamentation of Italian art and architecture – and on the other, he lauds van de Velde's desire to incorporate only *necessary* design features. His criticism of the replication of ornament is Nietzschean in tone. It is, he says, a 'disgusting masquerade', it lacks 'intellectual conscience' and is a product of 'vain illusion' and a 'depraved imagination'. Historicist architecture subsequently has an 'immoral effect', as it impedes the contemplation of 'honesty and unity'. The 'parasitic parts' of a new building designed in historical styles 'disturb' its overall 'clarity and logic', thereby establishing an unhealthy distance between it and us (1904:34).

Kühn parades van de Velde's work as the much-needed Nietzschean antidote to cultural malaise. Villa Silberblick will enrich life through the unity of its work as a Gesamtkunstwerk that will integrate and elevate the spirit, not only of those who visit the building but of modern culture generally through its adoption of van de Velde's 'new style'. In Kühn's description we find that this 'new style' speaks to Nietzsche's notion of the grand style, and it does so principally through the rhythmic energy of van de Velde's 'line-force', which incites in the onlooker a meaningful, uplifting bodily experience. This is achieved, Kühn argues, through van de Velde's masterful use of the line and in his respect for the organic features of the materials he uses. While the playful lines evoke a 'force', the quality of the materials – whether it be the villa's use of stone, iron, wood, brass or plaster – creates, Kühn says, a 'certain movement' that is specific to the material's nature (1904:28,30). Together they establish an evocative rhythm and mood that enlightens and invigorates.

Van de Velde's choice of materials and the lines he creates with them are never arbitrary, but at every moment 'necessary', and as such, they convey, Kühn says, a 'richer, more vivid and deeper effect', which enables a mimetic identification between the material design and the instincts of the onlooker. Of van de Velde's use of line he writes:

> By crossing or touching straight or crooked lines, the network of these lines is more varied, the ascending movement of the vertical line is

increased by the force of the movement by increasing the number of lines and their height. Other times, the horizontal lines are also increased. This increase and variation are not arbitrary and unlimited, but a logical development of the first curve that is introduced.

(1904:28–9)

The linear movement or force is further encouraged by the organic features and qualities of the materials that he employs, as if the materials directed him into fashioning a design to emphasize their nature. As Kühn puts it, 'creative thoughts grow out of the material itself' (1904:31). Van de Velde subsequently 'awakens' his materials, to ensure 'the spirit of heaviness leaves them' and their joyful nature is revealed (1904:30,31). Although not explicitly mentioned by Kühn, these ideas are strongly reminiscent of Zarathustra's desire to overcome the spirit of gravity and to awaken the human spirit from its slumber in stone. Every material has, Kühn says, a different 'movement value', so that 'a stone tower with a protruding shape', for instance, evokes a 'more emphatic movement for us than a lighter object of the same shape' (1904:30). Van de Velde is sensitive, he asserts, to the nature of the materials he uses so that he can facilitate their natural beauty. Once you 'discover that the beauty of the wood is in its veining, and the delicacy of its inlay', you will no longer think 'to cover large, smooth surfaces with ornaments' (1904:30) – something that Förster-Nietzsche had yet to discover, given her penchant for covering the surfaces of the main room with her flowerpots and tablecloths!

When awakened material is fashioned into forceful lines, the design becomes 'armed' with a powerful unity and rhythm that 'imparts strength and life' (1904:23). The rhythm is musical, creating an 'absolute impression of unity' akin to a 'symphony' (1904:26). As such, van de Velde appeals through these harmonious impressions, Kühn notes, to the experience of 'joy' which Nietzsche describes as arising 'at the sight of anything regular and symmetrical in lines, points, and rhythms' (OM,119). This joyful impression of harmony has a corresponding physiological effect on the visitor to the house, encouraging the integration and unity of their self-awareness. Paralleling Nietzsche's definition of art as a 'frenzy of an overarched and swollen will' leading to feelings of 'increased strength and fullness' (TI, IX,8–9:93), Kühn describes how van de Velde's architecture incites a 'latent force' which 'swells the limbs from the inside' and causes the visitor to the house to 'feel a play of forces flowing through and directed by a central will' (1904:26).

Kühn would have us believe that van de Velde's redesign of Villa Silberblick exemplifies Nietzsche's grand style, as one 'born in the spirit of Nietzsche's Zarathustra', and the 'visionary beauty of Zarathustra' (1904:35). When we enter its rooms, we are 'animated by Zarathustra's dance rhythms' (1904:14), and we relive its powerful harmonizing rhythms as an emotional and physiological experiences (1904:20–1). Zarathustra associates 'the highest things' with the power of dance, and in Villa Silberblick our soul and body are 'moved rhythmically' and 'our attitude to life is transformed, heightened, strengthened and refined' as a result (1904:21). Aschheim aptly notes that van de Velde establishes at Villa Silberblick a 'Nietzschean aesthetic in architectural terms' by conveying 'higher redeeming values' and 'regenerating powers of art and the spirit' (1994:48).

Kühn's dramatic interpretation of van de Velde's redesign of Villa Silberblick as Nietzschean philosophy translated spatially into architecture was dismissed by van de Velde for its hyperbolic gesturing (Emmrich 2000a:58). Nevertheless, van de Velde concedes that his design was inspired by Nietzsche's ideas:

> During the weeks of working on my drawings for the renovations, I could touch with my fingers the work of Nietzsche [...] I had absorbed his spirit from reading the first aphorism, the first paragraph of *Thus Spoke Zarathustra*. I had the original manuscripts, the notebooks full of annotations made by Nietzsche [on his walks] in the mountains; I could turn the pages of the books he had read and the notes he had written in the margin.
> (van de Velde 1995:155)

I believe, however, that it wasn't until he started to plan the Nietzsche memorial with Kessler that he starts to grapple more seriously with the notion of a 'Nietzschean architecture' and what this might involve. I will revisit this point later. His design for Villa Silberblick is, I think, more influenced by the reverence Nietzsche had inspired in van de Velde than Nietzsche's ideas per se. His deep respect for Nietzsche is apparent throughout his memoires. He surmised, 'had fate not struck Nietzsche too early, he would have found in my generation the students that his impatient genius longed for' (van de Velde 1995:359); Nietzsche was 'one of the most eminent and undoubtedly the most courageous of thinkers' (van de Velde 1995:66). Van de Velde recounts the occasion he confessed to Förster-Nietzsche the 'veneration' he felt for her brother, which made him very emotional when he arrived at Weimar station in August 1901, en route to accompanying Förster-Nietzsche and Kessler to Nietzsche's grave in Röcken (van de Velde 1995:61,66). He recalls how, when stood before Nietzsche's grave, he felt profound 'disappointment at not being able to bow to a sufficiently imposing monument' to honour Nietzsche properly (van de Velde 1995:66). Months later, he appears to attempt to rectify the situation in part through his designs for Villa Silberblick, to impart to it a 'solemn and monumental appearance', akin, he says, to 'a "*Schatzkammer*" [a "treasure chamber"]' (van de Velde 1995:155,n.1).

A 'modest Nietzsche temple' memorial building

After the Villa's refurbishment, Förster-Nietzsche invited van de Velde on 29 December 1910 to join a committee she was establishing to discuss ideas and raise funds for the construction of a memorial to her brother to be completed in time for the seventieth anniversary of his birthday in 1914. Van de Velde enthusiastically accepted on 31 December, and she wrote to him on 9 January 1911 to outline her vision for the memorial and to invite him to design something appropriate. Förster-Nietzsche envisioned a modest 'temple' on land she intended to purchase just below the Villa. The new temple-building would house the archives, freeing the Villa for her own domestic arrangements.

She asks van de Velde to refrain from designing something 'huge', since 'there is no money for it under any circumstances'. The monument could be 'something like a temple, but shouldn't be too expensive, since the money that's collected has to pay also for beautiful furnishings'. She is less concerned about the 'size' of the building and more with its 'grace'. Nevertheless, it must be sufficient to accommodate various rooms and functional spaces, including 'a large hall in the middle with works of art', the 'entire library of Nietzsche', a 'steel chamber with compartments' of the kind found in 'banks' to house manuscripts, 'an archive room for the archivist', a 'spacious cloakroom', 'a beautiful, solemn entrance', and a 'small apartment' in the basement for the 'Catellan' and the 'central heating system'. 'That is all', she says, 'nothing more is needed' (cited in Neuman 2015:93).

Förster-Nietzsche remarks that Villa Silberblick, the 'house where my brother died', 'must remain as it is now', but 'everything that belongs to the Nietzsche archive – that is: manuscripts, library, works of art, etc.' must be removed from the house. My wish, she says is to 'separate the place of death from the archive' (cited in Neumann 2015:557). Kostka suggests that Förster-Nietzsche probably intended the Villa as the 'house of death' [*Sterbehaus*] to become a 'philosopher's museum', sat next to the archives or 'Treasure House' of Nietzsche's work (2000:41). Kostka alludes to a rumour that the Villa was intended as a mausoleum to accommodate Nietzsche's body following its transfer from Röcken to Weimar but maintains there is no evidence to corroborate this. We do know, however, from Kessler's diary that in early August 1897, Förster-Nietzsche's sought to have her brother's remains buried in the garden of the Villa (Kessler 1880–1918/2011:187), and in 1900 her official request for a special permit to bury her brother there was apparently rejected (Cancik 1987:414). Stamm mentions that an elaborate cortège was planned to move Nietzsche's body to Weimar (1973–5). We know that in September 1913, Förster-Nietzsche agreed to offer support for the Nietzsche-stadium project on the formal condition that her brother's ashes be interred into the Villa's garden. I return to this point later.

The idea of memorializing Nietzsche the man and Nietzsche's works in separate buildings has important precedent in the arrangement of Goethe's house on Freuenplan (less than a mile from Villa Silberblick) and the Goethe-Schiller Archiv, inaugurated in 1896, when Elisabeth Förster-Nietzsche had begun to establish the Nietzsche-Archiv. Förster-Nietzsche may have wanted to replicate this arrangement in her quest to elevate Nietzsche's status to the level of Goethe's.

In a letter now lost, written on 2 February 1911, Förster-Nietzsche outlines to Kessler her intentions for the temple-building and asks him to join the memorial committee to oversee its design and construction. We know from a letter sent by Kessler to van de Velde on the same day that Kessler accepted the invitation but on certain conditions. Most notably, he insisted the designs be enhanced and developed into a more 'worthy' temple-building – suggestions he makes also to van de Velde. Kessler would soon take over the project and the designs for the building would become increasingly complex and grandiose. I will examine the evolution of these plans shortly, but I want first to consider how Förster-Nietzsche's 'modest' temple-building might have looked before Kessler intervened.

On 7 February 1911, Kessler asks van de Velde to bring his designs for the monument – 'if you have any' – to Förster-Nietzsche's house the following day for the three of them to discuss over lunch (KV,308:560). In his diary entry from the following day, Kessler alludes to two different architectural designs drawn up by van de Velde in response to Förster-Nietzsche's invitation. The first involved a 'remodelling of the archive' to add a 'great reception hall' to Villa Silberblick and thereby establish it as a new 'memorial'. The second was a 'memorial in the open air', separate to the Villa (Kessler 1880–1918/2011:505). Kessler notes that while van de Velde preferred the first plan, both he and Förster-Nietzsche preferred the second, and the second was subsequently adopted. Had Kessler not been party to the plans at this stage, van de Velde may have convinced Förster-Nietzsche to adopt the first design.

Unfortunately, the drawings for the two designs no longer survive, and it is not clear how the temple-building in either case would have looked. We may infer some basic characteristics of what van de Velde had in mind from his proposals for a later temple memorial for Nietzsche, whilst bearing in mind these were heavily influenced by Kessler, who managed the project. If I imagine what Förster-Nietzsche herself had in mind for a modest temple-building, there are two buildings – one real, one imagined – that may well have shaped her thoughts and expectations. The first is a drawing from 1898 of building to honour Nietzsche by German architect Fritz Schumacher (Figure 4.3). Schumacher mentions that Förster-Nietzsche and Nietzsche's intimate friends valued his design, so much so that Förster-Nietzsche invited him to visit her with a view to carrying it out (1935/1949:250). The second is the Ernst Abbe Memorial building in Jena, designed by van de Velde in 1908 and completed in 1911, just months after Förster-Nietzsche invited

FIGURE 4.3 Nietzsche-Denkmal. Temple des Lesben/'Temple of Life'. Charcoal sketch (Fritz Schumacher, 1898).

him to design her Nietzsche Memorial (Figure 4.4). Förster-Nietzsche was certainly familiar with this building. Furthermore, elements of its design appear as if replicated in van de Velde's drawings for his later temple to Nietzsche. To my mind at least, this building, or one like it, is probably the closest fit we have for the 'modest' temple building he proposed to Förster-Nietzsche. I shall consider these two buildings in turn before examining van de Velde's temple designs for Kessler's more ambitious proposal.

Temple to Nietzsche, Fritz Schumacher (1898)

Schumacher attended Nietzsche's funeral ceremony at Villa Silberblick the day before his burial at Röcken, and he wasn't impressed with the occasion, finding it insufficiently profound for Nietzsche's intellectual

FIGURE 4.4 Ernst Abbe-Denkmal, Jena (b.1908–11, Henry van de Velde). Exterior view from the South. Author's photograph.

stature. 'Seldom have I experienced a grimmer moment', he reports, 'Scholarship pursued this man to the grave. If he had revived, he would have thrown the speaker out of the window and chased us out of the temple' (1935/1949:252). When Schumacher alludes to Nietzsche's final home as a '*Tempel*', he may have had his own drawing of a Nietzsche temple in mind. Drawn two years earlier, Schumacher intended his sketch, titled, *Nietzsche-Denkmal. Tempel des Lesbens* ('Nietzsche Monument. Temple of Life') to convey the profundity of Nietzsche's teaching. The drawing was part of an exhibition of 40–50 charcoal drawings that toured various German cities in 1900 to rave reviews. Schumacher published it alongside nineteen other sketches in a folio of ideal designs for monuments, and sacred and secular buildings.

Schumacher describes the building as a 'quiet round temple in a lonely plateau; above, a genius of humanity longs to stretch its arms, below, dark giants stretch in their fetters' (1935/1949:250). He notes there were errors in the printing of his drawing, which led to stronger tonal contrasts than he intended (1935/1949:249). This may have inadvertently made its image appear more striking, as it probably did to Paul Kühn, who praised Schumacher's design for its 'simple lines' which produced the 'strongest effects' (1899:227). According to Kühn, Schumacher's temple expresses the rich soul life of Nietzsche's personality and provides artistic clarification of his 'spirit' (1899:223).

Arthur Seidl, an editor in the Nietzsche-Archiv from 1898 to 1899, was involved in a fundraising campaign to supplement the Archiv with a 'Nietzsche Museum' or 'artistic place of worship' for Nietzschean ideas, and it was in this context that he endorsed Schumacher's design, regarding it as 'ingenious' (1901:398–9). Seidl presents an evocative account of the design, with an imagined guided walk through its architecture. His description suggests the kind of experience that Förster-Nietzsche and others intended for her Nietzsche temple.

> Above all, we find a high-lying massive, open hall stone building, with pillars that aren't too high, upon which rests a strong, but flat dome crown; on both sides of this dome, above and outside, an eagle rests, ready to fly, and in front, exactly on the main front (probably not in the traditional symmetrical manner nicely in the middle, for example on the highest dome) stands upright [...] an eloquent human figure, who expresses the spirit of the whole, who [...] with raised hands appears to want to 'take away the abundance of the sun', or depending on the weather, is 'waiting for the first flash' [of lightning]
>
> (1901:397–8)

The staircase, he notes, has a 'peculiar artistic effect' – it is 'very dignified' and 'reverent', and evokes the 'sacred'. At the bottom of the staircase, we are 'greeted' by 'slave people' who are 'bound by morals'. As we climb the stairs, 'our gaze passes a 'mysterious sphinx in front of the pillared hall' before we have full view of the 'high man', depicted as if 'solemn' and 'lonely' but taking 'delight' in the horizon before him, with a view of 'the whole, wide surroundings' (1901). According to Colin Trodd the figure at the summit of the temple is the 'ecstatic Zarathustra, a heliotropic hero emerging from a sea of darkness', and the temple itself seeks to evoke 'solitude, inner reality, and revelation' (2018:27).

The temple Seidl describes is a building designed to encourage self-reflection or a spiritual awakening through its dramatic introspective walk into the heights. Krause (1984) similarly suggests that the sculptural figures of this building – the 'combative' emblems of Zarathustra's eagle and the rising sun – were intended to inspire and educate its prospective visitors. When viewed 'out of context', the monument, he says, 'gives the impression of a cramped melodrama', but when considered as a monument to Nietzsche, the images help us to differentiate this building from any Christian cult building, and the recognizable images, such as the Sphinx and the praying youth, he says, would make it easier for the public to enter Nietzsche's world of ideas and to engage in a personal educational and spiritual experience. This personal experience is depicted in Schumacher's sketch, Krause suggests, by the singular 'priest-like' disciple of Nietzsche taking the walk up the 'holy' staircase on his own (Krause 1984:166,170). This walk, Aschheim notes, is an 'ascent from *Sklavenmenschen* to *Höhermenschen*', a walk past the figure of the slave to the master (1994:48).

Schumacher describes how, during his visit to Villa Silberblick, he initially refrained from meeting Nietzsche personally for fear that Nietzsche's enfeebled condition would taint his impression of Nietzsche's ideas, and perhaps, also his powerful temple design. But this changed when Nietzsche himself – when prompted by a servant – indicated that he would like to meet Schumacher. Schumacher recounts how he was struck by the sense of calm serenity that pervaded Nietzsche. Seidl praised Schumacher's design for 'completely refraining from' depicting 'Nietzsche's physical appearance' (1901:398), but Schumacher nevertheless captures in his design, his romanticized view of Nietzsche's persona – a view which did not diminish after he met the ailing philosopher, propped up in his bed. The watchful figure depicted in his sketch echoes Schumacher's account of Nietzsche, whose 'watchful eyes' look 'deeper into the abysses of the human heart and higher to the icy peaks of his longings than those of another living person' (Schumacher 1935/1949:250).

Ernst Abbe Memorial, Jena, Van de Velde (1908–11)

Ernst Abbe (1840–1905) was a German physicist, industrialist and social reformer, who worked at the University of Jena and helped to establish the corporation *Zeiss*, which continues to manufacture optical systems to this day. Van de Velde's memorial to him is in Carl-Zeiss Platz, named after Carl Zeiss, Abbe's colleague, and original founder of *Zeiss*. The building's lack of distinctive historical style would have found favour with Nietzsche. Van de Velde's notes, 'no form is borrowed from antiquity. If we destroyed this building, each piece of debris would carry the signature of our own time' (1995:303). Art historian, Thomas Föhl, remarks that its design is a 'construction of van de Velde's creative will', which in turn 'illustrates the culture of his time'. He continues, the building 'has no real role model and defies the familiar criteria of architectural description', as such it exemplifies van de Velde's ambitions as a 'social reformer' and architect of a 'new style' (1996:66). Although Föhl is not writing with Nietzsche in mind, his descriptions of the Abbe Memorial portray a building that expresses through its design the will to power of its architect and are suggestive of an architecture in the grand style. In similar vein, Alexandre Kostka recognizes in the building van de Velde's ability to encourage a personal encounter with the ideas and spirit of a 'great individual', and this, she maintains, paves the way for similar success in his designs for a Nietzsche monument (2000:42,43,46). Förster-Nietzsche invited van de Velde to design her Nietzsche temple a few months prior to his completion of the Abbe memorial. It is probable that she had this building – or something very similar – in mind. Aside from the closeness of their dates, this notion is suggested by similarities between the Abbe memorial and van de Velde's later designs for a Nietzsche monument in Weimar for the project managed by Kessler. For instance, their similar exterior façades (Compare Figures 4.4 and 4.9) and elements of their interior ornamentation, including a herm designed by Max Klinger of the man honoured by the monument, and large bas-reliefs placed on the walls depicting themes pertaining to the man's ideological legacy. Van de Velde was instructed in the initial planning for both buildings to design a suitable architecture to integrate specific sculptures – four large bas-reliefs by Constantin Émile Meunier for the Abbe memorial, and a figurative sculpture by Aristide Maillol (1861–1944) and large bas-reliefs by Klinger for the Nietzsche memorial. Both buildings were intended as a Gesamtkunstwerk, integrating architecture and sculpture into a cohesive unity.

Certain restrictions were placed on the installation of Meunier's four reliefs known as *Monument au travail* (1890–1902), which subsequently influenced van de Velde's design for the building. A contract (1903) between Meunier and the Belgian state stipulated that only the city of Brussels was permitted to erect a full-size version of the ensemble, and that only smaller reproductions could be installed elsewhere (van de Velde 1995:299,n.3). Van de Velde consequently used bronze casts of the four reliefs at half their monumental size, and he was also persuaded by Meunier's intention to display the original reliefs on a convex wall in a specific sequence. This arrangement may have led to the octagonal shape of the building (Levine 1996:58–9,n.54; van de Velde 1995:297).

The building takes the shape of a Greek cross, which is intersected by four portals, each treated equally to establish an octagonal shape similar on all sides. The interior walls curve inward to enable the bas-reliefs to be presented as they were intended, and this gives the interior its almost circular shape. The portals hold four large copper-coloured doors. When open they treat the visitor to a different view of Klinger's herm and to the integration of sculpture and architecture. When closed, the concrete dome acts as a skylight, brightening the interior and animating the herm and bas-reliefs with playful shadows. When sufficiently bright, the light shines down on the herm, as if imbuing it with mystical or divine qualities.

The exterior conveys a solid mass of stone regulated by three-quarter pillars that flank each portal and protrude to clearly distinguish between the vertical walls and the simple low-rising crowning cap. The pillars contrast strikingly with the wall surfaces, each of which has four recessed lancet shapes, giving the impression of a rib cage. This is most noticeable when the exterior is lit at night. The lancets point upwards and give the building the impression that it is pushing itself upwards. According to Kostka, elements of the exterior design – specifically the lancet shapes – are reminiscent of features of the main room of Villa Silberblick, but 'turned inside out' (2000:44). He is probably alluding here to the vertical wooden strips that run along the four walls of the Villa's room, which bend to follow the curvature of the cavetto moulding – like the lancet shapes of the Abbe Memorial which point upwards and meet the curvature of the wall at their base where the wall bellows outwards. We might also add that the cavetto moulding of the room is suggestive of the grooved shallow roof of the Abbe Memorial. In his analysis, Kostka suggests there is a traceable trajectory in van de Velde's designs, from the Abbe Memorial to the interior of Villa Silberblick, and to the later Nietzsche temple.

Arguably, the Abbe Memorial embodies elements of Nietzsche's grand style. It is reminiscent of the Palazzo Pitti with its emphasis on solidity and physiological immediacy, and in its rhythmic play of repetitive features. It is reminiscent also of the Mole Antonelliana with its desire to push upwards to overcome the weight of its mass. Botho Graef (1857–1917), an art historian from Jena, writing a year after the memorial's inauguration, describes the powerful tensions of the curvature of its interior, which shape not only the room but also our 'mental life' in correspondence with 'the laws of its own rhythm' (1912:220). According to Graef, the building speaks to its visitors, encouraging them to participate in the festive play of its design. The building

FIGURE 4.5 Nietzsche-Archiv main room, with Nietzsche herm (1905, Max Klinger) and detail of vertical wooden strips and cavetto moulding by van de Velde. Author's photograph.

also speaks, as Föhl suggests, of the creative will of its architect, who utilizes its building materials to express his will to power. Echoing remarks made by Kühn in relation to van de Velde's design for Villa Silberblick, Graef asserts, 'Everyone knows how inventive van de Velde becomes when he awakens the artistic form of the material, bringing it to life' (1912:220). But for Graef, it is with the exterior of the Abbe Memorial where van de Velde's 'creative urge' is most viscerally felt, especially with the imposing cornices over the doors – the 'most striking feature of the building' – where the creative urge 'has increased almost to the point of fighting' (1912). Unlike the interior design, which was largely directed by the artworks exhibited inside, the exterior provided van de Velde greater opportunities to express himself.

The interior is relatively restrained to heighten the contemplative experiences of the sculptural artworks. Meunier's reliefs alternate with four doors which are each framed by block-like pillars and entablatures of untreated exposed concrete. The skylight is captured by octagonal ribbing that corresponds with the structure of the exterior, and the marquetry floor which presents itself as a pattern of concentric spiral circles. Van de Velde believed the effect of the interior was heavily compromised by the size and design of Klinger's herm at the centre of the room. Klinger's herm is more exaggerated in style compared to his Nietzsche herm, and while van de Velde was critical of the large proportions of the latter, he was viscerally upset with the size and ornamentation of the Abbe herm: 'I wish other decorative elements had not been introduced to my "sacrarium". If the effigy of Abbe were absolutely essential, I would have liked Max Klinger to have given up his decoration of the stele' (cited in Grohé 1996b:32,n.43). Van de Velde was upset by its 'overwhelming' size, and the 'soft, somewhat fake grace of the bas-reliefs' on the three sides of the herm, which 'does not match the rhythm of powerful virility' of Meunier's reliefs and failed to match the 'rhythm of the whole' edifice (van de Velde 1995:302).

The Abbe Memorial was completed in the spring of 1911 and inaugurated on 30 July of the same year with a procession and festive activities in the nearby Volkshaus. Van de Velde invited Kessler to attend a special preview of the building the evening before its official inauguration (29 July 1911; KV,327:585). Kessler attended and congratulated van de Velde on the monument in a letter sent the following day: 'it is an absolute success; I am very, very happy' (31 July 1911; KV,328:585). His praise for van de Velde's memorial is somewhat overshadowed by Kessler's other reasons for writing. For his praise for the Abbe monument feeds into instructions he wishes to convey for his plans for the Nietzsche Memorial. The Nietzsche monument, he insinuates, will be even more impressive. 'I hope', Kessler writes, 'that the Nietzsche monument will allow you to draw upon the consequences' of the Abbe building 'in large'. Furthermore, Kessler hopes van de Velde can develop a memorial to Nietzsche that is distinctly more 'joyful' and 'serene' and less 'sad' and 'grave' than the Abbe Memorial was allowed to be (KV,328:585).

Van de Velde's plans for a Nietzsche temple were never realized, largely because Kessler's desire for ever larger and costly designs departed considerably from the more manageable vision expressed by Förster-Nietzsche for a 'modest' temple. Kessler would come to envision a large architectural complex that would serve as an international centre for something akin to a Nietzsche cult, paralleling in reputation, Richard Wagner's Festspielhaus in Bayreuth. As Föhl notes, if we were to compare the Abbe memorial with the plans for the Nietzsche memorial, the Abbe memorial 'appears as a purified preliminary stage' of what soon became a 'megalomaniac' project (2000:68). To this project I now turn.

Nietzsche temple complex, Weimar: Kessler and van de Velde (1911–13)

The planning for this temple exposes some of the ideological tensions among those keen to promote Nietzsche's legacy following his death. The alliance between Kessler, van de Velde and Förster-Nietzsche was uneasy from the start, and any latent tensions that were initially felt between them came to the fore during their efforts to realize a memorial to Nietzsche. While the cosmopolitan Count and the Belgian architect were aiming for a modernist reform of art and life in the spirit of Nietzsche, Förster-Nietzsche as Director of the Nietzsche-Archiv was fabricating her own Nietzsche-mythology around her brother as a secular saint. Kessler is scathing in his criticism of Förster-Nietzsche in his diaries: 'Basically, she is a little philistine, pastor's daughter, who swears to be sure upon the words of her brother but is upset and angry as soon as you try to transform them into deeds. She justifies much of what her brother said about women' (Diary 20 April 1911; Kessler 1880–1918/2011:526). Van de Velde is more muted in his complaint: 'It seems quite impossible to march against her' (27 October 1911; KV,350:606). Although Kessler had a long, close relationship with van de Velde, it was heavily tested during the turbulent planning of the Nietzsche temple. As Kostka puts it, Kessler's unrealistic expectations of van de Velde 'masked and suffocated' the architect's 'own creative power' (2000:44).

A more worthy temple: A small temenos (February 1911)

Prior to Kessler's visit to Weimar to discuss with Förster-Nietzsche and van de Velde the two design proposals for the modest temple, Kessler wrote to them both to express his desire for a more 'worthy' temple building. Earlier I noted that Kessler initially approved of van de Velde's plan for 'a memorial in the open air' separate to Villa Silberblick, and this plan was subsequently adopted by the three of them. But Kessler would quickly press for a more elaborate design, and he would, for the time being, get his wish. Plans for the temple developed rapidly with van de Velde struggling to match Kessler's evolving vision for it.

Kessler initially imagined the temple as a Greek *temenos*. In letters from February 1911 to van de Velde and to his Austrian friend and essayist, Hugo von Hofmannsthal (1874–1929), Kessler describes his desire for a 'marriage between' the greenery of a small 'sacred wood' and van de Velde's 'little temple at the centre' with its 'terraces, its stairs, its statues'. There would be a wall that encloses the wood and architectural features to demarcate the area 'dedicated to the hero'. He envisaged a Gesamtkunstwerk combining architecture, sculpture and nature: a 'renewal of the ancient Greek heroic cult' infused with Nietzsche's spirit. By way of illustration Kessler alludes to the 'grandiose temples' of Nikkō, Japan (which he visited in 1892), with their 'solemn staircases', 'large alleys of pine trees' and 'sacred lanterns' dedicated to their ancestors. 'We should', he says, 'do something similar' but 'smaller' with the 'beautiful view and the beautiful sloping site beneath the Nietzsche-Archiv'. He alludes also to a 'small (very small) *temenos* devoted to [Hermann von] Helmholtz made by [Adolf von] Hildebrand' near Berlin. The wall that encloses this monument is, he says, 'very dignified and beautiful'. He suggests van de Velde visit this tomb when he gets the chance (KV,310:563–4).

From the outset Kessler sought to shift the project's emphasis away from the purely architectural to consider its sculptural ornament, which, as he saw it, would heighten the Nietzschean message. Indeed, there is a sense throughout Kessler's correspondences on the project that the sculptural programme remained his central concern and priority. Near the dissolution of the project, he concedes to van de Velde, 'I believe a temple is essential only to place the statue of Nietzsche there' (14 April 1912; KV,353:610–11). So keen was he to commission the French sculptor, Aristide Maillol, to design a large figure of the '*Übermensch*' to stand in front of the building, that he made the services of Maillol a condition of his involvement in the project. Given Kessler's wide network of social influence and his skill for securing financial subscriptions, Förster-Nietzsche would have found it difficult to argue against his vision. Nevertheless, their difference of opinion on the general design for the Nietzsche temple continued throughout the life of the project.

At first their disagreement was about the value of the sculptural additions to the building. On 5 February 1911, Kessler wrote to Förster-Nietzsche exclaiming, 'You must have misunderstood my letters; otherwise, I don't quite understand how our views could "diverge". Because a monument without plastic [three-dimensional mouldings] is not conceivable'. He alludes to the Abbe monument to underscore his point – thereby supporting my contention that this building was regarded by Förster-Nietzsche as influential in her vision for a modest Nietzsche temple. Kessler remarks, 'the

Abbe monument is even more plastic than most other monuments', and he continues to clarify his own desire for the temple:

> What I wanted was that, as with van de Velde as its architect, we secured one or, if necessary, two first-class sculptors, Maillol and possibly Klinger, for the execution right from the start. As I know you, it seems unthinkable that there should be a fundamental difference of opinion between you and me. Everything else was just suggestions [...]
> (Cited in Neumann 2015:94)

A few weeks later we find Kessler still trying to convince Förster-Nietzsche of the value of Maillol's sculpture. This time he tries to justify their inclusion on the grounds that they express the spirit of her brother's philosophy. His reasoning is somewhat unconvincing: 'Maillol is the only artist whose world view completely and instinctively coincides with that of your brother.' He is 'the resurrected Greek in all its warmth; not neo-classical, not even reinterpreted Roman or Latin-Italian, but with the entire content of sensuality, feeling, sunshine and thirst for life, as expressed in the works of the great sculptors of the fifth and sixth centuries.' He concludes, they would be responsible for a 'flawed' project if they failed to include Maillol's work, which 'embodies exactly what your brother always long for' (18 February 1911; cited in Neumann 2015:97–8). Kessler also argues his case to van de Velde in the hope that he might convince Förster-Nietzsche of Kessler's plan. To van de Velde, he exclaims that Maillol 'alone can achieve the "Übermensch", the heroic Spring, which would symbolize the dynamism of Nietzsche' (8 February 1911, KV,309:562).[9]

Kessler's initial instructions for the monument requested a 'beautiful image of the young "Übermensch"' positioned at its centre. This would be 'a superb triumphant nude by Maillol in the style of his first sketch of his Blanqui monument (albeit a young male figure, since Nietzsche never had anything feminine).' The figure would stand three metres high and would help to create 'something great and immortal' (2 February 1911; KV,306:556–7).

Just a day later, Kessler shifts the Nietzschean focus away from the *Übermensch* to 'the glorification of the Dionysian and Apollonian principles as its central theme'. The naked figure by Maillol would now 'embody the Apollonian principle, and two bas-reliefs by Klinger on the sides would represent the Dionysian principle'. According to Kessler, the Apollonian can only be symbolized in the form of a cheerful and well-composed statue, while the Dionysian requires the 'freer style' of a bas-relief (3 February 1911; KV,307:559). Kessler seeks to portray the creative relationship between Nietzsche's Apollonian and Dionysian principles through the proximity of their distinctive artistic styles, of plastic restraint on the one hand, and unrestrained expression on the other, in one free-standing monument.

Although the architectural designs would develop significantly and rapidly throughout the project, the relationship between the Apollonian and Dionysian remained a prominent theme. Kessler's management of the project sees the design grow ever grander, reflecting increases in financial support from enthusiastic benefactors, but a more nuanced reading of its evolution may suggest a development in Kessler's reflections on the creative tensions between the Apollonian and Dionysian, and how best to portray this in architectural form. A week after proposing their representation as contrasting art forms, his focus turns to their essential spatial relationship by positioning the works of Maillol and Klinger at a distance and at contrasting areas of the temple: 'In order *not* to have Maillol and Klinger be next to each other, I proposed to construct the memorial as a temple *in front* of which would stand a statue or statues by Maillol, while in the interior a bust of Nietzsche by Klinger would stand along with reliefs by Klinger' (Diary, 8 February 1911; Kessler 1880–1918/2011:506).

There are several points of interest here. First, I think Kessler's reflections on the spatial relationship between the Apollonian and Dionysian helped him to extend his focus beyond the sculptural elements of the building to consider its architectural design more broadly, and, as we shall see, to envision how other architectural edifices could enhance the Nietzschean spirit of the site.

Second, Kessler not only regarded the artworks of Maillol and Klinger as representations of Apollonian and Dionysian forces respectively, but also of the artists themselves. As Kessler tells van de Velde, their works together would symbolically unite 'the Mediterranean, Apollonian spirit in the person of Maillol with the northern Dionysian musical spirit, in that of Klinger'. Van de Velde's role, as Kessler saw it at this time, was to unite the two in the architectural design: 'as a Romano-Germanic Belgian, you would combine the two with your German-classical architecture. We absolutely have to achieve this goal' (3 February 1911; KV,307:559).

Third, we know little about Klinger's bust of Nietzsche (aside from the fact that van de Velde had not informed Klinger of its required dimensions), but it is probable that Kessler had in mind a herm like the one Klinger had created two years earlier at Kessler's behest for the Nietzsche-Archiv. Perhaps the intention was simply to fashion a bronze cast from one and the same mould (we know Klinger had made several casts of the Nietzsche bust and that Kessler thought the height of the new bust could be raised or lowered as required with steps). Klinger's herm of Nietzsche is perhaps a closer representative of the Dionysian principle than Kessler may have realized given the herm of Dionysus painted by Genelli, which, as we saw, so captivated Nietzsche and may have shaped Nietzsche's conception of the Dionysian spirit.

Kessler rounds up his instructions for the consortium of artists he proposed for the temple's ornamentation and describes their layout. It would have 'dimensions of a chapel' (1 April 1911; KV,312:566) with three rows of stone seats on the right and left for 200–250 people, and the Nietzsche herm standing at the back, placed on a stage like an altar in a church.[10] There would be three large bas-reliefs by Klinger in white marble on the walls above the seating, separated by three pilasters, and on either side of these would be large panels, also in white marble, with inscriptions of Nietzsche-sayings designed by Eric Gill, a British artist known for his typography skills. 'So, all in all, six reliefs (three on each wall) and twelve panels' (Letter to von Hofmannsthal, 16 April 1911; cited in Stamm 1973-5:311–12). These would be illuminated by light from a large window above the entrance door and through low side windows above each relief.

Kessler sets out his plans for raising the necessary funds for his proposals, including donations from wealthy benefactors, cultural events (theatre performances, concerts and lectures to be held around Europe), selling special facsimile editions of Nietzsche's works, and the creation of a 'Working Committee for the Establishment of the Nietzsche Memorial' to oversee these activities. The committee would comprise wealthy financiers, the intellectual elite, and members of Nietzsche's family, but notably, *not* Förster-Nietzsche (presumably to prevent her from having too much influence over the project).[11] As elected president of the committee (on 12 March 1911), Kessler had assumed direct leadership of all decisions for the architectural design and financial planning of the Nietzsche temple building.

A large international centre with stadium (April 1911–June 1912)

Subscriptions from leading industrialists, businessmen, bankers and public intellectuals incentivized Kessler to desire a temple much larger than the small *temenos* for individual contemplation he originally envisaged, and by April 1911 he began to think in terms of an international Nietzsche centre to educate the masses. As Kostka notes, 'It was now Kessler's aim to improve the German "type"' en-masse, using the temple to encourage the creation of a 'higher people' and to establish 'Zarathustra as a state philosopher' (2000:45–6). The location Kessler selected for this larger temple played into his ideological strategy, for it would be positioned immediately opposite the Bismark tower (which was built in 1909 and destroyed in 1949) on the south slope of the Ettersberg hill. Kessler intended the façade of his Nietzsche temple to point towards the Bismarck tower to establish, as Stamm notes, 'a visual integration of Bismarck's political genius with Nietzsche's philosophy' (1973–5:310). With the temple's association also to Goethe in Weimar, the placement of Kessler's building established, as Kostka puts it, a 'magic triangle', linking the past (Goethe), present (Bismarck) and future (Nietzsche), with the Nietzsche building poised to direct the German nation towards a heroic future (2000:48).

Within a month, the project evolved to include ambitious proposals for a large stadium, connected to the temple. To try to encourage financial support for the increase in projected costs, Kessler invited former Chancellor Bernhard von Bülow to be honorary chairman of the Committee (Kostka 2000:46).

The stadium

With the inclusion of the stadium, Kessler accentuated the dichotomy of Apollonian and Dionysian forces within the project, with each now represented by the activities planned for the two different, but interconnected buildings on site. The stadium would embody the Apollonian with the power and beauty of human physicality through the various competitive games, races and matches that would take place there, while the temple, announced first by the Apollonian figure by Maillol at its entrance, would exude a Dionysian energy through the musical performances and dances held inside and in the mysterious aura suggested by its intentional placement. Its westerly orientation sought to capture the setting sun, illuminating it with a warm glow and enticing the play of shadows across its features and Maillol's free-standing sculpture – a setting for nature's own mysterious dance (see Stamm 1973–5:310).

The aesthetic contrast between the Apollonian physicality of the stadium and the Dionysian mystery of the temple is suggested also by the respective designs of each structure – between, Kessler says, the 'imposing stadium walls and the gracious temple form' (5 September 1911; Kessler 1880–1918/2011:561). Kessler wanted to convey in the temple's design a lightness to contrast with the heroic energy of the stadium. He instructs van de Velde on this matter throughout the project. On 3 May 1911, he writes, 'for the façade of the temple it will be necessary to avoid two pitfalls: heaviness [*la lourduer*] and thinness [*la maigreur*]' for: '[h]eaviness is what Nietzsche hated most in life! And thinness is the enemy of serenity. It is above all, serenity and sensuality, sensual beauty, that I have to look for; obviously a sensual beauty disciplined by reason [...]' (KV,321:578). But, as we shall see, still twelve months later, Kessler is troubled by the 'oppressively heavy and empty effect' of van de Velde's temple design (24 March 1912; Kessler 1880–1918/2011:588).

Kessler intended for his temple and stadium complex a place of mass pilgrimage and gatherings, with the stadium enabling 50,000 people to participate at any one time (Kostka 2000:47). According to Stamm, the ideological motivation for this architecture was to replace Christ with Nietzsche as the centre of spiritual life. It was intended that 'the initiated elite' would undergo 'constant and emotional renewal' inside the temple, 'while masses of young people [who] performed in the name of Nietzsche in the stadium' would celebrate the '"beauty of vigour and force"'. He notes that it is difficult to imagine in Europe prior to 1914 a 'more intimate relation between monumental architecture and ideological manipulation on a mass scale' (Stamm 1973–5: 314–15). According to Kostka, the complex was designed to contribute to the furtherance and completion of the German Empire with New Weimar at its centre. Its vast capacity to gather people in their thousands has unfortunate associations, making one think, Kostka remarks, of 'the Nuremberg Party Rally' (Kostka 2000:46). However, as I note below, Kessler was vehemently critical of the rise of National Socialism and deeply saddened by the later infiltration of the Nazis in the Nietzsche-Archiv.

Kessler envisioned a horseshoe-shaped stadium similar in design to Torben Grut's stadium for the 1912 Olympic Games in Stockholm. Grut's plans were widely published before April 1911 and were generally regarded as the most successful example of a modern stadium (Stamm 1973–5:313). Kessler's enthusiasm for Grut's stadium was matched by his interest in the newly restored ancient stadium in Athens. He sent publicity materials for both stadiums to van de Velde to inspire him. Their Nietzsche stadium would sit behind the temple. It would be 185 metres in length, 400 metres wide, with a grandstand of steps reaching up to 100 metres. Three ceremonial pathways or *Feststraßen*, each 500–800 metres long, would lead the visitors up to the site with steps at various levels.

Given the sudden growth of the project, Kessler begs both van de Velde and Förster-Nietzsche not to be alarmed by the idea, and in letters to each (14 April 1911 to van de Velde, and a day later to Foster-Nietzsche), he outlines his rationale for the stadium and supplements it with a simple sketch that he refers to as 'the ideal scheme'. He presents the stadium as the architectural embodiment of Nietzschean spirit with its emphasis on the beauty of physical strength. To Förster-Nietzsche he writes: 'Your brother was the first [...] to teach joy in one's body, on physical strength and beauty; the first who brought physical culture, force, and grace back into relation with the spirit and the highest things. This relation I would like to see realized in this monument' (Easton 2006:187). To van de Velde, he writes:

> Nietzsche was the first great modern thinker to preach the beauty of strength and the joy of feeling alive [...] and this idea allow us to address all sports clubs, all those who are interested in sports, and to build a bridge between the culture of the body and the spirit on this hill, which will become a 'holy hill' once we have established our temple and our games there.
>
> (KV,317:572–3)

Kessler's idea of including a stadium in a memorial to Nietzsche is not altogether surprising. In general terms, around 1910, the education of the body was a subject of many life reform movements, and Nietzsche was a key point of reference for these ideas (Kostka 2000:48). Stadiums extolled the aesthetics of sport, uniting it with art. The modern Olympic Games had been taking place since 1896, and Kessler's journal *PAN* regularly featured artworks by Ludwig von Hofmann (1861–1945) of arcadian scenes with heroic nude males. Most significant, perhaps, is an essay Kessler wrote in 1909, titled *Griechischer Frühling* ('*Greek Spring*'). In this essay he celebrates sport for its capacity to invigorate the spirit and to master the ego and there he outlines his hopes for ushering in a new era of culture grounded in 'cheerfulness', and cheerfulness, he argues, is associated with 'the highest possible physical and mental strength' (cited in Kostka 2000:48). In his letter to Förster-Nietzsche, Kessler expresses his hope that the Nietzsche stadium would play its part in arousing such cheerfulness, spirit and joy to levels of intensity that have not been experienced since the times of ancient Greece. Months later he writes to van de Velde describing the stadium-temple as an '*idea*, or more precisely *feelings* of heroism and joy, the feelings that form the basic spirit of Nietzsche's works'. The buildings themselves will comprise a 'great form that breathes heroism and joy' (Diary 30 November 1911; Kessler 1880–1918/2011:572).

Although Förster-Nietzsche and van de Velde disliked the idea of a stadium, Kessler found support with Committee members, and it was proposed that gymnastics clubs and sports leagues in the region could help finance its construction. Kessler arranged a loan of 60,000 marks to purchase a new site for the temple-stadium complex in a 10-hectare plot of land in the hills in southwest Weimar, behind Villa Silberblick and close to a small strip of woodland. The change in location required Kessler to rethink his ideological focus for the site. As Stamm notes, the Bismarck Tower as an essential component of the setting was now replaced with Weimar itself, with Maillol's statue positioned to look over the city (1973–5:313). The *Feststraßen* would present a visual link between city and monument, presenting different vistas of the city to visitors en route.

Kessler estimated the total cost of the project to be in the region of 1 million marks. But he had his sights on a larger sum to enable him to extend the site to include an additional building: one that would function as an 'Institute for "Genetics," for the beautification of the race' (Diary, 5 September 1911; Kessler 1880–1918/2011:561). Again, allusions to the National Socialist agenda may spring to mind – to the Lebensborn campaign and Heinrich Himmler's castles of the SS – but it is important to note that eugenics was rife in Europe and the United States long before the Nazis rose to power. Furthermore, Kessler's reasoning is probably influenced by Nietzsche's own ideas about the development of higher types (see for instance AC, 3). As Kostka notes, 'the ideological core of the Nietzsche monument' is grounded in the idea of a 'better future resulting from human reform', and its organization and planning was directed by 'an international group of "higher men", with the public largely excluded'. This Nietzschean idea, Kostka says, 'wouldn't have been lost on Kessler' (Kostka 2000:51;cf. 50).

Förster-Nietzsche responded to the new plans with both excitement and horror, and she accused Kessler and van de Velde of concocting them behind her back (see Kessler diary entries 20 April, and 28 April 1911; Kessler

1880–1918/2011:526, 527). She was reticent about the project throughout its life and lent it her support so long as it continued to suggest an income stream for the Nietzsche-Archiv. According to Easton, Förster-Nietzsche sought at various times to jettison the plans for fear of losing control of the Archiv, and out of a general dislike for the international focus of the proposal (cited in Kessler 2011:376). Later that year, in October, she wrote a terse letter to Kessler to oppose his plans, citing philosophical justification from Nietzsche himself. There she quotes from a letter she purports to have been written by Nietzsche where he expresses his disapproval of watching competitive games in an 'arena or stadium'. She also recounts the occasion when a man, called 'Rudolf Lenke or Menke' from Leipzig, visited her in August to inform her that a group of young artists were very hostile to Kessler's plans for the memorial and wanted to use van de Velde's plans instead (presumably the original plans he drew up at her request for a modest temple). The visit by Herr Lenke (or Menke) encouraged Förster-Nietzsche, she reports, to seek advice from family members Richard Oehler (1878–1948) and Max Oehler (1875–1946). Unsurprisingly, we learn that they, too, were against Kessler's plans. She cites Richard's complaint as follows: 'You [Kessler] had already donated the most beautiful and worthy monument to Nietzsche in the Herm by Klinger and placed it here [in the Archiv] in noble secrecy. Why now design a monument in the opposite sense?'[12]

Upon receiving this letter, Kessler notes in his diary:

> Unbelievable letter from Förster-Nietzsche, who asks me to give up the plan for the memorial because 'a Herr Lenke or Menke' (she cannot recall the name) visited her and spoke against the project. The 'forthright indignation' of this 'Nietzsche worshipper' has affected her deeply, and 'she herself cannot do anything now other than to oppose it'.
> (Diary 20 October 1911; Kessler 1880–1918/2011:564)

Kessler responded to Förster-Nietzsche with a terse letter of his own, outlining the financial implications of cancelling the project – implying that she would have to pay off the loan acquired for the purchase of the land, with an acknowledgement that she lacked the funds to do so. He also suggested that she refrain from valuing the opinion of a man whose name she couldn't remember (Diary 20 October 1911; Kessler 1880–1918/2011:564)

Van de Velde's evolving plans of the temple complex (February 1911–June 1912)

It is difficult to chart the evolution of van de Velde's designs from his initial drawings of the 'modest temple' of February 1911 for Förster-Nietzsche to the final design that was accepted by Kessler and the Working Committee in June 1912. Many of van de Velde's sketches, plans and photographs for the project have been preserved in the archives of the *Harry van de Velde Collection* in Brussels, but several are lost.[13] Only a small selection of images is replicated in the relatively few scholarly works that consider the subject. Van de Velde rarely dated his drawings, which puts the onus on scholars to resort to informed guesswork when judging the evolution of his designs. This is helped considerably by the publication of the correspondence between Kessler and van de Velde (Neumann 2015), and by Kessler's dated diary entries where he alludes to the project, and to lesser degree, descriptions in the posthumous memoirs of van de Velde and in correspondence between Kessler and von Hofmannsthal.[14] Correspondence between the two men on the aims of the building and its ideological rationale as the design remit changes is useful for assessing its potential as a 'Nietzschean' architecture in the grand style.

Van de Velde's plans for the temple, stadium and *Feststraßen* are now lost (Neumann 2015:590), but he describes them in a letter to Kessler on 19 August 1911 with an apology for their delay. There he refers to a *Feststraße* – of approximately 200m in length that leads from the Berka-chaussée (*Berkastraße*) to Maillol's statue with the temple behind it, and the stadium behind that. The sides of the temple would remain uncovered, and the terrace would overhang the side paths with balustrades at its edge. Kessler responds, describing the plans as 'interesting' but notes that van de Velde has forgotten to include the colonnades that connect the temple to the stadium. Kessler includes in his response a sketch (now lost) of his own to demonstrate the desired direction of the *Feststraßen*, which could be supplemented, he writes, with a line of statues of athletes. He also suggests the inclusion of an open-air swimming pool, surrounded by trees or statues (August 1911; KV,335:591–2).

From early October 1911 van de Velde began work on a large-scale model of the site to ensure its correct portions, basic shape, and spatial relations of the temple and stadium within the hill site. Kessler saw the model for the first time on 16 December 1911. He approves of it and delights in the dimensions of the stadium – which replicate 'the one in Athens' – and especially the relationship between the temple and stadium, which he found 'surprisingly beautiful, beautiful and grandiose' (Kessler 1880–1918/2011:574).

Van de Velde did not tweak the plans for the monument in accordance with Kessler's suggestions until November. He gave the excuse of other work commitments, but around this time his correspondence with Kessler expresses his growing resistance to the idea of a stadium for the Nietzsche monument. He suggests the public will be 'baffled' by the paradoxical coupling of a temple with a stadium: a place of contemplation and a place of exhibition (van de Velde 1995:353–5). And in a long letter to Kessler, he argues against the stadium on practical grounds, citing the fact it will quickly lose its appeal, becoming a 'lifeless, irrelevant' museum-like object. He also cites Förster-Nietzsche's opposition to it (KV,350:603–6; see also van de Velde 1995:355). Interestingly, van de Velde explains how he had several times meditated 'on what the Nietzsche monument should be' and from this series of reflections he came to realize that the original idea of a modest temple was most appropriate. Furthermore, he maintains, it was closer to his *own* 'taste' [*goût*]. He mentions that he drew several sketches at this time that helped him arrive at these conclusions.

To try to garner favour with Kessler on this matter, he cites Kessler's earlier letter to him where Kessler outlines his original vision for the Nietzsche monument as a *temenos*, with all the 'moving and mysterious serenity of the Japanese temples, hidden in hundred-year-old parks' – *this*, van de Velde says is the way forward, as he sees it. Van de Velde alludes to the trees on the current site as lending themselves to the idea of a mysterious *temenos*. They are, he says, 'more beautiful than anywhere else in Germany!' His temple design, still with the statue in front of it, will be entrusted and informed, he says, by the mystery suggested by the trees and the idea of the 'Sacred Wood' [*Bois sacré*]. He goes on to describe the evocative nature of a tree-lined alley, which refuses to disclose its destination to those who venture along its pathway. In van de Velde's design it will gradually reveal its secrets, first the vision of the statue, then the temple, and finally, the high plateau with its sky and the hills. Upon receipt of this letter, Kessler writes in his diary: 'A letter from van de Velde in which he expresses, in wounded tones, his opposition to the stadium project' (Diary 5 November 1911; Kessler 1880–1918/2011:568). A day later, Kessler's diary mentions a 'lengthy, partly somewhat heated' conversation with van de Velde, which eventually led van de Velde to 'pledge his support for the stadium idea'.

Van de Velde's reflections for a Nietzschean temple

There are several drawings that fit van de Velde's description of those he said he had sketched during his meditations on Nietzschean architecture, each of which includes the temple and tree-lined alley, and each giving emphasis to the trees – the 'sacred wood' – in their composition (see Figures 4.8 and 4.12, and most notably, Figure 4.6 where the trees are most prominent, wild, and uncultivated). Van de Velde's memoirs describe how his meditations were directed by his reading of Nietzsche's published works and handwritten notes in the archives at Villa Silberblick, which he consulted 'to discover whether the philosopher had arrived at an image of architecture, and if he had defined an aesthetic system of the "grand style"' (van de Velde 1995:357).

We know that van de Velde had read a selection of Nietzsche's writings prior to this occasion, and that his renovations of Villa Silberblick were influenced by his reverence for Nietzsche's philosophy. But it is in his preparations for the Nietzsche temple design – and, particularly, his growing doubts over the value and relevance of the stadium – that van de Velde turns directly to Nietzsche's comments on architecture and the grand style for guidance. Although van de Velde indicates that he consulted various editions and manuscripts at the Nietzsche-Archiv, Anne van Loo, editor of his memoires, thinks it more probable that he consulted his copy of *Pages Choisies*, a volume of selected passages from Nietzsche's writings, translated into French by Henri Albert (van de Velde 1995:357,n.2). This is because the passages by Nietzsche that van de Velde cites in his memoires were marked (among others) in his copy of this volume.

Van de Velde paraphrases from *Twilight of the Idols* (TI, X.11:94–5) to highlight features that, in his mind, highlight 'the aesthetic system of the "grand style"' in relation to architecture. He refers to the notion that such an architecture has 'no need to please', that 'it must show pride in its victory over heaviness', and that it is 'a kind of eloquence, sometimes persuasive

FIGURE 4.6 Nietzsche Temple design (1911–12, Henry van de Velde). Phase 1. Sketch of front elevation resembling Doric temple, with *Feststraßen* and statue, 1911. Collection ENSAVE – La Cambre, Bruxelles, inv.1503. © Henry van de Velde Foundation (Pays-Bas).

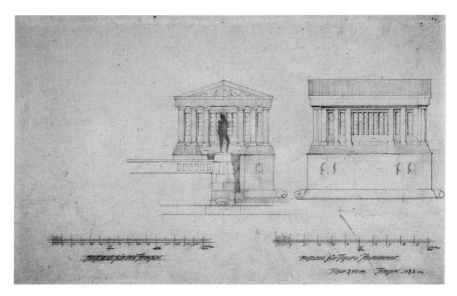

FIGURE.4.7 Nietzsche Temple design. Phase 1. Sketch of front and side elevations with statue, 1911. Collection ENSAVE – La Cambre, Bruxelles, inv.4519. © Henry van de Velde Foundation (Pays-Bas).

and flattering, sometimes cutting' (1995:357). He also draws attention to *Human all too Human*, to some 'obvious axioms' about the failure of truth and the 'beautiful in itself', and to Nietzsche's experiences of 'dematerialiality' [*dématérialité*] when encountering the soul-enchanted stones of the temple in Paestum (cf.HH I,145). Nietzsche's description, van de Velde writes, 'confirmed my own feelings, which I struggled to make clear to my students in Weimar' (van de Velde 1995:357–8).

Van de Velde's sketches of a temple (Figures 4.6 and 4.7) resembles the Doric second temple to Hera at Paestum, and his addition of the bellowing trees – which he regarded as mysterious and beautiful – suggests van de Velde's sought to convey with his design the kind of soulful and animated architecture that he was so pleased to have discovered in Nietzsche's accounts. The overall impression van de Velde presents is a *temenos* or sacred grove of the type he tried to impress upon Kessler: 'Since I have been so intensely concerned with the idea of the Nietzsche monument, it is to the mystery that magnificent and suggestive trees compose [...] the mystery of the "Sacred Wood", that I would like to entrust to the temple, the temple and the statue!' (KV,350:605). Van de Velde's design addresses Nietzsche's desire for spaces for self-reflection. The tree-lined path leading upwards to the temple with views over the city and finally to the sky is conducive to the meditative mountain walks that Nietzsche sought. As Stamm puts it, 'The Nietzsche admirer, being surrounded by nature on his way to the sanctuary [would be] constantly exposed to the "Master's" world, at least in principle, and [would have] experienced a kind of catharsis' (Stamm 1973–5:314).

Architectural phases of the temple

A few scholars have attempted to order van de Velde's illustrations of the temple-complex according to distinctive stages in its design evolution coupled with a vague timeline. Günther Stamm's account (1973–5) is often cited as an authority in this regard, and although compelling in its consideration of the development of the design, the timeframes he suggests are confusing and occasionally out of step with the written evidence available with the correspondence between Kessler and van de Velde, Kessler's diary, and van de Velde's memoirs.[15] Following Stamm, there is a tendency to assume there are four distinct stages or phases in the design of the temple-complex. I shall consider these in turn.

First and second design phases (19 August–29 November 1911)

Although Neumann suggests the first design is lost, Stamm and others regard two sketches (Figures 4.6 and 4.7) – which I associate with van de Velde's period of 'Nietzschean' reflection (sometime between 20 August and 27 October 1911) as the *first phase* of the design, the details of which he sent to Kessler on 19 August 1911 (see Föhl 2000:22–3; Hollis 2019:189; Stamm 1973–5:315–6; van de Velde 1995:354[16]). Certainly, we can identify in these sketches various features described by van de Velde in his accompanying letter to Kessler, including the tree-lined *Feststraße* leading to Maillol's statue, with a temple – sides uncovered – and the balustrade on a terrace. The stadium, however, is wholly absent from the sketches. Perhaps additional sketches were included, now lost, along with the plan of the site (with its missing colonnades, as Kessler remarked).

Stamm recognizes the influence of classical Greek architecture on the first design, but in stark contrast to van de Velde's desire for it to evoke a mysterious atmosphere, Stamm describes it as 'strikingly "conservative", completely unoriginal and impersonal' (1973–5:316). He acknowledges the trees but seems unaware of their symbolic significance for van de Velde. Stamm merely draws attention to the 'charm' of their composition, drawn with late Art Nouveau technique, and contrasts this with the 'cold simplicity of the temple façade, which serves as a strictly tectonic frame for Maillol's statue' (1973–5:316).

Stamm dates the designs for phase 1 of the project between 14 April and 3 August 1911, and phase 2 between 3 August and December 1911. However, the correspondence between Kessler and van de Velde suggests the first formal designs for the monument were not discussed between them until 19 August, with van de Velde taking a break from the project soon after and not returning to consider a revised design (the second phase) until early November.

According to Stamm, phase 2 is illustrated by a plan and the sketch of Figure 4.8. The contrast between the façade of this temple and the one he attributes to the first phase is sufficient, he maintains, to regard them as different phases of the project rather than variations of a theme drawn on the same occasion. Although the temple of phase 2 continues to be inspired by ancient Greek forms, Stamm suggests it has lost its former tectonic austerity. He continues:

> The newly employed curvature, the extension of the lower parts of the side elevations and the more monumental accentuation of the lower corners demonstrates the desire to transcend the classic or neoclassical vocabulary of *Phase I* and to create a less rigid frame-like arrangement for Maillol's *Apollo*. The monumental figure visually gains a greater degree of freedom in relation to its architectural background and the temple façade moves towards a more original solution.
> (Stamm 1973–5:320)

The trees, by contrast, seem more constrained and less mysterious in their clipped form. Their shadows are predictably rectangular, and unlikely to dance. Stamm interprets them more positively as complementing the character of the new temple façade and enabling the organic relationship between nature and architecture from Phase 1 to continue. The plan now includes the colonnades to connect the temple and stadium. But, as Stamm notes, the proportions of the temple, stadium and *Festraße* are problematic at this stage: the stadium is excessive in relation to the temple, and the *Festraße* is too short. He maintains that van de Velde will rectify this in subsequent design phases.

While Kessler is rather subdued in his response to the first design (21 August 1911), taking the opportunity to list omissions and potential additions, he is more vocal and critical of the second design. Following his examination of it in van de Velde's studio on 29 November, he records in his diary: 'I really didn't like them.'

> [They] have all been designed from the inside out. You recognize in the façade, cloakrooms, the shape of the hall, etc. mere petty details that lack the monumental feeling: everything according to the principle of the comfort of the English country home and expressing nothing further. But clearly this principle does not suffice to create a monument.
> (29 November 1911; Kessler 1880–1918/2011:571)

Kessler instructed van de Velde to 'reverse' his normal design procedure, to focus less on the functional needs of the building and to 'subordinate' all features to the 'spirit' and 'ideal expression' of the façade. At this stage, Kessler began to think the project exceeded van de Velde's creative talents. Kessler writes, he is '"out of his depth" with this commission' for 'his imagination falters without the aid of utility. Clearly, he hasn't much heart for the job' (Kessler 1880–1918/2011:571). When van de Velde presents Kessler with modifications of the temple (unaddressed by Stamm), which to Kessler's mind now make the temple look like a 'municipal museum' – 'just a lot of little, gossipy forms, unimportant things, cloak rooms, a hall with skylights, etc.' – Kessler outlines a new design process for van de Velde intended to enhance van de Velde's creative flare (30 November 1911; Kessler 1880–1918/2011:571-2). Exasperated, Kessler writes, 'I told him we can't continue this way.' The exterior of the monument 'must not express any goal', other than '*feelings*, heroism and joy, the feelings that form the basic spirit of Nietzsche's works [...] We must therefore have a great form that breathes heroism and joy, and then fit the hall to it from behind' (Kessler 1880–1918/2011:571-2).

Somewhat unsurprisingly, the new design method Kessler proposes uses sculpture as its guiding principle. He first instructs van de Velde to imagine his temple as a statue, and then as a backdrop or platform for a statue, for 'the façade is just the same as a statue', it is 'above all a work of art'. Kessler recommends van de Velde meditate on a small statue that he would send to him (of Kessler's lover, 'Colin'), which resembled in style Maillol's Apollonian statue to encourage van de Velde to design the temple as its exhibitory backdrop (Kessler 1880–1918/2011:571-2). Kessler imagined this process would help van de Velde to be more expressive and less conventional in his temple design. Of course, van de Velde was already familiar, to some extent, with Kessler's proposed method, having designed the Abbe memorial to accommodate Meunier's bas-reliefs. While Kessler praised the monument as a success, he was keen, as I noted, for the Nietzsche temple to be distinctly more dramatic, joyful and serene.

According to Stamm, the only evidence we have for the second phase of van de Velde's design is a sketch of the front elevation with *Feststraßen* (Figure 4.8) and a plan of the site. If that is correct, the building conveyed in Figure 4.8 is, in Kessler's estimation, a petty building akin not to a monument but to an English country home. Unless the design was significantly changed between 28 and 30 November (Kessler's diary offers no clarification on the matter), they also convey to Kessler a municipal museum.

Kessler supplemented his instructions for the revised design method, with details of what he had in mind by a 'heroic, joyful' temple to Nietzsche. First and foremost, the 'Memorial and especially the temple' ought to express 'the transposition of Nietzsche's personality into a grand architectural formula'. It must be 'an *expressive* rather than constructive architecture, a grand formula inspired by Nietzsche's personality alone'. Kessler suggests van de Velde look to Wilhelm Kreis' monument to Otto von Bismarck as a successful example of the translation of a heroic personality into a powerful

FIGURE 4.8 Nietzsche Temple design. Phase 2. Sketch of front elevation with *Feststraßen*, 1912. Collection ENSAVE – La Cambre, Bruxelles, inv. 4521. © Henry van de Velde Foundation (Pays-Bas).

design. According to Kessler, Kreis was able to convey in his monument a 'massive and balanced force, which was the personality of Bismarck: something like a stormy and armoured serenity, concentrated, threatening too, but more defensive than offensive'. By the same token, Kessler thought van de Velde could do the same with Nietzsche's personality in a temple building that would express, he says, 'the unity of the immense feeling of lightness, joy, and strength', with 'lyrical rhythm' (12 December 1911; KV,351: 607–8; Kessler 1880–1918/2011:573–4).

Kessler concedes it is easier to design to express sensations of 'lightness' than emotions of 'joy', and he recommends to van de Velde that he start with a light structure in mind: ideally, 'a light monument, soaring, so to speak, on its heights before the massive stadium'; an 'aerial monument' like 'certain Italo-Muslim monuments of the Indies that appear constructed by djinns, but nervous and strong and even slyly massive beneath this appearance of lightness' (Kessler 1880–1918/2011:573–4). If Kessler had stopped here his suggestions may have been useful, even persuasive to van de Velde, especially if Kessler had been aware and referred to Nietzsche's love of the Mole Antonelliana with its massive appearance combined with its desire for the heights, and aerial vista, looking towards the mountains. But Kessler refers instead to a temple that expresses 'the physiognomy of Nietzsche himself, with his formidable Bismarckian bone structure under the exquisitely delicate Greek surfaces of his brow and mouth'. Kessler concludes: 'I would like not only joy but almost irony in the monumental expression of this opposition, the triumph of finesse over force. A complete orchestration of these two motifs leading to a joy and serenity, an almost ironic purity and lightness' (Kessler 1880–1918/2011:573–4).

Van de Velde certainly has his work cut out! Such abstract and subjective requirements are, as Hindley notes, 'almost impossible to realize' (2012:50). Not only must he transpose the ideas of Nietzsche into a building, he is tasked also with imbuing it with the physiognomy and personality of the philosopher himself. Unsurprisingly, the pressures of design brief made him unhappy. As Föhl notes, although van de Velde was enthusiastic in his works 'and loyal to his hero', Nietzsche, he was 'also grumpy in the tow of Kessler, who constantly changed the requirements and goals in the course of the project to include comprehensive requirements' (2000:15).

Third and fourth design phases (30 November 1911–June 1912)

These phases of the design are van de Velde's response to Kessler's instructions for a more expressive architecture. According to Stamm, the start of phase 3 is marked by van de Velde's rejection of the classical architectural canon, which had provided inspiration for the first two phases, for it 'excluded any potential for expressive architectural statement on a monumental scale' (1973–5:323). Such a move, away from utilitarian architecture and historical style, is itself more conducive to Nietzsche's grand style. Within this context, the rejection of the template of a classical Greek temple – albeit one now modified into a more idiosyncratic rendition of one – is no loss. There is no loss even if one were to regard van de Velde's Greek temple design as a mediation on Nietzsche's experiences at Paestum. This is because the classical temple style does not itself convey the grand style, rather Nietzsche (and van de Velde, too) is concerned with the experiences that a design evokes in us. In other words, in terms of the Greek temple, they value the noble Greek spirit that was expressed through its design – a spirit that Nietzsche experienced in Paestum, and one van de Velde sought to capture in the spatial relationship between temple and sacred wood. To build in the grand style is to evoke a sense of spirit through the architect's will to power. This may result in a building of any given design or style, but it is most probably not going to be felt in those that merely replicate an historic style or conventional design as these tend to require less creative effort, and by the same token, a more diluted will to power.

Kessler visited van de Velde's studios on 22 March 1912 to view the new design. The next day he took Eberhard von Bodenhausen, co-founder of *PAN*, to see them.[17] According to Stamm, this design constitutes its third phase, illustrated here by a perspective drawing of the temple with the stadium behind it (Figure 4.9) and floor plans showing the gallery (Figure 4.10). The temple is massive and compact. It is highly suggestive of

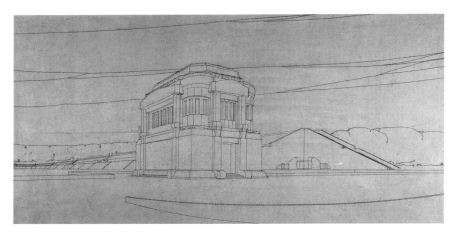

FIGURE 4.9 Nietzsche temple design. Phase 3. Perspective sketch with stadium behind, 1912. Collection ENSAVE – La Cambre, Bruxelles, inv.1505. © Henry van de Velde Foundation (Pays-Bas).

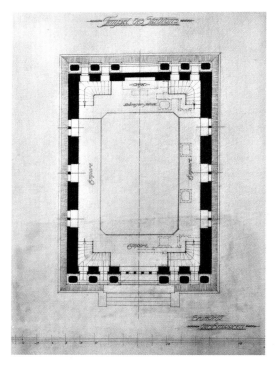

FIGURE 4.10 Nietzsche temple design. Phase 3. Sketch, plan of lower floor with gallery, 1912. Collection ENSAVE – La Cambre, Bruxelles, inv.2213. © Henry van de Velde Foundation (Pays-Bas).

van de Velde's Abbe monument but extended to include an additional floor. Stamm describes the building as '"Assyrian" grandeur' and 'architectural brutality' (1973–5:324). According to Stamm, the contrast between its carefully structured upper elevation and the lower parts, which are totally closed off, is a feature apparent in the first phase of the design, and probably also the second, but is now more prominent. This amendment, in Stamm's view, gives the building a 'higher degree of monumental expressiveness' than earlier designs – a summation that ought to have appealed to Kessler.

The plans appear to incorporate the various requirements Kessler outlines in his letters to van de Velde and to von Hofmannsthal in early April 1911, including three rows of stone seats on the side walls on the right and left (where 200–250 people would sit), and positioned above these, the large white marble bas-reliefs by Klinger and panel inscriptions by Gill. The main wall at the back forms a Nietzsche 'altar', where Klinger's herm or bust would be placed. In addition, we find an organ above the altar, and four staircases that present a continuous gallery.

According to Stamm, the shape and dimensions of the temple underwent a further two changes, from a strictly rectangular plan (Figure 4.10) to a modified rectangular outline, both of which Stamm assigns to phase 3, and then to a square plan (see Figure 4.11) in the final design, the fourth and final phase of the development according to Stamm.

Kessler was disappointed with the design; he reports that von Bodenhausen was too. Kessler describes the temple as 'an enormous, tall, Bismarck-tower-like structure', with 'enormously complicated articulation'. Although it was Kessler's idea that van de Velde turn to Kreis' Bismarckian tower for inspiration, and although he concedes that van de Velde had managed to overcome his problematical approach by creating a powerful façade, it failed to exude the feelings of lightness and joy that Kessler instructed. It was the exact opposite: 'an oppressively heavy and empty effect'. Kessler proceeds to blame van de Velde's inability to design an appropriately evocative architecture. 'The truth' of the matter is, he writes, 'our age lacks any tradition and handle on decorative architecture. This complete failure of van de Velde, after repeated efforts, to find an architectural expression for a pure and aimless joy in life and lightness proves it' (23/24 March 1912; Kessler 1880–1918/2011:588).

With a sense of resignation and a realization that the inability to design a building to evoke Nietzschean spirit lies not with the individual architect, but with modern culture at large, Kessler instructs van de Velde – in sarcastic tones – to design a more simplistic temple: just 'four walls and a roof' and 'the beauty of the walls as walls'. Van de Velde agrees. He had, after all, argued for a modest temple all along. But by now, his enthusiasm was understandably waning. Indeed, Kessler recounts, how van de Velde, now exhausted, was keen to 'forgo the temple entirely and build only a platform as a background for the statue' (Diary 24 March 1912; Kessler 1880–1918/2011:588).

Van de Velde presents the final design to Kessler in June 1912 (Figures 4.11,4.12,4.13). Both men seem disillusioned by the project. Kessler's diary is surprisingly quiet at this time with no explanation as to why he supported this design, which seems just as heavy as its immediate predecessor, and more like a 'Bismarckian tower' with its square shape. According to Krause, the designs (of phases 3 and 4) 'convey the exact opposite of grace and cheerfulness in the sense of Nietzsche's Zarathustra'. The final design resembles 'a grave or place dedicated to a cult of the dead, and certainly not one suitable as a Dionysian place of dance, music and singing as was intended' (1984:204–5).

FIGURE 4.11 Nietzsche Temple design. Phase 4. Perspective sketch, 1912. Collection ENSAVE – La Cambre, Bruxelles, inv.1508. © Henry van de Velde Foundation (Pays-Bas).

FIGURE 4.12 Nietzsche Temple design. Phase 4. Sketch of front elevation with *Feststraßen*, 1912. Collection ENSAVE – La Cambre, Bruxelles, inv.1507. © Henry van de Velde Foundation (Pays-Bas).

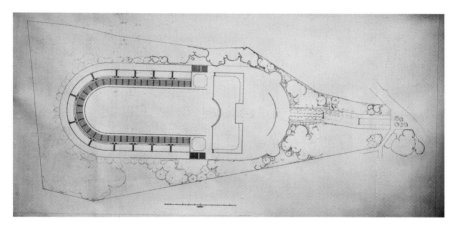

FIGURE 4.13 Nietzsche Temple design. Phase 4. Sketch of site plan, 1912. Collection ENSAVE – La Cambre, Bruxelles, inv. 2210. © Henry van de Velde Foundation (Pays-Bas).

The plan of the temple continues to meet requirements outlined by Kessler in April 1911. The exterior present similar façades to the previous design, apart from the entrance, and continues the pronounced contrast between the upper part and the more austere, closed-off lower part. Stamm finds the 'somewhat Neo-Romanesque' character of the elevation to be far richer and more expressive than previous designs (1973–5:330). This presents a more conducive relationship between the temple and the statue, allowing both to 'serve as independently formed, evocative, and expressive symbols of the ideological conception' (1973–5: 330). He commends, too, the proportions of the terrace that provides a careful balance between the temple and the 'decorative shape' of the swimming pool behind it. The shape of the pool acts as a visual connection between the stadium and terrace, taking on a straight edge where it meets the terrace and a concave shape to continue the rounded edge of the stadium grounds. The stadium provides twelve secondary entrances (the primary entrances are via the terrace), each of which is marked by a statue of an athlete. These lead to seats in the grandstand. Below the grandstand are spaces for restaurants, changing rooms and washrooms for athletes, and other relevant facilities. In Stamm's assessment, the entire composition of temple, statue and *Festraße* achieves an 'organic and pleasant unity' (1973–5:330).

The trees, although still significant in the sizeable space they occupy in van de Velde's sketches (Figure 4.12), appear cloud-like, as if blanketed out. Their outline is their key feature, which is employed to draw attention away from them and to the statue as the central focus of the composition.

This was the final design, which was quickly approved by the Working Committee on 9 June 1912, despite extensive anticipated costs of just over 2 million marks to complete the work. The minutes of the meeting record that van de Velde's plans were met with 'full applause from the assembled people' (Stamm 1973–5:325).

This would be the last positive move for the temple-complex, which was never built. Kessler became preoccupied with writing and with a ballet production for the rest of the year and into the next. Förster-Nietzsche played a tangible role in obstructing its progress through her mismanagement of the Nietzsche-Archiv, leading to substantial financial debts. She argued that financial support for the Archiv was being channelled into an unnecessary and extravagant memorial. Eberhard von Bodenhausen was called upon to negotiate a compromise. On 21 December 1913, they drew up a legal contract to ensure the building of the temple-complex was postponed until the financial situation was clarified. The contract included the proviso that the Archiv be transferred to the Nietzsche Foundation along with the land bought for the stadium. It also stipulates that once the archiv is financially stable, Nietzsche's body would be transferred to Weimar, and that van de Velde would be commissioned to design a suitable monument for the grave (van de Velde 1995:362,n.1).

The First World War marked the end of this project. Nietzsche's body would remain in the family plot in Röcken, Saxony-Anhalt, and van de Velde would never design Nietzsche's grave monument.[18] Sembach suggests that this project 'would not have lasted long even if the First World War had not broken out', because the designs van de Velde were asked to produce were so out of character for his work (1989:152). Had Kessler not become involved in managing the design, there may well be a modest temple-building in the garden of Villa Silberblick today, designed by van de Velde in a manner more conducive to Nietzschean ideas.

In his memoirs van de Velde speaks highly of Kessler's Nietzschean intentions, describing Kessler as an enlightened aesthete (Esthète éclairé), who 'relied on the philosophical principles of Nietzsche to try to forge the new type of man, which we aspire to achieve' (van de Velde 1995:57–8). But we also know van de Velde disliked and was frustrated by Kessler's design briefs, and on one occasion he asked their mutual friend, Eberhard von Bodenhausen, to be extremely discreet after confiding in him his feelings about them (Kostka 2000:46). Kessler's design brief grew into a grandiose spectacle. The designs have been described as 'megalomaniac' (Grohé 1996b:32); 'absurd fantasies', 'insanely soaring heights', 'presumptuous megalomania' and 'cloud cuckoo land' (Föhl 2000:15); a 'wild plan' and a 'desperate attempt to bring about the impossible' (Sembach 1989:94); and a 'symbol' of 'illusory and contradictory attempts to enforce the impossible' (Grupp 1999:201). Sembach notes how van de Velde's approach to Nietzsche for his designs for Villa Silberblick on the one hand, and for the temple-stadium complex on the other, was wholly at odds. Van de Velde's considerations of Nietzsche were incorporated into the Villa in a 'very subtle' way, hitting the 'perfect tone', but forced in 'an almost violent manner' with 'thunderous tone' in his designs for Kessler. Sembach continues to note, the designs for Kessler misunderstand Nietzsche and this misunderstanding leads to a 'puffed-up' and 'husk-like' architecture (Grupp 1999:152).

Arguably, Kessler's design brief loses its crucial sense of grounding. Its plans continued to morph into ever more complex and expensive elaborations until the energy behind it petered out, leaving individuals exhausted and resentful.[19] Like Antonelli, the architect lauded by Nietzsche for building ever higher despite the odds, Kessler refused to compromise on his vision, despite increasing costs and threats to his reputation. But unlike the Mole Antonelliana, Kessler's project ran out of steam. It lacked the will to power to realize itself and the creative energy, evident at the start, dissipated into the inflated heights.

Nietzsche Memorial, Kröller-Müller's 'Museum Park', Holland: Van de Velde (1925)

Van de Velde would have another opportunity to design a Nietzsche memorial, and this time, with a modest design brief. In 1920, modern art collector Helene Kröller-Müller commissioned van de Velde to design a 'Grand Museum' on her private estate – now, De Hoge Veluwe National Park. Due to financial setbacks the building was never constructed. In 1921 van de Velde designed for Kröller-Müller a 'museum park' for her collection of sculptures, which was intended as a scenic entrance for the museum building. She requested he also design a monument to Nietzsche in an area of wasteland within the park but van de Velde was adamant from the start that he would 'submit architectural composition and nature (vegetation) projects to her rather than sculptural compositions' (cited in Stamm 1973–5:334). With this remark, one senses that van de Velde is keen to distance himself and his project from the problematic approach to the temple-stadium design, which, as we saw, prioritized sculpture at Kessler's insistence. Indeed, free from the constraints of an over-bearing project manager, van de Velde was able to design a modest building (Figure 4.14). His plans are simple and reminiscent of the tomb to von Helmholtz, which Kessler recommended van de Velde visit when the idea of a *temenos* for Nietzsche was first raised between them. It also brings to mind the tomb or grave monument to Nietzsche that van de Velde would have been commissioned to design as stipulated in the legal contract mentioned above.

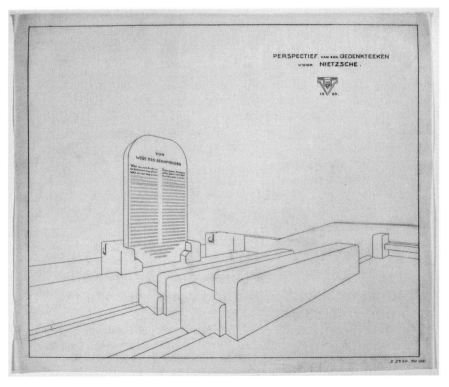

FIGURE 4.14 Nietzsche Memorial, Kröller-Müller's 'Museum Park', Holland (1925, Henry van de Velde). Sketch. Collection ENSAVE – La Cambre, Bruxelles, inv.4583. © Henry van de Velde Foundation (Pays-Bas).

The focus of van de Velde's monument is a stone tablet engraved with teachings of Zarathustra. The tablet is flanked by two sets of steps leading to a platform, and its position on a natural bulge in the ground gives the impression of an ancient cromlech. At the fringes of parkland, it would be a place discovered by walkers in quiet contemplation. The simplicity of the design and its relatively isolated surroundings addresses Nietzsche's notion of empty form to encourage the visitor to self-reflect with guidance from Zarathustra. A perspective drawing of the inscribed tablet reveals the quotation selected by van de Velde is from the chapter, 'Of the Way of the Creator' ('Vom Wege des Schaffenden') in *Thus Spoke Zarathustra*. The drawing depicts two columns of text tapering into one. Apart from the chapter heading, the drawing reveals only the impression of text, but the extent of it suggests the chapter would have been inscribed in full. In this chapter Zarathustra defines the qualities of creative individuals and emphasizes that few will be able to tolerate and affirm the solitude that true creativity requires. The message draws the visitor's attention to themselves, to the monument and to their shared remote setting, establishing an intimate relationship between them.

In a later chapter of *Thus Spoke Zarathustra*, titled, 'On Old and New Tablets', we find Zarathustra sitting in wait, with broken tablets of the old laws scattered around him, and with new tablets half written. He sits in wait for the occasion when the new laws can be completed by the arrival of a new style of creative individual who is able to compose them. Sadly, this monument to Nietzsche by van de Velde remained unfinished too. I shall revisit it in the final chapter where I discuss it in relation to Bruno Taut's design from 1919, *Monument des Neuen Gesetzes* (Monument to a New Law).

Nietzsche Memorial Hall, Weimar: Paul Schultze-Naumburg (1934–44)

After the War Förster-Nietzsche joined the German National People's Party and throughout the 1920s she solicited admirers of Nietzsche with far-right political beliefs, especially those who could contribute financially to the Nietzsche-Archiv.[20] From May 1934 she began to receive a monthly allowance of 300 reichsmarks from Hitler's private funds 'for her services in preserving and publicising Nietzsche's work' (Galindo 1995:182). Kessler recorded his disgust of the increasing Nazification of the Archiv in his diaries: 'in the archives, everybody from the servant up to the major is a Nazi.' It is enough to make 'one want to cry' (Diary, 7 August 1932; Kessler 1918–37/1961:681–3).

Förster-Nietzsche first met Hitler in January 1932 at the premiere of Mussolini's play, *Campo di Maggio* (100 days of Napoleon), at the National Theatre in Weimar. She invited him to the Archiv at Villa

Silberblick for the following day. He accepted, and was accompanied by his architect, Paul Schultze-Naumburg. Hitler would visit Villa Silberblick with various Nazi officials, including Albert Speer (architect and Minister of Armaments), Fritz Sauckel (Reich Governor and Gauleiter of Thuringia), and Wilhelm Frick (Reich Minister of the Interior). It is unclear when the plans for a Memorial Hall to Nietzsche were first discussed, and whose idea it was, but it is assumed to have been Hitler's initiative with full support from Förster-Nietzsche and her colleagues at the Archiv. We know that following Hitler's visit to Villa Silberblick on 2 October 1934 he donated 50,000 Reichsmarks from his private funds to establish a 'Nietzsche Memorial Fund', with its remit to construct a Memorial Hall next to the Villa with Schultze-Naumburg as its architect (Figs. 4.15 and 4.16).[21] A committee was established to oversee its design, comprising Schultze-Naumburg, its architect, and representatives from both the Nazi Party (Fritz Schaukel) and Nietzsche Archive Foundation (including Förster-Nietzsche). Förster-Nietzsche died five years before the hall was completed. Hitler attended her funeral,[22] and the building would never be used for its intended purpose.

FIGURE 4.15 Nietzsche Memorial Hall, Weimar. Main entrance. View from Luisenstrasße (now Humboldstraße). Author's photograph.

FIGURE 4.16 Nietzsche Memorial Hall and the Nietzsche-Archiv, Villa Silberblick. View from Luisenstrasße (now Humboldstraße). Author's photograph.

An ambiguous priority for Hitler

The myth of Nietzsche as a prophet of Nazi ideology was fabricated in large part by Förster-Nietzsche and others – such as Alfred Rosenberg (1893–1946) and Alfred Bäumler (1887–1968) – by their twisting of Nietzsche's words and ideas to fit Nazi political agenda. The extent of Nietzsche's influence on Hitler and the Nazi movement is uncertain, but it is widely recognized that Hitler barely read Nietzsche and had little interest in Nietzsche's ideas beyond a profoundly flawed interpretation of the *Übermensch*, the master race, and the will to power as justifications for the domination and subjugation of others.[23] The Nietzsche Hall project as a proposed cultural centre for the Third Reich presents us with a useful case study for assessing the extent to which Hitler valued Nietzsche's ideas and philosophical legacy in their own right and as a useful political commodity.

Schultze-Naumburg, the architect entrusted with the design of the Nietzsche Hall, was a founder of the Deutscher Werkbund, and director of the State College for Architecture and Crafts in Weimar – a newly installed institute to replace the Bauhaus School of architecture and art.

Schultze-Naumburg's architecture was informed by principles of *Blut und Boden* ('Blood and Soil') and his buildings were influenced by German rustic 'homeland' styles, often modelled on the traditional farmhouse and village community.[24] In 1928 he published *Kunst und Rasse* (*Art and Race*), and two years later he put his ideas into practice with Wilhelm Frick by systematically purging the Weimar Schlossmuseum of its 'degenerate' modernist paintings. Despite Schultze-Naumburg's dismissal of radically modern art and architecture, his career with the Nazi Party was heavily tainted when he spoke out against the architectural style that was increasingly employed by the regime as excessive in its monumentalism. He described such buildings as 'wantonly parvenu' and was duly punished for it (Kitchen 2017:31). After 1935 he received no major contracts, and he was forced into retirement from his position in Weimar. The Nietzsche Hall commission would be his final large building. In Chapter 5, I revisit Schultze-Naumburg's views about architecture within the context of Nietzsche's position in the ideological struggle for a new German architecture.

It is widely assumed that Schultze-Naumburg was Hitler's choice of architect for the Hall but given Förster-Nietzsche's long-standing friendship with the architect over several decades, his selection may have been at her request. If Schultze-Naumburg had been Hitler's choice, it would strongly suggest the Nietzsche Hall was a relatively low priority for him, and by extension, that he did not perceive Nietzsche's legacy as a powerful resource to further his political agenda. Had the Hall been of greater interest to Hitler, he would probably have assigned the project to one of his more trusted architects, to Albert Speer, Paul Ludwig Troost (1878–1934) or Hermann Giesler (1898–1987).

Hitler certainly seemed enthusiastic at the start of the project, and even took time for an impromptu visit to Villa Silberblick in October 1935 to reassure Förster-Nietzsche personally that the building would go ahead. Just a month before, Hitler gave his lecture, *Kunst und Politik* (Art and Politics) – delivered as the second address of his annual culture lecture series (*Kulturtagung*) at the seventh National Socialist Congress at Nuremberg on 11 September 1935. There he described his intention to revive the creative powers of the nation through architecture. There is no better way, he proclaimed, to convey the creative powers of the nation, than through the construction of grand buildings (*Grossartiger Gebäude*) in homage to the 'few' creative German individuals who have reached 'the highest pitch of human achievement' (1936:41). These buildings, he says, will 'imprint' the 'cultural stamp of the German race' for all time (1936:42). Although Hitler doesn't name these creative individuals, he says enough for Richard Oehler to believe Hitler had given his public endorsement for a monument to Nietzsche, or at least, justification for one. Oehler subsequently writes to Förster-Nietzsche on 16 September, with his 'delight' upon hearing the 'wonderful, grand speech of our dear leader', because 'it corresponds entirely to my view that Nietzsche in particular, but also Richard Wagner, ought to receive great building structures as documents for posterity to characterise the present time' (GSA, 72/2597). The timing of Hitler's impromptu visit, so soon after the Party Congress, to confirm his desire for the Nietzsche Hall suggests Hitler may have had Nietzsche in mind when he gave his speech.

As time went on, the building seemed to become less important to Hitler. In his memoires, Speer alludes disparagingly to the project and its architect:

> Hitler undertook to finance an annex to the old Nietzsche house, and Frau Förster-Nietzsche was willing to have Schultze-Naumburg design it. 'He's better at that sort of thing, doing something in keeping with the old house,' Hitler remarked. He was plainly pleased to be able to offer the architect some small sop.
>
> (1970/2009:109)

It is telling that Hitler, who was normally eager to oversee the smallest of details of construction projects in Germany, deferred all decisions about the design of the Nietzsche Hall to its Committee members – to the Nietzsche Archive Foundation, Fritz Schaukel and Schultze-Naumburg. At the time, Hitler was more interested in the design of the huge *Gauzentrum* in Weimar. Designed by Giesler, this would be the first of the *Gauforen* (Gauforum) buildings, and as such, its design was a model for others planned for each Gau capital in Germany, and thus also an architectural symbol of the governing centres of power in the Third Reich. Schultze-Naumburg, keen to win favour with Hitler, submitted a design proposal for the Gauforen, which Hitler 'threw away' and subsequently set in motion a competition for its design among Hitler's preferred architects (Speer 1970/2009:108). Speer suggests that Schultze-Naumburg's awful plans for the Gauforen led Hitler to give him the Nietzsche Hall project as a consolation prize. Speer recounts Hitler's vicious rejection of Schultze-Naumburg's design for the *Gauforen*, with Hitler describing it as 'an oversized marketplace for a provincial town' and describing Schultze-Naumburg as better suited to developing 'old houses' (Speer 1970/2009). Speer recalls Hitler's 'total disregard' for Schultze-Naumburg's reputation, with Hitler disallowing Schultze-Naumburg the opportunity to defend his proposal (Speer 1970/2009).

There would be no competition for the Nietzsche Hall; Hitler simply assigned it to an architect he held in relatively low esteem. The unfavourable perception of Schultze-Naumburg continued within the Nietzsche Hall Committee and among Nietzscheans, whom Krause argues, 'consoled themselves by pointing to the weak will of the architect' whenever they 'felt uneasy about Schultze-Naumburg's plans' (1984:223). Indeed, Adalbert Oehler sought to remove Schultze-Naumburg from the project and open the commission to competition among other architects on the grounds that 'Professor Schultze-N was once, but today is no longer the man who can create such a task [...] in accordance with the spirit of the new age, and the artistic ideals of National Socialism' (Letter to Förster-Nietzsche, 9 August

1935; GSA, 72/2597). His brother, Max, intercepted his plans, insisting: 'You can't! The Führer ascertained that Schultze-Nbg should carry out the construction' (Letter to Adalbert Oehler, 3 March 1936; GSA,72/2598).

Whatever enthusiasm Hitler had for the Nietzsche Hall waned significantly from October 1939. While other construction projects were hastened and forced through, even during the first years of war, the Nietzsche Hall was put on hold. By this time, the shell of the building was mostly complete, and during the topping out ceremony on 3 August 1938 (which was attended by Nazi officials other than Hitler, including Josef Goebbels as the Reich Minister for Public Enlightenment and Propaganda, and Fritz Sauckel as Gauleiter of Thuringia), only the stone inscription, hastily installed, represented Hitler's endorsement for the building (See Figure 4.24). It read: '*Nietzsche zum Gedächtnis – Erbaut unter Adolf Hitler – Im VI. Jahre des III. Reiches*' (Nietzsche in Memory – Built Under Adolf Hitler – In the 6th Year of the Third Reich).

A hall of ambiguity and contradiction, lacking unity of style

The ambiguity of Hitler's concern for the Hall was mirrored in the ambiguity of its design and function. At the start it was unclear whether the Hall was intended as a memorial to honour Nietzsche as a prophet of the Third Reich or as a National Cultural Centre of the Third Reich, whether it be a 'cult' building and place of pilgrimage or a place of study with utility rooms for archival work. Plans for the building developed to suggest a curious hybrid to accommodate all the above. The absence of a clearly defined project and strong management to see it through created a mishmash of competing opinions on how the Hall should look and function. It was impossible to second guess how the Führer would like the Hall to appear, and there was no official or distinctive architectural style of the Nazi Party to provide a useful guide. The Nietzsche Hall project suffered from the start from inconsistency and incoherency among those invested in the project. There was no unity of conviction – no organizing instinct or will to power – to shape the design, but a collection of contradictory wills and aspirations. As discussed, a key criterion of the grand style, the *one needful thing*, is to govern and to form with 'a single taste' – 'Whether this taste were good or bad is less important than one might suppose, if only it were a single taste!' (GS,290). In this respect, the Nietzsche Hall exemplifies the architecture that Nietzsche disparages for its lack of style and conviction, for its mere *assembly* of forms and opinions.

Fritz Sauckel and members of the Nietzsche-Archiv Foundation championed the Nietzsche Hall even after Hitler apparently lost interest in it. Sauckel wanted a prestigious ceremonial Hall to rival other cultural centres of Germany like Bayreuth. He saw in this project an opportunity to construct a grand monument of national significance to exemplify the spirit of National Socialism. For him, the Nietzsche Hall would respond directly to Hitler's rallying call for such buildings at the recent Party conference. To construct such a building so soon after Hitler's speech in Weimar (the capital city, and first Nazi capital city, and city of Sauckel's jurisdiction as *Reichsstatthalter* of Thuringia) would have been eminently satisfying for Sauckel. In stark contrast to Sauckel's vision, Förster-Nietzsche had in mind something more modest: although still 'magnificent', she wanted a building in a 'simple style', similar in dimensions to Villa Silberblick to house the practical work of the archives (Letter to Schultze-Naumburg, 21 July 1935; GSA,72,2597).

There were contrasting views within the Nietzsche camp too. Adalbert Oehler took issue with van de Velde's renovations for Villa Silberblick and wanted for the Hall a completely different style, one less abstract and more representative of the German Volk. To Förster-Nietzsche he writes: 'The symbolism of the architecture of a Henri van de Felde [sic] must certainly not be used here' (4 August 1935; GSA,72,2597[25]). He wanted the Hall to be a site of 'pilgrimage' and 'sanctuary for the German people' in the style of 'Nordic Germanic architecture' and of grand proportions like 'new, large buildings of the National Socialist Party' in Munich (GSA,72,259). Adalbert Oehler envisioned the Hall as a monument to National Socialism, with Nietzsche playing a secondary role as its spokesperson. He wanted to select various maxims of Nietzsche, which anticipated – as he interpreted them – ideals of National socialism, such as, he says, 'ideas of advanced breeding' (*Idee der Höherzüchtung*). He thought these abstract sayings, rather than the personality of Nietzsche, could be made the 'objects of veneration' for the masses of people who would come here on pilgrimage (GSA,72,259). Richard Oehler, by contrast, praised van de Velde's work at Villa Silberblick as a building of 'creative power' that makes people feel 'at home' irrespective of whether they consider themselves a disciple of Zarathustra (1935/1938:12). On 15 October 1934, just thirteen days after Hitler visited Villa Silberblick and donated funds for the Nietzsche Memorial Fund, Richard Oehler presents his vision for the Nietzsche Hall at the Nietzsche-Archiv as a lecture, as part of the commemorations for Nietzsche's ninetieth Birthday (Wollkopf 1991). He also wrote a pamphlet titled, *Gedanken über die Nietzsche-Gedenk-Halle* ('Thoughts on a Nietzsche Memorial Hall'). His vision was a sacred hall to function alongside Villa Silberblick to 'preserve and strengthen' the 'non-religious, intellectual, artistic, cultural, creative and living movement' of Nietzsche (1935/1938:13). Together the two buildings would establish a 'cult site' intended to 'awaken creative experiences' in those who visited.

The sculptural programme for the Nietzsche Hall was also a focus of dispute for the Committee overseeing it, with no clear vision of which Nietzschean motif should take centre stage – should it be Zarathustra, Dionysus and Apollo, or Nietzsche himself? And how best to convey its symbolic value? Schultze-Naumburg's designs for the Hall invited continual critique and interventions by Sauckel, Förster-Nietzsche and the Oehlers.

The evolving design

Elisabeth Förster-Nietzsche died on 8 November 1935, but not before Schultze-Naumburg had circulated the first designs for the Hall for comment. Sketches for the initial design from March 1935 show a building or corridor connecting the Hall to the Villa. The Hall is announced with a pillared portico and large French doors with a circular motif above (Figures 4.17 and 4.18). The entrance to the Memorial Hall itself opened to another corridor, this one was long and thin with high walls clad in wood in a diagonal arrangement. The corridor was described as *Philosophengang* ('Philosopher's walk') and it was intended to function as a ceremonial passageway featuring a gallery of portraits of thinkers who had inspired Nietzsche, or 'ancestors of Zarathustra' (Oehler 1935/1938:14) (see bottom of Figures 4.18 and Figure 4.19). The walkway would open to a large festive room with a semi-circular apse that would house a large statue of Nietzsche or Zarathustra (see Figure 4.20). The intended effect of the passageway was to evoke for the visitor a spiritual experience guided by Nietzsche's philosophy, presented here as an eternal philosophy, with its roots in revered cultural traditions of the past and its vision firmly set on a creative future. The walker's attention would be given to the looming statue in front of them, which would become ever larger with each step, and by busts of thinkers at their side as important

FIGURE 4.17 Nietzsche Memorial Hall and Villa Silberblick with connecting building, Weimar. Sketch by Paul Schultze-Naumburg, March 1935. © Goethe und Schiller Archiv. Foto: Klassik Stiftung Weimar. GSA 72/2599.

BUILDINGS TO 'HONOUR' NIETZSCHE

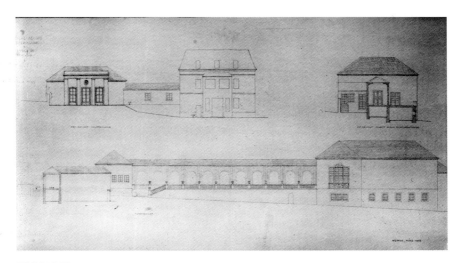

FIGURE 4.18 Nietzsche Memorial Hall and Villa Silberblick, with connecting building, from the East (top left). Cross section of Philosopher's walkway from East (top right). Memorial Hall, showing the Philosopher's walkway, from the North (bottom). Plans by Paul Schultze-Naumburg, March 1935. © Goethe und Schiller Archiv. Foto: Klassik Stiftung Weimar. GSA 72/2602.

FIGURE 4.19 Nietzsche Memorial Hall, Weimar. View from the Philosopher's walkway, looking towards the apse in the Main Hall. Photograph, 1943. © Goethe und Schiller Archiv. Foto: Klassik Stiftung Weimar, 1943. GSA 72/2610.

FIGURE 4.20 Nietzsche Memorial Hall, Weimar. Festive room with apse. Photograph, 1943. © Goethe und Schiller Archiv. Foto: Klassik Stiftung Weimar. GSA 72/2620.

stations, marking the wider cultural ground of the ceremonial walk. This feature is reminiscent of van de Velde's temple design for Kessler, with its evocative walkway that led to an altar with a statue or herm of Nietzsche. According to Richard Oehler, the Hall was designed to 'uplift' the visitor and encourage them to participate in the architectural spectacle. The Nietzsche-Zarathustra sculpture was integral to this experience, intended to captivate the visitor with its 'spell', so they would leave with an 'unforgettable experience' (1935/1938:14).

It was unclear at the time whether the festive room would have a specific function. Writing three years after its initial design, Richard Oehler still questions the kinds of activities that would take place there, but he refers to the room as a lecture hall and meeting room, and he proposes its use for educational activities to establish 'communities of higher men' (1935/1938:13). Running parallel to this room is a terrace with a stone balustrade, providing unbroken views to the city (Loos 1999:183,189; Bogner 2018:53).

The initial design of the Memorial Hall was rejected by the Committee. Sauckel thought them too simplistic and 'meagre' and unworthy of Nietzsche's significance (Krause 1984:223; Loos 1999:186). Förster-Nietzsche objected to the connecting corridor to the Villa, and she requested that in addition to the large room, there ought to be offices, conference rooms and a library. She also insisted that the building should reflect the dimension of Villa Silberblick and have a similar 'solemn portal'. Förster-Nietzsche had clearly moved on from her earlier desire for a temple-building, for she explicitly requests that the Hall not look like a temple, for this, she says, would 'ruin' the 'whole style of the area and its simple style', and although the style is 'unfortunately, a bit petty bourgeois' it 'has to be maintained because it corresponds to the time my brother lived there!' (Letter to Schultze-Naumburg, 21 July 1935; GSA,72,2597). Förster-Nietzsche supplements her requests to Schultze-Naumburg with a sketch of a staggered sequence of rooms, including a lobby, a library and conference room, the original festive room with the terrace facing the city, and two pavilions at the corners of the room (Bogner 2018:53).

The plans were returned to Schultze-Naumburg, who presented a revised design with two variants in October 1935. Neither was accepted. 'Solution A' appears more restrained. It no longer includes the connecting corridor to the Villa or the *Philosophengang* (Loos 1999:189). The revised plan features two

FIGURE 4.21 Nietzsche Memorial Hall, Weimar. Model, with figures of Apollo and Dionysus flanking the main entrance. Photograph, January 1937. © Goethe und Schiller Archiv. Foto: Klassik Stiftung Weimar. GSA 72/2610.

storeys, and includes, on the ground floor, the apse and terrace, cloakrooms, work rooms, meeting rooms and the central festive room with a skylight. The library would occupy the upper floor. The plans for 'Solution B' are now lost (Bogner 2018:53; Loos 1999:185), but the minutes of a meeting of the Nietzsche Memorial Foundation suggest that 'Solution B' was the preferred choice, and that with substantial developments it would be presented to Hitler for inspection and approval without delay (Loos 1999:185).

Schultze-Naumburg's third design substantially changes the placement of the office spaces, now separated from the ceremonial spaces with their own wing and made accessible from the entrance hall. These draft plans were finalized and a model of them was made (for Hitler was known to appreciate architectural models more than drawn plans) in time for Hitler's visit to Weimar for the Nazi Party rally in July 1936 (Figures 4.21 and 4.22). But it took several months for the plans to be approved. On 16 March 1937, Speer wrote to Sauckel to confirm Hitler's approval of the design, and

FIGURE 4.22 Nietzsche Memorial Hall, Weimar. Model, showing apse. Photograph, January 1937. © Goethe und Schiller Archiv. Foto: Klassik Stiftung Weimar. GSA 72/2610.

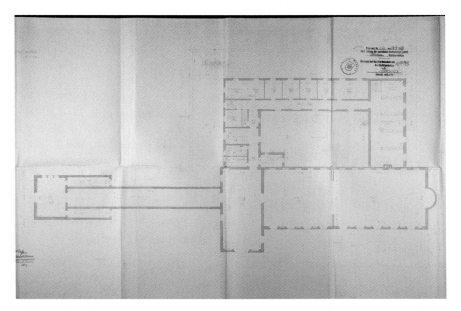

FIGURE 4.23 Nietzsche Memorial Hall, Weimar. Ground floor plan of final design. July 1937. © Goethe und Schiller Archiv. Foto: Klassik Stiftung Weimar. GSA 72/2602.

Schultze-Naumburg confirmed the good news to Max Oehler two weeks later. On 24 June 1937, after two years of planning, the building contract was awarded to Schultze-Naumburg (Bogner 2018:58, n.54). The plans from July 1937 correspond approximately to the final design (Figures 4.23 and Figure 4.16). Construction began in mid-July 1937 with the laying of the foundation stone in the presence of senior Nazi officials and its construction continued intermittently during the War.

The final design

The Nietzsche Hall is a rather plain and austere next-door neighbour of Villa Silberblick. The brick building clad in natural stone is on an east-west axis, approximately 90 metres in length and a floor area of almost 5,000 metres square. The main entrance is accessible from the street, set off from the road by a gate. Life-sized statues of Dionysus and Apollo were intended to flank the limestone portal of the main entrance (see detail of Figure 4.21). This leads to a one-storey cloak room, which was intended to have parquet flooring and busts of Nietzsche and Hitler, each made from black marble. The cloak room opened to two narrow reception rooms, either side of the

30m corridor. The corridor would be aligned with sixteen busts on plinths of Nietzsche's 'spiritual ancestors', of poets, thinkers and musicians, each alternating with display cases of memorabilia from Nietzsche's family. A glazed skylight in the ceiling provided natural light from above (see Figure 4.19). The corridor led to a small hall that could hold 200 people (the lecture hall and meeting room that Richard Oehler describes). This room had a coffered ceiling, and at its northern end, was a simple high French window with a rounded arch. The window had a small balcony to allow the visitor to step outside and view the garden of Villa Silberblick, and adjacent to the window was a glazed door which led out to the terrace, with extended views of the Villa's grounds and across to Weimar.

The hall led to a larger festival hall, almost 8 metres in height that could hold up to 600 people (see Figure 4.20). The hall could be divided into two rooms with a door set into a partition. Both parts of the room had a floor-to-ceiling French window that led to the terrace, running parallel to the hall. The terrace had a single staircase to the garden. The main hall was intended to have just one decorative feature: the huge Nietzsche-Zarathustra sculpture in a semi-circular apse, positioned in the line of sight of the main entrance. The layout of this part of the building encouraged the visitor to engage in ceremonious activities. They would enter the building via the large formal portal announced by Nietzsche's gods, walk with reverence along the corridor of Nietzsche's intellectual heroes lit from above, with an uninhibited view of the ever-looming statue of Nietzsche.

Connected to both halls is the second wing of the building, which would house the library and office spaces on two storeys, with a caretaker's apartment on the lower floor. This wing was intended for everyday use, and its aesthetic style conveyed the functional utility of its rooms. While the ceremonial wing would have parquet and marble floors, the flooring of its administrative areas was cork. The U-shaped administrative wing connects with the ceremonial wing to establish a small atrium in the centre of the complex.

After its completion, the national press described it variously as a 'castle of the German spirit' (*Burg deutschen Geistes*), a 'church' and a 'monastery' with rooms for 'contemplation' and its atrium reminiscent of a cloister (Bogner 2018:54). The idea was floated to turn the complex into a mausoleum for Nietzsche. Earlier I noted that Förster-Nietzsche wished for her brother's bodily remains to be moved from his grave in Röcken to Villa Silberblick, and we find the idea resurface in connection with the Hall as a site for his grave. Adalbert Oehler suggested that 'a young couple of Nordic-Germanic character [...] who want to get married' could do so in front of 'Nietzsche's tomb' (Letter to Förster-Nietzsche, 4 August 1935; GSA, 72,2597). The tomb would depict Nietzsche's Zarathustra with the legislation of marriage or a mighty eagle who holds the bill in its talons (see Krause 1984:205–6,224). Presumably the tomb would replace the anticipated huge Nietzsche-Zarathustra sculpture at the end of the building.

Sculptural disarray

The 'topping out' ceremony of the Hall took place on 3 August 1938 (Figure 4.24), and the exterior was mostly built by 1939. The interior fittings – the floor, stairs, and stonemasonry and marble work – continued into the following year but plans for the Nietzschean-Zarathustra sculpture went on for another four years. The construction work was never fully completed. Because the Nietzsche Hall was not a priority for Hitler, its financial support was not guaranteed and rising costs were not met. Sauckel's interest in the building waned significantly from 1939. On 19 January 1940 he reported that the construction would not continue for the foreseeable future, and in 1943 he announced that no financial investment in the building would be made during the war (Bogner 2014:63; Loos 1999:192–3). Despite this, the Nietzsche Foundation, through the Oehlers, continued to push to find a suitable sculpture for the Hall. Bogner (2018) suggests that the search for the sculpture caused Hitler to distance himself further from the project. Certainly, Richard Oehler suspected that Hitler was not keen on the idea of a symbolic rendition of Nietzsche's ideas in the guise of a Zarathustra. To his brother, Max, he remarks that Hitler preferred a portrayal of Nietzsche's physical likeness (8 October 1940; GSA,72,2613-2).[26]

The search for suitable sculptures for the Hall was marked with frustration and disagreement. The German sculptor Emil Hipp, renowned

FIGURE 4.24 Nietzsche Memorial Hall. Topping out ceremony, 3 August 1938. Photograph. © Goethe und Schiller Archiv. Foto: Klassik Stiftung Weimar. GSA 72/2610.

for his neo-classical style, was invited by Schultze-Naumburg and Max and Richard Oehler to produce working sketches of a large Nietzsche sculpture for the main hall, and also for a sculpture of Zarathustra's two animals, the eagle and snake, to adorn the two pillars of the entrance gate. They invited other sculptors to design busts of Hitler, Dionysus and Apollo for the entrance hall, and the sixteen busts for the *Philosophengang*. They also sought to purchase older sculptures of Nietzsche, including a herm that Max Klinger had designed in 1914 for the publisher Alfred Kröner (Dietrich and Erbsmehl 2004:162–4). Max Oehler was disappointed with the various proposals that had been submitted. He was particularly amused by the sculpture proposed by Fritz Müller-Camphausen (1901–55) of a seated Nietzsche with a rather 'tame' looking eagle and lion. While Schultze-Naumburg wanted the Committee to endorse Müller-Camphausen's design and to have him design the sixteen busts, Max Oehler preferred Georg Kolbe's (1877–1947) sculpture of Zarathustra. Hitler quickly rejected Kolbe's Zarathustra in September 1940 as 'completely unsuitable', without explanation.[27] According to Krause, the sculpture may have been too modernistic and abstract for Hitler's tastes (1984:231–2). Emil Hipp (1893–1965) crafted models for the figures of Apollo and Dionysus for the entrance to the Hall, which were dismissed by Richard Oehler as bizarre 'dancing dervishes': 'Nobody can understand what these dancing dervishes up there are supposed to be doing' (Letter to Max Oehler, 26 January 1940; GSA 72/2612).[28] Müller-Camphausen was commissioned to design the busts, but only five were cast in bronze, and others in metal were discontinued due to the war.

By April 1942, the year of Nietzsche's 100th birthday, decisions about the main sculpture had not progressed. At this point Georg Lüttke (1884–1963), a publisher of Schultze-Naumburg, suggested the idea of placing an authentic antiquity in the apse of the main hall in reverence to Nietzsche, and Benito Mussolini – a great admirer of Nietzschean philosophy – responded by gifting a Roman replica of a Greek statue of a clothed and bearded Dionysus by Praxiteles, which he had required illegally from the National Museum of Rome. Its transportation to Weimar proved cumbersome due in part to the collapse of fascism in southern and central Italy in the summer of 1943. It eventually arrived in Weimar on 29 January 1944, at a time when Weimar was under attack from US aircraft. Remarkably, Max Oehler brought the antique statue of Dionysus from the train station in Weimar to Villa Silberblick in a horse-driven cart under a hail of bombs. But it turned out to be far too large for the hall! (Bogner 2018:48). It was subsequently buried in its transportation box in the garden of Villa Silberblick (Emmrich 2000a:68) and then kept in a storeroom in Villa Silberblick until 1954, after which it was exhibited in the Pergamon Museum in Berlin before returning to Italy in 1990 (Block 2006:147).

The Nietzsche Hall would be used for many activities, but never for its intended uses as a ceremonial hall and for archival study. During the war it became an air-raid shelter, and took on various functions, including 'home rooms' (*Heimaträume*) for the Hitler Youth, a training office for the Gau and a military hospital. After the war, the Nietzsche-Archiv was recognized as a dangerous centre for National Socialist propaganda and Villa Silberblick was closed; Max Oehler as director of the Archiv was imprisoned by the Soviet Military Administration in Germany. On 21 October 1949 the Archiv was transferred to the Goethe und Schiller Archive in Weimar, and the rooms of Villa Silberblick were converted for use by the Working Seminar for Young Scientists in the German Democratic Republic (Arbeitsseminar für den Wissenscharftlichen Nachwuchs der Deutschen Demokratishcen Republik). The Nietzsche Hall was used by the National Research and Memorial Centres of Classical German Literature in Weimar (Nationalen Forschungs und Gedenkstätten der klassischen deutschen Literatur in Weimar) and was later converted into a broadcasting studio for a radio station serving Weimar. An extra floor was added at this time, and the Hall was converted into two rooms with seating areas and a stage, with the offices developed into sixty rooms for the workers. The windows, walls and apse of the main hall were sealed with sound-proof cladding.[29]

CHAPTER FIVE

Nietzsche and the new style

Many claims are made about Nietzsche's influence on modern architecture, some are significant, others generalized and vague. We are told, for instance, that Nietzsche was the forerunner of modern architecture (Garnham 2013:70; Kostka and Wohlfarth 1999); that his ideas about aesthetics underpin the aspirations of architectural theories of the late nineteenth century and designs of the early twentieth century (Breitschmid 2001:6); that decades after Nietzsche's death, architects were inspired by his nod towards reductionist designs without ornament (Buddensieg 1999:266; Neumeyer 2001/2004:184–5); and that architects sought to give practical expression to his philosophy through the creation of real and imagined Nietzschean 'life styles' (Aschheim 1994:33).

Nietzsche's name occasionally appears in commentaries by or about popular modern architects. According to Heinz Wirz, Nietzsche had unmistakable influence on the history of architecture after his death at the turn-of-the-century, and helped to shape the architectural ideas of 'Louis H. Sullivan,[1] Otto Wagner,[2] Adolf Loos, Peter Behrens,[3] Ludwig Mies van der Rohe, Erich Mendelsohn,[4] Henry van de Velde,[5] Le Corbusier,[6] Jacobus Johannes Pieter Oud, [and] Theo van Doesburg' (2001:5). Nadir Lahiji notes, 'The list of twentieth-century architects who took up the task of reading Nietzsche is long. It runs from Henry van de Velde to Peter Behrens,[7] Bruno Taut,[8] Walter Gropius,[9] Mies van der Rohe, Ludwig Hilberseimer,[10] Le Corbusier, Erich Mendelsohn, Richard Neutra, and many more' (2019:78). Buddensieg notes, 'In no context was [Nietzsche's] experience of chaos and anarchy so intense as in the architecture and décor of cities and private houses; and so it is no wonder that around the turn of the century, architects and designers such as Henry van de Velde, the Arts and Crafts reformers in Munich, the artists' colony in Darmstädt, Karl Ernst Osthaus in Hagen, and the German Werkbund all cited the same texts by Nietzsche' (1999:261). Neumeyer notes, 'By 1914 – as can be seen by their letters, diaries, and other utterances – Bruno Taut, Le Corbusier, Walter Gropius, Ludwig Hilberseimer, Erich Mendelsohn, and Richard Neutra had all passed through a Nietzschean experience that was to influence their subsequent architectural ideas' (1999:288).

When Nietzsche's name is discussed in the contexts of these architects, there is often little attempt to solicit evidence to corroborate a direct or explicit influence of Nietzsche's ideas on them. In such cases we must concede that Nietzsche's influence was at best implicit or probable. Nevertheless, valuable insights have been made into common ideas and concerns of Nietzsche and those architects who may have been influenced by him and who went on to have a formidable impact on the development of modern architecture.

To arrive at a nuanced assessment of Nietzsche's influence on architects and architecture in the first half of the twentieth century is difficult. According to Elie Haddad, van de Velde approached Nietzsche's ideas as a convert, rather than a scholarly critic (2005:93), and the same could be said for many architects I consider here. Because Nietzsche's ideas were pervasive throughout Germany and further afield around this time, they were often adopted without acknowledgement or critique. Consequently, when Nietzsche is identified as an influence on the theories and designs of the architects discussed here, closer scrutiny may reveal the influence to be much broader or general than has otherwise been suggested. The architect may have had passing familiarity with Nietzsche's ideas – perhaps a popular reading of a general theme or specific motif in his writings, rather than a substantial engagement with his philosophical position. One often finds a 'pick and mix approach' to Nietzsche's ideas to fit the aspirations of the architect or client – with Nietzsche's vision of the *Übermensch*, his rejection of historicism coupled with the desire for a new dawn, and the will to power as the most popular. Again, in the context of van de Velde, but applicable to other architects, Haddad concedes that van de Velde's revolt against current taste and 'decadence' never translates fully into a distinctly *Nietzschean* revolt against morality or an open challenge to social and religious norms (2005).

Similarly, when it is claimed that an architect in the early twentieth century had read Nietzsche, it is often revealed that they dipped into Nietzsche's most popular work – *Thus Spoke Zarathustra* – or perhaps an anthology of Nietzsche's aphorisms, which were translated into several languages and widely available throughout Europe at the time. Zarathustra's rousing call upon artists to create a new style or way of being may have been inspiration enough for many aspiring architects at the time to claim Nietzsche as an influence: 'O my brothers, I direct and consecrate you to a new nobility: you shall become begetters and cultivators and sowers of the future – ' (Z, III,12[12]:220). Of the architects named above, we know several had read parts of *Thus Spoke Zarathustra*, with some annotating their copies of the work and referencing it in their own writings. Some have suggested that Le Corbusier and Sullivan went further by emulating its lyrical style and prophetic tone in their own writings and may even have modelled themselves on the figure of Zarathustra. I analyse this in the next chapter.[11]

Because Nietzsche's architectural ideas are scattered throughout his writings, not as self-contained reflections on aesthetic design but interlinked with his wider philosophical vision, they are difficult to grasp. I have understood them in the context of his notion of the grand style, which draws upon his views on art and German culture, often in response to Wagner and his readings of Semper and others who sought to revive the German spirit. It is therefore difficult to extract a definitive Nietzschean theory of architecture, and when we examine the influence of Nietzsche's ideas on modern architects and architectural movements, we need to bear in mind that this influence often extends to those who Nietzsche himself identified with, either through agreement or critique. For instance, Miller Lane (1985) in *Architecture and Politics in Germany, 1918–1945* identifies the Wagner Cult as a key 'ancestor of the radical architects of the 1920s', for 'Wagner's view on the role of music in society resembles the radical architect's definition of the new architecture' (1985:7). From this it is but a small step for us to imagine how Nietzsche, Wagner's confidant and severe critic, was drawn by name into debates about the new architectural style, with the focus not so much on the content of Nietzsche's ideas but their general appeal to the common cause.

Inevitably, the ambiguous and elusive nature of Nietzsche's writing style contributed to contrasting interpretations of his philosophical vision by modern architects, especially those who utilized Nietzschean ideas in piecemeal fashion, appropriating or misappropriating them according to their own aspirations. For instance, the relationship between Nietzsche's rejection of historicism and his championing of empty form has been variously interpreted by architects who were supposedly influenced by his ideas. While Le Corbusier and Ludwig Mies van de Rohe emphasized the building's function and the simplicity of its materials, often with large areas of transparent glass and stark white surfaces as if a tabula rasa without reference to past traditions, others lifted symbolic imagery directly from Nietzsche's writings to incorporate Nietzsche's message literally within the fabric of their buildings as ornamental motifs, as we see, for instance, with Peter Behrens' 'Zarathustra' house (1901) and Bruno Taut's *Monument des Neuen Gesetzes* (1919). I will explain why I think these approaches fail to capture crucial nuances of Nietzsche's ideas. Nevertheless, it is important to recognize that the mere mention of Nietzsche's ideas by architects at this time – irrespective of whether the ideas were faithfully interpreted – demonstrates Nietzsche's potential influence in the development of modern architectural design. Furthermore, the various and diverse applications of the ideas he popularized have helped to extend and propagate the cultural legacy of Nietzschean thought more generally. And the fact that Nietzsche's ideas were actively adopted by a broad range of architectural ideologies and contrasting styles and designs suggests a creative openness entirely in keeping with the spirit of Nietzsche's philosophy with its call for creativity through the plurality of perspectives.

In this chapter I will examine some of the ideological concerns that were common to Nietzsche and to prominent early modern architects and movements that have been linked to Nietzsche, before I evaluate, in the next chapter, the extent to which some of these architectural theories and designs were genuinely influenced by Nietzsche and his idea of the grand style.

Competing for a 'new' style

The architecture that Nietzsche criticized during the latter half of the nineteenth century was fussy, with highly decorated façades cluttered with eclectic ornament. The degeneration of culture was conveyed through a profusion of gables, turrets and mouldings in a mishmash and recycling of historical styles, often favouring the Gothic and Baroque. The result was an inauthentic appeal to the Dionysian spirit – a superficial attempt to evoke a meaningful response in the onlooker, akin to the parody of affect that Nietzsche identified in Wagner's music. Architecture of this kind was thought by Nietzsche to bewilder and alienate, inviting people to reflect rationally on abstract ideas rather than entice them into more instinctual responses that enliven and encourage self-exploration. This decadent architecture colluded with the problematic gap, as Nietzsche saw it, between the intellectual mindset, which had come to dominate the culture of his day, and the instinctive body, which had been repressed.[12]

The resounding call for a new architectural style to elevate German culture and revive its spirit was interpreted and acted upon by an array of architects, whose responses were as varied as the styles and designs that necessitated their remedy. Nevertheless, common to most was the desire to move away from historical styles to a more organic architecture that would reflect the spirit of the times.

Figuring out the aesthetic details of this 'new style' of architecture led to inevitable political and ideological rifts and heated debates over whether, for instance, it ought to be wholly new and distanced entirely from historical tradition, and distinctly German or open to international influence. Nietzsche's ideas were cited in such discussions, often as philosophical justification for starkly different viewpoints and across a spectrum of designs proposed for the 'new style' – from utilitarian cubic or modular styles promoted by socialist and internationalist groups to 'German' styles, rooted in conservative narratives of race. The competitive struggle for styles would have appealed to Nietzsche's perspectivism and his desire for creative tension, but he would insist that no style or approach can credibly lay claim to be definitive as the one and only new style.

Germany was a fertile country for developments and experiments in modern architectural design due in large part to its identity crisis in the lead up to the First World War and the Weimar Republic that followed. The human horrors of the Great War marked for many a distrust of conventional values and systems of truth and meaning, and with that came a widespread rejection of traditional aesthetic styles. Radical values, rapid industrialization, and technological innovations in the production and use of new materials for building construction were all toyed with in the experiment for a new, more meaningful, architectural style.

The Deutscher Werkbund, the artist's colony at Darmstädt, and the Bauhaus

Of the architectural organizations associated with the origins of modern architecture and discussions of Nietzsche's ideas, the Deutscher Werkbund (*c.*1907–49), Darmstädt Colony (1899–1901) and the Bauhaus (1919–33) are most prominent.

The Deutscher Werkbund, which had developed out of the Dresden Exhibition of the Third German Applied Arts in 1906, is commonly regarded as the beginnings of twentieth-century modern German architecture and design. The Werkbund's aim was to invigorate German industry, enabling it to compete with its successful British and American counterparts, by making high-quality goods for mass-consumption that could improve and ennoble everyday objects[13] and raise the cultural expectations of ordinary German people. The Werkbund involved a diverse array of approaches and experiences of reform initiatives, voiced by an association of architects, artists, craftsmen, manufactures, and government officials from across Bavaria, Hessen, Württemberg, Saxony-Weimar-Eisenach and Saxony (Maciuika 2008:25).

Scholars are quick to associate the aims of the Werkbund with those of Nietzsche. Peter Bernhard, for instance, asserts the Werkbund 'ties directly to Nietzsche' [*knüpft unmittelbar an Nietzsche*], specifically to Nietzsche's criticism of the 'chaotic confusion forced by historicism of all styles' and its resolution in a 'unity of artistic styles in all expressions of life' (2008:274). But I think there are more interesting correspondences to be found, particularly with specific buildings that were showcased by the Werkbund. After the Great War the Werkbund focused almost exclusively on promoting its architectural vision of the new style within art journals and its exhibitions, in Cologne in 1914 and 1949, and in Stuttgart in 1927. In Chapter 7, I examine two notable buildings from its first exhibition in Cologne, which have been discussed in relation to Nietzschean ideas, a theatre by van de Velde and Bruno Taut's *Glashaus*.

In 1899, prior to the establishment of the Werkbund, Grand Duke Ernst Ludwig of Hessen (1868–1937) formed by decree a colony of artists in Darmstädt to transform through architectural experiment the small provincial Ducal capital into a pioneering centre of modern German culture. The duke, influenced by the British Arts and Crafts movement and its belief in the socially transformative power of the applied arts, recruited leading artists and architects from Germany to take up residence in a hilltop site known as the *Mathildenhöhe*, overlooking Darmstädt. The colony was simultaneously intended as a home and workplace for each artist and as an exhibition of an ideal life that is completely infused by art. Each artist was given a salary but was required to purchase the land upon which to build their house at rates subsided by the duke. Among architects who received contracts were Joseph Maria Olbrich (1867–1908), Otto Wagner (1841–1918) and Peter Behrens.

Although presented to the public as an ideal, egalitarian community where artists were free to develop their individual styles, the colony was largely shaped by Ducal policies and by hierarchical fractions among the architects due to their unequal salaries. Those on larger salaries were able to design more buildings and had greater access to higher quality materials. Olbrich, for instance, was commissioned to design the master plan of the site and most of the buildings, including its exhibition buildings and most of the artist residences that were on show for the first Darmstädt exhibition in 1901. The second most prominent architect in the established hierarchy was Peter Behrens, who had full control over the design of his own home, a building known as the 'Zarathustra house' due to its incorporation of symbolic motifs from Nietzsche's *Thus Spoke Zarathustra* – a building I examine in Chapter 7.

Nietzsche's inspiration at the colony is thought to extend beyond Behrens' house to the colony as a whole. Maciuika, for instance, goes so far as to claim that its architects 'competed to cast themselves as bearers of modern "Nietzschean" values' for the opening ceremony of the 1901 Exhibition (2008:40). This ceremony was called *Das Zeichen* (The Sign), and its intention was to announce the arrival of a new era for German art through the staging of its rebirth with great fanfare and theatrical drama. Behrens, working with the poet Georg Fuchs (1868–1949), choreographed a sombre ritualistic procession against the architectural backdrop of Ernst Ludwig's House (by Olbrich), with its imposing staircase that led up to a portal flanked by two 6-metre stone statues of a man and woman – husband and wife (by Ludwig Habich; 1872–1949), representing together strength and beauty (*Kraft und Schönheit*) (Figure 5.1). This design is reminiscent of the portal of the Nietzsche Memorial Hall with its statues of Dionysus and Apollo designed decades later by Paul Schultze-Naumburg. The artistic procession centred around the unveiling of a large crystal by a prophetic figure who appeared from the portal, while accompanied by a Greek chorus who sang Fuch's paean to the creative powers of the human soul.

Both the ritualistic nature of this ceremony and the symbolism of the crystal have been tenuously linked to Nietzsche's notion of Dionysian rebirth (see Aschheim 1994:33; Bletter 1981:30–1; Maciuika 2008:38–9).

FIGURE 5.1 Opening ceremony, Darmstädt Colony, *Das Zeichen*, 1901, with Ernst Ludwig House (1900–01, Joseph Olbrich). Photograph. © Institut Mathildenhöhe, Darmstädt Municipal Art Collection.

According to Bletter, for instance, the symbolism of the crystal as 'the sign' is a clear allusion to the last section of *Thus Spoke Zarathustra* – titled 'The Sign' ('*Das Zeichen*') – where Zarathustra emerges from his cave to embrace a new dawn (1981:31). Oddly, Bletter goes on to decode the meaning of Behrens' crystal as a desire to 'escape from reality', which is an interpretation Nietzsche would reject outright as metaphysical nonsense. In Chapter 7, I go on to examine various architectural projects that have been associated with Nietzsche on grounds of their extensive reference to crystal and glass symbolism. I subsequently evaluate the extent to which crystal motifs are distinctly *Nietzschean*.

The Darmstädt Colony received mixed reviews. According to Maciuika, they were as varied as contemporary interpretations of Nietzsche's philosophy tend to be (2008:42). Some celebrated its popular appeal, others – van de Velde and Harry Graf Kessler among them – denounced it as an elitist project, which compromised its own objectives of cultivating artistic freedom through its enormous expenses and curatorial approach. Either way, the buildings of the colony sought to elevate domestic German architecture and design through its festive appeal.

From 1916, nearly two decades after the Darmstädt project, Walter Gropius was in the throes of preparing a new socially conscious architecture, the 'new style' as he called it, intended to express a new culture, new society, and 'new man' through simplistic designs and a romanticized interpretation of industry. In 1919 he established the Bauhaus School ('building house'), housed in Weimar in the building designed by van de Velde in 1905–6 for the Grand Ducal Saxon School of Arts and Crafts. Juliet Koss goes as far as to note that 'a romantic Nietzscheanism lurked at the Weimar Bauhaus inhabiting the souls of its artistically inclined idealists' (2003:738).

The Bauhaus promoted a purging or emptying of traditional styles, rather than introduce a single identifiable style. The goal was to create an all-inclusive Gesamtkunstwerk that could bring the arts and people together, and inform all building types in Germany, from industrial and commercial buildings to churches, housing estates and individual residential dwellings. Their designs stressed a radical simplification of architectural forms with an emphasis on spatial relations between fundamental geometric shapes. Cubic forms were favoured in asymmetrical arrangements, with flat roofs, terraces and balconies, white walls, large glass areas and open interiors. The asymmetrical arrangement of forms meant greater opportunities for their dynamic interplay, which was further enhanced by changes to the observer's line of sight and different lighting conditions. Shadows across unexpected spatial arrangements can captivate the unwitting onlooker, and dance differently along the sheen of glass compared to the solidity of bare walls. The playful juxtaposition of these materials together with the use of balconies and roof top areas to unite interior and exterior spaces were simple ways to encourage connections between people and their environments. In comments reminiscent of Nietzsche's call in the wake of God's death to design only what is necessary, Gropius describes the approach of the Bauhaus as an architecture with 'no lying façade and trickeries', 'free of superfluous ornament' and made 'effective only through the cubic composition of the masses' (1923). 'The morphology of dead styles has been destroyed; and we are returning to honesty of thought and feeling' (1936:19).

The Bauhaus School in Weimar was sponsored by the state government, and from 1924, during a period of economic stability in Germany, large government-sponsored commissions were given to Bauhaus architects, including large housing estates which were intended to relieve the critical housing shortage following the war. Consequently, there were greater opportunities for progressive architects in Germany to experiment with designs for a 'new style' in a public arena compared to their counterparts in other countries. By the same token, the radical 'new style' being developed by Bauhaus architects became synonymous with the agendas of the communist and socialist municipal governments that sponsored their work (Miller Lane 1985:4). Housing projects of the Bauhaus were publicized extensively in popular journals and promoted in the public press as the 'new architecture', expressive of a 'new era' in Germany. Architects of the Bauhaus promoted their designs in public exhibitions and published theoretical works (notably Gropius and Bruno Taut). By 1930, designs of the Bauhaus were touted in many circles as 'the new *German* style' and celebrated as a national accomplishment.[14] But they were denounced in equal measure, provoking heated criticism, not least from the conservative press who ridiculed them as by-products of their left-wing sponsors.

Opposition to the Bauhaus shifted its focus from academic criticism of its aesthetic designs to the political arena so that by 1924 a smear campaign was launched against the Bauhaus, accusing it of favouring socialist-communist agendas aimed at suppressing individual enterprise and local design industries to support large-scale communalized industry (Miller Lane 1985:80). Bauhaus architecture was widely referred to as 'bolshevist architecture' by political opponents. Their economic cubic designs were reinterpreted in political terms as expressions of mass-urbanization driven by machine technology, and as a ploy to promote function, utility, and materialism as the only meaningful criteria for design. Conservative right-wing groups subsequently campaigned for the buildings of modern Germany to be informed by a more traditional and historical aesthetic, rooted to rustic 'folk' traditions of German's past.

Increased opposition to the Bauhaus forced Gropius in 1924 to move the School from Weimar to the politically neutral city of Dessau, and then again to Berlin in 1932 under the directorship of Mies van der Rohe after the Nazi Party gained control of Dessau's Council. One of the first acts of the first member of the Nazi Party to hold a ministerial post, Wilhelm Frick (Minister of the Interior and Education in the state of Thuringia) was to dissolve the state-sponsored Bauhaus School in Dessau, and establish the State College for Architecture and Crafts in Weimar, with Paul Schultze-Naumburg as its director.[15] Schultze-Naumburg alongside Frick ousted most of the original Bauhaus staff, and purged the Weimar Schlossmuseum of its 'degenerate' modernist paintings, replacing them with nineteenth-century works. Mies van der Rohe sought to continue the Bauhaus School in Berlin without political ties or interference, but after a few months, it closed for good in July 1933 with pressure from the Gestapo. Following its demise, several exponents of the Bauhaus – including Mies van der Rohe and Hannes Meyer (1889–1954) – left Nazi Germany for other countries where the international appeal of their design principles continued to inform architecture, leading to the name 'international style'.

The Nazi Party appropriated the 'anti-bolshevist' architectural campaign to enhance their national appeal and to further their rise to power. But after 1928 they found themselves in the tricky situation of seeking to establish their own cultural programme and, by extension, their own distinctive architectural style, expressive of Nazi ideology. The result was a confusing and contradictory array of architectural styles – a situation which seemed to reflect the internal discord of the Nazi Party itself. Their buildings expressed styles reminiscent of the German Romanesque buildings of the

Middle Ages alongside the 'eternal values' of neo-classicalism, and regional 'folk' styles of rural Germany alongside radical designs which intended to convey the new era of their regime. As Miller Lane notes, the Nazis ironically appropriated as part of their cultural programme, 'buildings which closely resembled the work of the radical architects whom the Nazis had opposed' (1985:9). Ultimately, the 'Nazi architectural style' comprised the kind of a mishmash of styles that Nietzsche wanted to reject, and its struggle for unity was channelled into an abuse of power which often translated into vast, grandiose buildings that overwhelm and alienate the individual.

Nietzsche within the conflict

Nietzsche's name and ideas were selectively drawn upon to support conflicting aesthetic and political ideals. His place in the sparring factions that oversaw the development of the new German style is complex. We see this played out, for instance in Gropius' reception of Nietzsche. Although Gropius is thought to have been influenced by Nietzschean philosophy, it is also reported that he disliked the little amount of it he read. Nevertheless, Gropius accepted an invitation by Föster-Nietzsche to Nietzsche's seventy-fifth birthday celebrations in October 1919 at Villa Silberblick (Bernhard 2008:277[16]). It is probable that she invited him in the hope of taking advantage of his potentially lucrative connections at the Bauhaus School rather than extending the courtesy to someone who may have been personally invested in her brother's philosophy. There Gropius enjoyed a lecture given in Nietzsche's honour enough to invite the speaker to present it to his own students. The speaker was Max Brahn (1873–1944), an editor of Nietzsche's *Der Wille zur Macht*, with expertise in experimental psychology in education, who, together with his wife, would later die at Auschwitz. Gropius invited two other scholars with links to the Nietzsche-Archiv and the Nazi Party to speak at the Bauhaus School (Bernhard 2008). These were Hans Prinzhorn (1886–1933), a German psychiatrist with expertise on the analysis of art by the mentally ill (who presented at the first Weimar Nietzsche Conference in 1927, and donated art to the Nazi propaganda exhibition, *Entartete Kunst* (Degenerate Art) in Munich in 1937), and Carl August Emge (1886–1970), director of the Nietzsche-Archiv between 1931 and 1936 and member of the Nazi Party.

The amicable exchange of ideas between figures associated with the Nietzsche-Archiv and staff and students in the early years of the Bauhaus School contrasts starkly to the destructive encounters between adherents of Nietzsche's ideas in the School's later years. Paul Schultze-Naumburg's brutal destruction of Oskar Schlemmer's murals above the central staircase of the van de Velde building in Weimar is a case in point. Schultze-Naumburg and Schlemmer were two prominent figures associated with Nietzsche's ideas but at opposite ends of the politically fuelled search for the 'new style'. Schlemmer was one of Gropius's first appointments to the Bauhaus School in 1922. His interest in Nietzsche was principally in the philosopher's understanding of the relationships between Apollonian and Dionysian forms, which Schlemmer subsequently sought to apply to his own understanding of movement in space. (In the next Chapter, I discuss how this relates to Schlemmer's concept of 'Triadic Ballet' [*Das Triadisches* Ballet], which he developed at the Bauhaus School.) Schlemmer's mural (since restored) reflects his interests in the geometric pathways of the body in space with its depiction of simple, abstract rounded human figures in various, overlapping dance poses that fill the space above the stairwell. Schultze-Naumburg had the mural whitewashed, presumably as part of his mass-purge of modern art (Day 2014:288,291; Dick 1984:111).

Nietzschean philosophy was used sparingly in support of very different visions of a 'new' architecture and the 'new' citizen who would benefit from these enhanced building spaces. These differences fall crudely into two distinct groupings. On the one hand, there were those who looked predominantly to the future, who envisaged Germany taking the lead in industrial innovation and production, and who tended to embrace utilitarian, minimalist and machine-like aesthetics. Le Corbusier's dictums, 'man is a geometrical animal' (1925b:83) and 'a house is a machine to live in' (1923b) are often cited in this context. And on the other hand, there were those who imagined a new Germany refashioned from more rustic and rural styles of its past. The contrasting approach of these two groups is symbolized by the roof styles each tended to favour – a contentious issue which attracted heated debate, with the more radical flat room pitted against the traditional gable roof. From a Nietzschean perspective, each approach had its merits and pitfalls.

The first approach presents architecture and its inhabitants as efficient systems. In this case, the building's function is the guiding design principle, with the juxtaposition of abstract, geometric shapes providing its aesthetic form. 'New' is interpreted as *wholly* new, driven by a vision of the future. This approach chimes with Nietzsche's call for simple and undecorated forms, which present to the user only that which is necessary and useful. The second approach idealizes the past and draws on myths and folk traditions of Germany. In this case, architecture and inhabitants are identified by their distinctly 'German soul', with one foot rooted to a romanticized interpretation of Germany's past and another striding purposely into its future. This resonates with Nietzsche's call for the revival of the creative spirit and instinct that underpinned the rituals and myths of Ancient Greece and to harness this energy in aesthetic forms that are relevant to the culture of the current day. By the same token, both approaches present conceptual difficulties from a Nietzschean perspective. The first is in danger of treating inhabitants of the new architecture as if mere cogs in the machine, stripping them of their individuality and relegating them to the herd, which is, to say, a position diametrically opposed to Nietzsche's vision of the creative individual. The second approach conveniently forgets Nietzsche's explicit criticisms about German nationalism and his championing of cosmopolitan cultures.

One might assume these contrasting approaches fail to express a viable Nietzschean approach to architecture due to their respective failures to address the creative tensions between Apollonian and Dionysian perspectives, which is, to say, that each approach promotes either the Apollonian or Dionysian perspective to the detriment of the other. To recall, the grand style is dependent on the creative tensions of both, and the problems of modern German culture that Nietzsche had identified can be attributed to its emphasis on Apollonian rationality and the suppression of the Dionysian instinct. Criticisms of this kind were widely levelled at the first approach for its emphasis on economical practicality, social utility and material values as the principal or sole design criteria, which invariably ignored, devalued, and supressed the instinctual and existential needs of the prospective inhabitants of their buildings. Architecture of this nature came to be known through critical commentary as 'functionalism'. German art historian, Ernst von Niebelschütz (1879–1946), writing in 1924, describes it as 'engineering architecture', which 'pays no attention to the requirements of feeling or sentiment'; and Czech philosopher, Emil Utitz (1883–1956), denounced its misplaced sobriety and simplicity on the basis that people 'require warmth and rejoicing, splendour and brilliance' (Miller Lane 1985:131).

I wish to claim, however, that even the most abstract of architectural designs can be open to Dionysian expression. Although Nietzsche himself alludes to architecture as the Apollonian impulse in its purest aesthetic form, a building cannot be perceived or experienced as exclusively Apollonian. As we saw with the Palazzo Pitti – Nietzsche's early example of the grand style – despite its overtly solid and rationalized mass, it expresses a Dionysian energy through its rhythmic play of forms. In the next chapter I explain how the simplest of surfaces can reveal Dionysian traits through the play of reflected light and shadow. The crucial factor in a building's power to evoke the Dionysian is its capacity to encourage a person to engage with their bodily selves and to feel instinctively related or connected to its design features. Key proponents of the radically new utilitarian architecture, such as Gropius, Bruno Taut and Le Corbusier, often spoke of the simplicity of their designs in quasi-spiritual terms as having an animate quality separate to their function, practicality, or economical construction. The conscious decision to expose construction materials, stripped of decoration, was often to garner an appreciation for their innate quality and unique characteristics. Greater attention to the materials themselves, to their mass, flexibility, shape, texture and colour – for instance to the specific hardness of the stone or the unique grain of the wood – was thought to contribute to the spatial effects of the overall design and its dynamic impact. Students in the Bauhaus School were taught that a deeper appreciation of the physical characteristics of materials and how they could be employed to encourage closer relationships between people and their buildings, uniting people with matter. These ideas chime with Nietzsche's notion that empty forms, purged from unnecessary and distracting features, will encourage a person to take stock of themselves, inviting them to self-reflect and to experience their embodied selves in place. Walter Müller-Wulckow (1886–1964), a member of the Deutscher Werkbund and Nazi Party, who authored a series of popular books on modern architecture, goes so far as to assert that pure architectural forms speak not so much to our body, but to our souls, connecting us to the very essence of reality. Radical new architecture, he says, is

> characterised by a passionate desire for pure forms, a desire which penetrates deeper into the idea and essence of reality than the mere love of ornament ever could. Strange as it may sound, these logically planned and constructed buildings embody a metaphysical yearning. These creations of the machine age reflect a new phantasy of the spirit and a new mysticism of the soul.
>
> (1925:10)

He refers to this desire for pure form as 'our generation's will to *sachlichkeit*' ('will to objectivity') (1925). By staking this claim he inadvertently appeals to Nietzsche's early ideas in *Birth of Tragedy*, where he describes the highest expression of art (Greek tragedy) as a 'metaphysical miracle of the Hellenic will', where Apollo and Dionysus are brought together in the highest creative tension. Earlier I explained that Nietzsche came to reject the metaphysical basis of this idea, believing the idea of the essence of reality as a fictional narrative appropriated by those who are too weak to create values for themselves. Nietzsche sought to relocate the creative union of Apollo and Dionysus from a transcendent, metaphysical realm to the physiological instincts of the creative artist.

How 'new' and how 'German'?

The contrasting positions that debated the new style were largely framed by conflicting opinions about the significance of historical example and national identity, leading to competing views about how 'new' the style ought to be and how 'German'.

As we know, Nietzsche wasn't a systematic philosopher. He didn't present us with a detailed architectural manifesto on buildings for the new era. His philosophy was instead anchored in the avoidance of telling us what to do, with the onus typically placed on his readers to interpret his ideas with loose guidance from various clues or signposts embedded in his writings. While this applies just as readily to the fundamental questions, 'how new' and 'how German', Nietzsche's general position on these issues is relatively clear. He suggests that historical styles should not be wholly overlooked or rejected when developing new styles and nor should they be copied, and while he thinks it is important for Germany to revive its creative powers, this should be achieved within a wider, cosmopolitan approach, and not a purely nationalistic outlook which is otherwise reductive and restrictive.

Nietzsche's intentions appear clearer on the occasions he criticizes approaches and ways of being that promote decadent and degenerate values and lifestyles. It is clear, for instance, that an aesthetic style created in *reaction* to another is devalued by Nietzsche. It can never aspire to the grand style, for it is created from a weak-will, one that expresses *ressentiment* – a toxic approach to life that underpins all slavish-values, and which signals an absence of positive will to power. In such cases, an individual or group of people will seek to undermine the values of those who create organically and freely in their own image by actively promoting and celebrating values that are diametrically opposite or contrary. This is a negative expression of creativity, which demonstrates a parasitic dependence on the vitality of others. Meaning in such cases cannot be established from one's own creative accomplishments, it must be derived from the creations of others. This is exemplified by the Nazi building programme, which was motivated not by the mastery of a will to power but in large part from a political attack on the principles of Bauhaus architecture.

One may subsequently think that novelty is a healthy way forward for realizing creative style. Novelty ensures one is not stuck in the past, driven by old regimes or reactions to others. Nietzsche appears to endorse novelty. In Zarathustra's first speech we are told that the creative spirit is most powerfully represented by a child. The significance of the child is its youthful, new beginnings. The child is 'forgetful' of the past, and consequently unhindered in their daring risks and playful experiments. By the same token, Dionysus, another of Nietzsche's figurative representations of the creative spirit, is a god of fertile, new beginnings. Nietzsche seeks the revaluation of values without resentment of present or past values to facilitate the free and uninhibited development of new ideas and styles. A 'new' architecture that can forget the past and can experiment without reaction or recourse to historical styles seems most apt. But there is an important caveat to this. If a new architecture is to express the spirit of the times, its forms must be recognizable, legible and comprehensible to people in the present. An effective architecture cannot be wholly new and innovative otherwise it will befuddle and alienate, causing people to disengage from it. Indeed, although Nietzsche rejects the imitation of past styles, he is critical of approaches that negate the past and are uprooted from it. In this respect, Nietzsche adheres to Semper's warning that that one should not discard conventional building types and styles and replace them with wholly new ones, 'but, rather', as Semper asserts, to 'try to express new ideas with the old types. This, and slavishly using old schemata that for centuries have belonged to history, are two different things' (cited in Herrmann 1989,158,160–1). Arguably, this is an approach that many progressive German architects adopted at the turn of the century, with their attempts to create new designs by abstracting specific elements of different historical styles and fashioning them into more simplified and coherent forms. Their designs were novel but visually related to the past. For instance, Gothic and Baroque features that had been integrated into the cluttered and chaotic designs of earlier decades, now featured with more restraint, often stylized into orderly patterned surfaces. Miller Lane cites as a common example the reduction of the vertical masonry grid – such as we find in Alfred Messel's pre-war buildings – to flat surfaces with regular window arrangements (see Miller Lane 1985:11,14,36). This general approach is apparent also in van de Velde's designs for the Nietzsche temple and Schultze-Naumburg's Nietzsche Memorial Hall.

According to Garnham, 'pioneering' modernist architects tended to misread Nietzsche's call for a 'revaluation of values', believing it to mean the total rejection of history and subsequently misinterpreting its application in their designs as an avoidance of all historical signifiers (2013:70). Garnham criticizes Buddensieg's (1999) interpretation of Le Corbusier in this context, in particular Buddensieg's understanding of Le Corbusier's *Plan Voisin* (1925), which is, to say, Le Corbusier's plans to redevelop central Paris by demolishing its Latin quarter and erecting several residential skyscrapers to house its citizens economically and efficiently. Buddensieg interprets Le Corbusier's plan as a prime example of Nietzsche's suggestion that the architect is legislator of new values (1999:310), but as Garnham rightly points out, Le Corbusier's vision clashes with Nietzsche's aspirations due to its 'exclusively rational planning and total obliteration of the historical form of the city'. Earlier, I described Nietzsche's praise for the Genoese architects, whom, as he puts it, 'in their thirst for something new, set up a new world alongside the old' (GS,291). Garnham employs Nietzsche's words in his criticism, for he notes that Le Corbusier's plans contravene Nietzsche's desire for 'a new world alongside the old'. Garnham notes too, the absence in Le Corbusier's plan for places 'where Nietzsche could "think his own thoughts" in any meaningfully human sense' (2013:70). Garnham concludes that the *Plan Voisin* represents a triumph of objectivity, leaving no place for the subjective emotion that Nietzsche demands.

We could target other architects for similar criticism from the list of notable architects cited at the start of this chapter who were each supposedly influenced by Nietzsche and Nietzschean ideas, especially those who are celebrated for experimenting with novel and radical designs, such as Peter Behrens for his 'Zarathustra' house in Darmstädt (1901) and Erich Mendelsohn for his *Einsteinturm* (Einstein tower) in Potsdam (1919–21). To the list we might add, Joseph Olbrich for his buildings at the Art Colony in Darmstädt, and Hans Poelzig for his *Großes Schauspielhaus* (Great Theatre) in Berlin (1919). Arguably, these buildings take risk and experiment too far, often confounding their onlookers, and having little influence on the development of 'new styles' beyond their striving for innovation.

The key, as Nietzsche stated, was to look to history and to past cultures for lessons on what could be nourishing for one's own. Ancient Greek culture was his prototype for the grand style that he envisioned for the future of Germany – not to replicate its art forms but to identify how it harnessed the creative spirit of its time, by successfully embodying in its art the dynamic tensions between Apollonian and Dionysian impulses. Nietzsche calls for the careful and critical use of historical example, and he lamented its appropriation in his day. There is, he asserts, an 'excess of history', which has 'attacked the shaping power of life'; people no longer understand how to 'utilize the past as powerful nourishment' (UM II.10). Not all approaches to history are useful. The accumulation of mere historical facts for its own sake epitomizes the approach of Nietzsche's character, the 'Last Man' (*letzter Mensch*) – a problematic person who has acquired a lot of knowledge but lacks the wisdom to put it to use (Z, prologue,5:45; KSA,10.4[171]:162). Rather than regurgitate information and replicate past styles, we must employ, Nietzsche says, a 'critical approach' to history, to 'unmask' the origins of its vital artistic forms so that we can learn how to use them to design effectively for our present and future (UM II.2).

The fact that Nietzsche was keen to look outside Germanic myths and traditions for his understanding of the spirit that underpins the grand style suggests that modern architectural designs that develop organically from out of this spirit will not be confined to Germanic architectural traditions. The styles of architecture that were established over time and across the regions and states of Germany's past are not indicative of the creative spirit that will revive the architecture of Germany's present. Indeed, as I have discussed, Nietzsche warns of the dangers of seeking to create within the narrow confines of national identity alone. Germany ought to cast its gaze further afield to 'digest' and 'absorb' the creative tendencies of other cultures (BGE,251; HH I.475). But Germany at the turn of the twentieth century was volatile and pressured to consolidate and refine an identity for itself during a period of radical changes. The advantages of a more expansive, more cosmopolitan outlook were more likely to go unrecognized at this time.

Schultze-Naumburg was one of the first to align new architecture with German racial purity. He fiercely opposed radically 'new' styles for their distinct lack of 'German' character, which, he claimed, would hasten the further fragmentation of the German people and an all-pervading sense of uprootedness (Miller Lane 1985:159). He first made a name for himself as an architect of country mansions in the Biedermeier style, half-timbered and reminiscent of the later Middle Ages, and his vision for the new German style incorporated features from German Volk traditions, such as the gable roof, and designs modelled on rural farm houses (Miller Lane 1985:16).[17] But it was through his publication of *Kulturarbeiten* (Works of Culture) (1901–17), an extremely popular guidebook to architecture, lavishly illustrated across nine volumes, that Schultze-Naumburg acquired a celebrity status. The aim of these books was to demonstrate the stark contrast of urban dwellings impoverished by modern industry and the vivacious character of historic cities, and subsequently to lead his readers to the conclusion that whole cities could be vastly improved if only modern architecture incorporated historic features in their designs.

Schultze-Naumburg's aesthetic vision for modern architecture shifted markedly in coming years to a position where a concern for historic style was not enough. What was required, he claimed, was a new aesthetic style grounded in racial purity. This led to his emotionally charged book *Kunst und Rasse* (*Art and Race*) (1928), where he puts forward the argument that radical modern architectural designs are racially impure. This book helped pave the way for a dangerous movement that understood cultural decadence as having a biological cause. Reminiscent of Nietzsche's remarks of the Genoese palazzi, within which he *sees faces* of bold and autocratic people (GS,291), Schultze-Naumburg calls for a return to a German architecture, from out of which 'there seemed to gaze the features of men upright, good and true' (1928:106–8). Schultze-Naumburg heavily petitioned for the gable roof as a necessary feature of modern German buildings because it is integral, he claimed, to German 'racial physiognomy' (see Miller Lane 1985:137–8). While he initially criticized the flat roof on practical grounds – it leaked, the cement cracked and stained, and the metal fittings rusted – he came to denounce it as wholly other, as 'immediately recognisable as the child of other skies and other blood' (1926).[18]

CHAPTER SIX

The grand style in modern architecture

Of all philosophers, Nietzsche is arguably one of the most self-conscious and self-reflective. Even Sigmund Freud, who was ambivalent about the value of philosophical insight, several times said of Nietzsche that 'he had a more penetrating knowledge of himself than any man who ever lived or was ever likely to live' (Jones 1957–7:344). In this respect, it is fitting that Nietzsche's ideas are cited in the context of modern architecture – an architecture that is conscious of its own modernity and the strivings for identity and change. However, as I mentioned, these citations often reveal a superficial reading of Nietzsche's philosophy, amounting to a caricature of his work or its misinterpretation. Architects who have been aligned with Nietzsche tend to fancy themselves, or are fancied by others, as powerful and prophetic 'Zarathustrian' artists who bring hope of a new way of living, or as *Übermenschlikeit* figures who exemplify the 'new man', driven by their will to power to design and build the new cultural edifice. In this chapter I delve deeper into relationships between Nietzsche's ideas and common themes in the early developments of modern architecture. I identify how key elements of his notion of the grand style are evident in the concerns of several prominent architects who have been associated with Nietzschean philosophy. I examine, in turn, the notion of empty form and festive rhythm, height instinct and bodily affect, and the heroic figure of the architect.

Empty form and festive rhythm

In *Modern Architecture* (1896), Otto Wagner defined modern architecture as the honest expression of materials and the rationalized structure and functional utility of the building. Key to this honesty was the eradication of unnecessary decoration. By the late 1930s, modern architecture became synonymous with the International Style, with cubic forms comprising stark white walls, flat roofs, large areas of glass, open-plan interiors, and the rejection or ornament and colour. Nietzsche's notion of empty form with the elimination of unnecessary and distracting details is cited by some as an intellectual forerunner to architecture of this character, and by extension, an influence on several prominent architects whose designs share an aesthetic resemblance to it.[1] The purging of distracting ornament and the idealization of pure white forms is, however, an age-old concern that extends far back in time to the likes of Plato, whose argument that temples should exclude distractive ornament and colour in favour of purity, simplicity and sacred whiteness was appropriated by Leon Battista Alberti in his fifteenth-century architectural treatise, *De re aedificatoria* (On the Art of Building) (*c.*1443–52).

Nietzsche does not call for the purity of architecture, nor for white buildings. Indeed, one might assume a whitewashed building is distinctly contrary to Zarathustra's taste: 'Deep yellow and burning red: that is to *my* taste – it mixes blood with all colours. But he who whitewashes his house betrays to me a whitewashed soul' (Z, III, 11[2]:212).[2] Note also, Nietzsche's description of 'princely' Turin where 'everything is either yellow or red-brown' (KSB,8.1013:285). But this is not a Nietzschean endorsement to paint buildings in deep yellows and reds or to construct them from materials of these colours, and neither is it a vilification of buildings painted or constructed in white. Architecture in the grand style depends not on colour alone, and nor does it depend solely on its general appearance. The grand style is conveyed in the spirit of its design and construction. Zarathustra alludes to yellows and reds as representations of flesh and blood, and it is our attention to these physiological aspects – more specifically, the fruits of bodily exertion – that Nietzsche calls for. Zarathustra continues in the passage above to describe the importance of bodily movement – of standing, walking, running, jumping, climbing and dancing – for self-discovery: 'With rope ladders I learned to climb to many a window with agile legs I climbed to high masts [...] I came to my truth by diverse paths and in diverse ways: it was not upon a single ladder that I climbed to the height where my eyes survey my distances.'

Nietzsche seeks a dynamic architecture that evokes exertions, risk, experiment and ultimately the self-discovery of its architect, which in turn will arrest others, inviting them through their designs to engage with this creative power, in the hope that they, too, will discover themselves and create anew. Following his reading of Semper, we can infer that Nietzsche seeks an architecture which somehow conveys through its surfaces the quality of ritual or festival, or put another way, an expressive rhythmic quality that connotes a Dionysian play contained within Apollonian forms. One way to emphasize this dynamic quality in a building is to remove decorative elements that would otherwise distract with their invitation to decode their meanings. With these removed, we are more exposed to its 'necessary' features, as Nietzsche puts it. Empty surfaces thereby prevent us from being preoccupied by our Apollonian sensibilities, which compel us to try to *understand* the building. This ultimately reduces the building to an object of intellectual enquiry, and places us at a distance to the building, thereby circumventing its more immediate and instinctive impact on us.

The question as to whether to incorporate or eradicate ornament is not an overriding concern for the grand style. Instead, what matters is the extent to which a building evokes a spontaneous physiological response. This is achievable in the plainest of surfaces and potentially within ornamental features too. It is simply the case that decoration is more likely to attract a person's attention to it and to invite them to question its significance, rather than tend to their own bodily and instinctual responses to the building. A Nietzschean architecture closes the problematic gap as he perceived it between abstract thought and bodily engagement and enables us to experience, assess and recreate ourselves more profoundly – our 'most sacred convictions' and 'supreme values' are, after all, simply the 'judgements of our muscles' (KSA,13.11[376]:169). Let us now examine briefly how some of our 'Nietzschean-inspired' architects have negotiated empty forms and festive rhythm.

Le Corbusier

Le Corbusier's name has come to be associated with Louis Sullivan's dictum, 'form follows function', Mies van de Rohe's 'less is more', and with the iconoclastic characteristics of the 'International architectural style'. The popularized image of Le Corbusier's architecture as purified spaces with white, reflective surfaces intended to cleanse its inhabitants by provoking meditative, self-reflection, puts him in conversation with Nietzsche's notion of empty form.

Echoing Adolf Loos' (1908) earlier indictment of ornament as a crime, Le Corbusier calls for a 'law of whitening' (*loi du blanchiment*), a compulsory whitening of buildings intended as 'a moral necessity, even more than a material one' to cleanse a person, improving their ability to discern the 'sincere truth' of things (cited in Janneau 1923:64). Ornament and decoration in architecture have become 'poisons that intoxicate' our capacity to think and to live well (Le Corbusier 1923a). The remedy he proposes is to impose on society plain, white surfaces to induce an inner cleanliness and to cultivate healthier, more intelligent people. Compulsory whitening will act as 'an X-ray of beauty. It is a court of assize in permanent session. It is the eye of truth', which makes 'each one of us a prudent judge' to rule on the quality of our individual lives, to call forth a healthy approach to living and 'joy of life' (1925/1987:187–90). Le Corbusier's law of whitening (also called 'Law of Ripolin', after a brand of white paint known for its anti-bacterial properties) would ensure every citizen's '*home* is made clean', that there are 'no more dirty corners':

Everything is shown as it is. Then comes *inner* cleanness, for the course adopted leads to refusal to allow anything at all which is not correct, authorized, intended, desired, thought-out: no action before thought. When you are surrounded with shadows and dark corners you are at home only as far as the hazy edges of the darkness your eyes cannot penetrate. You are not master in your own house. Once you have put Ripolin on your walls you will be *master of yourself.*

(1925/1987:188)

Le Corbusier's intention was to evoke spiritual reflection in the inhabitants of his buildings, to encourage them to turn from the distractions of materiality and engage in sustained self-reflection. Although the goal appears to be self-mastery, the spiritual power that Le Corbusier speaks of and which he attributes to whitening is – contra Nietzsche – authoritarian and controlling. It enforces a 'correct' way of being and does not allow for opposing and competing perspectives. It is an approach that smacks of the 'will to truth', a regime that *enslaves* the individual, cutting them off from their own instinctive and aesthetic impulses.

Le Corbusier's desire to control citizens continues in his plans for the Ville Radieuse dating from 1924, the ideal 'Radiant City', where people live in high-rise blocks, within concrete cell-like apartments. The design has been criticized for proposing an oppressively ascetic lifestyle, with 'the death of the street', where social spaces are severely limited to reduce chance encounters with others. Le Corbusier was especially keen to eliminate theatres and cafés (Nietzsche's favourite haunts!). According to Simon Richards, Le Corbusier's Radiant City seeks to eradicate the social world on the grounds that it distracts people. Its removal would subsequently compel citizens into solitude, to withdraw into themselves in search of higher values (2003:4). Like Nietzsche, Le Corbusier regarded isolation as necessary for self-reflection and a prerequisite for creativity: 'The man of initiative, of action, of thought, the FOREMAN', Le Corbusier writes, 'demands that his meditation be sheltered in a space that is serene and solid, a matter essential to the health of elites' (1923/2016:98). While Nietzsche found suitable places within the quiet city spaces, and at times even a room in a busy, ordinary guest house, Le Corbusier appears to seek secluded isolation. The quiet shelter he desired for himself as he worked was a nine-foot rectangular building, cell-like with blank walls, but as Charles Jencks notes, Le Corbusier projected his need for isolation onto society and to every citizen (1973:27). The result contrasts starkly with Nietzsche's aspirations. To coerce individuals or whole communities into isolation will cripple and stifle their creative freedom.[3] Isolated and ascetic lifestyles can promulgate the problematic and unhealthy split between inner reflective worlds and the material fabric of the natural and built environment, especially to those who already have poor mastery of their instincts. It can effectively dissolve one's sense of bodily materiality.

Crucially, however, Le Corbusier allows the expression of individual taste and a degree of spontaneity within the interiors of his city buildings. Although the structure of the building is standardized with an exterior that is as economical and efficient as possible to divest it of socially constructed meanings, inhabitants are encouraged to fill out the interior for themselves (Richards 2003:16). And, it would seem, inhabitants are free to experiment with colour. Thus, in relation to the purity of whiteness, Le Corbusier elsewhere concedes: 'To tell the truth, my house will only appear white' alongside 'the active forces of colours'. 'White, which makes you think clearly, relies on the powerful tonics of colour' (1926:49,52). Colour accentuates the qualities of white; paradoxically 'a house that is completely white' is ineffectual, resembling, he says, a banal 'cream jug' (1925b:146).

While Le Corbusier is popularized as a purist and purveyor of stark white spaces, this is only half the story. He has also been characterized as an architect of contradictions and a dualist (Cohen 2007:15; Jencks 1973:29; Richards 2003:204; Sharr 2018:57–8). As Cohen puts it: 'Nobody was less "Corbusian" than Le Corbusier himself' (2007:15). While Le Corbusier's supposed links to Nietzsche tend to be discussed in relation to the eradication of distracting ornament and the practical simplicity of his 'engineering aesthetic', we could equally argue for a 'Nietzschean aesthetic' in Le Corbusier's lyrical use of colour and texture, such as we find in his Unité d'Habituation in Marseilles, France (completed in 1952) – a building that echoes, in the words of Adam Sharr, 'the swelling shapes of Corbusier's latest artworks inspired by full-bodied naked figures, and the so-called "primitive" art of folk cultures' (2018:75). The contrast between this description and the criticisms I outlined in relation to the Ville Radieuse connotes important distinctions between an Apollonian approach to architecture with its concern for abstraction and isolation and the more sensual and festive approach of the Dionysian. It is perhaps in Le Corbusier's capacity to maintain the tensions between such competing perspectives that he best demonstrates his Nietzschean sensibilities – through the 'blending', as Sharr puts it, of 'practicality with the yearning for primeval mysticism' (2018:58) and the balancing of the 'intellectual' and 'lyrical', according to Jencks (1973:29).

Given the close proximity that Le Corbusier maintains between a person's inner world and the design of their home, it is perhaps unsurprising that Le Corbusier's contrasting approaches to design was reflected in his presentation of himself as a person with contrasting personalities. Up until 1917 he identified himself as Charles-Édouard Jeanneret, and with Le Corbusier, Corb or Paul Boulard after that. In a letter (to Josef Červ) from 18 January 1926, he presents Le Corbusier as a kind of Apollonian figure and Jeanneret as a person more closely aligned with the Dionysian:

> Le Corbusier works exclusively in architecture. He pursues disinterested ideas. He has no right to compromise himself through betrayals and accommodations. He is an entity freed from the weight of the flesh […]

Ch. Édouard Jeanneret is the man of the flesh who has experienced all the adventures – whether thrilling or heart-breaking – of a rather eventful life.
(cited in Cohen 1999:331,n.34)

According to Jencks, Paul Boulard represented the philosopher with the hammer: he 'carried out the Nietzschean injunction to burn what he loved in order to create something totally new and superhuman […] through opposition and moving from one attack to the next he would crystallize a stage in his own positive development' (1973:59). Boulard appears to personify an aspect of the wider personality that required isolation to fuel creativity. As Jencks notes, he 'continually cut himself away from his friends and society, rejecting them' in order 'to realise his own individualised view of truth', and 'as with Nietzsche's superman', he sought to 'restructure social values' accordingly (1973:181). Although Le Corbusier – together with his other personas – can be read in Nietzschean terms as a multi-perspectival artist who unites Apollonian and Dionysian impulses with a view to encouraging a personal and cultural revaluation of values in others, it is difficult to align his design strategies with Nietzsche, not least his desire to enforce spiritual elevation and in every person through spatial isolation.

Dancing with van de Velde and Bauhaus architecture

A building that evokes Dionysian instinct will induce in its onlookers a bodily identification with it. When this happens, the onlooker becomes a participant with its design, and the building is no longer an object perceived at a distance, but an architectural *festive event* which celebrates building and person alike (see Huskinson 2018). Nietzsche describes this as a physiological frenzy – 'the frenzy of feasts' and 'frenzy of an overarched and swollen will' – which leads to 'feelings of increased strength and fullness'. From out of these feelings, he suggests a person 'lends' themselves to the evocative object – in this case the building – until it 'mirrors their power'. In the process, 'one enriches everything out of one's own fullness: whatever one sees, whatever one wills is seen swelled, taut, strong, overloaded with strength' (TI, IX,8–9:92–3). A person's self-awareness is heightened, and the experience is reviving and affirming.

Nietzsche conveyed Dionysian energy as rhythmic and frenetic bodily movements using metaphors and analogies of running, jumping, dancing and climbing, often to the heights and to connote experiences of self-discovery and self-development. Movement and rhythm express the festive spirit, and it is perhaps in monumental architecture, where heaviness, gravity and inertia are most obviously felt, that the festive spirit is most poignant or surprising. As we saw with Nietzsche's experience of the Palazzo Pitti, colossal buildings can convey festive spirit through the rhythmic juxtapositions of shapes and surface textures. In other words, even heavy buildings can dance.

From its early beginnings, the Bauhaus School was known for its exploration of expressive dance and its creative possibilities for the configuration of geometric forms. A chief proponent of this was Oskar Schlemmer (1888–1943), one of the first appointments to the teaching faculty in 1920, as Master of Form. Significantly, Schlemmer was influenced by his readings of Nietzsche, referring to him in 1929 as 'the philosopher of my youth' (Schlemmer 1990:24), and he would remain an influence on Schlemmer's work throughout his life (see Bernhard 2008:278).

'Let the world belong to the dancer, as Nietzsche would say' (Schlemmer 1990:77). This remark by Schlemmer in 1919 makes a suitable epigraph to Schlemmer's contribution to architecture through his experimental investigations into spatial and rhythmic relationships between geometric forms and dance. He is perhaps best known for *Das Triadisches Ballett* ('Triadic Ballet'), which he choreographed for the theatrical stage at the Bauhaus School. The dancers of his ballet were dressed in colourful, minimalist costumes, each resembling one of three fundamental shapes: triangle, square and circle. The costumes were designed to restrict the dancers, leading to robotic-like movements intended to express the geometric pathways of colour and shape moving in space.

Schlemmer's Triadic Ballet and his theories of spatial relations are widely thought to have been influenced directly by his reading of Nietzsche, in particular Nietzsche's notions of Apollo and Dionysus and their aesthetic interplay.[4] In support, commentators of Schlemmer's works have cited as evidence various comments Schlemmer makes in his diaries, letters and teaching notes. However, it is uncertain whether Schlemmer sought in his experiments of spatial relationships the creative union of the two aesthetic principles as Nietzsche himself had intended. For instance, while Susanne Lahusen is adamant that 'the main theme' of Schlemmer's work is 'the reconciliation of polarities' (1986:67), Rachel Straus convincingly argues that Schlemmer's aim was 'in its final form' a 'strictly Apollonian' abstract dance form (2019:272; Schlemmer 1990:128). Straus demonstrates how Schlemmer's aesthetic goal was to present people with a choice between the 'Apollonian *or* Dionysian', and not their creative antagonism or union (2019:259; see also Schlemmer 1990:69). This approach is articulated in the opposition Schlemmer establishes between German expressive dance, on the one hand, which he describes with derision as a chaotic, Dionysian aesthetic. And ballet on the other hand, which he sought to reinvent as an abstract art form, valorized in terms that are distinctly Apollonian (Schlemmer 1990:69). If Schlemmer intended to repress Dionysian expression in favour of a purely Apollonian art form, he exemplifies modern tendencies that Nietzsche vilified and sought to overcome.

Arguably, van de Velde's interest in the power of line and its capacity to animate surfaces and spaces complements Schlemmer's concern for suggestive geometric forms through dance. In his essay 'Die Linie' (1902a), van de Velde elaborates his understanding of line as the script of evocative, voluptuous gestures and dances, and as we saw in Chapter 4, Paul Kühn (1904) in his official guide to the Nietzsche-Archiv extends this notion to van de Velde's renovations of Villa Silberblick to explain how its use of linear ornament leads to an exuberant Zarathustrian dance between the building and its visitors.

Van de Velde criticized the lack of architectural ornament as a denial of life itself. It leads, he suggests, to ascetic buildings akin to 'a convent, where men and women live in constant negation' of life, aspiring to a 'decadent ideal', which 'posits the renunciation of life as a condition of sanctity' (1895). Van de Velde regarded the line as the most visceral, elemental, and rhythmic of forms that can bring life to architecture and to those who engage with it. Van de Velde argues that the true festive origin of architecture is linear ornament, and not geometric ornament as Semper had claimed through his valorization of textile cladding. Van de Velde writes:

> Let us not forget that the origin of ornament corresponds to the need to 'animate' surfaces, to practice on the object the accomplishment of the *rite of incarnation of life* […] This was not any different in ornamentation than in the dance. It appears as such from the moment that, accompanied by the clapping of hands or the instruments of music | … | man sprang forth, moving exuberantly his arms, his legs, balancing his body or swaying it | … | In the same manner, ornament only appears the moment we realize that a phenomenon of lines and spots has taken possession of the space that is given them to conquer and to fill in the same way that a dancer fills with his gestures and movements the space in which he moves.
> (van de Velde in Haddad 2003b: 132–3)

The line has a 'powerful rhythm of penetration, circulation, convolution and growth', which compels us, he maintained, to be 'carried along' by its movements 'without fatigue' and 'with the voluptuousness of a dancer balancing, turning her body, throwing her arms and her legs in the air' (van de Velde 2003:160).

Starting from a series of curved lines, van de Velde would develop more sophisticated linear formations to create simple, repetitive sequences and rhythmic patterns of space and line. These patterns would animate wall surfaces when carefully applied to them. He believed that lines together possessed the same relations as musical notes, and in their rhymical motions they can lift us and raise our souls in similar manner to song and dance. In this respect, the significance of line-ornament 'is identical to that of dance' (van de Velde 2003). Ornamental lines were not intended simply to decorate a surface and to please the eye, but as a visceral force, which expresses – to recall Kühn's commentary – all that is 'necessary' to impart 'strength and life' and a 'life-awakening function' to the observer (Kühn 1904:23). Van de Velde's lines express the will to power. For him, the line is a vital and creative carrier of human energy, which draws its power from its creator, the architect, to animate the qualities of the materials selected for the design and powerful physiological feelings in those who experience it. Stanford Anderson describes this uniting power as a kind of "possession experience", where the vibrant personality of architect and observer 'play back and forth' upon the design form 'until subject and object are indivisibly fused' (2000:10). This is primarily a bodily experience, Kühn notes, which 'swells the limbs from the inside' and causes the observer to 'feel a play of forces flowing through and directed by a central will' as their body becomes 'animated by Zarathustra's dance rhythms' (1904:14,26). According to Zarathustra, dance leads us to consider 'the highest things', and according to Kühn, through van de Velde's use of line-force, 'our attitude to life is transformed, heightened, strengthened and refined' (1904:21).

Louis H. Sullivan and visceral ornament

Sullivan claims as 'self-evident' that 'a building, quite devoid of ornament, may convey a noble and dignified sentiment by virtue of mass and proportion', akin, he says, to a human body that is 'natural, vigorous and wholesome', 'strong', 'athletic' and 'comely in the nude' (1892/2014:187). A building with ornament, however, can evoke, he claims, an emotional quality that brings together the architect, the building, the observer and inhabitant into harmonious relationship.

Joining the likes of Semper and van de Velde, Sullivan describes the making of ornament as a fundamental instinct of human will and creativity.[5] Underpinning this is a notion of self-mastery that is reminiscent of Nietzsche's idea of will to power, and specifically, Nietzsche's requirement for the grand style that one employ a 'single taste' to govern and form every large and small aspect of the work (GS,290). This is most apparent in Sullivan's essay, 'Ornament and Architecture' (1892/2014) where ornament is conveyed as the character and individuality of the architect. Sullivan surmises that if the architect can master their instincts, they will create noble and harmonious designs that will uplift and invigorate others. An effective, powerful building is one that harnesses the 'emotion' and 'spirit' of its ornament so that the ornamental design 'flows harmoniously' throughout the building (1892/2014:188). The ornament in this context will appear as if an organic feature growing out of the architectural surface and not merely '"stuck on"' (1892/2014:189). As such, the ornament and surface will express the same spirit, each enhancing the value of the other (1892/2014). Sounding like Semper, Sullivan notes that buildings 'clad in a garment of poetic imagery, half hid as it were in choice products of loom and mine, will appeal with redoubled power, like a sonorous melody overlaid with harmonious voices' (1892/2014:187). Thus, while Sullivan maintains that 'an excellent and beautiful building may be designed that shall bear no ornament whatever', he believes 'just as firmly that a decorated structure, harmoniously conceived, well considered, cannot be stripped of its system of ornament without destroying its individuality' (1892/2014:188).

Crucial to harmonious architecture is the integrity of the architect, who must be sufficiently imaginative and powerful. The architect's will to power comes into play here. As Sullivan contends, the architect requires 'a high and sustained emotional tension, an organic singleness of idea'. They must be able to concentrate on the 'subtle rhythms' of a single idea without distraction (1892/2014). A weak architect is indecisive, unable to commit to a singular idea and susceptible to 'imitative' designs and historical styles that cannot 'wholly satisfy' (1892/2014). Only an architect at 'the culmination of his powers' can 'impart to passive materials a subjective or spiritual human quality', which they themselves have received by 'opening' themselves 'in enlightened sympathy' to 'the voice of our times' (1892/2014:187). The architect's power of concentration is paramount here. To the modern architect, Sullivan writes: 'Everything is against you. You are surrounded by a mist of tradition which you, alone, must dispel', to 'reduce all thoughts, all activities, to the simple test of honesty' (1906/2014:232).

In Sullivan's scheme, the work of the powerful architect may lead to a revaluation of cultural values. 'You will be surprised', he says, 'to see how matters that you once deemed solid, fall apart; and, how things that you once deemed inconsequential take on a new and momentous significance. But in time your mind will clarify and strengthen' and will have the 'intellectual power' to discriminate 'between those things which make for the health' and 'illness of a people' (1906/2014). Suggestive of Nietzsche's comments that architecture is the 'eloquence of the will' and 'power' in 'spatial form' (KSA,14[117]:425), Sullivan asserts that the most effective buildings will be those 'designed with sufficient depth of feeling and simplicity of mind, the more intense the heat in which it was conceived, the more serene and noble will it remain forever as a monument of man's eloquence' (1892/2014:188). Sullivan's ornamental design has been characterized as an 'architecture of striving' (Van Zanten 2000:119). Their 'arabesque' forms convey, as Van Zanten puts it, 'a moving, twisting line that transforms, struggles, and evolves as it extends', giving rise to a 'repeated compression followed by release', and resulting in a pattern that 'pushes through confining grids and border', finally to 'explode' in a 'starburst of buds flowers and acanthus fronds' (Van Zanten 2000). Such reeling arabesque forms are reminiscent of a stylized Greek acanthus plant (and incidentally, to the patterned wallpaper of Nietzsche's bedroom in Villa Silberblick).

Sullivan was perhaps most known for his skyscrapers, a type of building which posed for him the conundrum as to how to give artistic meaning to such vast structures that have the tendency to appear 'sterile', 'crude', 'harsh' and 'brutal', due to the emphasis they place on sheer volume compared to surface elaboration (1896/2014:202). As we shall see, his solution draws on ideas that are pertinent to Nietzsche's notion of height instinct. For Sullivan, the architect's will to power is made visible in buildings of this type through the dramatic forces of their ornamental features. Compression, tension and vertical thrust are rendered visible and tangible in Sullivan's skyscraper designs, pulling the observer into their visceral drama by activating similar forces experienced as muscular sensations in the observer's body. Vincent Scully asserts this is most evident in Sullivan's Guaranty building (Prudential building) in Buffalo, New York (1894–5) – a building thought by many as Sullivan's demonstrable solution to the high-rise problem he poses (Figure 6.1). 'Because of its ornament', he notes, the 'Guaranty Building becomes more than the simple skeleton of slender steel members and acts instead as a skeleton cladded with what appears to be integral force, stepping out towards its corner, standing, stretching, and physically potent' (Scully 1959:75). Scully continues, 'One can feel, in Sullivan's buildings, a curious power of potential action'. 'Turn [your back] around' and 'the Guaranty [building] may take its giant step across the square' (Scully 1959:80). Let us now consider Nietzsche's notion of height instinct in this context.

FIGURE 6.1 Guaranty building (later Prudential building), Buffalo, NY (b.1894–5, Louis H. Sullivan). East elevation. Author's photograph.

Height instinct

Nietzsche takes issue with those who desire the heights for their own sake, lest one lose one's grounding and become inflated by a grandiose desire to be the tallest, strongest and most vast. Like Zarathustra's animals, the eagle and snake – with one who resides in the skies and the other on the ground – one must reach for the heights while grounded if one is to master and contain creative experiences. Nietzsche suggests that German artists endure physical 'cramps' symptomatic of unrealized desires for the 'heights and super-heights' and a deep desire to 'rise beyond' (GS,105). To realize these heights we need, he asserts, to live like the Greeks – in other words, 'to stop bravely at the surface, the fold, the skin; to adore appearance, to believe in shapes, tones, words' (GS, preface, 4). Nietzsche criticized the German desire for tyrannical size, for the bloated and gigantic (D,161), and the modern incapacity to express joy and beauty in restraint as the ancient Greeks had done: *'The Hellenic is very foreign to us* [...] one stands astonished at the *smallness of the masses* by means of which the Greeks know how to express and *love* to express the sublime' (D,169). Zarathustra similarly remarks, 'One has to speak with thunder and heavenly fireworks to feeble and dormant senses' (Z, II,5:117). According to Mark Bolland, Nietzsche regarded the desire for excessive mass as the 'aesthetic aberration of the nineteenth century' (1996:87). And Nietzsche's criticism surely extends to architecture of our day and ongoing technological innovations in the construction industry and new materials which together enable buildings to extend ever higher. Such feats are impressive, but at what existential cost? Vast buildings overwhelm human proportions and outgrow us. As Immanuel Kant warned, buildings should not be too vast as to fail to impress upon us their sublimity and our powers of reasoning. A notable case in point to flout such advice is Albert Speer's ambitious plans for Germania, the Nazi capital city of the world. Its Great Hall was so large that it would have generated its own atmosphere and weather conditions. The vastness of Germania's buildings sought to overpower the individual, rendering individuals insignificant and submissive in the face of its totalitarian regime.

The skyscrapers that made Sullivan famous, at ten storeys high, were not particularly tall even by contemporaneous standards. Nevertheless, the surge in technological innovations at this time, such as the introduction of reinforced concrete, steel frames and the elevator, encouraged Sullivan to question how to design artistically for those buildings that are growing ever taller, becoming more expansive and potentially more sterile. His solution, as I noted, was to apply his ideas of ornament to their vast structures to enable people to engage viscerally with their vertical forces and massive surfaces.

In a very short chapter titled, 'Zarathustra in Chicago', Tilmann Buddensieg claims, 'Nowhere does Nietzsche's "height drive" – Zarathustra's dream of towers that "rise up" – find a more powerfully built figure than in the work of the great American architect Louis Sullivan' (2002b:188). He goes on to describe Sullivan's Wainwright building in St. Louis as an embodiment of the 'formal and linguistic emotion of a Zarathustrian and Antonellianian "absolute height instinct"'. It has a '"power"' and expresses the '"gigantic power of man to build"'. Buddensieg ascribes to the Wainwright building the height instinct that Nietzsche had experienced in the face of the Mole Antonelliana – two buildings completed within three years of each other. Furthermore, as Buddensieg notes, Sullivan adopts a distinctly Zarathustrian tone when considering the implications of the height of tall office buildings. He cites Sullivan's description of their loftiness as their chief characteristic:

> This loftiness is to the artist-nature its thrilling aspect. It is the very open organ-tone in its appeal. It must be in turn the dominant chord in his expression of it, the true excitant of his imagination. It must be tall, every inch of it tall. The force and power of altitude must be in it, the glory and pride of exaltation must be in it. It must be every inch a proud and souring thing, rising in sheer exaltation that from bottom to top it is a unit without a single dissenting line – that it is the new, the unexpected, the eloquent peroration of most bald, most sinister, most forbidding conditions.
>
> (Sullivan 1896/2014:206)

According to Buddensieg, Sullivan's words are suggestive of Zarathustra: 'One believes to hear', he says, 'Zarathustra's "exultant" "overcoming" of the darkest conditions, "from the ground up to the highest height"' (2002b:189). Arguably, Sullivan is more expressive of the 'Zarathustrian spirit' in this work than Buddensieg suggests. Take for instance, Sullivan's assertion that the 'man who designs in this spirit and with the sense of responsibility to the generation he lives in must be no coward, no denier, no bookworm, no dilettante. He must live of his life and for his life in the fullest, most consummate sense' (1896/2014:406). See also, from Sullivan's *The Autobiography of an Idea* (1924/2009): 'The appeal and the inspiration lie, of course, in the element of loftiness, in the suggestion of slenderness and aspiration, the soaring quality of a thing rising from the earth as a unitary utterance, Dionysian in beauty' (1924/2009:313–14).

Jörg H. Gleiter is of the view that Nietzsche's height instinct 'announces the ideas of the modern high-rise building', but he refutes Buddensieg's suggestion that Nietzsche was a direct influence on Sullivan's work in the development of the American skyscraper (2009:155). The skyscraper was the direct result, he asserts, of new construction methods and materials during a period of technological advancement, the results of which 'hardly required Nietzsche's inspiration' (2009:161). Gleiter's account appears to misinterpret the significance of Nietzsche's notion of height instinct and Buddensieg's appreciation of Sullivan's skyscrapers in relation to it. The significance of height and loftiness for Sullivan's skyscrapers is, as Buddensieg rightly notes, in the powerful and noble quality of their elevation with their capacity to 'overcome the darkest of conditions', and not, as Gleiter reads Buddensieg, its geometric proportions. The two concerns are not mutually exclusive of course: innovations in the construction industry and the capacity to build ever higher involve the risks and daring feats of overcoming that Nietzsche sought. But Nietzsche's height instinct does not build ever higher because advances in methods and materials make it feasible. The height instinct is *willed* on its own grounds, it requires no proof or external validation, and does not come about passively or by happenstance.

Uplifting forces of the Marshall Field Wholesale Store, the Wainwright, and Guaranty buildings

Sullivan's architectural inspiration for his first designs, including the Auditorium Building in Chicago (b.1886–7), the Wainwright in St. Louis (b.1890–1) and the Guaranty in Buffalo (b.1894–5), is widely thought to have been the Marshall Field Wholesale Store in Chicago (designed by Henry Hobson Richardson, b. 1885–7, destroyed in 1930; Figure 6.2).[6] His discovery of this building is pertinent to our enquiry and befitting of Nietzsche's notion of grand style, for Sullivan reports that upon seeing it he felt a strong bodily reaction, which led him to fantasize about the architect's will to power. The Marshall Field building stood before Sullivan in similar manner as the palazzi of the Genoese merchants stood before Nietzsche – as an imposing presence and 'virile force' of an upright, noble man and master of his trade. Sullivan writes:

> [H]ere is a *man* for you to look at. A man that walks on two legs instead of four, has active muscles, heart, lungs, and other viscera; a man that lives and breathes, that has red blood; a real man, a manly man; a virile force – broad, vigorous and with a whelm of energy – an entire male. I mean that stone and mortar, here, spring into life [...] a mind rich-stored with harmony [...] Four-square and brown, it stands, in physical fact, a monument to trade, to the organized commercial spirit, to the power and progress of the age, to the strength and resource of individuality and force of character; spiritually, it stands as the index of a mind, large enough, courageous enough to cope with these things, master them, absorb them and give them forth again, impressed with the stamp of large and forceful personality; artistically, it stands as the oration of one who knows well how to choose his words, who has somewhat to say and says it – and says it as the outpouring of a copious, direct, large and simple mind.
>
> (1901/2014, VI:29–30)

The Marshall Field building elevates the architect to a position of immense power in Sullivan's mind. Reminiscent also of Nietzsche's awe

FIGURE.6.2 Marshall Field and Co. Wholesale Store, Chicago, IL, 1887. Henry Hobson Richardson, Shepley, Rutan and Coolidge. J.W. Taylor, photographer. J.W. Taylor Photograph Collection, Ryerson and Burnham Art and Architecture Archives © Art Institute of Chicago. Digital file #199303_120806_032.

at the power of the Palazzo Pitti – a building that Nietzsche suggests was constructed by colossal giants – the Marshall Field building presents itself to Sullivan as the kind of 'tall graven building' which 'shows that once there were giants on the earth' (Caldwell 1956:12). As Alfred Caldwell notes, 'Like Nietzsche', Sullivan 'conceived of man as an infinite possibility, of man the creator surpassing the creature man' (Caldwell 1956).

Of the designs thought to have been influenced by the Marshall Field building, it was specifically the Wainwright and Guaranty buildings, which were thought to exemplify Sullivan's 'solution' to the artistic problem he posed in his essay, 'The Tall Office Building Artistically Considered' (1896/2014). It is in this essay that Sullivan first articulated his famous dictum, 'form ever follows function', discussed in the context of artistic ornament and its application in his designs for the Wainwright and Guaranty buildings. Where other architects may have attempted to mask the structure of tall office buildings with decorative cladding, Sullivan exposes the internal steel frame, making it visible through his use of ornament. This has led critics to suggest Sullivan's architecture attempts to be more 'honest' in its design and construction. As David Andrew notes, compared to Sullivan's buildings, those 'that use internal steel construction but cloak that construction in traditionally trabeated or arcuated forms are "dishonest" and ought to be relegated to less distinguished positions in the history of architecture' (1985:93). An appeal to honesty complements Nietzsche's desire to unmask imitations and parodies of organic forms and to create only that which is necessary.

The Wainwright building incorporates ornamental features that accentuate the building's function and structure (Figure 6.3). Its wide openings onto the street pavement are required to make the shops that accommodate the first floor more accessible to customers. The wide windows that define the second floor are required by the public offices that occupy this space. Above this are several floors with identical windows for a series of smaller offices, and finally, at the top is a closed floor to screen the water tanks and machinery of the building. The pronounced vertical movement of the sandstone exterior is achieved by a light skeletal structure of equally spaced piers, with bases and capitals, making them look like thin columns. These mark the broad window fields and draw the eye upwards to the overscaled cornice, which is abrupt and sharply incised, making it easily seen from the street, ten storeys below. Its overall impression, Carl Condit notes,

FIGURE.6.3 Wainwright building, St. Louis (b.1891, Louis H. Sullivan), East elevation. © Reading Tom (flickr), 2011.

'is movement, the dynamic transcendence of space and gravitational thrust' (1959:91).

But just how 'honest' is this building? After all, the top floor is screened off to hide its vital machinery, and every other pier is a formal addition with no practical function. Indeed, according to Andrew:

> [I]t fails on several counts to fulfil a 'functional' definition: it has two pilasters for every internal column; the second story is treated differently in elevation from those above it, even though its plan is no different from theirs; the floor just beneath the cornice – site of the toilets, ventilation equipment, and elevator motors – is actually the floor that receives the richest decoration on the outside.
>
> (1985:94)

While the Wainwright building has been regarded as 'one of the most remarkable exhibitions of sheer architectural originality in his own or any age' (Condit 1959:80), a few years later its formal character was refined and enriched in Sullivan's Guaranty building in Buffalo, a building that has been called his 'most perfect skyscraper' (Caruso 2012). In the Guaranty building we find greater emphasis on verticality, not simply because it has six additional floors, but in large part due to its ornament, which, compared to that of the Wainwright building, is not as wide, with recesses not as deep. Andrew notes, the Guaranty building is 'more the "proud and soaring thing" than the cubical Wainwright'. Its 'cornice is thinner, and instead of meeting the walls abruptly at right angles, it emerges as a graceful, continuous, curviplanar swelling of the walls themselves. The overall effect is one of stretching and attenuation' with walls that appear 'membranous and not lithic' (1985:102).

The heroic architect

Architects of the new style are heroic figures, who take it upon themselves to elevate cultural taste and to create a new community ripe for a new modern era. Architecture in the grand style is synonymous with the architect who designs in this mode; it is the spatial expansion of this architect's will. In this respect, the 'new man' is the 'new building', and both must be constructed in the grand style. In Nietzsche's later works, the architect is a favoured role model for the 'new man' – replacing the Greek tragedian of his earlier writings and the 'monumental figures' from his *Untimely Meditations* – and he glimpses evidence of the architect's grand style in the palazzi of Genoa and the Palazzi Pitti of Florence, before experiencing it more forcibly in the Mole Antonelliana in Turin.

In the early part of the twentieth century the figure of the architect was revered as a natural leader, a teacher, even as seer or prophet akin to

Zarathustra, as one uniquely gifted with the power to discern the spirit of the age and to create forms that symbolize and evoke the spirit for others. The architect had the technological wizardry to render the spirit of the age visible and tangible to others. The cultural goal, as Whyte puts it, was the 'reachable man-made paradise, which would be created by the architect or by the *geistig* leader, rather than by political revolution' (1982:224). The architect was promoted as a leader on grounds that he was 'uniquely qualified to reconcile and bring harmony with the higher truths of Geist and the demands of the Volk' by mastering 'the objective laws of function and technology' (1982:225).

The architect as heroic prophet and leader was an established trope long before Nietzsche gave expression to it. For instance, in the Renaissance period, the architect Giorgio Vasari in *The Lives of Artists* (c.1550) depicts architects as visionary geniuses working against the odds. But aside from Antonelli, whom Nietzsche praised by virtue of conceiving 'the most ingenious structure that might ever have been built' (KSB,8.1227:565), Nietzsche regarded the architects of his day as lacking the creative genius to harness the spirit of the times. Prior to his discovery of Mole Antonelliana, Nietzsche laments contemporary artists, who lack the will to build and are themselves unsuitable as building material (GS,356). But he senses optimism in the air: 'Already a new odour floats about, an odour that brings health and a new hope,' says Zarathustra. 'From you, who have chosen out yourselves, shall a chosen people spring, and from this chosen people, the Superman' (Z, I,22[2]:103). In the meantime, Zarathustra waits in his mountain cave for those who will discover his lofty terrain, waiting for those to arrive 'who are higher, stronger, more victorious, and more joyful, such as are built right-angled in body and soul' (Z, IV,11:294). Whether Alessandro Antonelli was the kind of person Zarathustra was waiting for is up for debate. Certainly, Nietzsche was thrilled to have found in Antonelli's work, the triumphant desire for the heights that Zarathustra had sought after.

The question remains as to whether the ideal of the heroic architect was realized among the modernist architects in the early twentieth century. Gropius, writing in 1919, suggests not: 'There are no architects today, we are all merely preparing the way for someone who will once again deserve the name of architect' (1919). Le Corbusier was ambiguous on the matter. On the one hand, he celebrates as fact that 'a great epoch has begun', that there 'exists a new spirit', and that 'a new style' is being determined 'day by day' (1923/2016:146–7), but on the other, he suggests that engineers are the ones who are leading the way, while architects, by contrast, are playing catch up. Engineering, he says, is 'at its full height' while architecture is in an 'unhappy state of regression'. He goes on: 'Engineers are healthy and virile, active and useful, balanced and joyful', while 'architects are disenchanted and idle, boastful or morose' (1923/2016:93–4). In Le Corbusier's eyes, modern engineering was flourishing and continually evolving with innovative technologies and machinery, and this was evident, he says, in the construction of airplanes, motorcars and steamships, while modern architecture seemed to be out of touch with the new resources available to it. In some respects, Le Corbusier's criticisms parallel Sullivan's concerns that a plethora of new resources would overtake and eclipse artistic vision. The failure to keep up with new ways of building led modern architects, Le Corbusier says, to regress in their designs by continuing to replicate styles of the past, notably 'the styles of Louis XIV, XV, XVI or Gothic' (1923/2016:101,109).

Francesco D'Alessio goes so far as to suggest that Le Corbusier's figure of the engineer is equivalent to Nietzsche's *Übermensch* on the grounds that both 'remain true to the earth' and both say a resounding 'yes!' to life through daring feats of self-overcoming (2016:17–18). Similar comparisons have been made albeit briefly by scholars between Nietzsche's *Übermensch* and the figure of the engineer in Louis Sullivan's writings (Menocal 2000:108; Snyder 2017:81). Sullivan, like Le Corbusier after him, celebrated the engineer as one who wields immense creative powers. In his autobiography Sullivan describes his early fascination with the energy exerted in the construction of bridges and railways in industrial America. They conjured for him images of heroic titans – akin to 'giants' who built the Marshall Field Wholesale Store – 'of naked mighty men, with power to do splendid things with their bodies' (Sullivan 1924/2009:79).[7] Writing in the third person, Sullivan asserts, 'the chief engineers became his heroes; they loomed above other men. The positive quality of their minds agreed with the aggressive quality of his own. In childhood his idols had been the big strong men who *did* things'. Later, his ideal of the most powerful type would evolve to those 'could *think* things', then to the 'expansive power of men who could *imagine* things; and at last he began to recognize as dominant', he writes, 'the will of the Creative Dreamer: he who possessed the power and vision needed to harness Imagination, to harness the intellect, to make science do his will, to make the emotions serve him' (Sullivan 1924/2009:247–8). This figure embodied a 'free spirit' (Sullivan 1924/2009:329), and 'the creator of realities', a 'lesser god, a humble god, no "ideal man", no "cosmic superman", just the maker of ornament' (Sullivan 1924:np).

D'Alessio characterizes Le Corbusier's engineer as an *Übermenschlich* figure who seeks continual self-overcoming by utilizing ever more advanced construction methods and technological materials to achieve optimum results (2016:18). While Sullivan's most powerful type was a present reality for him, embodied in those who master their emotions in the creation of architectural ornament, D'Alessio suggests that for Le Corbusier, the architect has not learnt how to master their emotions, but is hopeful they one day will, and that this will subsequently lead to more innovative architectural designs. This is because, according to Le Corbusier, architects are provoked into an emotional response as and when they observe engineers asserting themselves through their own bold initiatives. In this respect, Le Corbusier's architect must draw on the powerful achievements of the engineer as rolemodels for their own design aspirations (2016:18–19).

Both Sullivan and Le Corbusier fancied themselves as innovative figures, embodying the types they idealized in their writings, and fashioned in large part in the style of Zarathustra. I mentioned in the previous chapter that Sullivan and Le Corbusier are thought by some to have intentionally emulated the prophetic tone and writing style of *Thus Spoke Zarathustra* in their own writings. But others have taken this notion further to suggest that they modelled their personalities on Zarathustra, or further still, regarded themselves as *Übermenschen*, the very fulfilment of Zarathustra's teaching. According to Cohen, *Thus Spoke Zarathustra* 'convinced' Le Corbusier of his own 'prophetic call' as the 'prophet of a new architecture' (1999:317). Stanislaus von Moos suggests that Le Corbusier saw himself in 'Nietzsche's image of the lonely superman, whose tragic destiny it was to be sacrificed for the sake of mankind' (2009:29). Charles Jencks claims Le Corbusier had 'a highly developed sense of his own destiny' drawn 'from Nietzsche's notion of the Superman' (1973:59; Brooks 1999:174,358).[8] Sullivan positions himself somewhat similarly as the heroic architect who could, he writes, 'concentrate the powers of will', 'shape character', 'make good citizens' and 'lay the foundation for a generation of real architects' (1902/2014:226). Menocal suggests that Sullivan's tragic destiny is apparent in his 'disenchantment' with 'the social and architectural trends of his day [which] ran contrary to his ideals', so that – as with Nietzsche before him – Sullivan became 'a prophet without an audience that exasperated and for a time silenced him' (1981:89,100). Van Zanten supports this idea, claiming that Sullivan 'became a strange, great, solitary figure alone in his spreading office at the top of the Auditorium Tower [which he had built], the subject of distant admiration and recrimination, but not of employment' (2000:7). In other words, feeling maligned and misunderstood, Sullivan retreated to his equivalent of Zarathustra's 'high-rise' mountain cave.[9]

Other notable architects could be discussed in this context alongside Sullivan and Le Corbusier, such as van de Velde who sought to create a new artistic elite, or Bruno Taut, who envisioned ideal cities overseen by elite artists, and not least, Philip Johnson who imagined himself as a 'Nietzschean *Übermensch*, a man above the crowd, a prophet leading the way toward a new aesthetic' and 'the coming of a new society of elite supermen' (Lamster 2018:51,37). Coupled with such lofty aspirations is a dangerous egoism, which easily arises when the desire to engage with the spirit of the times turns into a desire to be recognized as the powerful individual who can master it. When this happens, the individual forfeits their creative potential. By the same token, it is relatively easy to mistake the will to power for political power, when one seeks not to master one's own instincts but to master other people. Architects who fail to integrate their instincts and creative powers, Sullivan asserts, will display a frenzy of energy, leading to the design of sick and neurotic buildings. These architects and artists tend to be preoccupied with petty gratifications and superficial whims clothed in grandiose desires to control others. Perhaps the most striking misappropriation of Nietzsche's notion of will to power is in the context of Nazi ideology, where the image of power is channelled into megalomanic buildings intended to express Hitler's 'heroic ideal' to remedy the decadence of Weimar society. In 1929 Hitler pledged to resolve the problematic absence of heroic feeling in Weimar and its disintegrating impact on the populace by providing Germany with his vision of a great architecture drawing on a 'political will to power' (see Miller Lane 1985:147). The architect as the 'new man' is subsequently interpreted as a badge of prestige and of political persuasion rather than a position drawn from creative and artistic skill. Nietzsche suggests architects are no longer given the opportunity to excel at their craft when the 'actors become masters' in society. When this happens, 'the strength to build' is 'paralysed', and 'great architects' become 'ever more disadvantaged' until they are 'finally made impossible' (GS,356).

CHAPTER SEVEN

Modern architecture inspired by Nietzsche

Charting Nietzsche's significance within architectural theory and practice is a speculative exercise. Nevertheless, Nietzsche was influenced by certain architects and buildings, and in turn, his philosophy has influenced a variety of prominent architects and designs. This chapter will examine examples of the latter. I have claimed that Nietzsche's ideas find their clearest architectural expression in the works of Henry van de Velde. Of all architects, van de Velde exerted most effort in designing buildings and monuments to honour Nietzsche. The frustrations he experienced with his unrealized stadium-temple complex would have taught him invaluable Nietzschean lessons in the struggles of creativity. And although his renovation of Villa Silberblick is the only architectural project to honour Nietzschean philosophy that he brought to completion, some suggest he was able to realize elements and features of his stadium-temple complex in the commission that immediately followed it – his Theatre for the 1914 Deutscher Werkbund Exhibition in Cologne.

This final chapter analyses specific designs of modern architecture which have been identified by scholars as making explicit reference to Nietzschean ideas. I draw upon the findings from previous chapters to evaluate their claims. I begin with van de Velde's Theatre for the 1914 Werkbund Exhibition before evaluating the romantic notions of cave and mountain often associated with Nietzsche and rendered architecturally into designs by Peter Behrens and Bruno Taut. Specifically, I examine Behrens' 'Zarathustra house' atop a hill at the Darmstädt Artist Colony (1899–1901) and his cave-like *Hamburger Vorhalle* (1902) for the Exposition of Decorative Arts in Turin. I also examine Bruno Taut's various crystal houses, conceived in his illustrated works *Alpine Architektur* (Taut 1919a) and *Die Stadtkrone* (1919/2015), as well as his celebrated *Glashaus* (1914), which stood hundreds of yards away from van de Velde's Theatre at the Werkbund Exhibition in Cologne, and his *Monument des Neuen Gesetzes* (1919).

Perhaps most pertinent to my investigation is Taut's search for a worthy building to 'crown' an entire city (*Stadtkrone*). Taut attempted to establish an architectural template for a city that maximizes and elevates the creative aspirations of its citizens in accordance with Taut's ideas about social hierarchies – ideas which resemble in part Nietzsche's own. Nietzsche's philosophy is often characterized as championing individuals who live and create for themselves in isolation from the masses. But this is a misleading caricature. Earlier I suggested that Le Corbusier's plans to enhance a person's creativity by isolating them and limiting their opportunities for spontaneous communal interactions with others were unlikely to inspire the creative freedom that Nietzsche himself sought and was more likely to compound the problematic gap that Nietzsche envisaged between a person's reliance on abstract thoughts and their disengagement with bodily experiences. In other words, while Nietzsche's exemplary artist requires a degree of isolation from unnecessary distractions, if they are to have a real and positive impact on their community by elevating its cultural value and standing, they must also be part of it. Taut reflects on how this balance is attainable through the architectural designs of city spaces. In Chapter 2, I suggested that a city in the grand style would contrast with those German provincial towns that assaulted Nietzsche's instincts with their 'flat and cowardly' architecture which cowered beneath their tyrannical religious buildings. Nietzsche allows for cathedrals and other religious buildings so long as they are stripped of their unhelpful symbolism, and thereby stripped of their oppressive power. By the same token, a city in the grand style would allow their elevated structures to stand alongside other distinctive buildings, each standing upright and self-assured. As I will argue, Taut's vision for the 'city crown' shares similar principles to architecture in the grand style.

Van de Velde's Theatre, Deutscher Werkbund Exhibition, Cologne (1914–18)

As with all buildings at the Deutscher Werkbund Exhibition of 1914, van de Velde's Theatre intended to showcase potentials for German design and technology for the new age (Figure 7.1). Nietzsche's affirmative ideas provided for many a rousing philosophy to herald the dawning of this new era. And while the exhibited buildings were not monuments to Nietzschean philosophy per se, there are several features of van de Velde's Theatre that are highly suggestive of Nietzschean ideas.

According to Anne van Loo, the editor of van de Velde's memoires, the Werkbund Theatre project arises for van de Velde precisely when the Nietzsche stadium-temple project is abandoned. Given this continuity of

FIGURE 7.1 Theatre, Werkbund Exhibition, Cologne (b.1914, Henry van de Velde). Front perspective. Photograph, 1914. © Bildarchiv Foto Marburg.

projects, Loo notes, it is unsurprising that the theatre design is informed by 'Nietzschean sources' (1995:377n.2). The principal design features which Loo identifies as distinctly Nietzschean are its overall 'zoomorphic character' and the 'dialogue between the Apollonian and Dionysian decoration of the interior'. Loo's remarks mirror comments by Dirk Teuber (1984). Teuber sheds some light on its supposed 'zoomorphic, natural character', as he also refers to it, by referring to a description of the Theatre by Carl Oscar Jatho (1884–1971), a German essayist who compared the building to 'beings of an unconscious nature that grow mysteriously out of the earth' (Teuber 1984:126). Teuber himself remarks that the building's entrance evokes images from Nietzsche's *Dionysian Dithyrambs*. He further notes that the pictorial programme of the building alludes to the 'rhythmic' interplay of Apollo and Dionysus (1984:125).

It is difficult to claim a direct influence of Nietzschean ideas on van de Velde's theatre design. As I explained in relation to Gottfried Semper and his Semperoper in Dresden, the distinctive use of Dionysian iconography within a theatre building designed by an architect who is both familiar with and favourable to Nietzschean ideas does not in itself indicate Nietzsche's influence. Just as Semper's interest in Dionysus as a god of the arts and master of the Muses can be traced to traditions and sources that precede Nietzsche's popularization of these themes, similar claims can be made for the incorporation of Dionysian imagery in van de Velde's Theatre. Indeed,

I am not entirely convinced that van de Velde's Werkbund Theatre was imbued with Dionysian themes to the extent that is sometimes suggested.

Katherine Kuenzli (2012) maintains that the Theatre is stylized after a 'Dionysian aesthetic formulated [by] Nietzsche', due to its figurative decoration, which makes explicit reference to 'Dionysian rituals of dance' (2012:256). Aside, perhaps from sculptures in relief of grape vines by Hermann Obrist (1862–1927), which adorned the mullions of the eye-shaped exterior windows, it is difficult to see how the pictorial programme of the Theatre is distinctly Dionysian. The main mural in the side foyer by Ludwig von Hofman appears to follow typical theatrical iconography with images pertaining to the Muses. Its depiction of dancers and a man wielding a sword before vulnerable women is reminiscent of the allegorical portrayals of 'La Danse' and 'La Tragédie' by Antoine Bourdelle (1861–1929), which are incorporated into his bas-reliefs of Apollo and the nine Muses (designed in 1912) for the Théâtre des Champs-Elysées by van de Velde. Van de Velde was obliged to incorporate Bourdelle's reliefs into the Théâtre, and there is evidence to suggest he was similarly hesitant about including some of the ornament for his Werkbund Theatre – not least, Obrist's grape vines, which obstructed natural light from entering the interior.

Perhaps it is more profitable to examine the building design itself for traces of Nietzschean influence. Kuenzli suggests that Dionysian principles are evident in the overarching 'ritualistic and dynamic character' of the building. Its architecture suggests to Kuenzli a Greek amphitheatre and a medieval cathedral, which combine to evoke a sense of festival. This festivity continues in its interior with its use of colour, light, and shadow. Its auditorium has an 'inner glow', and the mobile lighting on stage creates a magical effect that 'dissolves actor and scenery into flickering patterns of light and shadow' (2012:260). Kuenzli's description is reminiscent of Semper's allusion to the 'haze of carnival candles' as the 'true atmosphere of art' – a phrase Nietzsche himself uses to describe the arousal of Dionysian instincts.

The most compelling suggestion of a direct link between Nietzschean ideas and the architectural design of this theatre is the visual correlation between van de Velde's drawing of its ground floor plan from 1913 (Figure 7.2) and a title cover he designed for an edition of Nietzsche's *Dionysos-Dithyramben* at the request of Elisabeth Föster-Nietzsche in 1914 (Figure 7.3). Earlier, I alluded to van de Velde's geometric illustrations for lavish editions of Nietzsche's works as reminiscent of architectural structures. There I suggested that the blending or merging of architecture, art, philosophical prose and poetry is illustrative of van de Velde's commitment to a Gesamtkunstwerk or total work of art. The symbiosis of the Werkbund Theatre floor plan and illustration for Nietzsche's book of poems continues this approach.

The striking similarity between the theatre's floorplan and frontispiece for *Dionysos-Dithyramben* is noted by Teuber (1984) and later by Sembach (1989). Sembach writes, 'If this design is turned upside-down, it is similar to

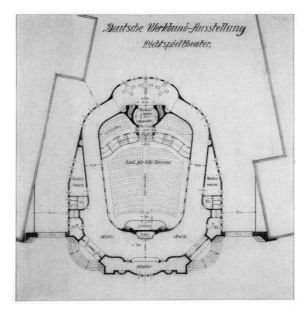

FIGURE 7.2 Theatre, Werkbund Exhibition, Cologne. Plan, 1913. Henry van de Velde. © Rheinisches Bildarchiv Cologne, RBA 194 095.

FIGURE 7.3 Frontispiece for an edition of Nietzsche's *Dionysos Dithyramben*. Henry van de Velde, 1914. Author's photograph.

the ground plan, not in every detail, but certainly in contour and movement. In both cases long, curving lines are juxtaposed with concentrated grammalogues, creating a state of tension' (1989:184; see also Teuber 1984:126–7). Teuber notes a correspondence between the four 'voluptuous' circular shapes at the top of the illustration and a mirror designed by van de Velde for the doors into the auditorium (1984:127).

Although it is tempting to imagine the Werkbund Theatre design as a direct chronological descendent of the Nietzschean temple-stadium project, it is more appropriate to consider it as part of a much larger, repository of design ideas that van de Velde had been reworking and developing for many years. Richard Hollis notes that van de Velde was 'constantly developing ideas on the design of theatres' (2019:191), and his Werkbund Theatre would have inevitably incorporated residues of his earlier theatre designs, such as his theatre for Weimar, intended to revival the Bayreuth Festspielhaus (b. 1903/4), his design for a competition for a theatre in Lübeck (b. 1908) and Théâtre des Champs-Elysées (b. 1910/11). His temple-stadium project would also have been in this repository of influential design ideas. In Chapter 4, I discussed van de Velde's tendency to incorporate interior design features of his earlier buildings into the exterior designs of his later ones. There I cited Sembach's assertion that design elements of the main room of the Nietzsche-Archiv at Villa Silberblick are replicated in exterior features of his unbuilt theatre in Weimar (1989:88), and Kostka's (2000) suggestion that he replicates these elements again in the outer skin of his monument to Ernst Abbe. I went on to note visual similarities between the exterior designs of the Weimar theatre, Abbe monument, and van de Velde's initial attempt to design a temple to honour Nietzsche in what would become the Nietzsche temple-stadium complex project. The point I wish to make is that it is difficult to identify in van de Velde's designs exactly where and when Nietzsche's impact begins and ends. What we find is the translation of van de Velde's own style articulated across different mediums, designs and building types – albeit a style that resonates with precepts of Nietzsche's grand style.

Zarathustrian caves and mountains: Peter Behrens and Bruno Taut

Thus Spoke Zarathustra was instrumental in popularizing the romantic image of the lonely wanderer, walking along treacherous icy mountain paths of self-discovery. I noted that this book sparked mass tourism in the early twentieth-century to Nietzsche's favourite mountain walks and a wider 'cult of mountains', which remained closely associated with Nietzsche and Nietzschean imagery, specifically from *Zarathustra* (Aschheim 1994:35; Maciuika 2008:42). Idealized alongside the heights of Zarathustra's mountain paths was his cave dwelling, where he lived with an eagle and snake, and from where he was greeted by the rising sun every morning. Nietzschean philosophy subsequently became identified with towering and cavernous structural forms. According to Wolfgang Pehnt, 'almost all reading and thinking artists of the era' were aware of 'the topography of the superman' as the intimate 'connection between tower and cave' (1994:58). Peter Behrens and Bruno Taut are two architects often mentioned in this context, and in their works, we find concerted efforts to translate this imagery into architectural forms, with expressed intentions to elevateced the cultural and spiritual aspirations of individuals and whole communities through their designs. Behrens and Taut were similarly drawn to the spiritual connotations of crystal and glass, and in their works, caves and mountains are morphed into glittering caverns and crystal peaks. While several designs by Behrens and Taut make explicit reference to Nietzsche's philosophy and *Thus Spoke Zarathustra* especially, their sparkling aesthetic should not be regarded – as it sometimes has – as distinctly 'Nietzschean' in its appeal.

Peter Behrens

Behrens' Nietzschean credentials are lauded by many, including Aschheim, who refers to Behrens' work as 'the most famous and striking' practical expression of Nietzsche's inspiration (1994:33), and by Buddensieg, who asserts that Behrens was the only visual artist of his generation 'who had the "grand style" prophesised by Nietzsche' (1980:37). Given Behrens' wide influence as a founding member of the Deutscher Werkbund and teacher to several notable architects of the modern era – including, Le Corbusier, Mies van der Rohe, Bruno Taut and Walter Gropius – we might expect his interests in Nietzsche to have inspired others, encouraging Nietzschean ideas to permeate far and wide.

Behrens personally thanked Elisabeth Förster-Nietzsche for her gift to him of writings by 'your immortal brother', and in response to her invitation to visit the Nietzsche-Archiv, he confesses, 'This fulfils a wish I have had for a long time. I consider myself fortunate to be able to pour out in your presence all my veneration and my deepest admiration for the Wise Artist.' He continues to note, 'I wish I had the strength to convert my feelings into works' (6 December 1902; cited in Buddensieg 1980:40). Despite Behrens' self-professed limitations, several commentators maintain he successfully translated Nietzsche's artistic vision into his designs. Most recognized in this regard are his designs that feature symbolic motifs drawn from *Thus Spoke Zarathustra*, such as Behrens' house on top of a hill at the Darmstädt Artist Colony (b. 1901) (Figure 7.4), and the cave-like vestibule of *Hamburger Vorhalle* in Turin (built in 1902) (Figure 7.5).

According to Rosemarie Haag Bletter, the positioning of Behrens' house on the Mathildenhöhe hill of Darmstädt is reminiscent of 'Zarathustra's cave at the top of a mountain', and suggestive of a Nietzschean stratification of society, which positions 'the artist' at 'the apex of the social pyramid', a place 'formerly occupied by the aristocracy' (1981:31). But it is Behrens' ornamental scheme for this house – notably, his stylized images of eagle and *Edelstein* (precious stone) – which has encouraged many to regard it as distinctly Nietzschean, and thereby to call it by its unofficial name, *Zarathustrahaus*, and to describe its architectural style as *Zarathustrastil* (see Bryant 2004:161; Buddensieg 1980; Maciuika 2008:39). Tilmann Buddensieg maintains that Nietzsche was of 'central importance' to the design of the house due to Behrens' representation of 'Zarathustra's favourite animal', the eagle and 'Zarathustra's diamond' (1980:39). Fritz Neumeyer regards Behrens' house as Zarathustra's 'architectural debut' due to its incorporation of 'Zarathustra motifs of the eagle and the crystal' (1999:288). While Neumeyer concedes that their allusion in the house is somewhat obscure, or as he puts it, 'more-or-less coded', Aschheim regards its 'symbols of the eagle and Zarathustra's diamond or *Edelstein*' as the most 'striking', 'practical expression' of Nietzsche's 'inspiration' (1994:33). John Maciuika maintains that the 'crystal, inspired by the writings of the philosopher Friedrich Nietzsche, was a symbol of artistic rebirth and creativity', and it was a symbol that 'Behrens enthusiastically embraced' in the form of a 'recurring diamond motif'. This recurring motif 'signified Nietzsche's *Edelstein*, intended to radiate "the virtues of a world that is not yet here"' (2008:38–9).

I am less convinced than most that Behrens' crystalline motifs and his inclusion of a portal that is stylized in abstract patterns that resemble wings

FIGURE 7.4 Peter Behrens' House, Darmstädt. Northeast elevation. © Bildarchiv Foto Marburg/Norbert Latocha.

of an eagle are indicative of Nietzsche's immediate influence. That we find similar stylized motifs of the eagle and diamond replicated by Behrens for his book cover of *Thus Spoke Zarathustra*, which he exhibited in 1902 at the First International Exhibition of the Decorative Arts in Turin (see below), certainly suggests their link to Nietzsche. While Mark Bolland incorrectly asserts that Nietzsche's 'symbolism skirted crystals entirely' (1996:108), I think his dogmatic assertion appeals to the fact that the relationship between crystals and Nietzsche's Zarathustra is not immediately evident, but more subtle and easily overlooked. When commentators speak of a Zarathustrian crystal or diamond, they tend to allude to a conversation Zarathustra has with an elderly woman about the value of women (in Part I of the book). There Zarathustra says a woman can discover within a 'true man' a playful child. To that end, Zarathustra calls upon women to become 'a plaything, pure and fine, like a precious stone [*Edelstein*], illumined by the virtues of a world that is not yet here'. He continues: 'Let the light of a star shine in your love! Let your hope be: "May I give birth to the Superman!"' (Z, I,18:92). The precious stone in this context has transformational properties that bring forth playful, creative possibilities. Another occasion where Zarathustra alludes to a precious stone is rarely mentioned by commentators in connection with Behrens' designs. This is the occasion in Part III, where Zarathustra calls upon his brothers to '*become hard*' like diamonds (*Diamanten*), 'For creators are hard', resisting and unyielding (Z, III,12[29]:231).[1]

Significantly, the symbolic meaning given to Zarathustra's crystal by commentators of Behrens' work, as a metaphor of divine wisdom and transcendence, can be traced to older, broader esoteric traditions, which are more persuasive and pervasive in their influence than Nietzsche's scant allusions to *Edelsteine* and *Diamanten* in *Thus Spoke Zarathustra* appear to be.[2] Indeed, it is not altogether clear how Behrens' house negotiates the significance of Zarathustra's *Edelstein*, which shines with the 'virtues of a world that is not yet here'. Contrary to Zarathustra's aspirations for the future and hopes for a new way of being, Behrens' three-storey square house has been described by some as a conventional domestic dwelling. John Maciuika, for instance, suggests its prominent gables and brick trim are indicative of vernacular architecture of Northern German traditions, and its interior plan – featuring music room, and dining and drawing rooms set off from a main entrance hall – as 'fairly conventional' for a single family (2008:43,39). But others highlight its eccentricity and uniqueness, with Barbara Miller Lane, for instance, describing the same curved gables and contrasting bands of masonry as 'a self-conscious striving for novelty' and a 'bizarre architectural experiment' (1985:19). Contrasting interpretations such as these, when accepted together in tension, are indicative of the creative outlook that Nietzsche himself sought. To that end, perhaps Buddensieg comes closest to a Nietzschean reading of the house in his recognition of its various 'contradictions', on the one hand as 'a theatre for the self-representation' and 'celebration' of Behrens as an 'artist', and on the other hand, its 'intuition of new possibilities' as 'the house of the future' (1980:44). In practical terms, the house is forward-looking, but it had not yet grasped the potentials of its modern design for architectural and industrial development. In this regard, Miller Lane asserts that Behrens' house remained a 'mere exercise' in 'the development of surface pattern and had little influence except insofar as [it] expressed a desire for innovation' (1985:19).

Behrens experimented with Zarathustrian imagery more overtly in his interior design, *Hamburger Vorhalle*, for the German section of the first International Exposition of Modern Decorative Arts in Turin in 1902. By doing so, he explicitly connects Nietzsche's message to Germany's aspirations for a new, powerful, and artistic culture and industry. The transitory nature of this installation, which was intended to last only for the duration of the exhibition (May to November), complements Nietzsche's characterization of identity as fleeting and in flux. Behrens designed a dark, cool, and damp chamber room with stucco walls and a ceiling moulded into stalactite forms to give the impression of a cave. But this was not intended as any given cave; it was Zarathustra's cave, for a large copy of *Thus Spoke Zarathustra* was exhibited at the centre of the room, bound with the cover designed by Behrens, mentioned above. The darkness of the cave was punctured by a shaft of light from a skylight of coloured glass. The skylight was draped with hanging plants and its light shone directly on to the book to highlight its sacred quality, as if the book were divinely selected or chosen by nature itself. Its sacred nature is further emphasized by the placement of the book within a square area enclosed by the folded wings of two angelic figures, who guard it reverentially. The prominent focus given to Nietzsche's Zarathustra presents Nietzsche's philosophy at the very centre of the aspirations for German industry. The two become synonymous in Behrens' design, sharing an altar, which is connected to the skies above, thereby suggesting the dawning of a new era for the nation. According to Anderson, the *Hamburger Vorhalle* translates into architectural space the concluding chapter of *Thus Spoke Zarathustra*, titled 'Das Zeichen' (The Sign). He quotes from the chapter in his description of Behrens' room: 'This is *my* morning, *my* day begins: *rise up now, rise up, great noontide!* Thus spoke Zarathustra and left his cave, glowing and strong, like a morning sun emerging behind dark mountains' (2000:32).

The *Hamburger Vorhalle* received strikingly mixed reviews by the public and artists alike. It was known by many by its unofficial, derogatory name, 'grave of the unknown Superman', while Georg Fuchs (1868–1949), an art critic and supporter of the Darmstädt Artist Colony, lauded it as the entrance hall to the 'House of Power and Beauty' (*Die Vorhalle zu Hause der Macht und der Schönheit*) (cited in Anderson 2000:33; Pehnt 1994:56; Whyte 2013:10). According to Fuchs, it was an architectural symbol of the contemporary German Empire, and expressed the 'intoxication of gratitude',

FIGURE 7.5 *Hamburger Vorhalle*, Exposition of the Decorative Arts, Turin (b.1902, Peter Behrens) © Bildarchiv Foto Marburg.

'the exuberance of noble power' and the 'fulfilment and completion of life' itself (Anderson 2000:33; Pehnt 1994:56; Whyte 2003/2013:10). Fuchs' eulogy to Behrens' design, Pehnt asserts, was nothing short of 'an embarrassing hymn to the will to power' (1994:56).

Behrens' architectural works throughout his career are characterized by their celebrational and festive qualities. Robert Breuer, one of Behrens' contemporaries and early critics, speaks of Behrens' 'will to raise everything, even the everyday, into the crystalline atmosphere of the sacred festival house' (1910:195). And it is his idealist quest to transform the everyday and mundane that attracts most criticism to his designs. Anderson concludes that while 'Behrens showed incessant interest in the zeitgeist', his works were 'often little adapted to the site and to other conditions of place and use […] With Behrens, architecture answered to "the Time", not to people'. He continues to note that 'in a strange way' Behrens' 'buildings were themselves celebratory without need of […] people' (2000:259–60). While Behrens' architecture may be regarded as an 'untimely meditation' insofar as it presents an architectural vision of the elevation of cultural values for a 'time that has not yet come' (GS,125), Behrens' disinterest in people as active participations in his designs ensures his designs fail to capture the essential dynamic of Nietzsche's notion of festival, and ultimately, the grand style.

Behrens' sense of festivity is heard most loudly in his *Hamburger Vorhalle*, while his house in Darmstädt presents us – if we accept Breuer's summation – with 'the crystalline atmosphere of the festival house'. But his desire to celebrate and elevate the mundane and the everyday is perhaps most evident in his most recognizable work, the Turbine Factory (b. 1909) in Berlin, which he designed for the electrical equipment company, Allgemeine Elektrizitäts-Gesellschaft (AEG) (Figure 7.6). Prior to this building design, factories tended to hide the industrial operations they housed within depersonalized and anonymous facades of steel and glass. Behrens' design, by contrast, sought to elevate the factory building to the level of art, as a celebration of the power of the machine. Gabriele Bryant notes that by fusing technology and art, Behrens reformulated the idea of Gesamtkunstwerk from its origins in the nineteenth-century Festspielhaus to the industrial corporation buildings of the early twentieth century (2004:162). According to architectural historians Manfredo Tafuri and Francesco Dal Co, the ceremonial character of this building is expressive neither of a Zarathustrian nor Dionysian sense

FIGURE 7.6 AEG Turbine Building, Berlin (b.1909, Peter Behrens). Photograph, 1910. © Bildarchiv Foto Marburg.

of festivity, but of a synthesis 'under the Apollonian signs of industrial organization'. In other words, Behrens' factory represents, they assert, Behrens' 'own, rather shrunken interpretation of Nietzsche: not the liberating rejoicing of Zarathustra, but a somewhat mournful quest for a New Order' (cited in Aschheim 1994:34). Behrens' Apollonian Turbine Factory building would come to have far greater impact on modern architectural designs than his Zarathustrian-inspired projects.

Bruno Taut's City Crown and Alpine architecture (1917–18, 1919)

Bruno Taut developed the crystal theme beyond mere motif in his designs of houses and towns constructed almost entirely from glass. Taut, like Behrens, regarded the crystal as a symbol of spiritual renewal. Similarly, glass for Taut was a precious material that reflected all colours of light as well as encouraging enlightenment and self-reflection in the onlooker. In 1919, at an exhibition for Unknown Architects in Berlin, Taut 'calls upon all those who believe in the future' to recognize that 'one day there will be a worldview and then there will also be its sign, its crystal – architecture' (1919/2002:47).

In June 1904, Taut wrote to his brother, the architect Max Taut: 'I've read Nietzsche's Zarathustra over the last three months – a book of enormous and serious vitality. I've learnt a lot from it' (Whyte 1982:85,n.19). Sadly, he doesn't elaborate on what Nietzsche taught him, but we get a sense of the ideas that impressed him from his brief allusions to the symbolism of *Thus Spoke Zarathustra*, and to Nietzsche's earlier work, *Untimely Meditations*, which Taut cites to support his own political critique of the problems of a centralized and militant state. Although one gets the impression that Taut's architecture would have been much the same had he not 'learned a lot' from Nietzsche, one can trace in Taut's writings and designs various elements that could be attributed to Nietzsche's influence. In addition to Taut's reading of Nietzsche's works, his interest in Nietzsche may have been reinforced in his conversations and exchanges with other architects and social critics who were interested in Nietzsche's philosophy, such as van de Velde, Behrens and the fantasy novelist, Paul Scheerbart, who was perhaps most influential on Taut's designs.

Of his designs, the most widely scrutinized are the *Glashaus* exhibited in Cologne (1914) and various large-scale residential housing estates in Berlin. Together they represent distinct architectural ideologies that sit comfortably within Taut's general approach. While the *Glashaus* embodies his utopian vision of artistic freedom and has no purpose other than to delight and inspire harmony with its festive play of coloured glass, Taut's housing estates are concerned with practical living. Underpinning both is Taut's desire for social reform and a revaluation of values, and while Nietzschean ideas could provide philosophical support to either ideology, it is principally in the context of Taut's glass architecture (a material deemed too expensive and impractical for housing estates) that Nietzsche's influence is most readily cited. Perhaps most widely cited in the context of Nietzsche's ideas is Taut's fanciful work, *Alpine Architektur* (1919a). There Taut envisions the construction of a vast array of crystalline buildings embedded in towering mountain peaks, gorges and geometricized natural formations. These buildings would capture unimpeded light from the sun to maximize the physical and spiritual properties of their glass for the communities who lived within these satellite glass cities. It is difficult to imagine Nietzsche approving of the transformation of natural mountain landscapes into sparkling palaces and grail shrines, and to cityscapes that are perhaps better suited to futuristic theme parks or fantasy novels than to daily living. Mark Bolland describes Taut's Alpine vision as 'decadent', and dependent on an 'elemental reverie' that is far from the 'mountain interests of Nietzsche' (1996:108). Nevertheless, many have attempted to identify Nietzschean ideas as a credible source for this fantastic vision.

For the rest of this chapter, I wish to show how Nietzsche's ideas are pertinent to Taut's architectural designs for communal living, especially in the spatial layout of Taut's utopian city and the prominent glass structures within it. As we have seen, Nietzsche's interest in mountains extends to their topographical arrangement, which – in the same vein as a towering building – provided him with a spatial metaphor to illustrate his notion of height instinct, and the hierarchical social placement of people according to their personal character or extent of their will to power, with exemplary artists residing at the heights and the mediocre herd in the valleys below. Taut presents similar principles in the spatial arrangements of his ideal city and it is in this respect that I find his aspirations closest to Nietzsche's. Taut places at the highest point of his city a beautiful *Kristallhaus* (crystal house), where the most powerful citizen, the creative artist, dwells.

My discussion begins with Taut's plans for an ideal city and its *Kristallhaus*. I then evaluate Taut's Alpine vision from a Nietzschean perspective before considering two potential candidates for the *Kristallhaus* from Taut's wider work. The first is perhaps Taut's most widely discussed building, *Glashaus* designed for the Cologne exhibition in 1914, and the second is *Monument des Neuen Gesetzes*, a sketch of a monument 'for the new law', which makes explicit reference to Nietzsche.

Die Stadtkrone (1919)

In *Die Stadtkrone* (City Crown), Taut outlines his philosophy of architecture with plans for an ideal city, the arrangement of which sought to place artistic activity at the epicentre of communal living to enhance the culture outlook of all citizens. Taut proposed his city as a replacement for the German state, which, since 1870, had centralized its power, seizing control from its citizens and putting it in the hands of a militaristic government. A centralized state was problematic, Taut argued, because it encouraged war between nations.

He cites from Nietzsche's essay 'Schopenhauer as Educator' (the third of the *Untimely Meditations*, 1874) to underscore his point: 'Nietzsche observed: "All those nations, in which people other than the statesmen must deal with politics, are poorly organized and they deserve to collapse"' (Taut 1919/2015:81). A peaceful and harmonious society can be ensured, Taut maintains, only when a cultural and spiritual elite are invested with authority to challenge existing leadership by identifying its failings and suggesting viable solutions. Taut singles out the architect as the person with the imaginative capabilities and strength of will to carry out such demands, for only the architect, he asserts, is attuned to the spiritual needs of the people, and able to translate or to 'crystallize' those needs into material, spatial form (1915:174–6; cited in Whyte 1982:48). Taut envisions the architect as a benign dictator, whose buildings will inspire and revive German society at large with powerful designs that evoke precisely what the people need.[3]

Various scholars have acknowledged some of the correlations between the spatial arrangement of Taut's city and Nietzsche's hierarchical and aristocratic conception of society, such as Chapman and Ostwald (2002), Bletter (1982), Whyte (1982:86), and Mindrup (2015:18). To these I wish to add my own assertions, principally that in Taut's utopian city we discover, I suggest, Nietzsche's height instinct rendered into an architecture of vertical stratification. Bletter's account of Nietzsche's influence on Taut's city plan is perhaps least helpful with her description of the latter as 'a kind of Nietzschean gigatomania' (1982:224).[4] As I have explained, Nietzsche was explicit about his distrust in the gigantic and those who seek it out. He concerns himself less so with the *size* of a thing, and more with the motivations that drive it. The desire for power is a desire for creativity, not of domination. I wish to claim that Taut's utopian blueprint in the *Stadtkrone* furnishes Nietzsche's height instinct with architectural detail and helps us to visualize the social relations between the Nietzschean artistic creator who dwells in the heights and the herd who reside in surrounding lowlands, as well as the motivations that underpin these relations. Taut's city is socially and spatially aligned as a 'pyramid of human stratification' (1919/2015:100). This 'crystalline image of stratification', he asserts, organizes people according to 'their inclinations and their dispositions' (1919/2015:88) – or, as Nietzsche would say, according to their will to power – with the intention of elevating the cultural standards of the entire community.

Taut's city is circular in form with a diameter of approximately 7 kilometres to house approximately 300,000 inhabitants. At its centre is a towering *Kristallhaus* (crystal house). Taut describes this building as 'pure architecture', on the grounds that it is a 'material expression' of the spirit of the community. The *Kristallhaus* subsequently 'reigns over' the whole city as a beacon of its hopes and desires (1919/2015:89). The *Kristallhaus* is located geographically at the highest point of the city, and its elevated position is enhanced by the city's pyramidal shape, which is established by its different functional zones, each of which gradually step down and away from the *Kristallhaus*. This building is the 'crowning' feature of Taut's city, and here the artistic genius lives at the height of the community. The centripetal arrangement of the zones of the city emphasizes Taut's vision of a city ruled by a new cultural elite, with the cultural and artistic facilities closest to the centre, radiating outwards and downwards to its residential, business and industrial zones.

Immediately surrounding the *Kristallhaus* in the central are four large buildings, arranged in the shape of a cross. The buildings and spaces here are designed to meet the artistic needs of the community by encouraging meditation and self-reflection. They include an opera house, theatre, large community building, and large and small meeting halls. Immediately beyond these are meeting houses with terrace gardens, aquarium, plant house, tree-lined squares and a sequence of courtyards and arcades. Attached to the outer courtyard is a museum and central library, which are connected by colonnades to two reading houses. Within the innermost colonnade of this complex is the *Kristallhaus*, elevated above all other buildings with a reinforced concrete and steel frame, filled with prismatic glass and coloured glass mosaics (1919/2015:90). This is the only building in the city that has no specific purpose, and as such it comprises 'nothing but a beautiful room' that remains 'quiet and empty' (1919/2015:90–1).

In the residential zones, away from the centre, are shops, cafés and restaurants. These housing units and communal gardens are constructed on a flat plane. Houses are low in profile, designed as terrace housing, each with a long garden. The residential zone marks the start of communal activities for most citizens, with areas for shopping, eating, socializing and relaxing. Citizens instinctively find their position in the city according to the 'direction to which [they are] drawn' (1919/2015:84). Chapman and Ostwald note, 'This spatiosocial tendency not only congregates those of the same rank together, eliminating conflict, but induces new levels of creativity that are unencumbered by the forces of cultural homogenisation' (2002:2). The *Kristallhaus* and its surrounding architecture reserved for the artistic elite is intended to inspire other citizens, who will see these elevated buildings from every angle of the city. The central focus of the *Kristallhaus*, Taut says, radiates its light onto every building in the city, right down to the simplest hut, and imparts to each one the 'depth and power' of its 'philosophy of life', causing them all to 'shimmer' in its brilliance (1919/2015:76).

Taut develops a community shaped by principles of meritocracy that appealed to Nietzsche, and he utilizes a similar pyramidal hierarchical topography to place its citizens according to their natural instincts or inclinations, with the noble artist positioned at the heights, and the masses in the lowlands. In his introduction to the English translation of *Die Stadtkrone*, Matthew Mindrup describes 'Nietzsche's vision of the artist as superman, elevated above normal humanity' as the inspiration for Taut's figure at the centre of his city (2015:18). Taut's scheme lends architectural detail to a Nietzschean conception of power relations, with power and influence extending from the heights to rouse and elevate those below. Unlike an aristocracy, where excellence is judged in terms of natural inequality, a meritocratic culture regards excellence as individual achievement. According to Nietzsche, few are artistic geniuses, but everybody can share in the fruits of this genius through shared culture (AC,57; BGE,258,259). Taut's city proposes the architectural infrastructure to facilitate the cultural elevation of all citizens, with each zone oriented towards the creative centre.

According to Taut and Nietzsche, creative individuals do not exploit the many; they seek to educate them with a view to advancing the excellence of the community. An effective community will want to cultivate creative excellence by upholding the talents of its exemplary individuals as role models to encourage ever new models of human excellence to develop. Taut's architect at the centre of the city is subsequently not wholly free to pursue their own creative agendas, but

> must remind himself of his noble, priestly, magnificent, even divine profession and try to raise the treasure that lies in the depths of the human soul. In complete self-abandonment, he must immerse himself in the soul of the Volk and discover both himself and his noble profession by giving – at least as a goal – a material expression for that which slumbers in all humankind. As it was at one time, a talismanic built ideal should again arise and make people aware that they are members of a great architecture.
>
> (1919/2015:84)

The *Kristallhaus* at the heights of the city is intended as a source of artistic aspiration for all citizens as its spiritual and intellectual centre, a creative beacon towering over the community. According to Taut, it should inspire people, no matter their position or rank to move 'towards the heights'. Echoing Nietzsche's insistence that the summit be treated not as a terminal point to be conquered but a creative struggle ever upwards and beyond, Taut maintains that the *Kristallhaus* is not 'an end in itself' but 'an encouragement towards the realisation and further establishment of goals' (1919/2015:84).

Although the creative individuals imagined by Nietzsche and Taut require detachment and segregation from the preoccupations of others to prevent unnecessary distractions, they are not so isolated as to be wholly out of touch with their communities and ineffective educators. As Whyte puts it, the two groups should be clearly demarcated from each other so they can enrich each other with their complementary resonances (1982:113). Thus, when we first meet Nietzsche's Zarathustra, we find him descending from his mountain cave after thirty years of isolation, driven by a compulsion to share his wisdom with the people in the lowlands. Similarly, Nietzsche's enlightened 'mad man' goes into the marketplace to convey to others the repercussions of the death of God (GS,125). Zarathustra observes: 'the lonely height may not always be solitary and sufficient unto itself', consequently, 'the mountain may descend to the valley and the wind of the heights to the lowlands' (Z, III,10[2]:208).

The education of the herd by the exemplary individual is described by Nietzsche and Taut as a struggle, and this frustration is borne out by the failures of both the madman and Zarathustra to convey the full meaning of Nietzsche's teachings to the people. 'Have I been understood?' Nietzsche laments in his final words in his final book (EH, XIV). In his address to the Werkbund in 1914, Taut similarly notes:

> [Art] represents a pyramid, which widens towards its base. Above, at the apex, stand the most able – the artists with ideas. The broadening base means nothing more than a levelling down of these ideas [...] I find it exceedingly depressing that we cannot bring ourselves always to trust simply in the artists at the top.
>
> (cited in Whyte 1982:85)

According to Chapman and Ostwald, Taut's *Kristallhaus* is reminiscent of Zarathustra's cave, not only in relation to those in the lowlands, but also to the path of the sun. Just as Taut intended its glass surfaces to meet the sun's trajectory to ensure it radiates maximum light, Zarathustra's cave is positioned high in the mountains where it greets the rising sun, infusing Zarathustra with its 'glowing and strong' nature (Z, IV,20:333). We can imagine Zarathustra having to squat to enter the terrace houses in the low-level zones at the edge of Taut's city, and Chapman and Ostwald picture him residing happily within the *Kristallhaus*. Taut's description of the inner chamber of the *Kristallhaus*, they say, introduces a distinctly 'Nietzschean dimension' to the building suggestive of Zarathustra's sunlit cave. Taut describes it as a place where all 'deep and great feelings will be awakened'. For there, 'in its space, a lonely wanderer discovers the pure delight of architecture. While ascending the steps to the upper platform, he will see the city at his feet and beyond to the sun rising and setting, towards which this city and its heart are so strongly directed' (1919/2015:90).

Taking the city into the mountains

Taut's concern for the stratified placement of elite artists in relation to other citizens is absent in his next work, *Alpine Architektur* (1919a). There artists live in glass mountain-communities isolated from the rest of society, so that crystal houses become the reserve of the artistic elite. As Chapman and Ostwald note, in contrast to the *Stadtkrone* where 'everything is accessible to everyone', Taut's *Alpine Architecture* 'had abandoned the masses completely, seeking safe haven in the air above the contaminated clutter of the cities' (2002:8). This situation appears to undermine the creative dynamics that Nietzsche sought between artists and citizens and his desire to elevate the culture of whole societies. While Taut is occupied in this work with drawings of fanciful, dream-like buildings to house his lofty artistic ideals, from 1920 his focus is on more utilitarian and pragmatic matters, with social solutions for those who reside in the 'lowlands', with his designs of several large housing estates in Berlin, including *Siedlung Schillerpark* (1924–6), *Hufeisensiedlung Berlin-Britz* (1925–33), *Onkel Toms Hütte* (1926–31) and *Wohnstadt Carl Legien* (1928–30).

Increasingly efficient methods of glass manufacture made glass more affordable and popular, and a conventional material in the construction of all building types. Glass was no longer the reserve of the elite artist. 'The jagged, crystalline forms, associated with the aesthetic purity of Taut's new elite', Whyte writes, subsequently 'exploded onto the streets' (1982:110). It was employed indiscriminately for a whole variety of different social utilities and functions, such as the Berlin nightclub *Skala-Tanzcasino* (1920), remodelled by Walter Würzbach (1885–1971), and renovations of *Luna Park* (1929) also in Berlin, where, as Chapman and Ostwald note, the 'imagery of the crystal-house' appears 'against a backdrop of rampant mass-culture' (2002:9). In this respect, Taut's 'crystalline pyramid of social stratification' is razed to the ground and differences are levelled out. According to Chapman and Ostwald, 'the pinnacle had been reduced to the level of the marketplace' (2002:9).[5]

Alpine Architektur is considered one of the most ambitious architectural treatises of the twentieth century. It is certainly a curious work. It comprises a table of contents and thirty annotated drawings of a variety of glass structures set into mountain ranges. These include temples, pyramids, cathedrals, domes, pillars, arches of emerald glass, arcades between waterfalls of ruby-red glass, balconies, terraces, open halls of glass, and crystal-lined caves and grottos – all of which are placed apart to encourage spaces for their inhabitants to meditate and self-reflect on their relationship with their environments. The drawings depict various types of community dwellings for artists, which ascend in size to suggest ever-increasing distances between the artists who reside in these places and other non-artists whose dwelling places are notably absent in this work. We are led from 'Crystal Houses' to 'Architecture of the Mountains', thence from 'Alpine Constructions' to 'Terrestrial Buildings', and finally to 'Astral Buildings'. The buildings appear fuzzy and disembodied in structure, giving the overall impression of grandiose utopian fantasy worlds. It is as if the book invites us to gaze upon the realms of elite artists with little explanation of their meaning – perhaps initiated or elite artists do not require explanations.

The sense of unreality begins on its cover page with an epigram that suggests architecture is an achievement that is higher than life itself: '*Aedificare necesse est vivere non est necesse*' ('Building is necessary, living is not necessary'). Nietzsche would have rejected this assertion outright, for nothing can be higher than life. For Nietzsche, to build is to express life, and architecture in the grand style expresses a life lived well, of giving style to one's character, but building and architecture cannot be placed *above* life. As Zarathustra maintains, life uses architecture to its own ends, to achieve height, for 'life wants to build itself high with columns and stairs' (Z, II,29:125). Taut's final drawing suggests we have been led throughout the work to consider progressive stages of unreality. There dotted lines resemble a cloud placed around the words, 'Sterne Welten. Schlaf. Tod. Das Grosse Nichts. Das Namenlose' ('Stars. Worlds. Sleep. Death. Immensity. Nothingness. Namelessness'). Beneath this cloud is one word: 'Ende' ('The End').

Nietzsche is not mentioned in Taut's annotations to *Alpine Architektur*, and those who regard its designs as distinctly 'Nietzschean' tend to focus only on the prospective inhabitants of these vast glass buildings or point merely to Nietzsche's general love of icy peaks.[6] Colin Trodd goes out on a limb, to claim brashly that Nietzsche is 'the prophet' of Taut's *Alpine Architektur*. He maintains that the 'crystal cathedrals at the summit of the Alps were an appeal to the pantheistic vitalism' of '*Thus Spoke Zarathustra*', and its landscapes were 'informed by the ecstatic dynamism outlined by Nietzsche'. He concludes that the work is nothing short of 'a vast Book of Nietzsche' (2018:27). Ironically, however, Trodd quickly undermines his own sweeping assertions as soon as he cites Zarathustra's speech where the prophet exclaims – contrary to Taut's epigraph – that architecture is not above life, but an expression of the power of life itself (Trodd 2018:27).

In the longest of the book's annotations, Taut spells out his pacifist rationale for his designs, and there, with his vilification of boredom and his desire to eradicate all social tensions and struggles, we discover a significant counter to Nietzsche's views on creativity. According to Taut, boredom is a notable psycho-social problem, which leads to 'quarrelling, strife and war', to 'lies, robbery, murder and wretchedness', and to 'blood flowing from a million wounds'. To ensure peace and harmony, we need, Taut claims, to eradicate boredom from peoples' lives. People only get bored, he maintains, when they have nothing constructive to occupy themselves with. To stave off boredom and prevent social unrest, every person must focus their efforts into building the glass structures that shape their Alpine communities. Boredom, according to Nietzsche, however, is vital to our creative awareness. 'Many people', he asserts, 'do not feel any boredom because they have never really learned how to work', while 'artists' and 'inventive spirits', by contrast, require 'much boredom if their work is to succeed' (HH I.391). In other words, while creative spirits 'endure' boredom, 'lesser natures' flee from it (GS,42). And, as if passing comment on Taut's vision of glass buildings constructed beside glacial mountain streams, Nietzsche starkly warns: 'Anyone who shelters themselves against boredom also shelters themselves from themselves: they will never obtain the most powerfully refreshing drink from their innermost fountain' (WS,200).

I noted that the final section of *Alpine Architektur* presents us with 'nothingness' and 'death'. This nihilistic stance in Nietzschean terms signals not the end of life, but a prelude to rebirth. Read this way, Taut's architectural Alpine vision is the beginning of a new architecture for a new community – a pacifist community that is rebuilding following the Great War. It spells the revaluation of values in the wake of war between communities and nations. Indeed, we discover the same caption that marks the end of *Alpine Architektur* – 'Sterne Welten. Schlaf. Tod. Das Grosse Nichts. Das Namenlose' – at the start of Taut's design, 'Monument to the New Law' (*Monument des Neun Gesetzes*, 1919; Figure 7.7). The design for this building makes explicit reference to Nietzsche, by incorporating a quotation from the chapter, 'Of Old and New Laws' from *Thus Spoke Zarathustra*. This design is one of two buildings by Taut, which are to my mind, potential candidates for his city crown.

City crowns

The city crown expresses the deepest values of its citizens, and since these values evolve over time and place the architectural design of the city crown will change too. Taut subsequently avoids discussions on specific architectural features of the crown beyond its materials, size and location so as not to influence later constructions, which may need to develop differently. The 'ultimate solution', he says, 'is comprised of many thousands of varied possibilities' (1919/2015:92). Taut presents forty examples of historic city crowns but warns his readers of the dangers of historicism: 'The study of old building styles does little to help the designer because they remain fixed on individual forms that are blind to the light that radiates through all magnificent things', not least the 'treasure' in the depths of the soul of the people (1919/2015:84). The historical examples he provides are mostly religious buildings (cathedrals, mosques, temples and pagodas), but these are no longer feasible as crowns for Taut's city. Taut, like Nietzsche before him, maintained that religion was no longer a viable force to bind communities together. Neither religion nor politics can adequately represent for Taut the spirit of a community. Taut's choice of city crown was modelled instead on the idea of a non-religious and non-political meeting house.

As a physical representation of the communal spirit that inspires citizens to turn from material concerns to artistic values and 'noble emotions', its architecture must be 'empty and pure', 'empty and quiet' and 'absolutely turned away from the daily rituals for all times' (1919/2015:91). Taut's city crown is akin to Nietzsche's empty architecture which frees people from unnecessary distractions to enable them to focus on noble ideas and values. Glass is Taut's favoured material for its construction due to its 'gleaming, transparent, reflective character', which makes it 'more than ordinary matter' (1919/2015:89–90). The *Glashaus* (1914) which Taut designed and constructed from glass for the entrance to the 1914 Werkbund Exhibition in Cologne is often cited as a building Taut had in mind when he came to write *Die Stadkrone* five years later.[7] I shall examine this design shortly, but not before I return to Taut's *Monument des Neuen Gesetzes*, a design that is rarely discussed, and which could be construed as a strong candidate for a city crown.

Monument des Neuen Gesetzes (1919)

Taut presents his design for this monument to a new law in a letter, dated 23 December 1919, to members of *Gläserne Kette* (Glass Chain) (see Taut 1985). This group was started by Taut and was comprised of a group of architects who shared amongst themselves via a chain letter (circulated between November 1919 and December 1920) their utopian visions of crystalline buildings, often depicted as dazzling structures that capture the light of a new dawn. Taut's initial letters express his uncertainties about the architecture of the future, and how it will convey the loss and overcoming of traditional values. His *Monument des Neuen Gesetzes* was intended to convey society at the point of change, with the dissolution of a political State and the promise of cultural flourishing.

The inscription above Taut's sketch of the monument repeats the final words of *Alpine Architektur* – 'Sterne Welten. Schlaf. Tod. Das Grosse Nichts. Das Namenlose' – to suggest this is a monument to mark an ending, a loss of meaning, a death. Indeed, it is a memorial to remember those who died in the Great War, and a monument to herald new beginnings. In a Nietzschean context, we could regard it as a monument to the revaluation of values. According to Taut, there should be little distinction between a war memorial and a memorial to a new law. The memory of the fallen 'can be handed down to posterity on plaques' or monuments, but the 'best' way to honour the dead, he says, is 'by striving in thought and deed to create something new out of the[ir] legacy' (1915:176). This monument to the 'New Law' is a symbol of such striving, and it employs poignant words said by Nietzsche's Zarathustra alongside those of six other 'exemplary individuals' to articulate its rationale. The artists who govern Taut's utopian city would not shirk from the horrors of war but would draw on their creative powers to discern significant lessons learnt from war and to cultivate viable alternatives to war. This monument would be well placed at the heart of Taut's city, as its crowning architecture to mark an age of liberation following the end of imperial rule after the Great War. It represents the dawning of a new era after death and beyond the nihilistic finality of *Alpine Architektur* with its dissolution of architecture into nothingness.

Monument des Neuen Gesetzes is pyramidal in shape and is composed of innumerable prisms that fit together to suggest a large crystal. The building tapers into a point, shaped like a mighty arrow aiming up into the sky. Taut has drawn rays of light reflecting downwards from its tip towards seven raised panels, placed at half-height of the building, each a different colour,

FIGURE 7.7 *Monument des Neuen Gesetzes* (1919, Bruno Taut). Illustrated letter with a drawing of a project for the Monument to the Dead. © Canadian Center for Architecture.

and which fan outwards and upwards. According to Taut's handwritten note beneath the sketch, the building is clad in majolica painted turquoise blue, with a white marble base, and the panels would be onyx with gold inlay. According to Dietrich Schubert, the base of the arrow-shaped point is star-shaped, and this creates a star-shaped pattern of light to illuminate the panels (1988:245). It thereby evokes Taut's allusion to 'Sterne Welten' (Star Worlds).

The panels are inscribed with quotations, which can be read clearly at ground level in the natural light of day and with artificial lighting at night. Taut briefly mentions at the bottom his choice of quotations:

> 1) Luther: Und wenn die Welt voll Teufel wär ... 2) Liebknecht: Sturm, mein Geselle ... 3) Nietzsche: Vom neuen Götzen 4) Haggai 1, 1–17 5) Scheerbart: Wo du auch hinüberfliehst ... 6) Offenbarung Joh. 21,9–27 7) Scheerbart: Lesabéndio Die Sonne – unser Gesetz!

> 1) Luther: And were this world all devils ... 2) Liebknecht: Storm, my companion ... 3) Nietzsche: Of the new idol 4) Haggai 1, 1–17 5) Scheerbart: Wherever you flee ... 6) Revelation Joh.21, 9–27 7) Scheerbart: Lesabéndio: The sun – our law!)

The passage that Taut selects from Nietzsche's writings is a long section from Part I of *Thus Spoke Zarathustra*, where Zarathustra denounces the State as a powerful adversary – as 'the coldest of all cold monsters' – and calls upon us to look beyond it to 'the rainbow and bridges to the Superman' (den Regenbogen und die Brükken des Übermenschen). One can imagine how Taut intended his glass monument to evoke a portal or bridge to the Superman through its kaleidoscopic movements, reminiscent of a rainbow.

There is, arguably, a more suitable passage from *Thus Spoke Zarathustra* that Taut could have utilized for this monument, and that is 'The Old and New Tablets of the Law' from Part III. There Zarathustra describes a 'new tablet' inscribed with words of the 'new law': that one must '*Become hard!*' like a diamond (Z, III, 12[29]:231). In other words, like Taut, Zarathustra presents in this passage a monument to a new law, and it is a monument that conveys the new law as diamond-like. Perhaps more significant still is the intriguing parallel we discover in this passage with Zarathustra's poetic description of his desire for the new law and notable design features of Taut's monument:

> That I may one day be ready ... ready for myself and my most deeply concealed will: a bow in hot desire for its arrow, an arrow in hot desire for its star – a star, ready and ripe in its noontide, glowing, pierced, enraptured by annihilating arrows of the sun – Myself a sun and an inexorable solar will, ready for annihilation as I conquer!
>
> (Z, III, 12[30]:231)

I think these words of Zarathustra would be very well placed on a glass panel of Taut's monument.

Taut's monument is similar in several respects to van de Velde's later memorial to Nietzsche (designed in 1925) for Helene Kröller-Müller's Museum Park in the Netherlands, which I discussed earlier. Both have engraved on their surfaces, words spoken by Zarathustra about the new law. But their intended audiences and aesthetic effects contrast significantly. Van de Velde's large stone tablet design is modest and simple compared to Taut's vast and intricate turquoise-glazed monolith. Van de Velde addresses through Zarathustra's words the importance of self-isolation for creativity (from 'Vom Wege des Schaffenden'/ 'Of the Way of the Creator', Part I). To emphasize Zarathustra's teaching, the monument would have been set in a relatively secluded rural location discoverable by the solitary walker, who may happen across the monument initially unawares. The potential surprise of its discovery by a walker (who is already primed for contemplative thought) would likely heighten the intended impact of Zarathustra's message. By contrast, Taut's monument would be situated in a prominent position for all to see, speaking to the people at large, calling them to embrace the dissolution of the State and to claim power for themselves. Approximately 18 m in height, its magnitude would have been greatly enhanced if placed at the highest point of the city.[8] While both monuments seek to encourage self-reflection, the direct and immediate presentation of Nietzsche's words – combined with notable others in the case of Taut's monument – may somewhat delimit the potentials for self-reflection, by directing people's thoughts too closely. This could feasibly undermine the fundamental principle of Taut's *Kristallhaus* as a 'pure architecture', as 'nothing but a beautiful room' that remains 'quiet and empty', and similarly 'perhaps' prove too distracting for Nietzsche's call for empty forms.

Glaushaus, Cologne Werkbund Exhibition, Cologne (1914)

Taut's *Glashaus* was placed prominently near to the entrance of the exhibition grounds of Rheinpark, hundreds of yards from van de Velde's Theatre, which was tucked away, behind the Haupthalle (Main Hall, by Theodor Fischer). Since the German glass industry had financed the construction of the building, it was meant to demonstrate how glass could be utilized innovatively in architecture. But Taut's own intentions for the building were more ambitious. For Taut, the *Glashaus* embodied qualities of 'something removed from material existence'. It was a pavilion for contemplative reflection and for heightening spiritual awareness to channel a person's 'longing for purity and clarity' (Taut 1917:222).

The *Glashaus* was a symmetrical fourteen-sided prism, constructed from concrete beams which lent support to glass bricks (Figure 7.8). The top half of the building formed a large dome reminiscent of a pineapple with a double glass layer. The exterior layer was composed of reflective glass and the interior layer was composed of floor-to-ceiling coloured glass prisms. Sadly, only monochrome photographs of the building survive. Nevertheless, Taut describes its kaleidoscope of colours as 'reflections of light whose colours began at the base with a dark blue and rose up through moss green and golden yellow to culminate at the top in a luminous pale yellow' (1919b:12). The *Glashaus* was a festive celebration of colour, which, if not analogous to the rainbow of the *Übermensch*, was certainly reminiscent of the shimmering lights of 'purity and transcendence' that radiated from the *Kristallhaus* of the *Stadtkrone* as a 'carnival of un-refracted, radiant colours' and 'as proof of the happiness in the new life' (Taut 1919/2015:69).

The entrance was reached by one of two concrete flights of steps on either side of the concrete plinth of the building, which gave to the building the impression of a temple. Inside, a person was met with two staircases created from metal and glass prisms, which led to the upper hall. As one walked up the stairs, a cascade of sparkling water flowed past, for between the two staircases was a waterfall. The waterfall tumbled over seven large steps, each lit from beneath, and thence, lower down, over a section of yellow glass before terminating in a recess of violet glass (Figure 7.9). The passage of the waterfall could also be viewed from a circular hole in the upper floor. The play of lights continued throughout the interior from the refracted natural light which passed through its glass skin, and from artificial lighting at night. The carnival light-effects were further enhanced with the installation of a mechanical kaleidoscope built into the back of the building.

Bletter (1981) provides a useful summary of some of the esoteric traditions that inform the symbolic meanings Taut attributes to glass, which include visions of the Temple of Jerusalem and medieval Grail legends. Although Nietzsche appears briefly in her account, it is not with reference to Zarathustra's *Edelstein*, which is somewhat surprising given she notes its potential influence on the work of Taut's colleague, Peter Behrens. Instead, Bletter draws attention to relatively nondescript images within *Thus Spoke Zarathustra*, which are neither central to its message nor distinctive to its symbolism, to suggest the significance of this work to Taut's *Glashaus*. Thus, she describes how the building's cascading waterfall with its playful lights and shadows together with its reflective surfaces find their influence in Zarathustra's mountainous cave dwelling, and to occasions when Zarathustra describes his soul as if it were a fountain and when a child held up to Zarathustra a mirror to encourage his self-reflection (1981:30).

If we were to identify a more convincing Nietzschean influence on Taut's design, it might have to come indirectly via the work of Paul Scheerbert (1863–1915), a fantasy novelist and social critic from Berlin, to whom Taut dedicated his *Glashaus*. Scheerbert's writings are highly suggestive of Nietzsche's influence, and Scheerbert himself was a decisive influence on Taut's glass designs throughout Taut's career. In the year *Glashaus* was constructed, Scheerbert reciprocated Taut's gesture, by dedicating to Taut

FIGURE.7.8 *Glashaus*, Werkbund Exhibition, Cologne (b.1914, Bruno Taut), front elevation. © Bildarchiv Foto Marburg.

FIGURE 7.9 *Glashaus*, Werkbund Exhibition, Cologne (b.1914, Bruno Taut), interior. © Bildarchiv Foto Marburg.

his published architectural manifesto, *Glassarchitektur* (1914/2014). A year later, following Scheerbart's death, Taut established the *Gläserne Kette* to honour Scheerbart, and to keep alive their shared utopian visions of glass architecture as the architecture of the future. Taut had asked Scheerbert to compose for the *Glashaus*, fourteen rhyming couplets that convey the utopian values of glass architecture, from which Taut chose three, which were subsequently engraved into a concrete frieze that wraps around the building's exterior.[9]

Scheerbart's utopian vision, much like Taut's, proposes the construction of entire glass cities and crystalline palaces festooned across Alpine peaks. In Scheerbart's cities, even the verges of its streets and highways are given a crystalline makeover, with columns of coloured lights replacing trees (Scheerbart 1914/2014:89). His fantasy novels depict architects and engineers eager to fulfil the heroic quest of designing an architecture that will transform people's lives and elevate whole communities to higher states of being. The main protagonist in his widely acclaimed novel, *Lesabéndio: ein asteroïden-Roman* (*Lesabéndio: An Asteroid Novel*) (1913/2012), has been compared to Nietzsche's Zarathustra and to Nietzsche's *Übermensch* due to the transformative experiences this character, Lesabéndio, undergoes in his attempt to build a steel tower ever higher and eventually into the stellar realms of 'higher truths' (See Partsch 2002:210). Once the fictional architect – who, incidentally, is not human, but a peace-loving, salamander-like creature, a 'Pallasian' – has achieved such heights, the narrative style of the novel changes to employ a stylistic refrain that mirrors *Thus Spoke Zarathustra*, by substituting ' ... – thus Spoke Zarathustra' with ' ... – and they did as he ordered' (Partsch 2002:210). It is perhaps significant to note that Lesabéndio does not heed Nietzsche's warnings of the dangers of the abyss, for soon after he completes his tower, he experiences a painful Dionysian dissolution of his body, becoming seemingly at one with the universe.[10]

But of course, Dionysus symbolizes both death and rebirth, just as *Alpine Architektur* ends where *Monument des Neuen Gesetzes* begins, with death and the namelessness immensity of star worlds. Curiously, Nietzsche and Scheerbart have been linked existentially to each other as reincarnations of Dionysus, with Dionysus first embodying Nietzsche before transitioning into Scheerbart's creative life upon Nietzsche's death. This idea appears in an article by Anselm Reust from 1919, titled, 'Von Geburt, Tod und Wiedergeburt des Dionysus: Ein Gedächtniskranz auf Paul Scheerbarts Grab' (On the Birth, Death, and Rebirth of Dionysus: A Memorial Wreath for Scheerbart's Grave). Reust's article begins with a quotation from *Birth of Tragedy*: 'The one truly real Dionysus appears in a multiplicity of forms ... ' and asserts that the 'fifteenth of October' is 'a date that will long be remembered by future generations' as 'the birthday of Nietzsche and the death-day of Paul Scheerbart'. He continues to note, 'In 1888, the year of Nietzsche's derangement, Scheerbart began for the first time to sound Dionysian, as if something were just then dawning' (1919/2014:267). Reust insinuates that while Nietzsche was unable eventually to contain the Dionysian spirit, Scheerbart was able to embody the Dionysian spirit, but only with the help of Taut – specifically, with his building of the *Glashaus*. Reust argues that by building for Scheerbart a version of his ideal *Glassarchitektur* – albeit not to the scale of his utopian fantasies – Taut could protect Scheerbart from being blinded by 'the unfathomable depths of his inner vision'. Taut's *Glashaus* worked 'like protective goggles' for Scheerbart, for which Scheerbart 'was so grateful'. Reust concludes that Scheerbart was the 'last Dionysus' we have witnessed, and he questions when, and in whom, Dionysus will rise again.

Reust raises the crucial point for any architect of the grand style: one must not encourage Dionysian elements at the expense of the Apollonian. If we are to speak of a 'Nietzschean architecture', we speak of an architecture that reveals new and unexpected perspectives not only in its material features but in the people who experience it. It is ultimately an architecture of *participation* which celebrates the spirit of individuals and whole communities within the shared festive spectacle.

NOTES

Introduction

1. See Bishop (2017); D'Iorio (2012:4–5).
2. Anacleto Verrecchia notes: 'According to others who speak of the episode as if they had been present, though without ever mentioning their sources, it happened in Piazza Carlo Alberto, in Piazza San Carlo, in Piazza Carlina, or even on Via Accademia delle Scienze' (1988:108). Verrecchia suggests 'the sudden collapse' of Nietzsche was probably fabricated by Nietzsche's sister, Elisabeth, and his friend, Overbeck, to lend credence to the idea that Nietzsche's 'madness' was sudden and unexpected, and not in evidence to those around him in the months prior to the supposed event (1988:106–7).
3. Neumeyer interprets Nietzsche's allusion to the Mole in his final letter as 'bait' to coax Burckhardt into visiting him in Turin (2001/2004:11). Scholars have incorrectly interpreted Nietzsche's allusion to Antonelli here as the Papal Secretary of State under Pius IX. For instance, Karl Schelechta (1966; cited in Neumeyer 2001/2004:12,n.12), and www.TheNietzscheChannel.com (accessed January 2024).
4. See, for instance, Leslie Chamberlaine's, *Nietzsche in Turin* (2022) which barely considers Turin or Nietzsche's perceptions of it.
5. The conference was held on Nietzsche's 150th birthday. Other chapters discuss such topics as the use of architectural metaphors in Western philosophy; metaphors of the mask and the labyrinth; Nietzschean themes within artworks by Gustav Klimt and Giorgio de Chirico; Nietzsche's influence on Dadaism; Nietzsche's search for home within alienating conditions of modernity; the cult-like status of van de Velde's interest in Nietzsche; the use of metaphor in Nietzsche's *Thus Spoke Zarathustra* and by Le Corbusier. The short book, *An Architecture Manifesto: Critical Reason and Theories of a Failed Practice* (2019) by Nadir Lahiji, features a chapter, 'Nietzsche and the architect' (72–88).
6. Nietzsche regarded architecture as "the foundation on which the unfolding of the other arts should be fully achieved […] The idea of the Gesamtkunstwerk must start from architecture" (Behrens 1987). For critical discussion on the meaning and philosophical implications of Gesamtkunstwerk, see Bryant (2004).
7. See Huel (2015:71,75:n.50,76,n.59).

Chapter 2

1. The daily work schedule is not prescribed by Nietzsche. However, he refers to one's need to identify aspects of oneself that seem ugly or weak and to reinterpret them as beautiful and strong, otherwise to conceal them (GS,290). This enables one to tolerate oneself, and later, to delight in oneself. Such transformation of ugliness into beauty and weakness into strength cannot be forced or involve pretence at any level. Grand style involves – for both people and buildings – an organic drive of rhythmic placement without fuss.
2. See Henry van de Velde's essays, 'Die Linie' (1902a) and 'Prinzipielle Erklarung' (1902b).
3. Nietzsche may have been influenced by Burckhardt's comments in *Der Cicerone* about the temples at Paestum, which Burckhardt describes as 'living beings' and 'not mere stone' (1855:2). Nietzsche probably visited Paestum in March or April of 1877.
4. In an unpublished draft – which Buddensieg describes as 'an astonishing variant' to GS,280 – Nietzsche suggests we rebuild those buildings that cannot be cleansed: 'Perhaps we could rebuild and decorate many [church] buildings in our own spirit and for our own purposes. For the time being, inside some sumptuous Catholic churches our capacity for thought is constrained – at least, I am not so crass as to be able to think *my* thought in such places' (KSA, 14.280:263).
5. Eleven days earlier, Nietzsche had written to his sister and mother with a more modest description of his initial lodgings: 'an attic room with an excellent bed: simple, healthy fare' where he can keep to himself (KSB,6.68:51). Prior to his stay in Genoa for a few months at the beginning of the 1880, he *did* live in an imposing palazzo – Palazzo Berlendis in Venice, at the end of Rio dei Mendicanti. Nietzsche recounts how he enjoyed his vast but cold room of marble, reached by an impressive marble staircase, with a 'view to the Island of the Dead', San Michele. (KSA 6, 18:13; KSA 6, 19–20:14–5).
6. Nietzsche was under the impression that the two men agreed on his own philosophical position (see his letter to Erwin Rohde of 29 May 1869; KSB 3.6:13). Martin Ruehl notes: 'Although he later denied having had much or any influence on the thinking of his younger colleague, Burckhardt lastingly shaped Nietzsche's understanding of the early modern period – and the emergence of modern subjectivity' (2015:59).
7. Nietzsche owned two copies of *The Civilization of the Renaissance in Italy*. In one Burckhardt inscribed the dedication, 'To Prof. Dr. Nietzsche, presented with reverence by the author'. Nietzsche annotated both copies, especially the first three sections titled, 'The State as a Work of Art', 'The Development of the Individual' and 'The Revival of Antiquity' (See Ruehl 2015:72). Nietzsche described *Cicerone* in a letter to Carl von Gersdorff as 'a book to rise up with and go to bed with: there are few books that so stimulate the imagination and prepare the ground for the artistic conception' (October 1872; KSA,4.264:68). Nietzsche presented his sister with a copy on 6 July 1883 (KSB,6430:391).

8   English editions also go by the name of *Architecture of the Italian Renaissance*.
9   Burckhardt describes this superhuman architect as a man susceptible to violence and contempt for the world. In this respect, he employs terms that have become associated with Nietzsche's conception of the 'superman' or *Übermensch*: the new, creative human being, who adopts a 'world despising' attitude to create for themselves a world they take delight in. By the same token, the 'last men' – whom Nietzsche associates with modern Europeans – are incapable of love, creation and longing, and unable subsequently to 'despise' themselves, choosing instead a 'wretched contentment' with mediocrity.
10 In the context of his views of liberal institutions, he similarly notes, 'We all know *what* they set in motion: they undermine the will to power, they are the levelling of mountain and valley exalted to a moral principle, they make everything small, cowardly and pleasurable – the herd animal triumphs with them every time' (TI,IX.38:112).
11 See, for instance, Henry-Russell Hitchcock's summation: 'Yet Antonelli arrived at no coherent expression of his structural innovations and, to judge from the successive purposes for which the structure has been intended to serve or has served, no real capacity to provide a functionally viable building. On the whole, as its name implies, this is a monument chiefly to its designer's megalomania' (1992:605,n.21).

Chapter 3

1   See Garnham (2013) and Mallgrave (1996:351). Fritz Neumeyer convincingly argues that Nietzsche consulted Semper's writings from Wagner's library. Wagner owned the entirety of Semper's works. After Wagner's move from Tribschen to Bayreuth, Nietzsche borrowed a copy of Semper's *Der Stil* from Basel University Library (on 8 December 1875).
2   Rykwert makes the passing remark that 'Wagner took Nietzsche to see Semper in his engraving workshop in 186? [*sic*], which must have been when the final illustrations were being prepared [for *Der Stil*]' (1989/2010:xvi).
3   It is possible that Burckhardt introduced Nietzsche to Semper's ideas rather than Wagner, for Burckhardt and Semper were distant colleagues at E.T.H. in Zürich from 1855.
4   See for instance, Stephan (1996:98); and Caroline van Eck, who asserts that Mallgrave's 'fundamental study' [1996] on Semper establishes Nietzsche 'as the main philosophical presence in Semper's work' (2006:136).
5   See, for instance, Fritz Neumeyer (2001/2004:121).
6   Semper in Herrmann (1981:MS 6, fol. 8). Also, Herrmann (1989:155).
7   Semper, 'Vergleichende Baulehre. Vorwort' in Herrmann (1981:BMS 19, fol.23). Also, Herrmann (1989:156).
8   Semper in Herrmann (1981:MS 2, fol. 7). Also, Herrmann (1989:156).

9   For a detailed account, see Manfred Semper (1906); Habel (1970); Newman (1945:409–37).
10 See Semper's brochure, *Wissenschaft, Industrie und Kunst*, and *Der Stil*.
11 Semper (1851/2010:78). Also, Herrmann (1981:MS 14, fol.5); Herrmann (1989:158).
12 Semper in Herrmann (1981:MS 25, fol. 258). Also, Herrmann (1989:159).
13 Semper in Herrmann (1981:MS 25, fol.53). Also, Herrmann (1989:155).
14 Semper in Herrmann (1981:MS 6, fol. 53). Also, Herrmann (1989:155).
15 Semper in Herrmann (1981:MS 55, fol.12). Also, Herrmann (1989:5).
16 Bacchus – the Roman equivalent of Dionysus – personifies similar aspects to Dionysus. In my later discussion of the Semperoper, I will cite Bacchus and Dionysus interchangeably.
17 See also Mallgrave (1996:350); McGrath (2013:142–8); and Nietzsche's allusions to Semper in the context of colour perception (KSA,9.4[95]:123).
18 Nietzsche himself indicates at the beginning of *The Birth of Tragedy* that it was not intended as a work of philological scholarship grounded in evidence from ancient texts or testimony but a work of 'vision' that employs 'intuition' to fathom the 'profound mysteries' of antiquity.
19 See also Wilamowitz's response to Erwin Rohde's critical retort, *Afterphilologie* (1872). For discussion of the inaccuracies of Wilamowitz's criticisms of Nietzsche, see Porter (2011). For Wilamowitz's review in English see Babich (2000).
20 For images of the quadriga, see Magirius (1987:91).
21 See Bartnig et al. (1995:35).
22 See Semper (1858) *Entwurf für das kaiserliche Theatre in Rio de Janeiro*, Theatremuseum München; especially plate 131, which depicts the quadriga with two figures for the theatre in Rio de Janeiro. See Habel (1985) for the following images. The quadriga for the Festspielhaus in Munich: plates 21, 27, 28, 29, 41, 47, 48, 58. Dionysus and Ariadne: plate 75.
23 See also McGrath (2013:70).
24 Genelli notes that his depiction of Dionysus or 'Bacchus' instead of Apollo in the company of Muses was influenced by Aloys Hirt's *Bilderbuch für Mythologie, Archäologie und Kunst* [*Picture Book for Mythology*] (1805). There Hirt notes: 'it is strange that there is not some sort of memorial where Bacchus appears at the same time as or among the Muses, since the Muses are said to have accompanied him on his travels, and since Bacchus is regarded as the author of theatrical plays' (1805:Vol.1:80; cited in Nielsen 2005:31). As if in response to Hirt, Genelli provides this memorial in visual form.
25 See Ebert (1971:172) and Mandel (1990:212). Vogel describes the composition as Genelli's most important work (1966:125).
26 See Silk and Stern (2016:259–60, 214–15) and Vogel (1966:142,147–8). Both Silk and Stern, and Vogel confuse the issue by stating incorrectly that Wagner and Nietzsche were influenced by Genelli's *Bacchus und den Musen* (not *Dionysos, von den Musen Apollos erzogen*). Vogel, however, includes the correct image in his study (plate 41).

27 See Vogel (1966:146). *Unsere Zeit* [*Our Time*] was published by Friedrich Brockhaus, Wagner's brother-in-law.

28 Art collector, Adolf Friedrich von Schack (1815–1894) owned a copy of this painting in oils, which Genelli completed in 1865/1866 (Magirius 1987:146). Genelli's composition, 'Die Geburt der Künste aus der Finsternis' was submitted to an open competition for the stage curtain in 1875. It came second out of sixty-eight submissions. An earlier version of the winning image (*Providentia memor* by Ferdinand Keller) includes features reminiscent of Genelli's *Dionysos, von den Musen Apollos erzogen*, such as a menacing herm covered in foliage to the left, and to the right, a serene Muse with a harp. See Magirius (1987:161) for an illustration of it.

29 It is thought that Genelli had composed the first version titled, *Bacchus unter den Musen* as a watercolour in Rome. This painting is now housed at Vienna's Albertina (see Ebert 1971:48).

30 Letter from Genelli to Hermann Härtel (15 January 1832; Archives of the German National Museum in Nuremberg; cited in Nielsen 2005:17). Genelli goes on to note that he plans to depict Bacchus seated in a grove, surrounded by Muses, some of whom are standing, some seated, others lying down, and with Amor and Pan, both half-drunk and dancing to strange, graceful music.

31 See Ebert (1971:62–9) and Vogel (1966:127). Genelli brought an unsuccessful lawsuit against Härtel in the summer of 1836.

32 In his study on Genelli's *Bacchus unter den Musen*, Siegfried Mandel does not mention Genelli's wish for his composition to grace a theatre curtain. However, Mandel appears to intuit as much in his suggestion that the painting gives 'the impression that a curtain is being raised to reveal an archaic Greek festival scene' (1990:221).

33 To Rohde, Nietzsche writes, 'You know that for [the idea of] the "Muses with Dionysus in their midst", I had in mind Genelli's watercolour which Wagner had in Tribschen'. Rohde responded in kind with his counter-criticism to Wilamowitz, which took the form of a letter addressed to Wagner: 'Thus, the brilliant Genelli knew very well what he was doing when he stole upon Dionysus in the midst of the Muses in his beautiful watercolour painting that I was once allowed to admire [11–13 June 1870] in your house, dear Master' *Afterphilogie* (Rohde 1872).

34 When I imagine Nietzsche gazing at the herm in Genelli's painting, I am reminded of Nietzsche's remarks in 'The Dionysian Worldview' (1870), which he composed between visits to Tribschen. There Nietzsche alludes to the creative play of Apollonian and Dionysian impulses in the context of a sculptor creating a statue: 'As a block of marble, the statue is something very real, but the reality of the statue as a dream figure is the living person of the god. As long as the statue hovers as a fantasy image before the artist's eyes, he still plays with reality, when he transfers this image into marble he is playing with the dream' (KSA,1.582).

35 The concept of a sunken orchestra had been proposed as early as 1775 in an essay by De Marette ('Mémoire sur une nouvelle orchestre de salle de spectacle'/'About a New Theatre Orchestra'). Wagner may have been the only one to have put the idea into practice by this time. See Baker (1998:263).

36 Cosima Wagner described the building as 'a fairy tale in the midst of clumsy reality' (24 September 1873; C. Wagner 1978:680).

Chapter 4

1. For examples of Nietzsche's association with various architectural styles, see the following. Classical style: Breitschmid (2001) and Neumeyer (2001/2004); Renaissance: Neumeyer (2001/2004); Totalitarian architecture: Hartmut Böhme (2001); Baroque: Buddensieg (1999); Brutalist architecture: Tirthika Shah (2020); Cyclopean style see Pehnt (1999); Internationalist Style: Buddensieg (1999); Medieval monastic architecture: Iñaki Ábalos (2016). Ábalos' reasons for claiming Nietzsche sought a monastery-type of architecture rests only on Nietzsche's insistence for a contemplative life.

2. On conversing with Förster-Nietzsche, Kessler notes in his diary entry of 31 January 1909, 'Try as you might to elevate the conversation to a higher level, it sinks with her gradually and hopelessly back to gossip. Evidently in part because she lacks entirely the foundations for purely cultural or philosophical discussion. This makes such a lunch with her extremely fatiguing' (1880–1918/2011:486).

3. *PAN* regularly published texts by and about Nietzsche, combining them with visual art. The first issue (1885) opened with an unpublished fragment of Nietzsche's poetry with the title, 'Zarathustra Vor Dem Köenige' ('Zarathustra before the King'), coupled with an etching by Hans Thoma (1839–1924) depicting Zarathustra's eagle and snake, a crystal, the rising sun and a lion. The second issue (1885) included an unpublished aphorism of Nietzsche's with the title 'Der Riese' ('The Giant'), accompanied by an etching by Ernst Moritz Geyer (1861–1941) of a melancholic Prometheus. The third issue included Curt Stoeving's (1863–1939) portrait of Nietzsche in Naumburg. The fifth and final issue which was published in 1900 included Hans Olde's (1855–1917) now famous etching of Nietzsche's head. The artists selected for these issues were closely associated to the Nietzsche-Archiv and overseen by Förster-Nietzsche.

4. Von Salis-Marschlins recalls how Nietzsche cast a 'golden shimmer' over her life, and she vowed always to promote his philosophy (Young 2010:390). Förster-Nietzsche agreed to pay von Salis-Marschlins a modest annual rent as long as her brother remained alive, with the possibility of buying the property after his death (Peters 1977:161).

5. While Nietzsche resided bed-ridden at the end of his life on the top floor of the Villa, visitors to the rooms below could sense his presence throughout the house. Architect, Fritz Schumacher notes, 'it was never forgotten that above, separated only by a layer of bars, were watchful eyes that looked deeper into the abysses of the human heart and higher to the icy peaks of his tendons than those of a second living human being' (1935/1949:250).

6. See Emmrich (2000c) for an 'imaginary tour' of the renovated Villa including the upper rooms of Förster-Nietzsche's bedroom and living room, and Nietzsche's bedroom, the so-called 'death room' [*Sterbezimmer*]. Nietzsche's

living room was organized by his sister as a space for work and living, with a desk and books laid out for Nietzsche, who would occasionally write when his illness allowed it. Busts of Nietzsche by Curt Stoeving and Max Klinger were displayed here, giving the room the appearance of a memorial. The room's décor was dark, perhaps to alleviate Nietzsche's ailments with his eyes, with heavy curtains, black furniture and brown wallpaper featuring a recurring chrysanthemum pattern (Emmrich 2000c:89–91). His sister's living room, by contrast, was lively and bright (Emmrich 2000c:100).

7   Sembach notes that the functional design elements in the main room of the Nietzsche-Archiv appear in van de Velde's theatre design but in inverted form, and 'the correspondence goes further', he notes, for the 'sweep of the sofa is repeated in the bulge of the façade, the cavetto moulding in the room corresponds to the rounded upper part of the façade' (1989:88). Kostka notes: 'The outer skin of the Abbe monument gently takes up individual design elements of the central meeting room in the Nietzsche-Archiv. The design elements are turned inside out' (2000:44).

8   When the Archiv opened on 15 October 1903, Klinger's herm was not on display. In its place was a bust of Nietzsche by Klinger that he loaned to the Archiv until the herm was ready. The bust would remain at the Archiv for two years. It was replaced in May 1905 with a plaster cast of the herm bust, intended as another 'placeholder'. This was kept on display until October 1905 when it was finally replaced by the marble Nietzsche herm, which remains at Villa Silberblick to this day. See Dietrich and Erbsmehl (2004) for discussion of Klinger's various busts and herms of Nietzsche produced between 1902 and 1914. In 1914 he designed a marble Nietzsche herm for Alfred Kröner. Kröner took over C.G. Naumann Verlag (Leipzig publishers of Nietzsche's works since 1886). Following Kröner's death, the herm was sold in 1938 to Max Oehler with the intention of displaying it in the Nietzsche Hall in Weimar.

9   Max Klinger is included in the sculptural programme for the project. Interestingly, he is described in the official guide to the Nietzsche-Archiv as having created in his statue of Beethoven, 'the embodiment of the Übermensch' – where the 'new ideal human type, of God in creative man, has become a reality. [Klinger's] Beethoven statue is the most splendid, jubilant, artistic affirmation of Nietzsche's Zarathustrianism' (Kühn 1904:10).

10   Letter to von Hofmannsthal 16 April 1911 (Dietrich and Erbsmehl 2004:14; Stamm 1973–5:311–12). See also letter to van de Velde, 12 April 1911 (KV,316:571).

11   Only Adalbert Oehler and Josef Kohler as representatives of Nietzsche's Archiv were included. Despite Förster-Nietzsche's absence from the committee, she seems to have welcomed the attention the project gave to her brother's legacy, and undoubtedly assumed it would have positive financial repercussions for the Nietzsche-Archiv (See Kostka 2000:45).

12   It is doubtful whether Nietzsche wrote the letter to which Förster-Nietzsche alludes (see Kostka 2000:54).

13   For a list of lost resources, see Neumann (2015:558,141,n.576).

14   An article by Günther Stamm (1973–5) was regarded for several years as the most accurate account of the different architectural phases of the project.

This work has been supplemented by a short book by Thomas Föhl and Alexandre Kostka (2000). Both studies are inevitably vague and speculative in their accounts without the invaluable resource of Neumann (2015). It should be noted that the memoires of van de Velde were not prepared by the author himself but comprise texts that have been reconstructed from several sources, occasionally rewritten in the first person by the editors posing as van de Velde.

15 For instance, Stamm suggests the drawings for the first phase of the design (Figures 4.6 and 4.7) were received by Kessler before 21 August 1911, but he also suggests Kessler received drawings prior to this date for phase 2 (e.g. Figure 4.8; see 1973–5:316,320). Subsequently, he leads us to imagine these drawings are variations of a singular phase ending in mid-August. Furthermore, Stamm suggests van de Velde's drawing of the temple plan for the second phase of the design (Figure 2.3 in his article) was probably the drawing that Kessler criticizes in his letter to van de Velde. However, the date of this letter (21 August 1911) doesn't chime with Stamm's suggestion that this drawing 'portray[s] the development of the Nietzsche monument after August 1911'.

16 The account given by Hollis tends to follow Stamm's account and is also confusing on its own accord. Oddly, he says the design which I depict in Figure 4.8 was intended 'for the first site' (Hollis 2019:189). By this he either means the original site intended for a Nietzsche memorial (land below Villa Silberblick: but this is unlikely given van de Velde's plans for this site are lost), or he means the *second* site, on the hill overlooking Weimar from the east. Hollis also claims the design which I depict in Figure 4.9 was 'the final design for [the] Nietzsche memorial' (2019:190) – an idea he may have taken from Sembach (1989:162).

17 Stamm implies that the plans are first announced by van de Velde in his letter to von Bodenhausen in April 1912. But Kessler reports that he took Bodenhausen to van de Velde's studio to see them a month earlier.

18 There were some suggestions that a statue of Nietzsche would be erected in the garden of Villa Silberblick, and Karl Donndorf's (1870–1941) depiction of Nietzsche – 'Säulenheilger' (the 'Pillar Saint') – was a distinct possibility. Karl Donndorf had already made a bust of Nietzsche to sit on a plinth in the veranda of Villa Silberblick. Donndorf presents Nietzsche as a solemn figure, dressed in priestly robes, in a sculpture that would extend approximately 6 m in height. The image epitomizes Förster-Nietzsche's mythology of her brother in stark contrast to Kessler's heroic stadium.

19 The street that would have marked the beginning of the *Feststraßen*, leading up to the temple-stadium site, was later named *Henry van de Velde Straße*. It is pleasing to think that van de Velde's investment in this site has, in some regard, been formerly realized.

20 Richard Oehler's 1935 work, *Friedrich Nietzsche und die deutsche Zukunft* (Friedrich Nietzsche and the German Future), aligned Nietzsche's ideas with Hitler's movement, by presenting Nietzsche as a prophet of the Third Reich, and the curators of the Nietzsche Archiv as Nietzsche's only legitimate administrators. Walter Kaufmann described it as 'one of the first Nazi books on Nietzsche' (2000:387). In 1895–1904 Elisabeth Förster-Nietzsche's influential but compromised biography of Nietzsche appeared. In 1901, with Heinrich

NOTES

Köselitz, she produced *The Will to Power* which included doctored material from Nietzsche's unpublished papers; another expanded volume appeared in 1906. Förster-Nietzsche helped to establish a simplistic, nationalized and politicized reading of Nietzschean ideas that would shape later interpretations and corruptions of Nietzsche's writings in fascist Italy and Nazi Germany.

21 The memorial building was principally financed by the Nietzsche-Archiv, the Reich Chancellery, the Thuringian State government, the city of Weimar, the Zeiss foundation in Jena (which funded the Abbe memorial) and the Wilhelm-Gustloff Foundation (a trust set up by the Nazi government in 1933, established from the Berlin-Suhl arms works).

22 Hitler and members of his cabinet attended Förster-Nietzsche's funeral – a ceremony elevated to a level normally reserved for crown heads of state. At the end of the ceremony, Hitler placed a large laurel wreath on her coffin. Details of the funeral were announced on the front page of the National Socialist newspaper, *Völkischer Beobachter* (*People's Observer*), on 11 November 1935. She was eulogized in hyperbolic terms by Fritz Sauckel as an indomitable German woman, revered by National Socialist Germany. The 1944 Nietzsche centenary would later be held under the patronage of Alfred Rosenberg, acting as Hitler's official representative.

23 See Berger (1999:177–94). The library of his Chancellery contained a set of Nietzsche's collected works but his reverence for the philosopher seems somewhat limited; he is said to have told Leni Riefenstahl that Nietzsche was more of an artist than a philosopher (Riefenstahl, 1902–2003, was known principally as a director of Nazi propaganda films).

24 Schultze-Naumburg was a member of a group of artists who established the *Jugendstil* movement of arts and crafts in Munich – albeit a rather conservative member – and later, a key figure in the *Deutscher Werkbund* and the nationalist German architecture and landscape preservation movement. Perhaps his most recognizable work is the Cecilienhof Palace in Potsdam (1914–17), commissioned by Wilhelm II for his son, Crown Prince Wilhelm. The palace takes the form of an English Tudor manor house, with steep pitched roof and neo-Tudor timbering. This building was the site of the Potsdam Conference from 17 July to 2 August 1945, where Winston Churchill, Harry S. Truman and Joseph Stalin gathered to make plans for the administration of Germany following the war.

25 The misspelling of van de Velde may not have been an intended slight. The error appears again in the land register for the Villa (see Föhl 2000:18).

26 Later, Hitler would acquire Josef Thorak's (1889–1952) Nietzsche bust from the *Große Deutsche Kunstausstellung* (Great German Art Exhibition) in Munich in 1944.

27 No project had occupied Georg Kolbe as extensively as the Nietzsche Monument for Weimar. Ursel Berger suggests Kolbe's 'obsessive' personal investment in a Nietzsche monument was therapeutic for Kolbe, who struggled to overcome his wife's suicide in February 1927. Nietzsche's affirmative philosophy helped Kolbe to find emotional stability, and to lead – Berger suggests – a life modelled on Zarathustra (1999:181–3). A total of twenty

Nietzsche sculptures by Kolbe can be identified, which vary the motif of an ascending man.

28 Their image and proposed position by the portal are reminiscent of the Courtyard of Honour of the New Reich Chancellery (designed by Speer in 1939, Berlin) with its two bronze statues, *Wehrmacht* and *Die Partei* ('Armed Forces' and 'The Party') by Arno Breker (1900–91).

29 See Bogner (2014) for details of the building's evolution from a Nietzsche memorial to broadcasting studio.

Chapter 5

1 For allusions to Nietzsche's influence on Sullivan, see: Hedges (1961:xiv); Menocal (1981:99–100, 195,n.30); Egbert (1950:363–8); Paul (1962:97–8); Condit (1959:84); Morrison (2001:255); Snyder (2019).

2 See Breitschmid (2001:18); Steiter, Breitschmid and Mallgrave (2000).

3 See Fischer (2013); Krawietz (1995:62); Anderson (2000); Bryant (2004).

4 See Pehnt (1998:53–4); Neumeyer (1999:298–9).

5 See Haddad (2005); Stamm (1973–5); Kuenzli (2012).

6 See Cohen (1999, 2007); D'Alessio (2016); Jencks (1973); Ottmann (2018:222); Brooks (1999:175); Richards (2003) argues that Le Corbusier was heavily influenced by the ideas of C.G. Jung. Jung was himself strongly influenced by Nietzsche's ideas (see Huskinson 2004).

7 See Bryant (2004:161); Buddensieg (1980); Maciuika (2008).

8 See Breitschmid (2007:75).

9 According to Fiona MacCarthy (2019), Gropius was 'not [...] a great admirer of Nietzschean philosophy', and he regarded Förster-Nietzsche as a 'local irritant'. By contrast, Gropius' first wife, Alma Mahler, described herself as a 'wild Nietzschean', having read him 'constantly' (Mahler-Werfel 2011:21,28). See also Kater (2014:166).

10 See Neumeyer (1999:288).

11 In the context of Le Corbusier's writing style, see Jencks (1973:25); Cohen (2007:1); Banham (1960:222–3); and for Sullivan's writing style, see Hedges (1961); Jordy (1975:165); Andrew (1985:34).

12 Architectural historian Alan Colquhoun naïvely and incorrectly interprets Nietzsche's desire for an architecture that evokes Dionysian instinct as an 'anarchistic urge', which seeks not 'to tame the disorder of modernity, but to plunge into its terrifying and nihilistic stream' (2002:61). While Nietzsche wishes to dismantle unhelpful and outmoded cultural values, he does so to create and build anew. He certainly does not wish to plunge culture into a terrifying and nihilistic chaos.

13 The motto of the Werkbund was '*vom Sofakissen zum Städtebau*': From sofa cushions to city-building'.

14 Despite the popularity of the Bauhaus and the large commissions they received, their architecture was never the most common, vernacular style in Germany. Most prominent were the conservative styles that developed out of pre-war progressive designs. These tended to adapt historicist styles by simplifying them and reducing them to more abstract forms.

15 On 20 September 1930, Wilhelm Frick replied to a letter from Elisabeth Förster-Nietzsche: 'Thank you kindly for your friendly congratulations on the NSDAP electoral success. I have not given up hope that you, dear lady, will attach yourself to the freedom movement of the German people, in the spirit of your highly commended brother, the warrior Nietzsche' (GSA,72, BW1496, GSA; Letter cited in full in English in Diethe 2003:151).

16 See note 9 above. Michael Kater (2014) notes that Gropius' 'understanding of Nietzsche was limited and he was unable to share Frau Elisabeth's distorted view of her brother. Therefore [...] no significant relationship developed. Never was there a lecture by a Bauhaus Master in the Villa Silberblick, never an exhibition of its art, and its members were not invited to soirées' (Kater 2014:166).

17 Schultze-Naumburg also designed houses that appear devoid of historical reference, with bare, white surfaces and symmetrical proportions. His Nietzsche Hall in Weimar is a good example, with its restrained design and with ornamentation reserved only for the sculptures inside.

18 While this quotation comes from Schultze-Naumburg's earlier work, the technical handbook, *ABC des Bauens*, he develops this prejudicial racism in *Kunst und Rasse*. Schultze-Naumburg's call for German racial purity appealed to the Nazi Party, and following his introduction to the Party by Wilhelm Frick, he became a spokesperson for Alfred Rosenberg's *Kampfbund für deutsche Kultur* (Fighting League for German Culture), which went on to publish his writings. The Nazi Party's opposition to the Bauhaus was largely due to the influence of Schultze-Naumburg's ideas (Miller Lane 1985:157). But as we saw in the previous chapter, despite Schultze-Naumburg's early influence on the Nazi's architectural policies, his services as an architect were widely dismissed by the Party.

Chapter 6

1 See for example, Neumeyer (2001/2004:184); Buddensieg (1999:266); Garnham (2013:65,69–70).

2 Kühn (1904) alludes to this passage in his praise of van de Velde's red furnishings for Villa Silberblick, as does Buddensieg (1980) in his comments on the furnishings of Behrens' house at the Darmstädt Artists' Colony.

3 For instance, 'Accept the fraternal feeling with great spirits!' 'No isolation!' (KSA9, 6[452]:315). Nietzsche warns of the disintegrating effect of philosophizing for those who are not strong enough to endure isolation. In such cases, 'Wherever an individual was willing to stand apart and erect a

4   See for instance, Scheyer (1970:48); Trimingham (2012:2).
5   Gottfried Semper is thought to have influenced Sullivan. According to Caruso (2012), Semper's theory of 'decorated structure' is evident in Sullivan's work, and with 'particular intensity' in Sullivan's 'development of a decorated structure' designed by him to give 'meaning to the apparent emptiness of the modern office building'. Caruso argues that Sullivan 'realised the potential of Semper's theory perhaps more powerfully than the work of [Semper] himself'.
6   The Marshall Field Wholesale Store was demolished to make way for a car park. It was U-shaped and red, and not 'four-square and brown' as Sullivan eulogizes. See O'Gorman (1978) for an historical account and description of the building conceived by its client.
7   In his autobiography, Sullivan describes himself as living in a 'maze of hero-worship'. See Menocal (1981) who briefly notes that Sullivan considered Michelangelo's work as expressive 'of the Nietzschean superman' (1981:18).
8   Allen Brooks takes a different stance on the matter: 'Jeanneret's personality, reinforced by his diverse reading, exhibited certain points in common with Nietzschean thought. But this does not mean that he comprehended, or was influenced by the Nietzschean vision as a whole. Furthermore, all of these so-called Nietzschean characteristics were a basic part of Jeanneret's personality long before he ever read Nietzsche' (1999:174).
9   Andrew offers an interesting counter-position, suggesting Nietzsche's characters of the last man or foaming fool (antagonists to Zarathustra) more closely resemble Sullivan's personality due to Sullivan's obsession for health and hygiene. According to Andrew, Sullivan was 'compulsive about recording year by year gains and losses in weight, bodily measurements, track timings, and swimming efforts'. Consequently, 'Sullivan seems to have ignored completely the opinion of one of his favorite philosophers in regard to this matter. In criticizing that "most contemptible" of creatures, the *"last man"*, Nietzsche includes a ringing indictment of the health obsession of such men' (1985:55). Andrew also claims that 'Sullivan denied his own true self' and failed to know himself and to love the city (1985:111–12), which is to say that Sullivan is akin to the foaming fool whom Zarathustra meets at the city gates. Andrew writes, 'Indeed, there is reason to believe that Sullivan, no matter how much his writings bear the tone of Nietzsche, neglected one of the passages in *Thus Spoke Zarathustra* that should have struck closest to home' (1985). This is the occasion in Part III where Zarathustra converses with a fool who describes to Zarathustra some despicable features of the city to encourage Zarathustra to walk away from it. Zarathustra silences the fool: 'I despise your despising; and if you warned me, why did you not warn yourself?' As a parting gift, Zarathustra remarks, 'where one can no longer love, there one should *pass* by' (Z, III, 7:195–8). According to Andrew, Sullivan was unable to follow Zarathustra's teaching: he was unable to love the city (1985:112).

Chapter 7

1. Zarathustra's teaching echoes earlier passages by Nietzsche, such as the provocative aphorism in *Daybreak*: '*How one should turn to stone* – Slowly, slowly become hard like a precious stone [*Edelstein*] – and finally lie there still and silent, to the joy of all eternity' (D,541). See also his discussion of Heraclitus and the nature of philosophers in 'Philosophy in the Tragic Age of the Greeks' [*Die Philosophie im tragischen Zeitalter der Griechen*]: 'The wall of his self-sufficiency must be made of diamond [*Diamant*] if it is not to be destroyed and broken, for all is moving against him' (KSA,1:833). See also a lecture by Richard Oehler given at the Nietzsche Archiv in 1935, titled *Friedrich Nietzsche und die deutsche Zukunft* ('Friedrich Nietzsche and the German Future'), where Oehler describes a 'strong will' and 'noble hardness' as requisites for creative living, citing the symbolism of the diamond and eagle to illustrate his point (1935/1938:7).

2. See Bletter (1981) for an account of this tradition. While Anderson's comprehensive study of Behrens' work concedes that Zarathustra's eagle companion was probably an inspiration for Behrens' fondness for the eagle motif (2000:49), he cites Stendhal's theory of crystallization as the philosophical inspiration for Behrens' penchant for crystal motifs (2000:29).

3. It is important to note that Taut's definition of socialism was different to the notion advocated by the political parties in Europe in the aftermath of the War. Taut endorsed an aristocracy led by elite artists who could cultivate the masses, elevating them above the working classes of proletarian socialism, Marxism, and democracy. Taut argued that the most gifted artisans ought to have greatest power in order that they may influence the most people. 'For all artistic questions, we should arrange to elect a recognised artist as a dictator, whose decision would be absolute [...] I am quite certain [...] that therein lies the possible way in which good, artistic values might be promoted' (1919/2002:3–4).

4. In support of Bletter's charge of gigantism against Taut – but not of Nietzsche – Wolfgang Pehnt suggests that the aesthetic effect of Taut's towering *Kristallhaus* on those who reside at ground level is dangerously close to totalitarian oppression rather than creative inspiration. Pehnt characterises Taut as having a 'fascination with size and mass', which results in monumental buildings that are 'wildly out of scale, with complete disproportion between the building and the people using it'. With specific reference to Taut's choice of visual illustrations for the *Stadtkone*, Pehnt remarks that the 'workers wend their way like pilgrims to colossal sanctuaries', and the 'people appear, if at all, as tiny dots' (1973:208).

5. Arguably, the *Kristallhaus* retains its symbolic status as a city crown irrespective of the popularization and prolific use of its glass material across all city zones, for the *Kristallhaus* transcends the material nature of glass. Furthermore, the presence of more glass throughout the city could extend and concentrate the reflective powers and reach of the *Kristallhaus*, encouraging other buildings to shimmer brighter with the brilliance it conveys.

6. See Maciuika (2008:42); Aschheim (1994:34); Whyte (1982:8).

7   See for instance, Chapman and Ostwald (2002:7); Pehnt (1994:60); Schubert (1988:252).

8   While van de Velde's monument sought to gently coax the onlooker to consider Zarathustra's message, Taut's monument is far from subtle. Interestingly, Taut considered himself an adversary of van de Velde's use of ornament more generally. In his annotations to another sketch he sent to the *Gläserne Kette* (titled, *Vivat Stella*/'Long Live the Star'), a day after he sent *Monument des Neuen Gesetzes*, Taut asserts that in contrast to van de Velde, who searches for style through shape or form, he himself discovers style through religious world views and religious symbols (Schubert 1988:241; Taut 1985:12).

9   The chosen phrases are as follows. 'Ohne einen Glaspalast ist das Leben eine Last' (Without a palace of glass, life is a burdensome task), 'Das bunte Glas zerstort den Hass' (Coloured glass destroys all hatred at last); and, 'Das Glas bringt uns die neue Zeit, Backsteinkultur tut uns nur leid'. (Glass brings us the new era, brick culture only makes us sorry.) See Scheerbart (1920/2014:130–43).

10 Others note the parallels of Nietzschean themes and the occasion of Lesabéndio's merging with the cosmos, such as Schubert, who asserts that Scheerbart 'shares with Nietzsche the priority of world affirmation and astral symbolism' (1988:246).

BIBLIOGRAPHY

Ábalos, I., November, 2016-last update. Architecture for the Search for Knowledge (The Walter Gropius Lecture. Harvard University Graduate School of Design). Available: https://www.gsd.harvard.edu/event/inaki-abalos-architecture-for-the-search-for-knowledge/ [January 2024].

Altenmüller, U., 2000. The City Crown: An Utopianist's Vision of a Better World by Bruno Taut. *Spaces of Utopia: An Electronic Journal*, 2, pp. 134–42.

Anderson, S., 2000. *Peter Behrens and a New Architecture for the Twentieth Century*. Cambridge, MA: MIT Press.

Andrew, D.S., 1985. *Louis Sullivan and the Polemics of Modern Architecture: The Present against the Past*. Urbana, IL: University of Illinois Press.

Aschheim, S.E., 1994. *The Nietzsche Legacy in Germany, 1890–1990*. Berkeley, CA: University of California Press.

Babich, B., 2000. Future Philology! By Ulrich von Wilamowitz-Moellendorff. *Articles and Chapters in Academic Book Collections, Research Library, Fordham University*, 3, pp. 1–33.

Baker, E., 1998. Richard Wagner and His Search for the Ideal Theatrical Space. In: M. Radice, ed, *Opera in Context*. Portland, OR: Amadeus Press, pp. 269–78.

Banham, R., 1960. *Theory and Design in the First Machine Age*. New York: Praeger.

Bartnig, H., Neidhardt, H.J., Krull, E. and Krull, D., 1995. *Semperoper: Gottfried Sempers Opernhaus Zu Dresden*. Dresden: Meissen.

Battista Alberti, L., 1998. *On the Art of Building in Ten Books*. Cambridge, MA: MIT Press.

Behrens, P., 1987. Die Form. In: W. Fischer, ed, *Zwischen Kunst und Industrie: der Deutsche Werkbund*. Stuttgart: Deutsche Verlags-Anstalt, pp. 181–4.

Berger, U., 1999. 'Herauf nun, herauf, du großer Mittag': Georg Kolbes Statue für die Nietzsche-Gedächtnishalle und die gescheiterten Vorläuferprojekte. In: H. Wilderotter and M. Dorrmann, eds, *Wege nach Weimar: Auf der Suche nach der Einheit von Kunst und Politik*. Weimar: Jovis, pp. 177–94.

Bernhard, P., 2008. Ich-Überwindung muß der Gestaltung vorangehen. Zur Nietzsche-Rezeption des Bauhauses. In: A.U. Sommer, ed, *Nietzsche – Philosoph der Kultur(en)?* Berlin and New York: de Gruyter, pp. 272–84.

Bishop, P., 2017. *On the Blissful Islands with Nietzsche and Jung: In the Shadow of the Superman*. London and New York: Routledge.

Bletter, R.H., 1983. Expressionism and the New Objectivity. *Art Journal*, 43(2), pp. 108–20.

Bletter, R.H., 1982. Global Earthworks. *Art Journal*, 42(3), pp. 222–5.

Bletter, R.H., 1981. The Interpretation of the Glass Dream-Expressionist Architecture and the History of the Crystal Metaphor. *Journal of the Society of Architectural Historians*, 40(1), pp. 20–43.

Bletter, R.H., 1975. Paul Scheerbart's Architectural Fantasies. *Journal of the Society of Architectural Historians*, 34(2), pp. 83–97.
Block, R., 2006. *The Spell of Italy: Vacation, Magic, and the Attraction of Goethe*. Detroit: Wayne State University Press.
Bogner, S., 2018. Die Nietzsche-Gedächtnishalle von Paul Schultze-Naumburg: den Ausbau und zugleich die Zusammenfassung der Nietzsche-Bewegung von Weimar aus und in Weimar. In: H. Meier and D. Spiegel, eds, *Kulturreformer. Rassenideologe. Hochschuldirektor: Der lange Schatten des Paul Schultze-Naumburg*. Heidelberg: Arthistoricum.net, pp. 47–59.
Bogner, S., 2014. Die ehemalige Nietzsche Gedächtnishalle in Weimar von Paul Schultze Naumburg – Von der Kultstätte zum Rundfunkhaus. *Weimar-Jena. Die große Stadt*, 7, pp. 52–71.
Böhme, H., 2001. Architektur im post-religiösen Zeitalter. *Der Architekt*, (März 3), pp. 16–23.
Bolland, M.E., 1996. Nietzsche and Mountains. Doctoral Thesis, University of Durham.
Breitschmid, M., 2007. Nietzsche's 'Architecture for the Perceptive'. From Sacred Space towards a Space for Reflection. *Spaces of Utopia: An Electronic Journal*, 4, pp. 74–87.
Breitschmid, M., 2001. *Der bauende Geist Friedrich Nietzsche und die Architektur*. Luzern: Quart-Verlag.
Breuer, R., 1910. Häuser, die Künstler sich bauten. *Über Land und Meer*, 105, pp. 195–7.
Brooks, A.H., 1999. *Le Corbusier's Formative Years: Charles-Edouard Jeanneret at La Chaux-de-Fonds*. Chicago: University of Chicago Press.
Bryant, G., 2004. Timely Untimeliness: Architectural Modernism and Idea of the Gesamtkunstwerk. In: M. Hvattum and C. Hermansen, eds, *Tracing Modernity: Manifestations of the Modern in Architecture and the City*. London and New York: Routledge, pp. 156–72.
Buddensieg, T., 2002a. *Nietzsches Italien: Städte, Gärten und Paläste*. Berlin: Wagenbach Verlag.
Buddensieg, T., 2002b, Zarathustra in Chicago. In: T. Buddensieg, *Nietzsches Italien: Städte, Gärten und Paläste*. Berlin: Wagenbach Verlag, pp. 188–9.
Buddensieg, T., 1999. Architecture as Empty Form: Nietzsche and the Art of Building. In: A. Kostka and I. Wohlfarth, eds, *Nietzsche and 'An Architecture of our Minds'*. Los Angeles: Getty Research Institute for the History of Art and the Humanities, pp. 259–84.
Buddensieg, T., 1980. Das Wohnhaus als Kultban. In: P. Schuster, T. Buddensieg and Klaus-Jürgen Sembach, eds, *Peter Behrens und Nürnberg Geschmack Wandel in Deutschland: Historismus, Jugendstil und die Anfänge der Industrieform*. München: Prestel, pp. 37–47.
Burckhardt, J., 2021. *The Civilization of the Renaissance in Italy*. Trans. S. Middlemore. Middlesex: Penguin.
Burckhardt, J., 1867/1987. *The Architecture of the Italian Renaissance*. Trans. J. Palmes. Middlesex: Penguin.
Burckhardt, J., 1867/1868. *Geschichte der Renaissance in Italien*. Stuttgart: Verlag von Ebner & Seubert.
Burckhardt, J., 1855. *Der Cicerone. Eine Anleitung zum Genuss der Kunstwerke Italiens*, vol. I. Architektur. 1869 edn. Leipzig: von E. Seemann.

BIBLIOGRAPHY

Caldwell, A., 1956. Louis Sullivan. *Dimensions*, 2(1), pp. 9–16.
Cancik, H., 1987. Der Nietzsche-Kult in Weimar. *Nietzsche-Studien*, 16(1), pp. 405–29.
Caruso, A., 2012-last update. The Tall Office Building .... Available: https://www.caruso.arch.ethz.ch/programme/fs-2012/studio [January 2024].
Chamberlain, L., 2022. *Nietzsche in Turin: The End of the Future*. London: Pushkin Press.
Chapman, M. and Ostwald, M., 2002. Laying Siege to the Stadtkrone: Nietzsche, Taut, and the Vision of a Cultural Aristocracy. *Additions to Architectural History: XIXth Annual Conference of the Society of Architectural Historians, Australia and New Zealand*. Sahanz, pp. 1–11.
Church, J., 2015. *Nietzsche's Culture of Humanity: Beyond Aristocracy and Democracy in the Early Period*. Cambridge: Cambridge University Press.
Cimorelli, D., 2016. *Mole Antonelliana Turin: Visitor's Guide*. Eds. F. Levi and R. Rolli. Verona: Salvana Editoriale.
Cohen, J., 2007. Introduction. In: *Toward an Architecture: Le Corbusier*. Trans. J. Goodman. Los Angeles: Getty Press, pp. 1–25.
Cohen, J., 1999. Le Corbusier's Nietzschean Metaphors. In: A. Kostka and I. Wohlfarth, eds, *Nietzsche and 'An Architecture of Our Minds'*. Los Angeles, CA: Getty Research Institute for the History of Art and the Humanities, pp. 311–32.
Cohn, P.V. and Förster-Nietzsche, E., 1931. *Um Nietzsches Untergang: Beiträge zum Verständnis des Genies. Mit einem Anhang von Elisabeth Förster-Nietzsche*. Hannover: Morris-Verlag; [L. Heidrich].
Colquhoun, A., 2002. *Modern Architecture*. Oxford and New York: Oxford University Press.
Condit, C.W., 1959. Sullivan's Skyscrapers as the Expression of Nineteenth Century Technology. *Technology and Culture*, 1(1), pp. 78–93.
D'Alessio, F., 2016. Twilight of the Styles: Unearthing Nietzsche's Notion of Death of God in Le Corbusier's Architectural Theory. Undergraduate Dissertation, BSc (Hons) Architecture, University of the West of England.
Day, L., 2014. Paul Schultze-Naumburg: An Intellectual Biography. Doctoral Thesis, Edinburgh College of Art, Edinburgh.
Dick, L.W., 1984. Art and Political Ideology: The Bauhaus as Victim. Masters Thesis, Department of History, Kansas State University.
Diethe, C., 2003. *Nietzsche's Sister and the Will to Power: A Biography of Elisabeth Förster-Nietzsche*. Chicago: University of Illinois Press.
Dietrich, C. and Erbsmehl, H., 2004. *Klingers Nietzsche: Wandlungen eines Portraits, 1902–1914; ein Beitrag zur Kunstgeschichte des 'neuen Weimar'*. Jena: Glaux.
D'Iorio, P., 2012. *Nietzsche's Journey to Sorrento: Genesis of the Philosophy of the Free Spirit*. Chicago: Chicago University Press.
Easton, L.M., 2006. *The Red Count: The Life and Times of Harry Kessler*. Berkeley, CA and London: University of California Press.
Egbert, D.D., 1950. The Idea of Organic Expression and American Architecture. In: S. Persons, ed, *Evolutionary Thought in America*. New Haven: Yale University Press, pp. 336–96.
Egbert, H., 1971. *Buonaventura Genelli: Leben und Werk*. Weimar: Hermann Böhlaus Nachfolger.
Emmrich, A., 2000a. Imaginärer Rundgang durch die Obergeschoßräume des Nietzsche-Archivs nach historischen Aufnahmen. In: S. Geske, ed, *Das Nietzsche-Archiv in Weimar*. München: Carl Hanser Verlag, pp. 88–106.

Emmrich, A., 2000b. Ein Rundgang durch das Erdgeschoß des ehemaligen Nietzsche-Archivs. In: S. Geske, ed, *Das Nietzsche-Archiv in Weimar*. München: Carl Hanser Verlag, pp. 72–87.

Emmrich, A., 2000c. 'zugleich ein Tempel und zugleich eine Häuslichkeit' Zur Haus – und Kunstgeschichte des Nietzsche-Archivs. In: S. Geske, ed, *Das Nietzsche-Archiv in Weimar*. München: Carl Hanser Verlag, pp. 39–71.

Fischer, O.W. and Pese, C., 2013. Bauen für den Übermenschen? – Peter Behrens, Henry van de Velde und die Suche nach einem Nietzsche-Stil. In: T. Föhl, ed, *Peter Behrens – Vom Jugendstil zum Industriedesign*. Weimar: Weimarer Verlagsgesellschaft, pp. 92–105.

Föhl, T., ed, 2000. *Ihr Kinderlein kommet ... : Henry van de Velde: ein vergessenes Projekt für Friedrich Nietzsche*. Ostfildern: Hatje Cantz.

Föhl, T., 1996. Das Ernst Abbe-Denkmal und sein Architekt. In: S. Grohé, ed, *Das Ernst Abbe-Denkmal*. Arnstadt: Rhino Verlag, pp. 60–71.

Förster-Nietzsche, E., 1914. *Der einsame Nietzsche*. Leipzig: Alfred Kröner.

Galindo, M.Z., 1995. *Triumph des Willens zur Macht: Nietzsche-Rezeption im NS-Staat*. Hamburg: Argument.

Garnham, T., 2013. *Architecture Re-assembled: The Use (and Abuse) of History*. London and New York: Routledge.

Gleiter, J.H., 2009. *Der philosophische Flaneur: Nietzsche und die Architektur*. Würzburg: Königshausen & Neumann.

Gnehm, M., 2017. Tropical Opulence: Rio de Janeiro's Theater Competition of 1857. In: C.M. Avolese and R. Conduru, eds, *New Worlds: Frontiers, Inclusion, Utopias*. São Paulo: Comité International de l'Histoire de l'Art, Comitê Brasileiro de História da Arte, pp. 146–64.

Graef, B., 1912. Das Abbedenkmal in Jena. *Kunst und Künstler: illustrierte Monatsschrift für bildende Kunst und Kunstgewerbe*, pp. 219–22.

Grohé, S., 1996a. Max Klingers Abbe-Herme – Eine Denkmal im Denkmal. In: S. Grohé, ed, *Das Ernst Abbe-Denkmal*. Arnstadt: Rhino Verlag, pp. 72–93.

Grohé, S., 1996b. Zur Geschichte des Janaer Ernst Abbe-Denkmals. In: S. Grohé, ed, *Das Ernst Abbe-Denkmal*. Arnstadt: Rhino Verlag, pp. 8–35.

Gropius, W., 1936. *The New Architecture and the Bauhaus*. Trans. P. Morton Shand. Cambridge, MA: MIT Press.

Gropius, W., 1923. *Idee und Aufbau des staatlichen Bauhauses Weimar*. München: Bauhausverlag.

Gropius, W., 1919. *Ausstellung für unbekannte Architekten: Berlin und Weimar*. Berlin: Neues Bauen.

Grupp, P., 1999. Geteilte Illusionen. Die Beziehung Zwischen Harry Graf Kessler und Henry van de Velde. In: H. Wilderotter and M. Dorrmann, eds, *Wege nach Weimar: Auf der Suche nach der Einheit von Kunst und Politik*. Weimar: Jovis, pp. 195–204.

Guillén, M.F., 2006. *The Taylorized Beauty of the Mechanical: Scientific Management and the Rise of Modernist Architecture*. Princeton, NJ: Princeton University Press.

Habel, H., 1985. *Festspielhaus und Wahnfried: Geplante und ausgeführte Bauten Richard Wagners*. München: Prestel.

Habel, H., 1970. Die Idee eines Festspielhauses. In: D. Petzet and M. Petzet, eds, *Die Richard Wagner – Bühne König Ludwigs II. München, Bayreuth*. München: Prestel, pp. 297–316.

Haddad, E.G., 2005. In Nietzsche's Shadow: Henry van de Velde and the New Style. *Architecture, Architectural Theory Review*, 10(2), pp. 88–99.

Haddad, E.G., 2003a. On Henry van de Velde's Manuscript on Ornament. *Journal of Design History*, 16(2), pp. 119–38.

Haddad, E.G., 2003b. The Realization of the Beautiful: On Henry van de Velde's Aesthetic Theory. *Fabrications*, 13(1), pp. 1–13.

Haskell, F., 1993. *History and Its Images: Art and Representation of the Past*. New Haven and London: Yale University Press.

Hedges, E., 1961. Introduction. In: E. Hedges, ed, *Democracy: A Man Search*. Detroit: Wayne State University Press, pp. vii–xxiv.

Heer, J.D. and Hall, G., 2009. *The Architectonic Colour: Polychromy in the Purist Architecture of Le Corbusier*. Rotterdam: 010 Publishers.

Herrmann, W., 1989. *Gottfried Semper: In Search of Architecture*. Cambridge, MA: MIT Press.

Herrmann, W., 1981. *Gottfried Semper Theoretischer Nachlass an der ETH Zürich. Katalog und Kommentare*. Basel: Birkhäuser.

Hindley, L., 2012. Nietzsche Is Dead, *Humanities*, July/August, 33(4). Available: https://www.neh.gov/humanities/2012/julyaugust/feature/nietzsche-dead [November 2023].

Hirt, A., 1805. *Bilderbuch für Mythologie, Archäologie und Kunst*. 2011 edn. Charleston, SC: Nabu.

Hitchcock, H., 1992. *Architecture: Nineteenth and Twentieth Centuries*. Fourth edn. New Haven: Yale University Press.

Hitler, A., 1936. Art and Politics. *Liberty, Art, Nationhood: Three Addresses Delivered at the Seventh National Socialist Congress, Nuremberg*. Berlin: Muller and Sons, pp. 30–53.

Hollis, R., 2019. *Henry van de Velde, the Artist as Designer: From Art Nouveau to Modernism*. London: Occasional Papers.

Huskinson, L., 2004. *Nietzsche and Jung: The Whole Self in the Union of Opposites*. London and New York: Routledge.

Huskinson, L., 2018. *Architecture and the Mimetic Self: A Psychoanalytic Study of How Buildings Make and Break Our Lives*. London and New York: Routledge.

Janneau, G., 1923. L'Exposition des arts techniques de 1925. *Le Bulletin de la Vie Artistique*, 4(3), pp. 61–5.

Jencks, C., 1973. *Le Corbusier and the Tragic View of Architecture*. London: Penguin Books.

Jones, E., 1957. *Sigmund Freud: Life and Works*, vol. 3. London: Hogarth Press.

Jordy, W.H., 1975. *American Buildings and Their Architects: Progressive and Academic Ideals at the Turn of the 20th Century*. New York: Doubleday.

Kater, M., 2014. *Weimar: From Enlightenment to Present*. New Haven: Yale University Press.

Kaufmann, W.A., 2000. *Basic Writings of Nietzsche*. New York: The Modern Library.

Kessler, H.G., 2011. *Journey to the Abyss: The Diaries of Count Harry Kessler, 1880–1918*. Ed. and Trans. L. Easton. New York: Knopf.

Kessler, H.G., 1961. *Tagebücher, 1918–1937*. Frankfurt am Main: Insel.

Kessler, H.G., 1909. Griechischer Frühling. *Die neue Rundschau*, XX, pp. 719–43.

Kessler, H.G. and Van De Velde, H., 2015. *Harry Graf Kessler – Henry van de Velde. Der Briefwechsel*. Ed. A. Neumann. Köln, Weimar, Wien: Böhlau Verlag GmbH & Cie.

Kirk, T., 2005. *The Architecture of Modern Italy. The Challenge of Tradition, 1750–1900*. New York: Princeton Architectural Press.

Kitchen, M., 2017. *Speer: Hitler's Architect*. New Haven: Yale University Press.

Koss, J., 2003. Bauhaus Theatre of Human Dolls. *The Art Bulletin*, 85(4), pp. 724–45.

Kostka, A., 2000. Eine unzeitgemässe Gabe für Weimar. Das Projekt eines Nietzsche-Tempels von Harry Graf Kessler und Henry van de Velde. In: T. Föhl, ed, *Ihr Kinderlein kommet ... : Henry van de Velde: ein vergessenes Projekt für Friedrich Nietzsche*. Ostfildern: Hatje Cantz, pp. 33–66.

Kostka, A. and Wohlfarth, I., eds, 1999. *Nietzsche and 'An Architecture of Our Minds'*. Los Angeles: Getty Research Institute for the History of Art and the Humanities.

Krause, J., 1984. *'Märtyrer' und 'Prophet': Studien zum Nietzsche-Kult in der Bildenden Kunst der Jahrhundertwende*. New York and Berlin: De Gruyter.

Krawietz, G., 1995. *Peter Behrens im Dritten Reich*. Weimar: Weimar und Datenbank für Geisteswissenschafte.

Kuenzli, K.M., 2012. Architecture, Individualism, and Nation: Henry van de Velde's 1914 Werkbund Theater Building. *The Art Bulletin*, 94(2), pp. 251–73.

Kühn, P., 1904. *Das Nietzsche Archiv zu Weimar*. Darmstädt: Alexander Koch.

Kühn, P., 1899. Studio News. Fritz Schumacher. *Deutsche Kunst und Dekoration*, 5, pp. 222–7.

Lahiji, N., 2019. *An Architecture Manifesto: Critical Reason and Theories of a Failed Practice*. London and New York: Routledge.

Lahusen, S., 1986. Oskar Schlemmer: Mechanical Ballets? *Dance Research: The Journal for the Society for Dance Research*, 4(2), pp. 65–77.

Lamster, M., 2018. *The Man in the Glass House: Philip Johnson, Architect of the Modern Century*. New York: Little, Brown and Company.

Lane, B.M., 1985. *Architecture and Politics in Germany: 1918–1945*. Cambridge, MA and London: Harvard University Press.

Laudel, H., 2003. Kaiserliches Theater in Rio de Janeiro. In: W. Nerdinger and W. Oechslin, eds, *Gottfried Semper 1803–1879: Architektur und Wissenschaft*. München: Prestel, pp. 333–6.

Le Corbusier, 1923/2016. *Toward an Architecture*. Trans. J. Goodman. Los Angeles: Getty Press.

Le Corbusier, 1925/1987. *The Decorative Art of Today*. Trans. J. Dunnett. Cambridge, MA: MIT Press.

Le Corbusier, 1926. Notes a la suite (sections VIII and XVIII). *Cahiers d'art*, 3, pp. 46–52.

Le Corbusier, 1925a. *Le Pavillon de L'Esprit Nouveau*. Almanach d'architecture moderne. Paris: G.Crès & Cie.

Le Corbusier, 1925b. *La Peinture Moderne*. Paris: Editions G. Crès et Cie.

Le Corbusier, 1923a. Salon d'automne (Architecture). *L'Esprit Nouveau*, n.p.

Le Corbusier, 1923b. *Vers une Architecture*. Paris: Editions G. Crès et Cie.

Levine, S., 1996. Constantin Meunier's *Monument au travail*. In: S. Grohé, ed, *Das Ernst Abbe-Denkmal*. Arnstadt: Rhino Verlag, pp. 36–59.

Loos, A., 1908/2019. *Ornament and Crime*. Penguin Classics. London: Penguin.

Loos, K., 1999. *Die Inszenierung der Stadt Planen und Bauen im Nationalsozialismus in Weimar*. Weimar: Universität Weimar.

Maccarthy, F., 2019. *Walter Gropius: Visionary Founder of the Bauhaus*. London: Faber and Faber.
Maciuika, J.V., 2008. *Before the Bauhaus: Architecture, Politics and the German State 1890–1920*. Cambridge: Cambridge University Press.
Magirius, H., 1987. *Gottfried Sempers Zweites Dresdner Hoftheater: Entstehung Künstlerische Ausstattung Ikonographie*. Guttenberg: Büchergilde.
Mahler, A., 2011. *Mein Leben*. Frankfurt am Main: Fischer Taschenbuch Verlag.
Mallgrave, H.F., 2006. Introduction. In: H.F. Mallgrave, ed, *Style in the Technical and Tectonic Arts; or Practical Aesthetics*. Los Angeles: Getty Press, pp. 1–70.
Mallgrave, H.F., 1996. *Gottfried Semper: Architect of the Nineteenth Century*. New Haven: Yale University Press.
Mandel, S., 1990. Genelli and Wagner: Midwives to Nietzsche's 'The Birth of Tragedy'. *Nietzsche-Studien*, 19, pp. 212–29.
Mcgrath, W., 2013. *German Freedom and the Greek Ideal: The Cultural Legacy from Goethe to Mann*. London: Palgrave Macmillan.
Menocal, N.G., 2000. The Iconography of Architecture: Sullivan's View. In: N.G. Menocal and T. Twombly, eds, *Louis Sullivan: The Poetry of Architecture*. New York: W.W. Norton, pp. 73–160.
Menocal, N.G., 1981. *Architecture as Nature: The Transcendentalist Idea of Louis Sullivan*. Madison: University of Wisconsin Press.
Mindrup, M., 2015. Introduction: Advancing the Reverie of Utopia. In: M. Mindrup and U. Altenmüller-Lewis, eds, *The City Crown by Bruno Taut*. Surrey: Ashgate, pp. 1–30.
Moos, S.V., 2009. *Le Corbusier, Elements of a Synthesis*. Rotterdam: 010 Publishers.
Morrison, H., 2001. *Louis Sullivan: Prophet of Modern Architecture*. New York: W.W. Norton.
Müller-wulckow, W., 1925. *Bauten der Arbeit und des Verkehrs aus deutscher Gegenwart*. Königstein im Taunus: Karl Robert Langewiesche.
Neumann, A., 2015. *Harry Graf Kessler – Henry van de Velde. Der Briefwechsel (Editor's Notes)*. Köln, Weimar, Wien: Böhlau Verlag GmbH & Cie.
Neumann, A., 2014. *Harry Graf Kessler – Henry van de Velde: der Briefwechsel*. Göttingen: Vandenhoeck & Ruprecht.
Neumeyer, F., 2001/2004. *Der Klang Der Stein: Nietzsches Architekturen*. Berlin: Gebr. Mann Verlag.
Neumeyer, F., 1999. Nietzsche and Modern Architecture. In: A. Kostka and I. Wohlfarth, eds, *Nietzsche and 'An Architecture of Our Minds'*. Los Angeles: Getty Research Institute for the History of Art and the Humanities, pp. 285–310.
Newman, E., 1980. *The Life of Richard Wagner*, vol. 3: 1859–1866. Cambridge Library Collection, Cambridge: Cambridge University Press.
Nielsen, E., 2005. *Bonaventura Genelli: Werk und Kunstauffassung. Ein Beitrag zur Kunst des Späten Klassizismus in Deutschland*, Ludwig-Maximilians-Universität München.
Nietzsche, F., 1888/2021. *The Case of Wagner, Twilight of the Idols, The Antichrist, Ecce Homo, Dionysus Dithyrambs, Nietzsche contra Wagner*. The Complete Works of Friedrich Nietzsche, vol. 9. Trans. C. Diethe and D. Large. Stanford, CA: Stanford University Press.

Nietzsche, F., 1886/2014. *Beyond Good and Evil/On the Genealogy of Morality*. The Complete Works of Friedrich Nietzsche, vol. 8. Trans. A. Del Caro. Stanford, CA: Stanford University Press.

Nietzsche, F., 1870/2013. *Das griechische Musikdrama/The Greek Music Drama*. Trans. P. Bishop. New York: Contra Mundum Press.

Nietzsche, F., 1886/2013. *Human, All Too Human, II: And Unpublished Fragments from the Period of 'Human, All Too Human II' (Spring 1878–fall 1879)*. The Complete Works of Friedrich Nietzsche, vol. 4. Trans. G. Handwerk. Stanford, CA: Stanford University Press.

Nietzsche, F., 1881/2011. *Dawn: Thoughts on the Presumptions of Morality [Daybreak]*. The Complete Works of Friedrich Nietzsche, vol. 5. Trans. B. Smith. Stanford, CA: Stanford University Press.

Nietzsche, F., 2005. *Sämtliche Werke: Kritische Studienausgabe*. München: Deutscher Taschenbuch Verlag.

Nietzsche, F., 2003. *Sämtliche Briefe: Kritische Studienausgabe, 8 vols*. München: Deutscher Taschenbuch Verlag de Gruyter.

Nietzsche, F., 1882/2001. *The Gay Science, with a Prelude in German Rhymes and an Appendix of Songs*. Trans. J. Nauckhoff. Cambridge: Cambridge University Press.

Nietzsche, F., 1873–76/1998. *Unfashionable Observations [Untimely Meditations]*. The complete Works of Friedrich Nietzsche, vol. 2. Trans. R.T. Gray. Stanford, CA: Stanford University Press.

Nietzsche, F., 1878/1997. *Human All Too Human I: A Book for Free Spirits*. The Complete Works of Friedrich Nietzsche, vol. 3. Trans. G. Handwerk. Stanford, CA: Stanford University Press.

Nietzsche, F., 1873/1996. *Philosophy in the Tragic Age of the Greeks*. Trans. M. Cowan. Reprint edn. Washington: Gateway, Regnery Publishing Inc.

Nietzsche, F., 1888/1995. *The Case of Wagner, Twilight of the Idols, The Antichrist, Ecce Homo, Dionysus Dithyrambs, Nietzsche Contra Wagner*. The Complete Works of Friedrich Nietzsche, vol. 9. Trans. C. Diethe and D. Large. Stanford, CA: Stanford University Press.

Nietzsche, F., 1994. *Frühe Schriften: Jugendschriften, 1854–1869*, vol. 5. München: Deutscher Taschenbuch Verlag.

Nietzsche, F., 1872/1993. *The Birth of Tragedy out of the Spirit of Music*. Trans. S. Whiteside. London: Penguin.

Nietzsche, F., 1883–1885/1969. *Thus Spoke Zarathustra*. Trans. R.J. Hollingdale. Middlesex: Penguin.

Oechslin, W., 1996. Politisches, allzu Politisches: Nietzschelinge, der Wille zur Kunst und der Deutsche Werkbund vor 1914. In: H. Hipp and E. Seidl, eds, *Architektur als Politische Kultur: philosophia practica*. Berlin: D. Reimer, pp. 151–90.

Oehler, R., 1935/1938. *Friedrich Nietzsche und die deutsche Zukunft*. Leipzig: Armanen-Verlag.

O'Gorman, J.F., 1978. The Marshall Field Wholesale Store: Materials toward a Monograph. *Journal of the Society of Architectural Historians*, 37(3), pp. 175–94.

Ottmann, H., 2019. Zarathustra – Spuren in Architektur, bildender Kunst und Malerei. In: M. Mayer, ed, *Also wie sprach Zarathustra? West-östliche Spiegelungen im kulturgeschichtlichen Vergleich*. Würzburg: Ergon-Verlag, pp. 217–41.

Ovid, 1989a. *Heroides*. New Haven: Harvard University Press.

BIBLIOGRAPHY

Ovid, 1989b. *Metamorphoses*. Books 1–8, vol. 3. New Haven: Harvard University Press.

Paden, R., 2010. Otto Wagner's Modern Architecture. *Ethics, Place and Environment*, 13(2), pp. 229–46.

Partsch, C., 2002. Paul Scheerbart and the Art of Science Fiction. *Science Fiction Studies*, 29(2), July, pp. 202–20.

Paul, S., 1962. *Louis Sullivan an Architect in American Thought*. Englewood Cliffs, NJ: Prentice-Hall, inc.

Pehnt, W., 1998. Reformwille zur Macht. Der Palazzo Pitti und der deutsche Zyklopenstil. In: R. Schneider and W. Wang, eds, *Moderne Architektur in Deutschland 1900 bis 2000. Macht und Monument*. Ostfildern: Ruit, pp. 52–9.

Pehnt, W., 1994. Turm und Höhle. In: A. Colquhoun, S. von Moos, and W. Pehnt, eds, *Moderne Architektur in Deutschland 1900–1950: Expressionismus und Neue Sachlichkeit*. Stuttgart: Hatje, pp. 50–67.

Pehnt, W., 1973. *Expressionist Architecture*. London: Thames and Hudson.

Peters, H.F., 1977. *Zarathustra's Sister: The Case of Elisabeth and Friedrich Nietzsche*. New York: M. Weiner Publishing.

Porter, J.I., 2011. 'Don't Quote Me on That!' Wilamowitz Contra Nietzsche in 1872 and 1873. *Journal of Nietzsche Studies*, 42(1), pp. 73–99.

Quatremere De Quincy, A., 1815. *Le Jupiter olympien, ou l'art de la sculpture antique considerer sous un nouveau point de vue*. 2018 edn. Paris: Hachette Livre-BNF.

Reust, A., 1919/2014. On the Birth, Death, and Rebirth of Dionysus: A Memorial Wreath for Scheerbart's Grave. In: J. Mcelheny and C. Burgin, eds, *Glass! Love!! Perpetual Motion!! A Paul Scheerbart Reader*. Chicago: Chicago University Press, pp. 267–71.

Richards, S., 2003. *Le Corbusier and the Concept of Self*. New Haven: Yale University Press.

Rohde, E., 1872. *Afterphilologie*. Leipzig: E.W. Fritzsch.

Romberg, J.A., 1845. *Conversations-Lexicon Für Bildende Kunst, Vols. 3–4*. Leipzig: Renger.

Rosenberg, A., 1889. *Die Deutsche Kunst, 1795–1889*. Leipzig: F.W. Grunoal.

Ruehl, M.A., 2015. Ruthless Renaissance: Burckhardt, Nietzsche, and the Violent Birth of the Modern Self. In: *The Italian Renaissance in the German Historical Imagination, 1860–1930*. Cambridge: Cambridge University Press, pp. 58–104.

Rykwert, J., 2010. Gottfried Semper: Architect and Historian. In: *Gottfried Semper. The Four Elements of Architecture and Other Writings*. Trans. H.F. Mallgrave and W. Herrmann Cambridge: Cambridge University Press, pp. vii–xvii.

Scheerbart, P., 1914/2014. Glass Architecture (*Glassarchitektur*). In: J. Mcelheny and C. Burgin, eds, *Glass! Love!! Perpetual Motion!! A Paul Scheerbart Reader*. Trans. J. McElheny. Chicago: University of Chicago Press, pp. 20–91.

Scheerbart, P., 1920/2014. Glass House Letters. In: J. Mcelheny and C. Burgin, eds, *Glass! Love!! Perpetual Motion!! A Paul Scheerbart Reader*. Trans. A. Posten and L. Lindgren. Chicago: Chicago University Press, pp. 130–44.

Scheerbart, P., 1913/2012. *Lesabéndio: An Asteroid Novel*. Trans. C. Svendsen. Cambridge, MA: Wakefield Press.

Scheyer, E., 1970. *The Shapes of Space: The Art of Mary Wigman and Oskar Schlemmer*. New York: Dance Perspectives Foundation.

Schlemmer, O., 1990. *The Letters and Diaries of Oskar Schlemmer*. Evanston, IL: Northwestern University Press.
Schubert, D., 1988. Bruno Tauts 'Monument des Neuen Gesetzes' (1919) zur Nietzsche-Wirkung im sozialistischen expressionismus. *Jahrbuch der Berliner Museen*, 29/30, pp. 241–55.
Schultze, S., 2019. Friedrich Nietzsche and the Artists of the New Weimar. In: *Friedrich Nietzsche and the Artists of the New Weimar*. Milan: Five Continents, pp. 11–38.
Schultze-Naumburg, P., 1928. *Kunst und Rasse*. München: Lehmann.
Schultze-Naumburg, P., 1926. *Das ABC des Bauens*. Stuttgart: Franckh.
Schumacher, F., 1935/1949. *Stufen Des Lebens. Erinnerungen eines Baumeisters*. Stuttgart: Deutsche Verlags-Anstalt.
Scully, V., 1959. Louis Sullivan's Architectural Ornament: A Brief Note Concerning Humanist Design in the Age of Force. *Perspecta*, 5, pp. 73–80.
Seidl, A., 1901. *Kunst und Kultur. Aus der Zeit – für die Zeit – wider die Zeit. Produktive Kritik in Vorträgen, Essais, Studien*. Berlin and Leipzig: Schuster & Loeffler.
Sembach, K., 1989. *Henry van de Velde*. London: Thames and Hudson.
Semper, G., 1869/2010. On Architectural Styles. In: F. Pellizzi, ed, *The Four Elements of Architecture and Other Writings*. Trans. H.F. Mallgrave and W. Herrmann. Cambridge: Cambridge University Press, pp. 264–306.
Semper, G., 1834/2010. Preface to Preliminary Remarks on Polychrome Architecture. In: F. Pellizzi, ed, *The Four Elements of Architecture and Other Writings*. Trans. H.F. Mallgrave and W. Herrmann. Cambridge: Cambridge University Press, pp. 45–73.
Semper, G., 1852/2010. Prospectus Comparative Theory of Building. In: F. Pellizzi, ed, *The Four Elements of Architecture and Other Writings*. Trans. H.F. Mallgrave and W. Herrmann. Cambridge: Cambridge University Press, pp. 168–73.
Semper, G., 1861/1862/2004. *Style in the Technical and Tectonic Arts; or Practical Aesthetics*. Trans. H.F. Mallgrave and M. Robinson. Los Angeles: Getty Press.
Semper, G., 1858. *Entwurf für das kaiserliche Theatre in Rio de Janeiro*. München: Theatermuseum.
Semper, M., 1906. *Das Munchener Festspielhaus*. Hamburg: von Conrad.
Shah, T., May, 2020-last update. Friedrich Nietzsche as an Architect. Available: https://www.re-thinkingthefuture.com/rtf-fresh-perspectives/a818-friedrich-nietzsche-as-an-architect/ [October 2020].
Sharr, A., 2018. *Modern Architecture. A Very Short Introduction*. Oxford: Oxford University Press.
Silk, M.S. and Stern, J.P., 2016. *Nietzsche on Tragedy*. Cambridge: Cambridge University Press.
Snyder, D.E., 2019. *Tender Detail: Ornament and Sentimentality in the Architecture of Louis H. Sullivan and Frank Lloyd Wright*. London and New York: Bloomsbury.
Speer, A., 1970/2009. *Inside the Third Reich*. Trans. R. and C. Winston. London: Widenfeld & Nicholson; Phoenix.
Stamm, G., 1973–5. Monumental Architecture and Ideology: Henry van de Velde's and Harry Graf Kessler's Project for a Nietzsche Monument at Weimar, 1910–1914. *Gentse Bijdragen*, 23, pp. 303–42.
Stendhal, 1975. *Love*. Middlesex: Penguin.

BIBLIOGRAPHY

Stephan, B., 1996. *Sächsische Bildhauerkunst: Johannes Schilling, 1828–1910*. Berlin: Verlag für Bauwesen.

Straus, R., 2019. *Reception and Analysis of Nietzsche's Apollonian and Dionysian Aesthetics in the Writing and Choreographic Practice of Six Dance Figures: 1900–1948*. Doctoral Thesis, Department of Dance, University of Roehampton, London.

Streiter, R., Breitschmid, M. and Mallgrave, H.F., 2000. *Contemporary Architectural Questions: A Collection and Examination of Various Views, Especially with Regard to Professor Otto Wagner's 'Modern Architecture' (1898)*. München: Delphin.

Sturm, H., 2003. *Alltag & Kult: Gottfried Semper, Richard Wagner, Friedrich Theodor Vischer, Gottfried Keller*. Basel: Birkhäuser.

Sullivan, L.H., 1902/2014. Education. In: *Kindergarten Chats and Other Writings*. Mansfield, CT: Martino, pp. 224–6.

Sullivan, L.H., 1901/2014. Kindergarten Chats. In: *Kindergarten Chats and Other Writings*. Mansfield, CT: Martino, pp. 17–174.

Sullivan, L.H., 1892/2014. Ornament in Architecture. In: *Kindergarten Chats and Other Writings*. Mansfield, CT: Martino, pp. 187–90.

Sullivan, L.H., 1896/2014. The Tall Office Building Artistically Considered. In: *Kindergarten Chats and Other Writings*. Mansfield, CT: Martino, pp. 202–13.

Sullivan, L.H., 1906/2014. What Is Architecture: A Study in the American People of Today. In: *Kindergarten Chats and Other Writings*. Mansfield, CT: Martino, pp. 227–41.

Sullivan, L.H., 1924/2009. *The Autobiography of an Idea*. New York: Dover.

Sullivan, L.H., 1922. *A System of Architectural Ornament, According with a Philosophy of Man's Powers*. New York: American Institute of Architects.

Synder, D.E., 2017. 'Louis H. Sullivan': That Object He Became. *Delft Architectural Theory Journal*, 11(2), pp. 67–85.

Taine, H., 1866/2020. *Italy: Florence and Venice*. Frankfurt: Salzwasser-Verlag GmbH.

Taut, B., 1919/2015. *The City Crown*. Trans. M. Mindrup and U. Altenmüller-Lewis. Surrey: Ashgate.

Taut, B., 1921/2014. Glass Architecture. In: J. Mcelheny and C. Burgin, eds, *Glass! Love!! Perpetual Motion!! A Paul Scheerbart Reader*. Trans. A. Posten. Chicago: Chicago University Press, pp. 118–22.

Taut, B., 1914/2014. Glass House: Cologne Werkbund Exhibition. In: J. Mcelheny and C. Burgin, eds, *Glass! Love!! Perpetual Motion!! A Paul Scheerbart Reader*. Trans. A. Posten. Chicago: Chicago University Press, pp. 98–110.

Taut, B., 1919/2002. New Ideas on Architecture. In: U. Conrads, ed, *Programs and Manifestoes on 20th-Century Architecture*. Cambridge, MA: MIT Press, p. 47.

Taut, B., 1985. *The Crystal Chain Letters. Architectural Fantasies by Bruno Taut and His Circle*. Trans. I.B. Whyte. Cambridge, MA: MIT Press.

Taut, B., 1920. *Die Auflösung der Städte, oder die Erde, eine gute Wohnung, oder auch: Der Weg zur Alpinen Architektur*. Hagen: Folkwang-Verlag.

Taut, B., 1919a. *Alpine Architektur des Architekten*. Hagen: Folkwang-Verl.

Taut, B., 1919b. Beobachtungen über Farbenwirkungen aus meiner Praxis. *Die Bauwelt*, 10(38), pp. 12–13.

Taut, B., 1917. Die Vererdung. Zum Problem des Totenkults. *Die Werkstatt der Kunst*, XVI(18), pp. 220–2.

Taut, B., 1915. Krieger-Ehrung. *Das Kungstgewerbeblatt*, XXVI(9), pp. 174–6.

Teuber, D., 1984. Henry van de Veldes Werkbundtheatre – ein Denkmal für Nietzsche? In: T. Konerding, W. Herzogenrath, D. Teuber, and A. Thiekötter, eds, *Der Westdeutsche Impuls 1900–1914. Die Deutsche Werkbundausstellung Köln 1914*. Köln: Kunstmuseum, pp. 114–32.

Trimingham, M., 2011. *The Theatre of the Bauhaus: The Modern and the Postmodern Stage of Oskar Schlemmer*. London and New York: Routledge.

Trodd, C., 2018. Revitalizing Romanticism; or Reflections on the Nietzschean Aesthetic and the Modern Imagination. In: P. Meecham and D. Arnold, eds, *A Companion to Modern Art*. New Jersey: Wiley & Sons, pp. 17–36.

Van de Velde, H., 2003. Manuscript on Ornament. Trans. E.G. Haddad and R. Anderson. *Journal of Design History*, 16(2), pp. 139–66.

Van de Velde, H., 1995. *Récit de ma vie. 1900–1917: Berlin – Weimar – Paris – Bruxelles*. Paris: Flammarion.

Van de Velde, H., 1902a. Die Linie. *Die Zukunft*, 40(49), pp. 385–8.

Van de Velde, H., 1902b. Prinzipielle Erklarung. In: *Kunstgewerbliche Laienpredigten*. Leipzig: H. Seemann, pp. 137–95.

Van de Velde, H., 1895. *Aperçus en vue d'une Synthèse d'art*. Brussels: Monnom.

Van Eck, C., 2006. Review: Gottfried Semper and the Problem of Historicism by Mari Hvattum. *Journal of the Society of Architectural Historians*, 65(1), pp. 136–9.

Van Zanten, D., 2000. *Sullivan's City: The Meaning of Ornament for Louis Sullivan*. New York: W.W. Norton.

Vasari, G., 1550/1997. *The Lives of Artists*. Trans. G. Bull. Penguin Classics. London: Penguin.

Verrecchia, A., 1998. Nietzsche's Breakdown in Turin. In: T. Harrison, ed, *Nietzsche in Italy*. Saratoga, CA: ANMA Libri, pp. 105–12.

Vogel, M., 1966. *Apollinisch und Dionysisch. Geschichte eines genialen Irrtums*. Regensburg: Gustav Bosse.

Wagner, C., 1978. *Cosima Wagner's Diaries, 1869–1877*. London: Collins.

Wagner, O., 1896. *Modern Architecture*. 1996 edn. Trans. H.F. Mallgrave. Los Angeles: Getty Press.

Wagner, R., 1966. *Richard Wagner's Prose Works*. Trans. W.A. Ellis. New York: Broude Brothers.

Wagner, R., 1963. *Mein Leben*, vol. 1. München: List.

Wagner, R., 1873. *Das Bühnenfestspielhaus zu Bayreuth: Nebst einem Bericht über die Grundsteinlegung desselben*. Leipzig: Fritsch.

Wagner, R., 1849. *Das Kunstwerk der Zukunft*. 2010 edn. Baden: Fischer, Klaus.

Whyte, I.B., 2013. *Modernism and the Spirit of the City*. London and New York: Routledge.

Whyte, I.B., 1982. *Bruno Taut and the Architecture of Activism*. Cambridge: Cambridge University Press.

Wigley, M., 2020-last update. Chronic Whiteness. Available: https://www.e-flux.com/architecture/sick-architecture/360099/chronic-whiteness/ [October 2021].

Wilamowitz, U.V., 1872. *Zukunftsphilologie! eine erwidrung auf Friedrich Nietzsches 'geburt der tragödie'*. Berlin: Borntraeger.

Winckelmann, J.J., 1756. *Reflections on the Imitation of Greek Works in Painting and Sculpture.* 1987 edn. La Salle, IL: Open Court.

Wirz, H., 2001. Bibliotheca 2 – Notat. In: M. Breitschmid, ed, *Der bauende Geist. Nietzsche und die Architektur.* Lucern: Quart Verlag, pp. 5–7.

Wolfenstein, A., 1920. *Die Erhebung.* Berlin: Fischer.

Wölfflin, H., 2021. *Prolegomena zu einer Psychologie der Architektur, 1886.* Basel: Schwabe Verlag.

Wollkopf, R., 1991. *Chronik Des Nietzsche-Archivs.* Weimar: Gutenberg Buchdruckerei.

Young, J., 2010. *Friedrich Nietzsche: A Philosophical Biography.* Cambridge: Cambridge University Press.

INDEX

Ábalos, Iñaki 226 n.1
Abbe, Ernst 92, 108, 111, 197; *see also* van de Velde works, Abbe Ernst memorial
Aeschylus 69
Albert, Henri 123
Alberti, Leon Battista 172
Alciati, Andrea 76
amor fati 59
Amor (god) 225 n.30
ancient Greek culture 12, 26, 62, 64–5, 67, 69, 129, 169, 182
Anderson, Stanford 179, 201, 202, 230 n.3, 233 n.2
Andrew, David 186, 187, 230 n.11, 232 n.9
Antonelli, Alessandro 8, 13, 54, 55–8, 135, 188, 221 n.3; *see also* Semper, works, Mole Antonelliana
Apollo, Apollonian 12, 14, 15, 16, 33, 38, 64, 66, 67–8, 70–3, 74, 75–6, 80, 81, 82, 83, 84, 85, 114, 115, 117, 126, 143, 149, 152, 159, 164, 165, 166, 169, 172–3, 175, 176, 177, 194, 195, 204, 220, 224 n.24, 225 n.34; *see also* Dionysus/Dionysian
architect as hero 9, 11, 18, 119, 171, 187–91
Ariadne 71, 72, 73, 74, 75, 224 n.22
Aristotle 1
art 12, 23, 38, 67, 69, 70, 74, 81, 83, 91, 92, 95, 102, 103, 115, 119, 127, 163, 177, 195, 203, 226 n.3; Bauhaus and art 231 n.16; Darmstädt colony and art 159; degenerate art 163, 164; fifteenth-century art 48; Greek art 65; Italian art 100; modern art 92, 98, 135, 140, 164; modern German art 62, 63, 70, 159, 169; Nietzsche and art 8, 12, 24, 39, 101, 112, 156; Renaissance art 47; Semper's approach to art 62, 63–5, 70, 195; Taut's approach to art 209; van de Velde and art 98; Wagner's approach to art 32, 33, 63, 81, 83; *see also* tragedy as highest art form
Art Nouveau 96, 127
Arts and Crafts 154, 159, 161, 229 n.24
Aschheim, Steven E. 2, 102, 108, 159, 198, 199, 233 n.6

Bacchus 15, 16, 71, 72, 74, 76, 77, 78, 79, 80, 224 n.16, 224 n.24, 225 n.30; *see also* Dionysus
Bachofen, Johann Jakob 67
Baroque architecture 5, 6, 24, 31, 42, 44, 54, 57, 65, 90, 157, 168, 226 n.1
Basel, Switzerland 48, 52, 68; University of 3, 47, 71, 223 n.1
Bauhaus, Bauhaus School 10, 17, 30, 139, 158, 161–4, 165, 167, 176–7, 231 n.14, 231 n.16, 231 n.18
Bäumler, Alfred 139
beauty, beautiful 18, 41, 44, 80, 89, 101, 117, 131, 179, 182, 183, 207, 222 n.1; and human strength 117, 118, 159
Beethoven, Ludwig van 29, 227 n.9
Behrens, Peter 10, 154, 159–60, 168, 192, 197–204, 217, 221 n.6, 231 n.2, 233 n.2
Behrens, works: AEG Turbine Building, Berlin 18, 203–4; book cover for *Thus Spoke Zarathustra* 200, 201;

Hamburger Vorhalle, Cologne 18, 201–2, 203; 'Zarathustra House', Darmstädt Artist Colony 18, 156, 159–60, 168, 192, 198–201, 203
Berger, Ursel 229 n.23, 229 n.27
Berlin, Germany 18, 95, 113, 152, 162, 168, 203, 204, 210, 229 n.21, 230 n.28
Bernhard, Peter 158, 177
Bernoulli, Carl Albrecht 98
Biedermeier style 169
Bing, Samuel 95
Bismarck, Otto von 116, 127–8
Bismark tower (Wilhelm Kreis) 127–8, 131, 132
Bismark tower, Weimar 116, 119
Bletter, Rosemarie Haag 161, 198, 206, 217, 233 n.2, 233 n.4
Bodenhausen, Eberhard von 129, 131, 134, 135, 228 n.17
body 31, 34, 38, 40, 53, 102, 118, 156, 164, 166, 178, 179, 181, 188, 219; *see also* Nietzsche's body; physiological experience/identification
Böhme, Hartmut 9, 226 n.1
Bolland, Mark 51, 53, 182, 200, 205
boredom 211
Boulard, Peter 175–6; *see also* Le Corbusier
Bourdelle, Antoine 195
Brahn, Max 163
Breitschmid, Markus 8, 9, 26, 43, 226 n.1, 230 n.2, 230 n.8
Breker, Arno 230 n.28
Brockhaus, Friedrich 78, 79, 225 n.27
Brockhaus, Heinrich 78
Brooks, Allen 230 n.6, 232 n.8
Brückwald, Otto 66, 82, 83
Brunelleschi, Filippo 47
Brutalism, brutalist architecture 90, 226 n.1
Bryant, Gabriele 199, 203, 221 n.6, 230 n.7
Buddensieg, Tilmann 8, 9, 40, 41, 42, 43, 47, 52, 54, 55, 154, 168, 182, 183, 198, 199, 200, 222 n.4, 226 n.1, 230 n.7, 231 n.1, 231 n.2
Bülow, Bernhard von 117
Burckhardt, Jacob 8, 9, 12, 47, 48, 49, 50, 56, 221 n.3, 222 n.6, 222 n.7, 223 n.9, 224 n.3; and the Palazzo Pitti 12–13, 49
Burckhardt, works: *Architecture of the Italian Renaissance* 12, 49; *Civilization of the Renaissance in Italy* 223 n.7; *Der Cicerone* 12, 48, 49, 222 n.3; *History of the Italian Renaissance* 49

Café Littéraire, Zürich 79
Caffe Baratti & Milano, Turin 6, 54
Caldwell, Alfred 185
Cancik, Hubert 94
Caruso, Adam 232 n.5
cave, imagery 2, 11, 30, 53, 160, 188, 190, 192, 198–9, 201, 208, 209, 210, 217
Cecilienhof Palace, Potsdam, Germany 229 n.24
Chapman, Michael 206, 207, 209, 210, 234 n.7
Chirico, Giorgio de 221 n.5
Christian buildings 49, 52, 108
Christianity 30, 41
Cimorelli, D. 58
Classical architecture 9, 12, 24, 44, 65, 90, 115, 125, 129, 226 n.1
Cohen, Jean-Louis 175, 190, 230 n.6, 231 n.11
Cologne, Germany 18, 52, 96, 158, 192, 193, 204, 205, 212, 216
colossal architecture 13, 40, 44, 49, 50, 176, 185, 234 n.4
colour, polychromy 65, 69, 90, 96, 97, 165, 172, 175, 177, 195, 213, 217, 224 n.17
Colquhoun, Alan 230 n.12
Columbus, Christopher 5, 45
Condit, Carl 186, 230 n.1
Cornelius, Peter 77, 78
cross 109, 207
crystal, crystal houses 18, 159–60, 192, 198, 199–200, 202, 203, 204–5, 206, 209, 210, 211, 213, 219, 226 n.3, 233 n.3; *see also Edelstein*; Taut works, *Kristallhaus*
Crystal Palace, London 66
cubic form 17, 157, 161, 162, 172, 187

cult 2, 10, 92, 107, 197, 221 n.5, 113, 132, 142, 143; Nietzsche cult 112; Wagner cult 156
Cyclopean architecture 50, 90, 226 n.1

Dadaism 221 n.5
Dal Co, Francesco 203
D'Alessio, Francesco 189, 230 n.6
dance 62, 70, 73, 80, 101, 102, 117, 126, 132, 164, 176, 177, 178, 179, 195
Darmstädt Colony, Germany 17, 18, 154, 158, 159, 160, 161, 168, 192, 198, 201, 203, 231 n.2
decadence, decadent values 9, 14, 16, 25, 26, 31, 33, 39, 42, 45, 51, 52, 56, 81, 82, 155, 157, 167, 170, 178, 191
degenerate art/architecture 10, 140, 162, 163, 167
Dessau, Germany 162
Deutscher Werkbund 17, 18, 96, 139, 158, 166, 192, 193, 195, 197, 198, 209, 212, 216, 229 n.24, 230 n.13
Dietrich, Conny 227 n.8
Dingelstedt, Franz von 79
Dionysus/Dionysian 14, 15, 16, 33, 38, 61, 66, 67, 68, 69, 70–7, 78, 79, 81, 82, 83, 84, 85, 114, 115, 117, 132, 143, 149, 152, 157, 164, 165, 166, 167, 169, 172, 175, 176, 177, 183, 194, 195, 203, 219, 220, 224 n.16, 224 n.22, 224 n.24, 225 n.33, 225 n.34, 230 n.12; *see also* Apollo/Apollonian
Doesburg, Theo van 154
Donndorf, Karl 98, 228 n.18
Doric order 124
Durand, Jean-Nicholas Louis 63–4, 68

E.T.H. Zürich, Switzerland 223 n.3
eagle 107, 150, 152, 182, 198, 199, 200, 226 n.3, 233 n.1, 233 n.2; *see also* snake
Easton, Laird 120
Ebert, Hans 78, 224 n.25, 225 n.28, 225 n.31
Edelstein 199, 200, 217, 233 n.1; *see also* crystal

Emge, Carl August 163
Emmrich, Angelika 89, 97, 98, 226–7 n.6
empty form 9, 10, 15, 18, 40, 41–3, 55, 57, 66, 137, 156, 166, 171–3, 207, 212, 216
epic poetry 38
Erbsmehl, Hansdieter 227 n.8
Eros 80
eternal recurrence 1

façades 29, 49, 50, 63, 82, 96, 97, 116, 117, 125, 126, 127, 131, 161, 227 n.7
Fancelli, Luca 12, 47
fascism 152
festive celebration 12, 14, 15, 18, 62–6, 70, 72, 73, 81, 110, 160, 171, 173, 175, 176, 178, 202, 204, 217, 220
Festspielhaus, Bayreuth 16, 33, 62, 63, 66, 75, 81–3, 92, 197
Festspielhaus, Munich 63, 66, 74, 75
First World War 17, 134, 158
Fischer, Theodor 216
Florence, Italy 12, 15, 41, 43, 44, 47, 49, 50, 54, 187
Föhl, Thomas 108, 111, 112, 129, 228 n.14, 229 n.25
Förster, Bernard 91
Förster-Nietzsche, Elisabeth 10, 91–6, 99, 101–5, 107, 108, 112, 113, 114, 116–21, 134, 137–47, 150, 198, 226 n.2, 226 n.3, 226 n.4, 226 n.6, 227 n.11, 227 n.12, 228 n.18, 228–9 n.20, 229 n.22, 230 n.9, 231 n.15
Franco-Prussian war 27
Freud, Sigmund 26, 67, 171
Frick, Wilhelm 138, 140, 162, 231 n.15, 231 n.18
Frosterus, Sigurd 97, 98
Fuchs, Carl 13, 49
Fuchs, Georg 159, 201, 202

Galleria Subalpina, Turin 6, 54
garden house (David Strauss) 14, 29, 31–2, 42
Garnham, Trevor 168, 223 n.1, 231 n.1

INDEX

Gast, Peter; *see under* Köselitz, Henrich
Gauzentrum, Weimar 141
Genelli, Giovanni Bonaventura 16, 33, 73, 76–81, 224 n.24, 224 n.25, 224 n.26, 225 n.28–34
Genoa, Italy 1, 2, 4, 5, 15, 41, 43, 44–7, 187, 222 n.5
Genoese palazzi 5, 15, 41, 43, 44–7, 53, 56, 110, 170, 184, 187
German nationalism, German nation 90, 162, 166, 169
Germania 10, 182
Gersdorff, Carl von 53, 222
Gesamtkunstwerk 62, 84, 96, 100, 109, 113, 161, 195, 203, 221 n.6
Geyer, Ernst Moritz 226 n.3
Giesler, Hermann 140, 141
Gill, Eric 116, 131
Gläserne Kette (Glass Chain) 213, 219, 234 n.8
glass 6, 54, 83, 98, 156, 160, 161, 172, 198, 201, 203, 204, 205, 207, 209, 210–13, 215–17, 219, 234 n.9
Gleiter, Jörg H. 8, 9, 56, 57, 183–4
God, death of 32, 161, 208
Goebbels, Josef 142
Goethe, Johann Wolfgang 29, 92, 93, 104, 116
Goethe and Schiller Archive 104, 153
Gothic architecture 42, 44, 99, 157, 168, 189
Graef, Botho 110, 111
Graf Kessler, Harry 5, 16, 91, 92, 93, 94, 95, 98, 102, 103, 104, 109, 111, 112–22, 124, 125, 126–9, 130, 131–3, 134, 135, 136, 137, 146, 160, 226 n.2, 228 n.15, 228 n.17
grandiosity, grandiose architecture 10, 28, 29, 50, 83, 104, 113, 121, 135, 163, 182, 190, 210
Gropius, Walter 10, 154, 155, 161, 162, 163, 165, 188, 198, 230 n.9, 231 n.16
Grut, Torben 118

Habich, Ludwig 159
Haddad, Elie 155, 230 n.5
Hähnel, Ernst 75, 78, 79
Halle, Germany 52

Härtel, Hermann 78–9, 225 n.30–1
Hasenauer, Karl von 66, 75
Haskell, Francis 50
Hegel, Georg Wilhelm 25
height instinct 13, 15, 18, 41, 43, 50–4, 58, 60, 171, 180, 181, 182–4, 205, 206
Heine, Heinrich 29
Helmholtz, Hermann von 113, 136
Heraclitus 52, 89, 233 n.1
herm 78, 80, 97, 98, 109, 111, 115, 116, 120, 131, 146, 152, 225 n.28, 225 n.34, 227 n.8
Hilberseimer, Ludwig 9, 154, 155
Hildebrand, Adolf von 113
Himmler, Heinrich 119
Hindley, Meredith 129
Hipp, Emil 151, 152
Hirt, Aloys 224 n.24
historicism 3, 27, 35, 49, 63, 155, 156, 158, 212
Hitchcock, Henry-Russell 223 n.11
Hitler, Adolf 17, 137–43, 148, 149, 151–3, 191, 228 n.20, 229 n.22, 229 n.26
Hofmann, Ludwig von 119
Hofmannsthal, Hugo von 113, 116, 131, 227 n.10
Hölderlin, Friedrich 67
Hollis, Richard 125, 197, 228 n.16
horizon 44, 51, 94, 107
Huebner, Julius 73
Huskinson, Lucy 176, 230 n.6

International style 10, 162, 172
Ionic order 23–4

Jatho, Carl Oscar 194
Jeanneret, Charles-Édouard 10, 175–6, 232 n.8; *see also* Le Corbusier
Jencks, Charles 174, 175, 176, 190, 230 n.6, 230 n.11
Johnson, Philip 190
Joseph Rykwert 14, 61–2, 223 n.2
Jugendstil movement 229 n.24
Jung, Carl Gustav 67, 230 n.6

Kant, Immanuel 182
Kater, Michael 230 n.9, 231 n.16

INDEX

Kaufmann, Walter 228 n.20
Keller, Ferdinand 225 n.28
King Ludwig II of Bavaria 14, 62, 80
Kirk, Terry 58
Klimt, Gustav 221 n.5
Klinger, Max 98, 109, 110, 111, 114, 115, 116, 120, 131, 152, 227 n.6, 227 n.8, 227 n.9
Kohler, Josef 227 n.11
Kolbe, Georg 152, 229 n.27
Köselitz, Henrich (Peter Gast) 4, 5, 6, 45, 53, 54, 56, 229 n.20
Koss, Juliet 161
Kostka, Alexandre 9, 97, 103, 108, 109, 110, 112, 116, 118, 119, 197, 227 n.7, 227 n.11, 227 n.12, 228 n.14
Krause, Jürgen 107, 132, 141, 150, 152
Kreis, Wilhelm 127, 128, 131
Kröller-Müller, Helene 92, 135, 216
Kröller-Müller Park, Holland 17, 135–6, 216
Kröner, Alfred 152, 227 n.8
Kuenzli, Katherine 195, 230 n.5
Kühn, Paul 15, 39, 40, 95, 96, 98–102, 106, 111, 178–9, 231 n.2

labyrinth 14, 29–32, 34, 42, 81, 221 n.5
Lahiji, Nadir 154, 221 n.5
Lahusen, Susanne 177
Lake Silvaplana, Switzerland 1
last man/last men 169, 223 n.9, 232 n.9
Le Corbusier 10, 18, 154, 155, 156, 164, 165, 168, 173–6, 188–90, 193, 198, 221 n.5, 230 n.6, 230 n.11; *see also* Jeanneret, Charles-Édouard
Le Corbusier, works: *Plan Voisin* 168; Unité d'Habitation, Marseilles, France 175; Ville Radieuse 174
line-force (van de Velde) 39, 95, 96, 98, 100, 179
lion motif 152, 226 n.3
Loo, Ann van 123, 193–4
Loos, Adolf 154, 173
Ludwig, Ernst 159, 160
Luna Park, Berlin 210
Lüttke, Georg 152

MacCarthy, Fiona 230 n.9
Maciuika, John 159, 160, 199, 200, 230 n.7, 233 n.6
Magirius, Heinrich 73, 74, 75, 78, 224 n.20, 225 n.28
Mahler, Alma 230
Maillol, Aristide 109, 113, 114–15, 117, 119, 121, 125, 126, 127
Mallgrave, Harry 74, 75, 82, 223 n.1, 223 n.4, 224 n.17, 230 n.2
Mandel, Siegfried 78, 80, 81, 224 n.25, 225 n.32
Marshall Field Wholesale Store, Chicago 184–5, 189, 232 n.6
mask, mask-like 11, 28, 29, 41, 70, 72, 112, 169, 185, 186, 221 n.5
mausoleum 14, 29, 30, 31, 42, 103, 150
megalomania 112, 135, 223 n.11
Mendelsohn, Erich 154, 155, 168
Menocal, Narciso, G. 190, 230 n.1, 232 n.7
Messel, Alfred 168
Meunier, Constantin Émile 109, 111, 127
Meyer, Hannes 162
Meysenbug, Malwida von 2, 3
Michelet, Jules 67
Mies van der Rohe, Ludwig 9, 154, 156, 162, 173, 198
Miller Lane, Barbara 156, 163, 168, 170, 191, 200, 201
Mindrup, Matthew 206, 207
modernist architecture 10, 43, 96, 112, 168, 188
Mole Antonelliana, Turin 6, 8, 13, 14, 15, 41, 43, 48, 53, 54–60, 61, 110, 128, 135, 183, 187, 188, 221 n.3
Monastic architecture 90, 226 n.1
Monumentalism, monumental architecture 50, 66, 90, 95, 96, 102, 118, 126, 129, 131, 140, 176, 233 n.4
Moos, Stanislaus von 190
mountain 1, 2, 5, 11, 38, 45, 50–4, 93, 94, 102, 124, 128, 188, 190, 192, 197–9, 201, 205, 208–9, 209–11, 217, 223 n.10
Müller, Karl Otfried 67
Müller-Camphausen, Fritz 152

Müller-Wulckow, Walter 166
Munch, Edvard 98
Muses 14, 16, 71–3, 75, 76, 78, 79, 80, 194, 195, 224 n.24, 225 n.30, 225 n.33
music 6, 12, 13, 14, 31, 33, 35, 36, 38, 49, 62, 69, 70, 71, 72, 75, 76, 79, 85, 91, 101, 115, 117, 132, 156, 178, 200, 225 n.30; *see also* Wagner's music
Mussolini, Benito 137, 152

Napoleon Bonaparte 29, 137
National Socialism 118, 141, 143; *see also* Nazi Party; Third Reich
Naumburg, Germany 3, 4, 42, 52, 91, 92, 93, 226 n.3
Nazi ideology 17, 92, 118, 137, 139, 143, 163, 167, 182, 191, 228–9 n.20, 229 n.23
Nazi Party 92, 119, 138, 140, 142, 148, 162, 163, 166, 231 n.18; *see also* National Socialism; Third Reich
necessary design 36, 39, 40, 43, 70, 100, 161, 164, 170, 172, 186
Neumeyer, Fritz 8, 9, 24, 39, 48, 57, 58, 69, 72, 73, 74, 75, 82, 83, 154, 199, 221 n.3, 223 n.1, 223 n.5, 226 n.1, 230 n.4, 230 n.10, 231 n.1
Neutra, Richard 154, 155
Nice, Italy 1, 3
Niebelschütz, Ernst von 165
Nietzsche, Friedrich: apartments of 6, 7, 47, 54, 93; building metaphors of 14, 16, 30–2, 34, 81, 205, 221 n.5; and construction of model buildings 3, 8, 63; as a flâneur 3; and love of architecture 3, 49, 128; mental breakdown 8, 48, 54, 56, 58, 221 n.2; and mistrust of large cities 3; Nietzsche's body 58, 103, 134; as a prophet 10, 35, 99, 139, 142, 211, 228 n.20; as a walker 1, 3, 5, 6, 51, 56, 94
Nietzsche, works: *The Antichrist* 6; *The Birth of Tragedy* 14, 15, 23, 33, 68, 70, 71, 72, 74–6, 80, 166, 219, 224 n.18; *Daybreak* 2, 5, 45, 233 n.1; *Dionysian Dithyrambs*

96, 194, 195, 196; 'The Dionysian Worldview' 68, 225 n.34; *Ecce Homo* 5, 8, 56, 91, 96; *The Gay Science* 5, 45, 89; *Genealogy of Morals* 89; 'The Greek Music Drama' 68, 69, 74; *Human, All Too Human* 41, 124; 'Philosophy in the Tragic Age of the Greeks' 233 n.1; 'Schopenhauer as Educator' 206; 'Socrates and Tragedy' 68; *Thus Spoke Zarathustra* 1, 2, 51, 53, 54, 56, 60, 96, 102, 137, 155, 159, 160, 190, 197, 198, 200, 201, 204, 211, 212, 215, 217, 219, 221 n.5, 232 n.9; *Twilight of the Idols* 5, 24, 38, 123; *Untimely Meditations* 25, 30, 187, 204, 206; *The Will to Power* 5, 229 n.20
Nietzsche memorial hall, Weimar 17, 92, 137–53, 159, 168
Nietzsche temple 16, 31, 103–12, 91, 92, 98, 168, 197, 228 n.15
Nietzsche temple-stadium 9, 112–35, 136, 192, 193, 197, 228 n.19
Nietzsche-Archiv 9, 15, 16, 39–40, 91, 92, 93–102, 104, 107, 110, 112, 113, 115, 118, 120, 134, 137, 139, 142, 143, 153, 163, 178, 192, 197, 198, 226 n.3, 227 n.7, 227 n.9, 227 n.11, 228 n.16, 228 n.20, 229 n.21, 231 n.2, 233 n.1; *see also* van de Velde works: Villa Silberblick
Nikkō, Japan 113
nobility/noble 5, 12, 23, 43, 44, 45, 47, 52, 53, 56, 59, 65, 67, 129, 155, 179, 180, 184, 202, 207, 208, 212, 233 n.1
Nueva Germania, Paraguay 91

Obrist, Hermann 195
Oechslin, Werner 90
Oehler, Adalbert 95, 141, 142, 143, 144, 150, 151, 227 n.11
Oehler, Max 120, 144, 149, 151, 152, 153, 227 n.8
Oehler, Richard 120, 140, 143, 144, 146, 150, 151, 151, 152, 228 n.20, 233 n.1

O'Gorman, James 232 n.6
Olbrich, Joseph Maria 159, 160
Olde, Hans 226 n.3
ornament 30, 39, 40, 41, 48, 95, 100, 113, 166, 172, 173, 175, 178, 179–81, 182, 185, 187, 189, 195, 234 n.8; ornament-free 9, 10, 13, 18, 30, 154; frivolous ornament 23, 157, 161; *see also* empty form
Osthaus, Karl Ernst 154
Ostwald, Michael 206, 207, 209, 210, 234 n.7
Oud, Jacobus Johannes Pieter 154
Overbeck, Franz 4, 44, 60, 98, 221 n.2
Ovid 76

Paestum, Italy 40, 124, 129, 222 n.3
Palazzi; *see under* Genoese palazzi
Palazzo Berlendis, Venice 222 n.5
Palazzo Madama, Turin 6, 7
Palazzo Pitti, Florence 12, 13, 15, 41, 43, 44, 47–50, 54, 56, 61, 110, 165, 176, 185, 187
Pan, the god 80, 225 n.30
PAN, the journal 91, 119, 129, 226 n.3
Pantheon, Rome 99
Pehnt, Wolfgang 2, 198, 233 n.4
physiological experience/identification 9, 15, 18, 24, 34, 39, 40, 41, 51, 66, 102, 101, 110, 166, 173, 179; *see also* body
Piazza Carlina, Turin 221 n.2
Piazza Carlo Alberto, Turin 221 n.2
Piazza Castello, Turin 6
Piazza San Carlo, Turin 6, 54, 221 n.2
Piazza di San Marco, Venice 89
picturesque, the 29
pilgrimage 92, 98, 117, 142, 143
Poelzig, Hans 168
Poussin, Martin 76, 80
Praxiteles 152
Prinzhorn, Hans 163
Prometheus 226

quadriga 71–5, 78, 82, 224 n.19, 224 n.20, 224 n.22, 224
Quincy, Antoine-Chrysostome Quatremère de 65

Raphael, Sanzio da Urbino 76
Rationalized construction/mindset 25, 31, 34, 38, 40, 65, 157, 165, 168, 171; *see also* Apollonian
Renaissance architecture 9, 24, 44, 47, 48, 54, 72, 90, 226 n.1
Reni, Guido 79
ressentiment 167
Reust, Anselm 219–20
rhythm, rhythmic play/form 2, 12, 13, 15, 18, 24, 34, 36, 38, 39, 41, 43, 44, 49, 50, 56, 78, 82, 83, 95, 97, 100, 101, 102, 110, 111, 128, 165, 171–3, 176, 177, 178, 179, 180, 194, 222 n.1
Richards, Simon 174, 230 n.6
Richardson, Henry Hobson 184–5
Richter, Cornelia 95
Riefenstahl, Leni 229 n.23
Röcken, Germany 3, 95, 102, 103, 105, 134, 150
Rohde, Erwin 45, 72, 75, 80, 222 n.6, 224 n.19, 225 n.33
Romanesque architecture 42, 133, 162
Rome, Italy 3, 65, 225 n.29
Rosenberg, Alfred 139, 229 n.22, 231 n.18
Ruehl, Martin 222 n.6, 222 n.7

Salis-Marschlins, Meta von 93, 95, 226 n.4
Sauckel, Fritz 138, 142, 143, 144, 146, 148, 151, 229 n.22
Schack, Friedrich Count von 78, 79, 225 n.28
Scheerbart, Paul 204, 215, 219, 220, 234 n.9, 234 n.10
Scheerbart, works: *Glassarchitektur* 219, 220; *Lesabéndio: ein asteroïden-Roman* 215, 234 n.10
Schiller, Friedrich 67, 93
Schilling, Johannes 72–6, 78
Schlemmer, Oskar 18, 163, 164, 177; and Triadic Ballet 164, 177
Schopenhauer, Arthur 29, 67
Schubert, Dietrich 215, 234 n.7, 234 n.10
Schultze, Sebastian 96

INDEX

Schultze-Naumburg, Paul 10, 17, 92, 137–41, 143, 144, 147–9, 152, 159, 162, 163, 164, 168–70, 229 n.24, 231 n.17, 231 n.18
Schumacher, Fritz 16, 92, 98, 104, 105–8, 226 n.5
Scully, Vincent 181
sculpture 8, 38, 65, 69, 72, 74, 75, 76, 98, 109, 113, 114, 117, 127, 135, 136, 195, 228 n.18, 230 n.27, 231 n.17; of Nietzsche-Zarathustra 98, 146, 150, 151–2
Seidl, Arthur 107, 108
self-reflection 24, 28, 41, 42, 55, 63, 90, 91, 107, 124, 173, 174, 204, 207, 216, 217
Sembach, Klaus Jürgen 97, 134, 135, 195, 197, 227 n.7, 228 n.16
Semper, Emanuel 72
Semper, Gottfried 9, 14, 15, 16, 33, 61–76, 78, 79, 83, 84, 156, 167, 178, 179, 194, 195, 223 n.2, 232 n.5; influence on Nietzsche 9, 10, 12, 14, 15, 33, 61–2, 66, 67, 68–72, 73, 74, 75, 156, 172, 223 n.1, 223 n.3, 223 n.4, 224 n.17
Semper, works: Festspielhaus, Munich 14, 16, 62–3, 66, 74, 75, 82, 83, 84; Hoftheatre/Royal Court Theatre, Dresden, 16, 66, 72, 75, 78, 79, 81, 82; K.K. Hoftburghtheatre, Vienna 66, 75; 'On Architectural Styles' 68, 70; 'Preliminary Remarks of Polychromy' 68, 69; Semperoper, Dresden 14, 15, 61, 63, 66, 70–6, 78, 81, 194, 224 n.16; *Style in the Technical and Tectonic Arts* 68, 69, 70, 74, 223 n.1; Theatre, Crystal Palace, London 66; Theatre, Rio de Janeiro, Brazil 66, 74, 224 n.22; Théâtre Royal de la Monnaie, Brussels 66; *Vergleichende Baulehre* 223 n.7; *Wissenschaft, Industrie und Kunst* 223 n.10
Semper, Manfred 82, 224 n.9
Silenus 78, 79, 80
Silk, M.S. 77, 224 n.26
Sils Maria, Switzerland 5
Skala-Tanzcasino, Berlin 210

slave 107, 108, 210
snake 152, 182, 198, 226 n.3; *see also* eagle
Sophocles 69
Sorrento, Italy 2, 33
Speer, Albert 10, 138, 140, 141, 148, 182, 228 n.15, 228 n.16, 228 n.17, 230 n.5
Stamm, Günther 103, 116, 117, 119, 124, 125, 126, 127, 129, 131, 133, 134, 136, 227 n.14, 228 n.15, 228 n.16
Stendhal 233 n.2
Stephan, Bärbel 72, 74, 76, 223 n.4
Stern, J.P. 77, 224 n.26
Stoeving, Curt 226 n.3, 227 n.6
stone 3, 13, 23, 24, 40, 41–3, 50, 52, 53, 60, 63, 70, 74, 80, 83, 96, 100, 101, 107, 109, 124, 137, 142, 149, 159, 165, 184, 216, 222 n.3, 233 n.1; *see also Edelstein*
Strasbourg, France 52
Straus, Rachel 177
Strauss, David Friedrich 14, 30–1
sublime 28, 30, 34, 49, 182
Sullivan, Louis H. 9, 10, 18, 54, 154, 155, 173, 179–81, 182, 183–7, 189, 190, 230 n.1, 230 n.11, 232 n.5, 232 n.6, 232 n.7, 232 n.9
Sullivan, works: Auditorium Building, Chicago 184, 190; *Autobiography of an Idea* 183; Guaranty building, Buffalo, New York 181, 184, 185, 187; 'Ornament and Architecture' 179; 'The Tall Office Building Artistically Considered' 185; Wainwright building, St. Louis 183, 184, 185, 186, 187
sun, motif 96, 97, 107, 117, 198, 201, 205, 209, 215, 226 n.3
Superman; *see under Übermensch*
surface 43, 65, 66, 68, 176, 178, 179, 180, 182, 201

Tafuri, Manfredo 203
Taine, Hippolyte 49, 50
Taut, Bruno 9, 10, 18, 54, 57, 137, 154, 155, 156, 162, 165, 190, 193, 197–8, 204–20, 233 n.3, 233 n.4, 234 n.8

Taut, works: *Alpine Architektur* 18, 192, 205, 209–12, 213; *Die Stadtkrone* 18, 192, 205–9, 213, 217–20, 233 n.4; *Glashaus*, Werkbund Exhibition, Cologne 18, 158, 192, 204, 205, 212, 216–20; *Hufeisensiedlung Berlin-Britz*, Berlin 210; *Kristallhaus*, as a concept 18, 205, 206–7, 208, 209, 216, 217, 233 n.4, 233 n.5; *Monument des Neuen Gesetzes* 18, 137, 156, 205, 212, 213–16, 234 n.8; *Onkel Toms Hütte* 210; *Siedlung Schillerpark*, Berlin 210; *Wohnstadt Carl Legien*, Berlin 210
Taut, Max 204
temenos 16, 112–13, 116, 122, 124, 136
Temple of Artemis, Ephesus 89
temple, as architectural type 16, 31, 89, 90, 91, 92, 98, 103, 107, 113, 119, 122, 129, 147; *see also* Paestum, Italy; Nietzsche temple; Nietzsche temple-stadium; Temple of Artemis
Teuber, Dirk 194, 195, 197
Third Reich 10, 17, 139, 141, 142, 228 n.20; *see also* National Socialism; Nazi Party
Thoma, Hans 226 n.3
Thorak, Josef 229 n.26
Tieck, Ludwig 73
Totalitarian architecture 9, 90, 182, 226 n.1, 233 n.4
tragedy, ancient Greek 33, 64, 84; as highest art form 69, 166; *see also* Nietzsche, works, *The Birth of Tragedy*
Tribschen, Switzerland 16, 33, 75, 76, 78, 80, 223 n.1, 225 n.33, 225 n.34
Trodd, Colin 107, 211
Troost, Paul Ludwig 140
Turin, Italy 4, 5, 6, 7, 8, 13, 15, 41, 43, 48, 50, 51, 52, 53, 54–7, 60, 172, 187, 192, 198, 200, 201, 207, 221 n.3, 221 n.4

Übermensch/Superman 2, 10, 13, 23, 40, 49, 53, 113, 114, 139, 155, 171, 176, 188, 189, 190, 198, 200, 201, 215, 217, 219, 223 n.9, 227 n.9, 232 n.7
unifying instinct 14, 26, 28, 29, 37
unity of taste/style 5, 26, 47, 57, 62, 64, 97, 101, 134, 142, 158, 163
Utitz, Emil 165

van de Velde, Henry 9, 10, 15, 18, 39, 40, 92, 95–105, 108–37, 143, 146, 154, 155, 160, 161, 163, 168, 176–9, 190, 192, 193–7, 204, 221 n.5, 227 n.10, 228 n.14, 228 n.17, 228 n.19, 229 n.25
van de Velde, works: *Dionysos-Dithyramben* (book cover) 96, 195–7; Die Linie' 177, 222 n.2; *Ecce Homo* (book cover) 96; Ernst Abbe Memorial, Jena 92, 97, 104, 106, 108–12; Maison de l'Art Nouveau, Paris 95; Nietzsche Memorial Kröller-Müller Museum Park, Holland 17, 92, 135–7, 216, 234 n.8; 'Prinzipielle Erklarung' 222 n.2; Théâtre des Champs-Elysées, Paris 195, 197; Theatre, Deutscher Werkbund Exhibition, Cologne 18, 96, 158, 192, 193–6, 216, 227 n.7; Theatre, Lübeck 197; Theatre, Weimar 97; *Thus Spoke Zarathustra* (book cover) 96; Villa Silberblick, Weimar 5, 16, 39, 40, 92, 93–104, 105, 108, 109, 110, 111, 112, 119, 122, 135, 137–8, 140, 143, 144, 146, 147, 149, 150, 152, 153, 163, 178, 180, 192, 197, 226 n.5, 226 n.6, 227 n.8, 228 n.16, 228 n.18, 229 n.25, 231 n.16, 231 n.2; *see also* Nietzsche-Archiv; Nietzsche temple; Nietzsche temple-complex
van Eck, Caroline 223 n.4
Van Zanten, David 180, 190
Vasari, Giorgio 188
Villa Silberblick, Weimar; *see under* van de Velde works; *see also* Nietzsche-Archiv, Weimar

Vitruvius 40
Vogel, Martin 77, 80, 224 n.25, 224 n.26, 225 n.27, 225 n.31

Wagner, Cosima 33, 68, 69, 70, 80, 226 n.36
Wagner, Luise 79, 80
Wagner, Otto 154, 159, 171
Wagner, Richard 2, 12, 14, 15, 16, 26, 29, 32–5, 38, 42, 56, 61, 62, 63, 64, 66, 67, 68, 70, 72–85, 92, 95, 112, 140, 156, 157, 223 n.1, 223 n.2, 223 n.3, 224 n.26, 225 n.27, 225 n.33, 225 n.35; Wagner's music 12, 26, 33, 34, 56, 61, 62, 64, 83, 84, 157; Nietzsche's rejection of 12, 29, 32–5, 38, 42, 81, 82, 83–5, 156
Wagner, works: *Die Kunst und die Revolution* 80; *Das Kunstwerk der Zukunft* 80; *Die Meistersinger* 72, 81; *see also* Festspielhaus, Bayreuth; Munich Theatre
Wahnfried, Bayreuth 80
Weimar Republic 17, 158
Weimar, Germany 5, 9, 15, 16, 17, 39, 91, 92, 93, 94, 95, 96, 97, 98, 102, 103, 109, 112, 116, 118, 119, 124, 134, 137, 139, 140, 141, 143, 148, 150, 152, 153, 158, 161, 162, 163, 191, 197, 227 n.8, 228 n.16, 229 n.21, 229 n.27, 231 n.17
white surfaces 65, 96, 97, 156, 161, 164, 172–5, 215, 231 n.17

Whyte, Iain Boyd 188, 206, 208, 209, 210, 233 n.6
Wilamowitz-Möellendorf, Ulrich von 71, 75
will to power 9, 10, 12, 13, 15, 32, 37, 38, 39, 40, 41, 42, 44, 47, 49, 51, 52, 58, 59, 95, 108, 111, 129, 135, 139, 142, 155, 167, 171, 178, 179, 180, 184, 188, 190, 191, 202, 205, 206, 223 n.10
will to truth 32, 174
Winckelmann, Johann Joachim 64, 65
Wirz, Heinz 154
Wohfarth, Irving 9
Wölfflin, Heinrich 15, 40
Würzbach, Walter 210

Zapfe, Rudolf 95
Zarathustra 2, 8, 11, 13, 14, 18, 23, 34, 51, 52, 53, 56, 59, 60, 91, 96, 101, 102, 107, 116, 132, 137, 143, 144, 146, 150, 151, 152, 155, 156, 159, 160, 167, 172, 179, 182, 183, 188, 190, 197, 198, 199, 200, 201, 204, 208, 209, 211, 213, 215, 216, 217, 219, 226 n.3, 229 n.27, 232 n.9, 233 n.1, 233 n.2, 234 n.8; Zarathustra's animals/companions: *see under* eagle, snake; *see also* Peter Behrens, works 'Zarathustra House'; Nietzsche, works *Thus Spoke Zarathustra*
Zeiss, Carl 108
Zürich, Switzerland 3, 79, 93, 223 n.3